OXFORD MONOGRAPHS IN INTERNATIONAL LAW

General Editors: Professor Ian Brownlie CBE, QC, FBA
Former Chichele Professor of Public International Law in the University of Oxford and Member of the International Law Commission, and
Professor Vaughan Lowe, *Chichele Professor of Public International Law in the University of Oxford and Fellow of All Souls College, Oxford*

UNIVERSAL JURISDICTION: INTERNATIONAL AND MUNICIPAL LEGAL PERSPECTIVES

OXFORD MONOGRAPHS IN INTERNATIONAL LAW

The aim of this series is to publish important and original pieces of research on all aspects of international law. Topics that are given particular prominence are those which, while of interest to the academic lawyer, also have important bearing on issues which touch upon the actual conduct of international relations. Nonetheless, the series is wide in scope and includes monographs on the history and philosophical foundations of international law.

RECENT TITLES IN THE SERIES

Just War or Just Peace?
Humanitarian Intervention and International Law
Simon Chesterman

State Responsibility for Transboundary Air Pollution in International Law
Phoebe Okowa

The Responsibility of States for International Crimes
Nina H. B. Jørgensen

The Law of International Watercourses: Non-navigational Uses
Stephen C. McCaffrey

International Justice and the International Criminal Court: Between Sovereignty and the Rule of Law
Bruce Broomhall

Human Rights in International Criminal Proceedings
Salvatore Zappalà

UNIVERSAL JURISDICTION

International and Municipal Legal Perspectives

LUC REYDAMS

OXFORD
UNIVERSITY PRESS

OXFORD
UNIVERSITY PRESS

Great Clarendon Street, Oxford OX2 6DP

Oxford University Press is a department of the University of Oxford.
It furthers the University's objective of excellence in research, scholarship,
and education by publishing worldwide in

Oxford New York

Auckland Bangkok Buenos Aires Cape Town Chennai
Dar es Salaam Delhi Hong Kong Istanbul Karachi Kolkata
Kuala Lumpur Madrid Melbourne Mexico City Mumbai Nairobi
São Paulo Shanghai Taipei Tokyo Toronto

Oxford is a registered trade mark of Oxford University Press
in the UK and in certain other countries

Published in the United States
by Oxford University Press Inc., New York

First published 2003

British Library Cataloguing in Publication Data
Data available

Library of Congress Cataloging in Publication Data
Data available

ISBN 0-19-925162-2

1 3 5 7 9 10 8 6 4 2

Typeset by Newgen Imaging Systems (P) Ltd., Chennai, India
Printed in Great Britain
on acid-free paper by
T.J. International Ltd., Padstow, Cornwall

To Griet and the children

General Editors' Preface

Dr Reydams writes that 'jurisdiction exercised by a State without its having any objective or legal link with either the offence or the offender erodes the very concept of jurisdiction'. Yet, in parallel with the establishment of international criminal tribunals, States increasingly assert universal jurisdiction in respect of serious crimes. Dr Reydams' detailed and scholarly study surveys these developments and offers a thoughtful analysis of their significance. His argument that unilateral exercises of universal jurisdiction over defendants *in absentia* risks weakening the very international order that it pretends to guard deserves careful consideration by those concerned with the development of international criminal law.

IB
AVL

Foreword

The exercise of universal jurisdiction reminds us of Mark Twain's famous comment about the weather: 'Everybody talks about it, but nobody does anything about it.' Luc Reydams has given the subject as exhaustive an examination as anyone previously – his book can claim to be the first major monograph on the subject in the English language – and it affirms the stunning paucity of national practice. For one reason or another, States rarely undertake prosecutions of crimes in the absence of a territorial or personal *nexus*, or an explicit treaty obligation to prosecute or extradite, no matter how horrible the criminal acts may be.

No more startling an example can exist than the sorry efforts of the United States of America to bring Pol Pot to justice for crimes committed while he was 'brother number one' of the Khmer Rouge regime in Cambodia, from 1975 to 1979. As initiatives to establish some form of accountability in Cambodia crystallized, in 1997, the United States thought it had a good shot at arresting the ageing and ailing tyrant.[1] The United States was itself unable to contemplate prosecution before its own courts, for while it takes perhaps the most generous view of all of its own territorial jurisdiction (courtesy of a broad notion of 'effects'), it has shown no inclination for genuine universal jurisdiction. So the United States went forum shopping. But one by one, those States that had enacted universal jurisdiction provisions into their codes of criminal procedure, such as Israel, Spain, and Canada, politely declined Washington's invitation. Pol Pot was never brought to justice and died shortly afterward, allegedly of natural causes.

It is a pity that none of the States that Washington approached ever took up the challenge, because this would have been a more or less 'pure' exercise of universal jurisdiction. None of the States concerned had any particular historic link with Cambodia, nor any national interest. And there's the rub. In virtually all of the cases where something resembling universal jurisdiction has been exercised, we find some special interest of the prosecuting State. Indeed, a cynic looking at the prosecutions of Rwandan *génocidaires* in Belgium or of Augusto Pinochet in Spain might argue provocatively that there is an additional category of jurisdiction in criminal law, to wit, criminal prosecution of crimes committed on the territory of a State's former colonies. There are a few examples of ostensibly disinterested prosecutions in countries such as Germany, but on closer examination these turn out to be the result of treaty obligations to prosecute or extradite (*aut dedere aut judicare*).

[1] Elizabeth Becker, 'U.S. Spearheading Effort to Bring Pol Pot to Trial', *New York Times*, 23 June 1997, p A1.

And yet to read much of the academic literature and the materials published by non-governmental organizations, universal jurisdiction is supposed to be uncontested and uncontroversial. Enormous material resources and personal efforts are devoted to building prosecutions and convincing national justice systems to proceed on this basis. Even in the United States, which prefers an expansive concept of effects jurisdiction to the typical forms of universal jurisdiction, there is much enthusiasm for civil suits against foreign criminals for acts committed elsewhere. Universal jurisdiction is often hailed as one of the magic bullets in the campaign against impunity. And yet to my knowledge essentially nobody is in jail as a result of the exercise of universal jurisdiction, and while the fabled alien tort claims in the United States lead to fabulous judgments, none of them is really enforceable.

On closer examination, even the legal underpinning of its exercise seems far less certain than many would claim. During the Rome Conference that established the International Criminal Court, delegates resisted a campaign led by Germany to entrench universal jurisdiction within the statute of the new tribunal. Germany's argument was well reasoned and seductive in its logic. If States individually could exercise universal jurisdiction over the most serious crimes of concern to the international community, such as genocide, crimes against humanity, and war crimes, why could they not delegate this jurisdiction to an international body of their own creation? But when the final draft was tabled, it stopped short of recognizing anything like universal jurisdiction. Was this a sign that the principle was perhaps not as widely accepted as had been purported?

Establishment of a customary rule recognizing the legitimacy of universal jurisdiction could only really come from a dictum of the International Court of Justice. Back in the 1920s, the Court had left the door open in a case dealing with a closely related issue, exercise of jurisdiction over crimes committed in international waters but against one's own nationals, when it indicated that international law allowed anything that was not specifically prohibited.

For human rights lawyers, the *Lotus case* was a double-edged sword, as dangerous as it was helpful. It worked well as an argument to justify universal jurisdiction, but was more than troublesome when it came to efforts to obtain a general prohibition of the use and the threat of use of nuclear weapons. In hearings on the International Court's advisory opinion on nuclear weapons, *Lotus* was the mantra of the nuclear powers seeking to justify the existence of their arsenals of weapons of mass destruction.

The *Arrest Warrant Case*, decided by the International Court of Justice in February 2002, confirmed the lingering uncertainties about the principle of universal jurisdiction that the debates at the Rome Conference had revealed. The applicant State, the Democratic Republic of Congo, curiously decided not to challenge Belgium on the question, twisting the litigation into a somewhat implausible debate about immunities. Yet universal litigation was central to the case, and whether or not the Congo's foreign minister enjoyed immunity from prosecution with respect to Belgian courts couldn't really arise until the legitimacy of Belgium's exercise of universal jurisdiction had been settled. So the plenary Court simply sidestepped the difficult issue, although this didn't stop some of the judges from expressing their individual opinions on the subject. Some of them had no trouble with universal jurisdiction. Yet others, including the president of the Court, Gilbert Guillaume, failed to find the requisite elements of international custom allowing States to prosecute crimes committed outside their territory by persons with no real connection to it.

In the years to come, it will be interesting to observe whether or not States with universal jurisdiction legislation have been unsettled by Judge Guillaume's analysis. But to be fair, we must also speculate about the reaction of States whose nationals are prosecuted by other States in the exercise of universal jurisdiction. It is important to recall that Congo, ultimately, declined to do battle with Belgium on the issue of universal jurisdiction. That may be because it assumed – rightly, as things turned out – that it had a winning argument on the immunity issue. But it may also have assessed its chances of succeeding on the jurisdictional issue as being slight. In the future, States whose nationals are prosecuted may well hesitate given the compelling arguments of Judges Higgins, Buergenthal, and Kooijmans.

Luc Reydams suggests that this may all be an interlude, what he calls an 'an aberrant intermezzo between Nuremberg and the ICC'. Many will quarrel with his cautious, conservative assessment of universal jurisdiction, yet on this point he has clearly hit the nail on the head. In what direction will the energies of the international community in the campaign against impunity be directed? There are many who believe that the existence of the International Criminal Court will energize efforts by national justice systems to exercise universal jurisdiction. If they are right, a decade from now the meagre list of examples of universal jurisdiction that Professor Reydams has identified will be considerably more impressive.

Certainly, it is a fact that many States, in the implementing legislation they have adopted to accompany ratification of the Rome Statute of the International Criminal Court, have also introduced provisions to allow for universal jurisdiction, or beefed up the existing legislation. Yet many of the reasons for their historic reticence to use universal jurisdiction, including the great cost and daunting complexity of prosecuting cases in far-away lands, cannot be said to have gone away. Only time will tell whether it is all symbolism, or if the pledge in the *Rome Statute*'s preamble that 'it is the duty of every State to exercise its criminal jurisdiction over those responsible for international crimes' means States will use the entire arsenal of mechanisms, including universal jurisdiction, to ensure accountability for serious violations of human rights. The overall scheme of the International Criminal Court is predicated on its subsidiary role (or 'complementarity') with respect to national justice systems.

The principal reason why we need the International Criminal Court is that States are unwilling or unable genuinely (the words are borrowed from article 17 of the Statute) to prosecute 'their own' offenders. It is targeted at the reluctance of Chile to prosecute Pinochet, or of Chad to prosecute Hissène Habré. The rationale of the Court has never been one of inciting States to exercise universal jurisdiction. Yet this may be precisely its effect. States parties to the *Rome Statute* may consider a ruling by the Court's Pre-Trial Chamber that they are unwilling or unable to prosecute an offender who may by happenstance be within their custody to be a blemish on their international profile. They may prefer to prosecute using universal jurisdiction than to essentially withdraw from their responsibilities and let the new Court do the work. Perhaps.

Luc Reydams tackles this subject at a time when its past is mysterious and its future uncertain. More than anything, this makes his research not only exciting but important. This is the enviable accomplishment of all legal academics, not only to describe the law as it is with accuracy and detail, but to contribute to its evolution.

William A Schabas
Oughterard, County Galway
December 2002

Acknowledgments

This book is based on my dissertation submitted in partial fulfilment of the requirements for the degree of Doctor of the Science of Law (JSD) at the Notre Dame Law School. I sincerely thank the members of my Advisory Committee: Professors Paolo Carozza, Carol Ann Moony, and Jimmy Gurulé. My work also greatly benefited from comments by two other Notre Dame Law School faculty members: Professor Barbara Fick and, in particular, JSD Program Director Professor Dinah Shelton. Her support and advice during the dissertation-to-book process are also greatly appreciated, as are the comments of the anonymous referee and the competence and efficiency of John Louth and his team at Oxford University Press throughout the publishing process.

I could never have covered such a wide range of sources without the generous help of numerous scholars, officials, practitioners, and advocates from many countries. I therefore offer the results of this study to the international legal community, to be taken up, refuted where necessary, nuanced, or elaborated. I am particularly indebted for providing me with key documentation to Kai Ambos (Max Planck Institute for Foreign and International Criminal Law and Albert-Ludwigs University Freiburg), William Bourdon (International Federation of Human Rights Leagues and Paris Bar), Eric Gillet (International Federation of Human Rights Leagues and Brussels Bar), Friedrich Hauptmann (Austrian Ministry of Justice), Menno Kamminga (University of Maastricht), Claus Kreß (University of Cologne), Christian Le Gunehec (French Court of Cassation), Rafaëlle Maison (University Paris II, Panthéon-Assas), Claude Nicati (Swiss Army), Jurjen Pen (Amsterdam Bar), Lars Plum (Danish Ministry of Justice and University of Copenhagen), Jean-Dominique Schouwey (Swiss Ministry of Justice), Caroline Stainier (Avocats Sans Frontières), Brigitte Stern (University Paris I, Panthéon-Sorbonne), Damien Vandermeersch (Catholic University of Louvain and Belgian Ministry of Justice), and Richard van Elst (Erasmus University Rotterdam and Dutch Supreme Court).

Important thanks also to the staff of the Kresge Law Library of the Notre Dame Law School for enthusiastically assisting me with many inter-library loans, to the Helen Kellogg Institute for International Studies at the University of Notre Dame for a Dissertation Year Fellowship, and to the Max Planck Institute for Foreign and International Criminal Law (Freiburg-im-Breisgau, Germany) for a residential research fellowship.

Special gratitude to my mentors Professors Filip Reyntjens (University of Antwerp) and Richard Buxbaum (University of California at Berkeley) and to my fellow JSD colleagues Ali Qazilbash (Notre Dame Law School) and Vincent Nmehielle (George Washington University) for their friendship and encouragement throughout the writing process. Finally, warm thanks to the Congregation of the Holy Cross at Notre Dame for its generosity and amity.

Text from the following publications was reproduced with the kind permission of Kluwer Academic Publishers and ASIL respectively: L Reydams, 'Universal Criminal Jurisdiction: The Belgian State of Affairs' (2000) 11 *Criminal Law Forum* 183–216; and L Reydams, 'Niyonteze v Public Prosecutor' (2002) 96 *Am J Int'l L* 231–6.

I could not have brought this undertaking to a good end without the unconditional love and support of my wife Griet. Her advice was simple: 'just do it!'

Luc Reydams
Notre Dame, Indiana, USA
October 2002

Contents

Abbreviations

ECHR	European Court of Human Rights
ETS	European Treaty Series
ICC	International Criminal Court
ICJ	International Court of Justice
ICTR	International Criminal Tribunal for Rwanda
ICTY	International Criminal Tribunal for the former Yugoslavia
ILC	International Law Commission
LNTS	League of Nations Treaty Series
OAS	Organization of American States
PCIJ	Permanent Court of International Justice
SAARC	South Asian Association for Regional Co-Operation
UN	United Nations
UNGA	United Nations General Assembly
UNTS	United Nations Treaty Series
WW II	World War II

Table of Official International Documents

Note: this Table lists only documents mentioned in the body of the text. Documents are listed in chronological order. Full references can be found where the document is cited in the text below.

Treaties

Other Documents

Table of Municipal Legislation

Note: this Table lists only the laws and statutes that provide for universal jurisdiction and that are mentioned in the body of the text. Thus other municipal legislation (eg active personality statutes, procedural statutes, extradition laws) is excluded. An English translation of a title in a foreign language can be found where the document is cited in the text below.

Table of Cases

Municipal Cases

Note: this Table cites only the cases that are dealt with in a separate section in the respective country studies. Cases mentioned in passing are excluded. Few of the cases listed have an official name (eg *Polyukhovitch* v *The Commonwealth*). For consistency, cases initiated by a private party are named after the first plaintiff and the principal defendant (eg *Abbas Hijazi* et al. v *Sharon* et al.) The letter X indicates that the identity of a party is unknown (eg *Javor* et al. v *X*). Cases launched by public authorities are named as follows: *Public Prosecutor* v *name of defendant* (eg *Public Prosecutor* v *Saric*), unless the case has a different official name (eg *United States* v *Yunis*). Full references can be found where the case is cited in the text below.

International Cases

Note: this Table cites only the cases that are mentioned in the body of the text. Full references can be found where a case is cited below.

Other international courts and tribunals

Introduction

'The exercise of criminal jurisdiction over foreigners is a sphere in which juridical literature and speculation abound and are conflicting even in the matter of first principles, but international precedent is rare and indecisive', WE Beckett.[1]

A. SUBJECT

This study is about the jurisdiction of a State to prosecute and punish foreigners who commit crimes abroad against foreigners.[2] The subject-matter first drew the author's interest in 1994 when news agencies reported that Rwandan refugees had filed criminal complaints in Belgium against other Rwandans for their alleged roles in the massacres in Rwanda earlier that year.[3] Since then judicial authorities in almost a dozen countries have investigated and sometimes convicted non-nationals for crimes committed abroad against non-nationals. More cases of 'universal jurisdiction' have been reported in the past decade than throughout the whole history of modern international law.

As a consequence, universal jurisdiction has become an important[4] yet controversial issue in international law. The international human rights movement embraces universal jurisdiction as a means to promote accountability for gross human rights violations;[5] a veritable 'transnational advocacy network'[6] organizes and strategizes for its effective implementation. By contrast,

[1] WE Beckett, 'Criminal Jurisdiction over Foreigners' (1927) 8 *British Ybk Int'l L* 108, 109.

[2] 'Foreigner' or 'alien' in this study means a person who is not a national or citizen of the forum State.

[3] Cf L Reydams, 'Universal Jurisdiction over Atrocities in Rwanda: Theory and Practice' (1996) 4 *Eur J Crime, Crim L & Crim Justice* 18.

[4] Eg International Law Association, 'The Exercise of Universal Jurisdiction in Respect of Gross Human Rights Violations: Final Report on the Exercise of Universal Jurisdiction in Respect of Gross Human Rights Offences', in *Report of the 69th Conference of the International Law Association* (2000) 403; an article version of the report by MT Kamminga, 'Lessons Learned from the Exercise of Universal Jurisdiction in Respect of Gross Human Rights Offenses' appeared in (2001) 23 *Human Rights Q* 940. Other collective scholarly initiatives include 'The Princeton Principles on Universal Jurisdiction' by the Princeton University Program in Law and Public Affairs, and 'Universal Jurisdiction in Theory and Practice' by the TMC Asser Institute for International Law in The Hague.

[5] Universal jurisdiction over gross human rights violations is now a common advocacy position of major human rights organizations; see eg Amnesty International, *Universal Jurisdiction: 14 Principles on the Effective Exercise of Universal Jurisdiction* (1999) AI Index: IOR 53/01/99; *Universal Jurisdiction: The duty of States to enact and implement legislation* (2001) AI Index: IOR 53/002-018/2001; Redress, *Universal Jurisdiction in Europe: Criminal prosecutions in Europe since 1990 for war crimes, crimes against humanity, torture and genocide* (1999); International Council on Human Rights Policy, *Hard cases: Bringing human rights violators to justice abroad—A guide to universal jurisdiction* (1999).

[6] Term coined and defined by ME Keck and K Sikkink, *Activists Beyond Borders: Advocacy Networks in International Politics* (1998) 1. N Roht-Arriaza, *Transnational Justice* (University of Pennsylvania Press; forthcoming 2004) specifically deals with the transnational advocacy campaign behind some of the cases discussed in this book.

a former United States Secretary of State strongly opposes the idea, warning against 'judicial tyranny'.[7]

In spite of this lively interest, existing scholarly publications on universal jurisdiction are either outdated[8] or do not take into account the recent State practice.[9] The time seems opportune, therefore, for a new analysis.[10]

Among the legal questions raised by a State's exercise of universal jurisdiction, this study considers two: (1) under what conditions is the country investigating or prosecuting the extraterritorial offence internationally competent, and (2) what is the basis in domestic or municipal[11] law for the exercise of jurisdiction? The goal of the study is to advance discussion on the subject and offer a frame of reference to decision-makers and legal practitioners, both national and international.

In its usual meaning, and in this study, 'universal jurisdiction' refers to the competence of *national* judicial authorities (as opposed to an *international* judicial body)[12] with respect to *crime* (as distinguished from *torts*). Universal civil jurisdiction, ie jurisdiction by courts in litigation between foreign private parties over extraterritorial torts,[13] comes close to the subject-matter of this study but it is excluded from the analysis. It should be noted, however, that what applies for criminal jurisdiction applies to some extent *mutatis mutandis* for civil jurisdiction, because the latter is considered less

[7] HA Kissinger, 'The Pitfalls of Universal Jurisdiction: Risking Judicial Tyranny' (2001) 80 *Foreign Affairs* 86. Some suggest that the former Secretary has more than an academic interest in the subject: see eg D Cassel, 'The World Reaches out for Justice', *Chicago Tribune*, 12 August 2002, s C p. 1.

[8] M Traub, *Das Universelle Schutzprinzip und das Prinzip der identische Norm, als ein regulierender Faktor der staatlichen Strafkompetenz* (1913); GF von Cleric, 'Das Weltrechtsergreifungsprinzip' (1920) 22 *Schweizerische Juristen-Zeitung* 345; G Solna, *Das Weltrechtsprinzip im internationalen Strafrecht* (1925).

[9] KC Randall, 'Universal Jurisdiction under International Law' (1988) 66 *Texas LR* 785; L Gardocki, 'The Principle of Universality' in N Jareborg (ed) *Double Criminality: Studies in International Criminal Law* (1989) 57; G Guillaume, 'La compétence universelle, formes anciennes et nouvelles' in *Mélanges offerts à Georges Levasseur: Droit pénal, droit européen* (1992) 23.

[10] When this book neared completion I learned about the publications of M Henzelin, *Le principe de l'universalité en droit pénal international* (2000) and L Benavides, 'The Universal Jurisdiction Principle: Nature and Scope' (2001) 1 *Anuario Mexicano de Derecho Internacional* 19.

[11] The terms 'national', 'domestic', and 'municipal' law are interchangeable in this study.

[12] 'Universal jurisdiction' led to controversy at the United Nations Diplomatic Conference of Plenipotentiaries on the Establishment of an International Criminal Court (Rome, 15 June–17 July 1998). Germany, several other countries, Amnesty International, and the International Committee of the Red Cross expressed preference for universal jurisdiction of the Court. China and the United States of America cited the Court's so-called universal jurisdiction as a reason for not signing the treaty; see the press releases of the Conference, in particular of 9, 13, and 17 July 1998. 'Universal jurisdiction' also appears in an *obiter dictum* in the landmark *Tadic* decision (at para 62) of the Appeals Chamber of International Criminal Tribunal for the former Yugoslavia: *Prosecutor* v *Tadic*, Decision on Jurisdiction, 2 October 1995, IT-94-1-AR72, reprinted in (1996) 35 *Int'l Legal Materials* 32.

[13] I am referring to litigation in the United States on the basis of the Alien Tort Statute 1789 (28 USC § 1350) and the Torture Victim Protection Act 1991; for a thorough analysis see B Stephens and M Ratner, *International Human Rights Litigation in US Courts* (1996); RG Steinhardt and A D'Amato (eds) *The Alien Tort Claims Act: An analytical anthology* (1999); see also JL Garwood-Cutler, 'Enforcing International Criminal Law Violations with Civil Remedies: The US Alien Tort Claims Act' in MC Bassiouni (ed) *International Criminal Law* (2nd edn, 1998) III, 343–91.

intrusive.[14] The presumption is that if universal criminal jurisdiction is permissible under international law, universal civil jurisdiction is also permissible (*qui peut le plus peut le moins*, the greater includes the lesser).[15] This being said, 'jurisdiction' refers hereinafter to criminal jurisdiction, unless otherwise indicated.

The present inquiry is about criminal jurisdiction of a State over *foreigners*, not over its nationals, and in respect of acts committed entirely *abroad* and without substantial impact on persons or property in the forum State. The jurisdiction which a country chooses to exercise over its own nationals in relation to acts performed at home or abroad is outside the sphere of international law.[16] Regarding aliens, it is a generally accepted rule of international law that a State possesses the right to try and to punish them for all infractions of its penal laws committed inside its territory.[17]

This study is not concerned with the expediency of universal jurisdiction, nor with the (international) legality of the investigation or proceedings, and nor with immunities under international law of certain foreign officials.[18] As for investigative acts, it suffices to say that a State cannot perform outside its territory acts auxiliary to the prosecution and trial of an offence (eg arrest of a suspect,[19] collection of evidence,[20] site inspection, or deposition of witnesses), unless explicitly authorized by the territorial State.

[14] Civil jurisdiction is considered less intrusive for several reasons. First, in civil cases with an extraterritorial element the application of foreign law is not excluded. Second, the government of the forum State plays no role other than adjudicating a suit brought by private parties. Finally, the stakes for the individual defendant in a civil trial are lower than in a criminal trial. A civil conviction results in damages, not in punishment. In reference to the latter, note that non common-law countries often refuse to enforce awards of punitive damages precisely because of the element of punishment; see D Shelton, *Remedies in International Human Rights Law* (1999) 283–4.

[15] An authoritative commentator, after examining State practice in respect of civil jurisdiction, declared: 'It is hard to resist the conclusion that (apart from the well known rules of immunity for foreign States, diplomats, international organizations, etc.) customary international law imposes no limits on the jurisdiction of municipal courts in civil trials': M Akehurst, 'Jurisdiction in International Law' (1972–73) 46 *British Ybk Int'l L* 145, 177.

[16] WE Beckett, 'The Exercise of Criminal Jurisdiction over Foreigners' (1925) 6 *British Ybk Int'l L* 44, 45; E Lauterpacht, *International Law: Being the collected papers of Hersch Lauterpacht* (1970) 488. But see E Rosswog, *Das Problem der Vereinbarkeit des aktiven und passiven Personalgrundsatzes mit dem Völkerrecht* (1965) 169–88.

[17] Cf article 15 of the Charter of the Organization of American States and article 9 of the Convention on the Rights and Duties of States.

[18] See generally D Oehler, 'Immunität, Exterritorialität und Asylrecht im Internationalen Strafrecht' (1979) 91 *Zeitschrift für die gesamte Strafrechtswissenschaft* 395; BJ George, 'Jurisdiction Over Embassies, Consulates, International Organizations and Their Personnel, and Armed Forces Stationed Abroad' in MC Bassiouni (ed) *International Criminal Law* (2nd edn, 1998) I, 107–144. See also *Arrest Warrant of 11 April 2000*, ICJ, 14 February 2002, reprinted in (2002) 41 *Int'l L Materials* 536.

[19] Literature arguing the illegality of extraterritorial arrest abounds; eg FA Mann, 'Reflections on the Prosecution of Persons Abducted in Breach of International Law' in Y Dinstein (ed) *International Law at a Time of Perplexity: Essays in Honour of Shabtai Rosenne* (1989) 407. A United States federal court recently held that State-sponsored abduction within the territory of another State violates customary international human rights law: *Alvarez-Machain* v *United States*, United States Court of Appeals for the Ninth Circuit, 11 September 2001, reprinted in (2000) 41 *Int'l L Materials* 130.

[20] See eg *Corfu Channel*, ICJ Reports 1949, 4, 34–5.

B. CONCEPTS

'Jurisdiction', a legal term *par excellence*, has various meanings. In municipal public law the term usually denotes the power of a court. In international law, however, jurisdiction is used much more liberally.[21] The term has been adequately defined as 'the legal power or competence of States to exercise governmental functions',[22] or 'a State's authority to subject persons (natural or juridical) and things to its legal order'.[23] In international criminal law and in Part I of this study, however, jurisdiction has a narrower meaning. The term refers primarily to 'a State's international capacity or competence under international law to prosecute and punish for commission of a crime'[24] or 'the sovereign power of one State *vis-à-vis* other States to make, apply and enforce its criminal law'.[25]

In contrast, jurisdiction in municipal law generally relates to the question 'whether a certain executive, legislative or judicial organ is competent in a given case under the applicable constitutional or statutory provisions'.[26] Part II below, which discusses and compares municipal penal statutes and cases, refers to the 'scope', 'ambit',[27] or 'extent'[28] *ratione loci* and *personae* of the domestic penal law as defined in the penal code, or to the competence *ratione loci* and *personae* under the municipal code of penal procedure of the judicial authorities *sensu lato*[29] over criminal offences. In most countries the competence *ratione loci* and *personae* of the judicial authorities is not explicitly determined[30] but follows

[21] Examples of broad use can be found in the constitutive texts of international organizations: I Brownlie, *Principles of Public International Law* (4th edn, 1990) 109 calls jurisdiction an *omnibus* term. For works on jurisdiction in international law, see FA Mann, 'The Doctrine of Jurisdiction in International Law' (1964) 111 *Receuil des cours de l'académie de droit international* 9; FA Mann, 'The Doctrine of International Jurisdiction Revised after Twenty Years' (1984) 186 *Receuil des cours de l'académie de droit international* 11; A Bos, 'The Extraterritorial Jurisdiction of States: Preliminary Report' (1993) 65 *Ybk Institute Int'l L*, I, 14; Akehurst (n 15 above).

[22] MW Janis, *An Introduction to International Law* (3rd edn, 1999) 322.

[23] Institute of International Law, 'Draft Resolution on the Extraterritorial Jurisdiction of States' (1993) 65 *Ybk Institute Int'l L*, I, 174.

[24] Harvard Research in International Law, 'Jurisdiction with Respect to Crime' (1935) 29 *Am J Int'l L* 435, 439. 'Prosecute' in this definition includes all the possible stages in a criminal proceeding, from preliminary investigation, through trial, to final adjudication on appeal in the tribunal of last resort; 'punish' includes both the execution of sentence and the remission of penalty.

[25] Law Reform Commission of Canada, *Extraterritorial Jurisdiction* (1984) 4.

[26] FA Mann (1964) (n 21 above) 9.

[27] Cf G Williams, 'Venue and the Ambit of Criminal Law' (1965) 81 *LQR* 276–88, 395–421, 518–38.

[28] Cf Law Commission (UK), *Report on the Territorial and Extraterritorial Extent of the Criminal Law* (1978).

[29] These authorities comprise the criminal courts, ie the judicial authorities *sensu stricto*, as well as the investigative and prosecutorial authorities. In some legal systems the investigative and prosecutorial authorities are part of the judiciary *sensu lato*, in others they fall under the executive branch of government.

[30] France and Spain are notable exceptions; see the country studies in Part II below.

from the ambit of the substantive penal law.[31] As a rule, it is sufficient that jurisdiction can be established either on the code of penal procedure or on the penal code.[32]

'Extraterritorial jurisdiction' is jurisdiction exercised over an extraterritorial offence, even when the whole process (investigation, prosecution, punishment) takes place within the forum State. Hence, the term does not imply that the forum State performs any official act outside its own territory.

'Universal jurisdiction' means that a State, without seeking to protect its security or credit, seeks to punish conduct irrespective of the place where it occurs, the nationality of the perpetrator, and the nationality of the victim. Negatively defined, it means that there is no link of territoriality or nationality between the State and the conduct or offender,[33] nor is the State seeking to protect its security or credit. Positively defined, a State exercises universal jurisdiction when it seeks to punish conduct that is totally foreign, ie conduct by and against foreigners, outside its territory and its extensions, and not justified by the need to protect a narrow self-interest.

C. TERMINOLOGY

For clarity, the following terms are used in the sense indicated. *Territorial State* is the State where an offence is committed, in whole or in part, also denoted by the Latin *locus delicti*, literally the 'place of the crime'. *Custodial State* is the State on whose territory an offender can be found or is present, even if only in a transitory way. It does not imply that the offender is under arrest in the custodial State. A Latin expression is frequently used in the latter respect: *judex* (*loci*) *deprehensionis*,[34] literally 'the judge (of the place) of arrest'.

[31] It should be observed that criminal courts do not apply foreign penal law. Thus, if a criminal court decides that the municipal penal law is not applicable in a case before it, it will not hear the case. See C Van den Wyngaert, 'De toepassing van de strafwet in de ruimte: Enkele beschouwingen', in *Liber Amicorum Frédéric Dumon* (1983) 501, 503; C Lombois, *Droit pénal international* (1971) 11; F Desportes and F Le Gunehec, *Le nouveau droit pénal* (1995) 276–77; K Cornils, 'The use of foreign law in domestic adjucation', in N Jareborg (ed) *Double criminality: Studies in International Criminal Law* (1989) 70; PO Träskman, 'Provisions on jurisdiction in criminal law: The reform of the law caught in the tension between tradition and dynamism' in R Lahti and K Nuotio (eds) *Criminal law theory in transition: Finnish and comparative perspectives* (1992) 511, 512. The application of national penal law concerns the substantive provisions and the penalties that may be imposed, the procedural rules, including the legal position of the parties, the rules of evidence, as well as the rules on the enforcement of court decisions. In some countries, however, the criminal courts apply the *lex loci delicti* for the assessment of damages to compensate the victim of a crime (eg Belgium).

[32] A rare exception is Canada where both the applicability of law and jurisdiction of courts must be provided for in the legislation if criminal conduct outside Canada is to be punishable by a court in Canada: Law Reform Commission of Canada, *Extraterritorial Jurisdiction* (1984) 3–4.

[33] Cf Gardocki (n 9 above) 62.

[34] The expression *judex deprehensionis* is traced back to the *Codex Justinianus*: H Donnedieu de Vabres, *Les principes modernes du droit pénal international* (1928) 135.

Forum State is the State investigating and prosecuting an extraterritorial offence. *Doctrine* stands for the teachings and writings of publicists.[35] *Jurisprudence* refers to the decisions of national and international courts and tribunals.[36] *Conventional law* means the law provided for in international treaties and conventions.

One of the most problematic terms in this book is *international offence* or *international crime*. A generally accepted definition[37] or list[38] of international crimes does not exist, and this study does not hazard one. The expression functions here as an umbrella term for other commonly used designations such as crime under or against international law, universal offence, or *delictum juris gentium*. This study only considers international crimes by individuals, not by States.[39] *Common* or *domestic offences* are crimes that do not rise to the level of an international offence. *Accused*, *suspect*, and *defendant* are used in a broad everyday sense, not in a legal-technical sense; thus the terms do not imply that the person is under official investigation or has been indicted.

D. CONTENT AND METHODOLOGY

This study centres around two questions: (1) under what conditions is a country exercising universal jurisdiction internationally competent, and (2) what is the basis in domestic law for the exercise of universal jurisdiction?

Part I deals primarily with the first question and consists of three chapters, each laying the groundwork for the following chapter(s). Chapter 1 outlines an international legal framework for the problem of extraterritorial jurisdiction in general. Chapter 2 presents the principal views on universal jurisdiction

[35] Cf the French version of article 38(1)(d) ICJ Statute.

[36] Cf the French expression *jurisprudence*.

[37] The problem of defining international crime is connected with the problem of defining international criminal law. In both expressions, the adjective 'international' is ambiguous as it can have either a material sense, or a formal sense, or both. See D Oehler, 'Perspectives on the Contents of the Special Part of the Draft International Criminal Code' (1981) 52 *Revue internationale de droit pénal* 407, 411–14. For a possible definition of the term international crime, see MC Bassiouni, *A Draft International Criminal Code and Draft Statute for an International Criminal Court* (1987) 55.

[38] One of the earliest comprehensive attempts to categorize international crimes is Q Saldaña, 'La justice pénale internationale' (1925) 10 *Receuil des cours de l'académie de droit international* 221, 285–346. Present-day scholarship distinguishes between international crimes *sensu stricto* and international crimes *sensu lato*; see eg the resolution of the XIVth International Congress of Penal Law (Vienna, 1989) reprinted in (1990) 61 *Revue internationale de droit pénal* 131–4; see also, extensively, O Triffterer, 'Efforts to Recognize and Codify International Crimes' (1989) 60 *Revue internationale de droit pénal* 29–88. It is generally accepted that the category of international crimes *sensu stricto* includes the three core ICC crimes: genocide, crimes against humanity, and war crimes. Some commentators identify well over twenty international offences, eg Y Dinstein, 'International Criminal Law' (1985) 20 *Israel L Rev* 206 and Bassiouni (ibid).

[39] I refer to article 19(2) of the Draft Articles on State Responsibility as adopted by the International Law Commission in 1976. The current draft no longer mentions international crimes of State.

in doctrine, putting the subject-matter in a theoretical and historical perspective. Chapter 3 examines universal jurisdiction in international texts.

Part II brings together, and makes accessible in English, detailed accounts of universal jurisdiction in fourteen countries. The results of Parts I and II are connected in the conclusions. The study ends with a postscript on the ICJ decision of 14 February 2002 in the case concerning the *Arrest Warrant of 11 April 2000*.[40]

In a way, the structure of this book corresponds with the various sources of international law as listed in article 38(1) of the ICJ Statute.[41] International conventions and the teachings of the most highly qualified publicists on the subject are considered respectively in chapter 2 and in the first section of chapter 3. International custom, which is sometimes advanced as a justification for universal jurisdiction,[42] is considered in the second and third sections of chapter 3 and in Part II.

What constitutes international custom, however, is controversial[43] and needs some explanation. Custom is generally considered to have two elements: State practice and *opinio juris*. According to the traditional understanding of customary international law, it was considered to come about through the emergence of a general (or extensive) uniform, consistent, and settled practice, more or less gradually joined by a sense of legal obligations, the *opinio juris*. For the purpose of verification, practice took priority over *opinio juris*; deeds were what counted, not just words. Traditional custom is evolutionary and is identified through an *inductive* process in which a general practice is derived from specific instances of practice. By contrast, modern custom is derived by a *deductive* process that starts from words—the text of a General Assembly

[40] N 18 above.

[41] Article 38(1) ICJ Statute provides:

The Court, whose function is to decide in accordance with international law such disputes as are submitted to it, shall apply:

a. international conventions, whether general or particular, establishing rules expressly recognized by the contesting states;
b. international custom, as evidence of a general practice accepted as law;
c. the general principles of law recognized by civilized nations;
d. subject to the provisions of Article 59, judicial decisions and the teachings of the most highly qualified publicists of the various nations, as subsidiary means for the determination of rules of law.

[42] Eg K Ambos and S Wirth, 'Genocide and War Crimes in the Former Yugoslavia Before German Criminal Courts' in H Fischer, C Kreß, and SR Lüder (eds) *International and National Prosecutions of Crimes under International Law: Current Developments* (2001) 769, 780; MP Scharf, 'Application of Treaty-Based Universal Jurisdiction to Nationals of Non-Party States' (2001) 35 *New England L Rev* 363, 377.

[43] My restatement of the controversy draws on the following sources: B Simma, 'International Human Rights and General International Law' in *Collected Courses of the Academy of European Law* (1993) IV, Book 2, 153, 213–23; M Koskenniemi, *From Apology to Utopia: The Structure of the International Legal Argument* (1989) 342–89; M Koskenniemi, 'The Pull of the Mainstream' (1990) 88 *Michigan L Rev* 1946; AE Roberts, 'Traditional and Modern Approaches to Customary International Law: A Reconciliation' (2001) 95 *Am J Int'l L* 757.

declaration, the provision of a treaty or of a draft convention—rather than from particular instances of practice. This approach emphasizes *opinio juris* rather than State practice because it relies primarily on statements rather than actions. Modern custom can develop quickly because it is deduced from multilateral treaties and declarations by international fora.

This study favours the inductive process and distinguishes between statements (*opinio juris*) and action (State practice). The more rigorous approach is adopted because of the need for legal security (*Rechtssicherheit, sécurité juridique*), particularly in criminal law.[44] The primary goal of chapter 3, which deals with *words* in multilateral conventions,[45] resolutions, and official drafts and studies, is to establish *opinio juris*. By contrast, Part II focuses on actual *deeds* of States. Because of the stated preference for the inductive method, greater weight is given in the conclusions to practice than to statements.

The research for this book was undertaken against the background of spectacular and rapid national and international legal developments, such as the establishment and practice of the *ad hoc* international criminal tribunals for Rwanda and the former Yugoslavia, the creation of the International Criminal Court, domestic prosecutions of international offences, national legislative initiatives, and the *Arrest Warrant* case referred to above. Empirical data are generally included until 1 July 2002. Many of the sources on which this study draws are non-English. All translations are by the author, except when otherwise indicated.

[44] The method preferred in this study may be called 'modern positivism'; cf B Simma and AL Paulus, 'The Responsibility of Individuals for Human Rights Abuses in Internal Conflicts: A Positivist View' (1999) 93 *Am J Int'l L* 302.

[45] Conventions obviously constitute a direct source of international law for the immediate parties but for the purpose of ascertaining custom they are here treated as statements; cf Roberts (n 43 above) 758.

PART I

Universal Jurisdiction in International Law

1

Working frame

Without a proper frame a topic is prone to manipulation. Framing 'universal jurisdiction' as an international legal issue turns out to be extremely tricky. This chapter frames the problem from a practical point of view, identifying the international legal issues that may arise when a State actually investigates and prosecutes an offence with a foreign element.

It starts with the *Lotus* case[1] of 1927, which remains the only international decision about a State's right to exercise criminal jurisdiction.[2] Next the consequences of *ultra vires* jurisdiction are examined, as well as possible remedies. After that it is demonstrated how extraterritorial jurisdiction, extradition, and human rights are closely connected. Then follows a discussion on the burden of proof in litigation regarding extraterritorial jurisdiction. Thereafter the so-called principles and forms of jurisdiction are considered. The chapter ends with some reflections on the impacts of globalization on jurisdiction.

A. THE *LOTUS* CASE

The question of extraterritorial jurisdiction under international law starts with this formulation: do we set out to examine whether extraterritorial jurisdiction is *permissible* or merely *not prohibited*?[3] The issue was presented in the *Lotus* case, which arose out of a collision on the high seas between the French steamer the *Lotus* and the Turkish steamer *Boz-Kourt*. Several Turkish sailors and passengers on board the *Boz-Kourt* were killed. Upon the arrival of the *Lotus* at Constantinople, Turkish authorities launched joint criminal proceedings in pursuance of Turkish law[4] against the French and Turkish commanders. A Turkish court found both guilty of involuntary manslaughter.

France challenged Turkey's jurisdiction before the Permanent Court of International Justice (PCIJ). The French government alleged that Turkey had acted in conflict with the principles of international law by asserting criminal jurisdiction over the French commander, and France claimed damages from

[1] 1927 PCIJ Reports, ser. A, no 10, 4.

[2] See below the postscript on the ICJ decision in *Arrest Warrant of 11 April 2000*.

[3] Cf G Fitzmaurice, 'The Law and Procedure of the International Court of Justice, 1951–54: General Principles and Sources of Law' (1953) 30 *British Ybk Int'l L* 7, 9–18. More generally, see M Koskenniemi, *From Apology to Utopia: The Structure of the International Legal Argument* (1989).

[4] The proceedings against the French commander were based on article 6(1) of the Turkish penal code, which provides for Turkish jurisdiction over extraterritorial offences to the prejudice of Turkey or of a Turkish subject, provided the foreigner is arrested in Turkey.

Turkey. France contended that the Turkish courts, in order to have jurisdiction, should be able to point to some specific entitlement to jurisdiction recognized by international law in favour of Turkey. Turkey, on the other hand, asserted that it had jurisdiction unless it was forbidden by international law.[5] The Court, by the President's deciding vote,[6] ruled in favour of Turkey. It held:

> International law governs relations between independent States. The rules of law binding upon States therefore emanate from their own free will as expressed in conventions or by usages generally accepted as expressing principles of law and established in order to regulate the relations between these co-existing independent communities or with a view to the achievement of common aims. Restrictions upon the independence of States cannot therefore be presumed.
>
> Now the first and foremost restriction imposed by international law upon a State is that—failing the existence of a permissive rule to the contrary—it may not exercise its power in any form in the territory of another State. In this sense jurisdiction is certainly territorial; it cannot be exercised by a State outside its territory except by virtue of a permissive rule derived from international custom or from a convention.
>
> It does not, however, follow that international law prohibits a State from exercising jurisdiction in its own territory, in respect of any case which relates to acts which have taken place abroad, and in which it cannot rely on some permissive rule of international law. Such a view would only be tenable if international law contained a general prohibition to States to extend the application of their laws and the jurisdiction of their courts to persons, property, and acts outside their territory, and if, as an exception to this general prohibition, it allowed States to do so in certain specific cases. But this is certainly not the case under international law as it stands at present. Far from laying down a general prohibition to the effect that States may not extend the application of their laws and the jurisdiction of their courts to persons, property, and acts outside their territory, it leaves them in this respect a wide measure of discretion which is only limited in certain cases by prohibitive rules; as regards other cases, every State remains free to adopt the principles which it regards as best and most suitable.
>
> This discretion left to States by international law explains the great variety of rules which they have been able to adopt without objections or complaints on the part of other States; it is in order to remedy the difficulties resulting from such variety that efforts have been made for many years past, both in Europe and America, to prepare conventions the effect of which would be precisely to limit the discretion at present left to States in this respect by international law, thus making good the existing lacunae in

[5] Compare the disagreement over the formulation of the legal issue in the *Lotus* case with the dispute about the phrasing of the question in the *Legality of the Threat or Use of Nuclear Weapons*, ICJ Reports 1996, 66, paras 20–2. The UN General Assembly put the following question to the Court: 'Is the threat or use of nuclear weapons in any circumstance permitted under international law?' The nuclear weapons States criticized the use of the word 'permitted' in the question on the ground that this implied that the threat or use of nuclear weapons would only be permissible if authorization could be found in a treaty or in customary international law.

[6] Resort to this procedure is highly exceptional. The PCIJ and its successor the ICJ have subsequently utilized it only twice. The second time was in *South West Africa* (ICJ Reports 1966, 6). The third time was in the above-mentioned *Nuclear Weapons* case.

respect of jurisdiction or removing the conflicting jurisdictions arising from the diversity of the principles adopted by the various States.

In these circumstances, all that can be required of a State is that it should not overstep the limits which international law places upon its jurisdiction; within these limits, its title to exercise jurisdiction rests in its sovereignty.[7]

...

The offence for which Lieutenant Demons appears to have been prosecuted was an act—of negligence or imprudence—having its origin on board the *Lotus*, whilst its effects made themselves felt on board the *Boz-Kourt*. These two elements are, legally, entirely inseparable, so much so that their separation renders the offence non-existent. Neither the exclusive jurisdiction of either State, nor the limitations of the jurisdiction of each to the occurrences which took place on the respective ships would appear calculated to satisfy the requirements of justice and effectively protect the interests of the two States. It is only natural that each should be able to exercise jurisdiction and to do so in respect of the incident as a whole. It is therefore a case of concurrent jurisdiction.[8]

Few decisions of the PCIJ and its successor have generated more debate.[9] The controversy focuses more on the *dicta* than the actual decision, which was mainly based on the ground that one of the constitutive elements of the offence, namely the effects, were produced on the Turkish vessel. Under international law a vessel is considered an extension of the territory of the State under whose flag it sails; therefore prosecution of the French commander was justified, according to the Court, from the point of view of the so-called territorial principle.

The discussion revolves in the first place around the dictum that '[r]estrictions upon the independence of States cannot... be presumed', which seems to proclaim a presumptive freedom of State action in general. Hence the expression '*Lotus* principle' for the view that States have a right to do whatever is not prohibited by an international convention or custom.[10] International law, in other words, would be merely regulative of State rights, not constitutive.[11] Underlying this view is the immanence theory, which is based on the Hegelian view that the State is the only creator of law.[12] Sovereignty thus precedes international law. States are vested with a natural liberty, and limitations on jurisdiction are always self-imposed and can be lifted at any time. The essence of international law is not to allocate competences but to establish duties as exceptions to the initial liberty. The opposite theory is the attribution theory, which holds that sovereignty is a quality allocated to certain entities by international

[7] *Lotus* (n 1 above) paras 18–19.

[8] Ibid para 31.

[9] See the lengthy bibliography of early comments on *Lotus* in World Court Reports (1927–1932) II, 20–1.

[10] M Koskenniemi, *From Apology to Utopia: The Structure of the International Legal Argument* (1989) 221.

[11] Cf Fitzmaurice (n 3 above) 9–18.

[12] GAM Strijards, *Internationaal Strafrecht: Strafmachtsrecht* (1984) 126.

law. The legal order pre-exists the sovereignty of the State and remains in control thereof; accordingly, a State will always have to show a specific rule of international law entitling it to act, or at least the absence of a prohibiting rule.[13] That the most prominent jurists remain divided over this legal-philosophical question was shown by the judgment and dissenting opinions in the *Nuclear Weapons* case.[14]

On the specific issue of State jurisdiction over crime, it appears that every condemnation of the *Lotus* judgment can be juxtaposed with a competing pronouncement defending it. One of the main critics is Mann who asserts that the *Lotus* passages that emphasize discretion 'have been condemned by the majority of the immense number of writers who have discussed them, and today they probably cannot claim to be good law'.[15]

Scholars who look primarily at State practice, however, do not readily share his opinion. The Rapporteur of the Commission on the Extraterritorial Jurisdiction of States of the Institute of International Law concludes that 'a spirit of free appreciation of the authority of the concept [of jurisdiction] pervades the atmosphere, and it is this spirit which must be responsible for the continuing popularity of the [*Lotus*] judgment'.[16] Another commentator persuasively argues that the non-referral by States of jurisdictional issues to the ICJ is itself an example of the continuing wish of States to retain freedom of decision.[17] States' disinclination to adopt a convention on criminal jurisdiction

[13] My distinction between immanence and attribution theory draws on the 'legal' and 'pure fact' approaches to sovereignty by M Koskenniemi, *From Apology to Utopia: The Structure of the International Legal Argument* (1989) 196–200.

[14] The Court's main strategy in the case was to find a specific rule prohibiting or authorizing the threat or use of nuclear weapons. A wide majority of the judges found neither. However, an evenly divided Court further concluded that 'in view of the current state of international law . . . the Court cannot conclude definitively whether the threat or use of nuclear weapons would be lawful or unlawful in an extreme circumstance of self-defence, in which the very survival of the State would be at stake': *Nuclear Weapons* (n 5 above) para 2E of the *dispositif*. According to some of the judges, this conclusion is in fact a pronouncement of *non liquet*, which could be advantageous to adherents of the *Lotus* principle. S Mahmoudi, 'The International Court of Justice and Nuclear Weapons' (1997) 66 *Nordic J Int'l L* 77, 95 notes that five pages of Judge Shahabuddeen's dissenting opinion are devoted to discussing and rejecting the *Lotus* argument and the thesis that what is not prohibited is permitted.

[15] FA Mann, 'The Doctrine of Jurisdiction in International Law' (1964) 111 *Receuil des cours de l'académie de droit international* 9, 35.

[16] A Bos, 'The Extraterritorial Jurisdiction of States. Preliminary Report' (1993) 65 *Ybk Institute Int'l L*, I, 14, 39. Likewise, L Gardocki, 'The Principle of Universality' in N Jareborg (ed) *Double Criminality: Studies in International Criminal Law* (1989) 57, 58–9; and P Peters, 'Volkenrechtelijke aspecten van extraterritoriale wetgeving' in P Peters and R Kotting (eds) *Extraterritoriale wetgeving* (1984) 3, 13. Recent monographs on extraterritorial criminal jurisdiction take the *Lotus* premise as a starting point: A Henrich, *Das passive Personalitätsprinzip im deutschen Strafrecht* (1994) 14–16; and C Pappas, *Stellvertretende Strafrechtspflege* (1996) 75–6. But I Cameron, *The Protective Principle of International Criminal Jurisdiction* (1994) 320–3, attributes limited relevance to the *Lotus* judgment for jurisdictional claims today.

[17] H Fox, 'Jurisdiction and Immunities' in V Lowe and M Fitzmaurice (eds) *Fifty Years of the International Court of Justice* (1996) 210, 212–15.

can be seen as a further example of this wish.[18] *Lotus* has also been sanctioned by Judge Fitzmaurice in *Barcelona Traction*[19] and by some domestic judicial decisions.[20]

The presumption of freedom, however, should not be taken literally. Without further elaboration, the judgment refers twice to 'limits' which international law places on jurisdiction and to 'principles'. The latter reference would have been superfluous had the Court taken the presumption of freedom literally.[21] Therefore, the controversial dictum that 'restrictions upon the independence of States cannot... be presumed' is perhaps not as far-reaching as critics of *Lotus* sometimes assume, at least not in respect of criminal jurisdiction.[22]

At this point, and despite the vagueness and generality of the Court's pronouncements, two conclusions of major importance for this study may be drawn from *Lotus*. First, international law governs the area of extraterritorial jurisdiction over foreigners.[23] If States had absolute discretion, extraterritorial jurisdiction would simply not be an issue. Second, international law recognizes (multiple) concurrent jurisdiction.[24] If States were forbidden from

[18] See this chapter, s B.

[19] *Barcelona Traction, Light and Power Company, Limited*, ICJ Reports 1970, 3; separate opinion of Judge Fitzmaurice at para 70:

'It is true that, under present conditions, international law does not impose hard and fast rules on States delimiting spheres of national jurisdiction [...], but leaves to States a wide measure of discretion in the matter. It does however *(a)* postulate the *existence* of limits—though in any given case it may be for the tribunal to indicate what they are for the purposes of that case; and *(b)* involve for every State an obligation to exercise moderation and restraint as to the extent of the jurisdiction assumed by its courts in cases having a foreign element, and to avoid undue encroachment on a jurisdiction more properly appertaining to, or more appropriately exercisable by, another State' (emphasis in the original).

[20] The Supreme Court of Israel in the *Eichmann* case and a United States federal court in the *Demjanjuk* case explicitly endorse *Lotus*. See the respective country studies in Part II below.

[21] This caveat applies to the *Eichmann* decision, which asserts discretion yet justifies Israel's competence under the universality principle, and to the work of those scholars who proclaim freedom of jurisdiction yet elaborate on the 'principles'.

[22] Cf RY Jennings, 'General Course on Principles of International Law' (1967) 121 *Receuil des cours de l'académie de droit international* 323, 518.

[23] For H Kelsen, *Principles of International Law* (2nd edn, 1966) 178, the determination of the sphere of validity of municipal law is the essential function of international law. Commentators supporting the opinion that international law governs the area of extraterritorial jurisdiction over foreigners include DW Bowett, 'Jurisdiction. Changing Patterns of Authority over Activities and Resources' (1982) 53 *British Ybk Int'l L* 1, 3; AMM Orie, JG van der Meijs, and AMG Smit, *Internationaal Strafrecht* (1991) 25; I Cameron 'The Protective Principle of Criminal Jurisdiction in Nordic Criminal Law' in R Lahti and K Nuotio (eds), *Criminal Law Theory in Transition: Finnish and Comparative Perspectives* (1992) 544, 562; Gardocki (n 16 above) 61; H Schultz, 'Compétences des jurisdictions pénales pour les infractions commises à l'étranger' (1967) 22 *Revue de science criminelle et de droit pénal comparé* 305, 306; E Roswogg, *Das Problem der Vereinbarkeit des aktiven und passiven Personalitätsgrundsatzes mit dem Völkerrecht* (1965) 37 (with more references to concurring doctrine).

[24] The view that territoriality of criminal jurisdiction is not a dogma was already taken by Brierly in his capacity as Rapporteur of the League of Nations Committee of Experts for the Progressive Codification of International Law. He wrote: 'The territorial basis of jurisdiction is not a mere dogma; it is justified normally because it is convenient that crimes should be dealt

extending the application of their criminal law and jurisdiction of their courts to persons and acts outside their territory, then extraterritorial, and *a fortiori* universal jurisdiction would be illegal and that would be the end of the discussion. So the extreme views, not uncommon a century ago,[25] seem to have been completely abandoned.

B. ABSENCE OF GLOBAL CONVENTION

One of the passages quoted from *Lotus* refers to efforts being undertaken at that time to prepare international conventions on jurisdiction with respect to crime. As of this date these efforts have borne no fruit, apart from a regional treaty between a number of Latin American countries.[26] The European countries successfully adopted a convention on jurisdiction in civil and commercial matters,[27] but tellingly failed to do so in the criminal field.[28] The International Law Commission at its first session in 1949 selected jurisdiction with regard to crimes committed outside national territory as a topic for codification but has discontinued its work on the matter. Thus, at present there is no global convention on criminal jurisdiction, and it seems unlikely that such an instrument will be adopted in the near future, if ever.[29] As suggested previously, the apprehension to adopt a general convention is an example of the continuing wish of States to retain some freedom of decision.

with by the State whose social order they affect most closely and this in general is the State on whose territory they are committed': JL Brierly, 'Report on Jurisdiction over Extraterritorial Crime' (1926) 20 *Am J Int'l L* 253, 255. See also I Brownlie, *Principles of Public International Law* (4th edn, 1990) 311; Roswogg (n 23 above) 40–2, with more references to concurring doctrine. Some publicists consider concurrency a desirable phenomenon as it can only enhance the international combat against crime, eg SZ Feller, 'Concurrent Criminal Jurisdiction in the International Sphere' (1981) 16 *Israel L Rev* 40, 42–3; C Shachor-Landau, 'Extra-Territorial Penal Jurisdiction and Extradition' (1980) 29 *Int'l & Comparative LQ* 275, 294. Others point to the risk of tensions between States and argue against, eg Strijards (n 12 above) 175.

[25] K Bindung, *Handbuch des Strafrechts: 1. Band* (1885) 347 argued that States have absolute discretion. L Oppenheim, *International Law: A Treatise, vol. I, Peace* (3rd edn, 1920) para 147, maintained the exact opposite:

> 'No right for a State to extend its jurisdiction over acts of foreigners committed in foreign countries can be said to have grown up according to the Law of Nations, and the right of protection over citizens abroad held by every State would justify it in an intervention in case one of its citizens abroad should be required to stand his trial before the courts of another State for criminal acts which he did not commit during the time he was under the territorial supremacy of such State'.

[26] The so-called Bustamente Code, annexed to the Havana Convention on Private International Law, entered into force on 1 January 1935 for the following States: Brazil, Bolivia, Costa Rica, Cuba, Dominican Republic, El Salvador, Chile, Ecuador, Guatemala, Haiti, Honduras, Nicaragua, Panama, Peru, and Venezuela; reprinted in (1935) 29 *Am J Int'l L* 642. It is not clear whether the Convention is still in force.

[27] Convention on Jurisdiction and the Enforcement of Judgments in Civil and Commercial Matters (Brussels, 27 September 1968; 72/454/EEC L 299 1972).

[28] See ch 3 s C below.

[29] Bos (n 16 above) 39.

Conversely, the international community of States has developed elaborate multilateral treaties on many specific crimes.[30] In addition, virtually all States have pledged to co-operate in suppression of all serious crimes by adopting bilateral and multilateral extradition treaties and treaties providing for mutual legal assistance in criminal matters.[31] The international community has thus committed itself to the suppression of crime through a variety of devices.[32] It may be said that a *co-operative* international law based on a community of interests has developed in the field of crime prevention and punishment.[33] Linking this development with the problem of extraterritorial jurisdiction, the Committee on Crime Problems of the Council of Europe takes the view that '[p]ublic international law does not impose any limitations on the freedom of States to establish forms of extraterritorial criminal jurisdiction where they are based on international solidarity between States in the fight against crime'.[34]

C. CONSEQUENCES OF *ULTRA VIRES* JURISDICTION AND REMEDIES

What are the consequences of and remedies for excessive jurisdiction? In the *Lotus* case it was the French State, not the French commander, which claimed damages from Turkey. An individual defendant lacks standing to challenge the jurisdiction of the forum State on the international plane. None of the human rights treaties that allow individuals to lodge a complaint against a State party before an international body provide the right of a defendant to be tried in the territorial State[35] or in the State of his nationality. There is thus no way for an individual to raise the jurisdiction issue *as such* at the international level. The present study therefore approaches the problem of extraterritorial jurisdiction primarily from the angle of the rights of States: looking at the issue through the lens of international law rather than criminal law or human rights.[36]

[30] See ch 3 s A below.

[31] GR Watson, 'The Passive Personality Principle' (1993) 28 *Texas Int'l LJ* 1, 42–3. [32] Ibid.

[33] On the evolution of international law from a law of co-existence to a law of co-operation, see W Friedmann, *The Changing Structure of International Law* (1964).

[34] Council of Europe. European Committee on Crime Problems, *Extraterritorial Criminal Jurisdiction* (1990) 27.

[35] Interestingly, the Bill of Rights of the United States Constitution, which inspired many an international human rights instrument, contains a clause to that effect. The Sixth Amendment provides:

'In all criminal prosecutions, the accused shall enjoy the right to a speedy and public trial, by an impartial jury of the State and the district wherein the crime shall have been committed, which district shall have been previously ascertained by law, and to be informed of the nature and the cause of accusation; to be confronted with the witnesses against him; to have compulsory process for obtaining witnesses in his favor, and to have the Assistance of Counsel for his defence'.

[36] On human rights issues related to extraterritorial jurisdiction, see AHJ Swart, 'Jurisdiction in Criminal Law: Some Reflections on the Finnish Code from a Comparative Perspective' in R Lahti and K Nuotio (eds) *Criminal Law Theory in Transition* (1992) 527, 529–33.

Excessive jurisdiction may, however, result in inter-State responsibility. The wrongful act can be regarded either as a *direct* violation of the territorial State's sovereignty (see section E below) or as an *indirect* violation of the right that its nationals be treated in accordance with international law.[37] Only the State of which the injured individual is a national has this right to intervene on his behalf (ie exercise diplomatic protection)[38] but other countries may treat an excessive exercise of jurisdiction as null for the purposes of recognition within their domestic law.[39] For instance, if a State issues an *ultra vires* arrest warrant, other countries can treat the warrant as invalid, and accordingly not execute it. They also may protest because acquiescence can amount to consent to a (nascent) customary rule.

The State of the individual concerned may resort to legal action after he has exhausted legal remedies under the law of the forum. The judicial body competent to adjudicate such a claim would ordinarily be the International Court of Justice because it is the only international tribunal with general jurisdiction.[40] It should be stressed that a State is entirely free to espouse the cause of its national.[41] A State may receive notice of a prosecution of a national abroad

[37] On the legal fiction that the State is the actual victim when one of its subjects is not treated in accordance with international law, see Nguyen Quoc Dinh, P Daillier, and A Pellet, *Droit Public International* (4th edn, 1992) 743–5. The Permanent Court of International Justice formulated this rule in *Mavrommatis Palestine Concessions*, 1924 PCIJ Reports, ser. A, no 2, at 12:

'It is an elementary principle of international law that a State is entitled to protect its subjects, when injured by acts contrary to international law committed by another State, from whom they have been unable to obtain satisfaction through the ordinary channels. By taking up the case of one of its subjects and by resorting to diplomatic action or international judicial proceedings on his behalf, a State is in reality asserting its own rights—its right to ensure, in the person of its subjects, respect for the rules of international law'.

[38] The International Court of Justice has articulated this basic rule of international law in *Barcelona Traction* (n 19 above) para 35:

'Obligations the performance of which is the subject of diplomatic protection are not of the same category [as obligations of a State towards the international community as a whole]. It cannot be held, when one such obligation in particular is in question, in a specific case, that all States have a legal interest in its observance. In order to bring a claim in respect of the breach of such an obligation, a State must first establish its right to do so, for the rules on the subject rest on two suppositions: "The first is that the defendant State has broken an obligation towards the national State in respect of its nationals. The second is that only the party to whom an international obligation is due can bring a claim in respect of its breach". (*Reparation for Injuries Suffered in the Service of the United Nations, Advisory Opinion, I.C.J. Reports 1949*, 181–2).' See also the *South West Africa* case (n 6 above) para 88 where the Court held that 'the equivalent of an "*actio popularis*", or right resident in any member of a community to take legal action in vindication of a public interest... is not known in international law as it stands at present...'

[39] RY Jennings, 'Nullity and Effectiveness in International Law' in *Cambridge Essays in International Law: Essays in honour of Lord McNair* (1965) 64, 82.

[40] See article 36 ICJ Statute. All other international courts and tribunals derive their jurisdiction from a treaty determining a specialized area of competence.

[41] See *Barcelona Traction* (n 19 above) para 79:

'The State must be viewed as the sole judge to decide whether its protection will be granted, to what extent it is granted, and when it will cease. It retains in this respect a discretionary power the exercise of which may be determined by consideration of a political or other nature, unrelated to the particular case. Since the claim of the State is not identical with that of the individual or

through consular notification. The Vienna Convention on Consular Relations (article 36)[42] and many bilateral consular conventions provide for a right of a foreign detainee to contact the diplomatic mission of his home State.

D. JURISDICTION, EXTRADITION, AND HUMAN RIGHTS

As noted above, human rights treaties do not restrict extraterritorial jurisdiction. They do, however, increasingly impact on extradition.[43] The 'breakthrough' for extradition and human rights on the international scene came with the *Soering* case of the European Court of Human Rights.[44] Soering, a German national, murdered his girlfriend's parents in Virginia and fled to the United Kingdom, from which his extradition was requested by the United States. After the United Kingdom ordered his extradition, he petitioned the European Commission of Human Rights, which referred the case to the European Court of Human Rights. The Court held that the United Kingdom was required by article 3 of the European Convention for the Protection of Human Rights and Fundamental Freedoms,[45] which prohibits torture and inhuman or degrading treatment or punishment, not to extradite Soering to the United States where there was a real risk that he would be subjected to inhuman or degrading treatment by being kept on death row for a prolonged period in the State of Virginia. The Court found that the fact that the actual human rights violation would take place outside the territory of the requested State did not absolve it from the responsibility for any foreseeable consequence of extradition suffered outside its jurisdiction. In such a case the requested State incurs responsibility because it has reasonable grounds to foresee that a violation of human rights will occur in the requesting State and, despite this, extradites the fugitive.

Other human rights that could thwart extradition include the prohibition on torture, discrimination, and the right to a fair trial.[46] States increasingly deny

corporate person whose cause is espoused, the State enjoys complete freedom of action'. A case in point is *Eichmann* wherein no State with any legal interest in the protection of the defendant interceded on his behalf; see the Israel country study in Part II below.

[42] Vienna, 24 April 1963; UNTS Nos. 8638–40, vol 596, 262–512.

[43] See, extensively, J Dugard and C Van den Wyngaert, 'Reconciling Extradition with Human Rights' (1998) 92 *Am J Int'l L* 187; see also C Blakesley, 'Autumn of the Patriarch: The Pinochet Extradition Debacle and Beyond—Human Rights Clauses Compared to Traditional Derivative Protections such as Double Criminality' (2000) 91 *J Crim L & Criminology* 1.

[44] *Soering* v *United Kingdom*, 161 Eur Ct HR (ser. A) (1989), reprinted in (1989) 28 *Intl' Legal Materials* 1063; see also *Chitat Ng* v *Canada*, Communication No 469/1991, UN Doc. CCPR/C/49/D469/1991 (1994).

[45] Rome, 4 November 1950; ETS No 5; 213 UNTS 221.

[46] Dugard and Van den Wyngaert (n 43 above) 196–206; see also the United Nations Model Treaty on Extradition: article 3(f) states that extradition shall not be granted 'if the person whose extradition is requested has been or would be subjected in the requesting State to torture or cruel, inhuman or degrading treatment or punishment or if that person has not received or would not receive the minimum guarantees in criminal proceedings, as contained in the International Covenant on Civil and Political Rights, article 14'.

extradition in the interest of these rights[47] even where such denial results in a violation of their obligations under an extradition treaty. The custodial State then faces a dilemma: leaving the fugitive in peace or prosecuting him before its own courts for a crime committed abroad. If the latter course of action were not allowed then both the interests of the custodial State and the requirements of justice would be seriously compromised.[48]

E. BURDEN OF PROOF

In litigation the onus of proof lies on the plaintiff (*actori incumbit onus probandi*).[49] In a dispute between States involving extraterritorial jurisdiction it is up to the State of nationality of the defendant to show that the criminal proceedings in the forum State are contrary to international law. The burden of proof in the *Lotus* case was accordingly cast on France, the challenger of jurisdiction. Turkey, the defendant State, had nothing to prove. It is important to remember, however, that the entire process complained of—the assumption of jurisdiction over a French national in respect of something done by him on the high seas—occurred in Turkish territory, ie in a Turkish court, in respect of a vessel and a person voluntarily present in Turkey.

How does the issue of burden of proof present itself when the dispute relates to an offence committed within the plaintiff State's own territory? The onus of proof still lies on the plaintiff State but it would not be too difficult for the plaintiff State to cause the onus of proof to shift if the following analysis is correct. The sovereign equality of States constitutes the basic constitutional doctrine of the law of nations.[50] A corollary of sovereign equality is the right of each State freely to choose and develop its political, social, economic, and cultural systems, including its criminal justice policy,[51] without interference in any form by another State.[52]

[47] See, most recently, *United States* v *Burns* [2001] 1 SCR 283, Supreme Court of Canada, 15 February 2001, reprinted in (2001) 40 *Int'l L Materials* 1034. The Court found that the right to life provision of the Canadian Charter of Rights and Freedoms concerned the potential consequences of extradition; extradition without assurances from the requesting State that the suspects would not suffer the death penalty would be a 'necessary link in the chain of causation' to the potential infliction of capital punishment.

[48] The requirement of justice was one of the reasons cited by the court in *Lotus* to justify concurrency of jurisdiction (n 1 above at 31).

[49] On the burden of proof in litigation before the ICJ, see extensively Fitzmaurice, (n 3 above) 9–18.

[50] Brownlie (n 24 above) 287.

[51] PO Träskman, 'Should We Take the Condition of Double Criminality Seriously?' in N Jareborg (ed) *Double Criminality: Studies in International Criminal Law* (1989) 135, 147–8.

[52] See the definition of 'sovereign equality' and 'non-intervention' in the Declaration on Principles of International Law concerning Friendly Relations and Co-operation among States in accordance with the Charter of the United Nations, UNGA resolution 2625 of 24 October

Couched in terms of international relations: a State may not interfere with another State's internal or domestic affairs. An exercise of jurisdiction by any State other than the territorial State violates *prima facie* the non-interference principle, which thus functions as an important limit on jurisdiction over crime.[53] The defendant State must then be prepared to show that its proceedings are nevertheless justified by international law, *either* by showing that it is pursuing its own legitimate interests *or* that the offence transcends the domestic affairs of the territorial State and falls in the sphere of international concern, and above all of international law. This leads to the 'principles of jurisdiction'.

F. PRINCIPLES OF JURISDICTION

The passage in *Lotus* that 'every State remains free to adopt the principles which it regards as best and most suitable' suggests that there are a number of clear and generally accepted principles on the basis of which States can exercise criminal jurisdiction in conformity with international law. Three questions arise: (1) which are the different principles of jurisdiction, (2) what is their meaning and function, and (3) under which principle(s), if any, can a State exercise jurisdiction over a non-national for a crime committed abroad against a non-national?

Doctrine identifies up to seven principles:[54] (1) the principle of territoriality, (2) the principle of the nationality of the offender (or active personality principle), (3) the principle of the nationality of the victim (or passive personality principle), (4) the principle of the flag, (5) the principle of protection, (6) the

1970, reprinted in DJ Djonovich, *United Nations Resolutions*, Series I, Volume XIII, 1970–71, 337–40; see also the Declaration on the Inadmissibility of Intervention in the Domestic Affairs of States and Protection of Their Independence and Sovereignty, UNGA resolution 2131 of 21 December 1965, reprinted in DJ Djonovich, *United Nations Resolutions*, Series I, Volume X, 1964–65, 107–8; see also the following instruments incorporating the non-interference and non-intervention principles: Convention on the Rights and Duties of States (article 8), Charter of the Organization of African Unity (article 3), Charter of the Organization of American States (articles 9, 16, and 18), Final Act of the Conference on Security and Co-Operation in Europe (Principle I), and Concluding Document of the Vienna Meeting 1986 of Representatives of the Participating States of the Conference on Security and Co-Operation in Europe (Principle 3).

[53] Scholars suggesting that the non-interference principle functions as an important limit on jurisdiction include Bowett (n 23 above) 14–18; Brownlie (n 24 above) 310; Pappas (n 16 above) 77–8.

[54] Two collective studies stand out: Harvard Research in International Law, 'Jurisdiction with Respect to Crime' (1935) 29 *Am J Int'l L* 435 and Council of Europe, European Committee on Crime Problems, *Extraterritorial criminal jurisdiction* (1990). The most comprehensive individual studies include M Travers, *Le droit pénal international et sa mise en oeuvre en temps de paix et en temps de guerre. Tome I. Principes.—Règles générales de compétence des lois répressives* (1920), H Donnedieu de Vabres, *Les principes modernes du droit pénal international* (1928), and D Oehler, *Internationales Strafrecht. Geltungsbereich des Strafrechts. Internationales Rechtshilferecht. Recht der Gemeinschaften, Völkerstrafrecht* (2nd edn, 1983). More recent and concise is CL Blakesley, 'Extraterritorial Jurisdiction' in MC Bassiouni (ed) *International Criminal Law* (2nd edn, 1998) II, 33–106.

principle of universality, and (7) the representation principle. For a long time the term 'international criminal law' meant the study of these principles.[55] A surge in academic interest in the principles could recently be noted.[56]

The first three principles are self-evident. The fourth and fifth can easily be described. The flag principle extends the application of a State's criminal law to conduct on board ships or aircraft flying its flag. Under the protective principle a State can take cognizance of an offence committed abroad with the intention of damaging its fundamental interests. The representation principle requires some explanation. According to the European Committee on Crime Problems the term refers to cases in which a State may exercise extraterritorial jurisdiction where it is deemed to be acting for another State which is more directly involved, provided certain conditions are met. In general, these conditions are a request from another State to take over criminal proceedings, or either the refusal of an extradition request from another State and its willingness to prosecute or confirmation from another State that it will not request extradition.[57] Defining the scope of the universality principle, according to which jurisdiction is exercised over extraterritorial offences, evidently without the links, criteria, or requirements underlying the previously mentioned principles being present, is one of the goals of this study.

What is the meaning and function of the principles? Before examining this question, a few preliminary observations are in order. First, these principles clearly grew out of decentralized sources—the domestic law and practice of States—rather than a centralized source.[58] Second, not every principle is readily recognized by doctrine. Only the principles of territoriality, flag, active personality, and protection are uncontested. Third, the principles, even the

[55] The best illustration is the classic one of Donnedieu de Vabres (n 54 above). For more references to doctrine identifying international criminal law with the study of the territorial scope of municipal criminal law, see G Schwarzenberger, 'The Problem of an International Criminal Law' in GOW Mueller and EM Wise (eds) *International Criminal Law* (1965) 3, 5–6.

[56] The following monographs have recently appeared: M Henzelin, *Le principe de l'universalité en droit pénal international* (2000) (on the universality principle); HD Wolswijk, *Locus delicti en rechtsmacht* (1998) (on the territoriality principle); Pappas (n 16 above) (on representation jurisdiction in German penal law); Cameron (n 16 above) (on the protective principle); Henrich (n 16 above) (on the passive personality principle in German penal law); H Li, *Die Prinzipien des internationalen Strafrechts: Eine vergleichende Untersuchung zwischen dem internationalen Strafrecht der Volksrepublik China und dem der Bundesrepublik Deutschland* (1991) (a comparative study of the principles of criminal jurisdiction in Germany and China). Older monographs include: S Shubber, *Jurisdiction Over Crimes On Board Aircraft* (1973); W Wendt, *Das passive Personalitätsprinzip* (1965) (on the passive personality principle); E Rosswog, *Das Problem der Vereinbarkeit des aktiven und passiven Personalgrundsatzes mit dem Völkerrecht* (1965) (on the compatibility of the active and passive personality principles with international law). See also T Vander Beken, *Forumkeuze in het internationaal strafrecht: Verdeling van misdrijven met aanknopingspunten in meerdere staten* (1999) (on the determination of the forum in international criminal law).

[57] Council of Europe. European Committee on Crime Problems (n 34 above) 14.

[58] GR Watson (n 31 above) 42–3; and according to Brownlie (n 24 above) 306 the principles are in substance no more than generalizations of a mass of national provisions.

uncontroversial ones, are capable of different constructions. Questions regarding the territoriality principle relate to the method of determining where an offence has been committed.[59] Nationality may seem a clear-cut criterion, yet questions arise.[60] The problem with the protective principle is that there is no internationally accepted definition of 'national security' or 'fundamental interests'. Regarding the universality principle, a cursory study of doctrine could lead one to believe that there are in fact several principles at work. For these reasons, it is doubtful that the principles of jurisdiction, at least the controversial ones, are hard and fast (international) legal rules.

To avoid a *petitio principii*, this book is entitled *Universal Jurisdiction* and not *The Universality Principle of International Criminal Jurisdiction*. This being said, it is impossible not to use the term 'principle' as applied to jurisdiction, given that it is part of the common language of international jurists and criminal lawyers. When the term is used, however, the aforementioned qualifications should be kept in mind.

If these principles do not constitute hard and fast (international) legal rules, then what are they? Pappas offers the following useful analysis of the principles' function and meaning.[61] The *function* of the principles is to indicate *either* a meaningful link (*sinnvolle Anknüpfungspunkt*) which describes an internationally legally permissible relation (*eine völkerrechtlich zulässige Nähebeziehung*) between forum State and offence or offender, *or* further international legal criteria (*weitere völkerrechtliche Kriterien*) which prevent an exercise of extraterritorial jurisdiction from infringing on another State's sovereignty. In addition, the principles rest on and are the typical results of a balancing of sovereignty between States and prohibited interference with internal affairs. As such, they make easier the difficult balancing task of legislatures and courts in a specific case: for legislatures the principles function as

[59] According to the doctrine of *ubiquity*, an offence as a whole may be considered to have been committed in the place where a part of it has been committed. Some States categorize only the acts, others also their effects. Thus, according to one interpretation of the *ubiquity* theory, a State has jurisdiction whenever any material element of an offence has occurred within its territory. According to another interpretation, a State has jurisdiction over crimes which, although committed by conduct wholly outside the territory of the forum State, caused substantial effects, whether intended or not, on persons or property within its territory. See, extensively, Wolswijk (n 56 above) 108–14 and Council of Europe, European Committee on Crime Problems (n 34 above) 8–9.

[60] Can the active personality principle be applied to a national who was born abroad, resides abroad, and is perhaps also a national of the country of residence? Can it be extended by analogy, as some States do, to extraterritorial offences committed by foreign residents? What are the consequences of a change in nationality (or residence) after the commission of the offence? The passive personality principle, in addition to these issues of dual nationality, extension to foreign residents, and change of nationality (or residence) raises specific questions. What role, if any, should the nationality of the victim play in the motive for the crime? Does the term 'victim' include persons other than the physically injured persons? If close relatives are included then diversity of citizenship between the victim *sensu stricto* and the victim(s) *sensu lato* is possible.

[61] Pappas (n 16 above) 85–7.

'signposts' when defining the scope (*Geltungsbereich*) of a norm,[62] for courts they function as standardized balancing devices (*standardisierte Abwägungshilfe*). The balancing and the resulting principles thus have a double function: they determine the international legal limits (*völkerrechtliche Grenzen*) for the general abstract criminal norm as well as for a specific case.

As for the *meaning* (*völkerrechtliche Gehalt*) of the principles, Pappas argues that they are neither simply the result of a categorization by scholars of domestic legal systems nor rules of customary international law. They have, however, some normative meaning at the international level. This follows necessarily from their origin and function according to which the content of the principles is only determined by international legal (balancing) criteria (*völkerrechtliche (Abwägungs-)Kriterien*).

If Pappas' analysis is correct, application of the principles to a specific problem will require further balancing of interests of the States involved and the requirements of justice. Moreover, in some cases the question will not be posed in terms of whether a State's claim to jurisdiction is illegal *per se*, but whether it is a *proper* exercise of jurisdiction, given the conflicting interests of two or more States as well as the consequences for the individual defendant. In short, the problem may be the more delicate one of balancing State interests and justice requirements rather than of applying a particular principle to the specific facts and producing a clear-cut answer. The need to combine the principles with a balancing of interests has been recognized by the Institute of International Law[63] and the American Law Institute.[64]

The answer to the third question includes obviously, and above all, the universality principle. But jurisdiction over a non-national for a crime committed abroad against a non-national can also be exercised on the basis of the representation principle. It differs, in theory, from the universality principle in that the decision to prosecute is not taken unilaterally, but requires a certain understanding, if not agreement, by the territorial State.[65] In practice, however, the distinction is often blurred. The present study focuses on practice, and therefore includes representation jurisdiction, exclusive of cases of transfers of criminal proceedings.[66]

[62] The 'signpost' idea (*Wegweiserfunktion*) comes from Henrich (n 16 above) 21.

[63] Article 4.1 of the Institute's Draft Resolution on the Extraterritorial Jurisdiction of States provides: 'Extraterritorial jurisdiction, whatever the specific title under which it is claimed, shall be exercised reasonably, while balancing the legal interests involved'. The Draft Resolution, which was adopted at the Milan session in 1993, is reprinted in (1993) 65 *Ybk Institute Int'l L*, II, 133–9.

[64] Section 403(1) of the Restatement (Third) of the Foreign Relations Law of the United States, as adopted and promulgated in 1987 by the American Law Institute, provides: 'Even when one of the bases for jurisdiction under § 402 is present, a State may not exercise jurisdiction to prescribe with respect to a person or activity having connections with another State when the exercise of such jurisdiction is unreasonable': American Law Institute, *Restatement of the Law (Third), The Foreign Relations Law of the United States* (1987) vol. 1, 244–5.

[65] Council of Europe, European Committee on Crime Problems (n 34 above) 14.

[66] A transfer of criminal proceeding supposes a request to prosecute from a State with jurisdiction and prosecution by the requested State on that basis. See, extensively, Vander Beken (n 56 above) 208–15.

G. FORMS OF JURISDICTION

Under the influence of American legal scholarship a number of distinctions regarding jurisdiction have become common, requiring some consideration. Most popular are the three-pronged distinction between legislative, judicial, and executive jurisdiction (by reference to the three traditional branches of State authority)[67] and the two-pronged distinction between prescriptive and enforcement jurisdiction (by reference to the substance of the powers exercised).[68] These different forms of jurisdiction would, in principle, be subject to different international legal regimes.[69]As rightly pointed out by some commentators, these distinctions are very rigid[70] and have little practical relevance because the enactment of rules by a State carries with it a presumption of future enforcement.[71]

In any event the issue of a State's international responsibility does not arise until there is a case or controversy,[72] ie until one of its organs initiates criminal proceedings regarding an offence involving an international or extraterritorial element.[73] When there is a case or controversy, international law is not concerned with the underlying abstract statute (if there is one) or how the municipal authorities have construed or applied it. It might well be that the prosecuting authorities or the adjudicating court have misconstrued their competence under the statute, and therefore acted *ultra vires* under domestic

[67] *Legislative* jurisdiction is the jurisdiction to establish in general the contents and scope of application of certain national norms and prescriptive rules. *Judicial* jurisdiction is the jurisdiction to apply established norms in a particular litigation or proceedings. *Executive* jurisdiction is the jurisdiction to enforce orders or prescriptive rules emanating from the judiciary or the legislature. See American Law Institute (n 64 above) § 401; Institute of International Law (n 63 above) 133; Council of Europe, European Committee on Crime Problems (n 34 above) 18; M Akehurst, 'Jurisdiction in International Law' (1972–73) 46 *British Ybk Int'l L* 145, 151.

[68] *Prescriptive* jurisdiction refers to the power to prescribe laws and regulations applying to situations, particularly those involving a foreign element. Such power can be exercised by either a legislature, an executive body, or a court. *Enforcement* jurisdiction refers to the power to perform acts pursuant to such rules and is exercised by either a court or an executive body.

[69] Sections 402 to 433 of the Restatement (Third) of the Foreign Relations Law of the United States spell out the legal regimes applicable to the three categories (n 64 above).

[70] Peters (n 16 above) 5 points out that there is overlap and that it is difficult to draw the dividing lines. The European Committee on Crime Problems (n 34 above) 19 observes that legislative jurisdiction does not perform its functions in isolation and that jurisdiction claimed by the legislature has to be implemented through the exercise of judicial and executive jurisdiction.

[71] HG Maier, 'Jurisdictional Rules in Customary Law' in KM Meessen (ed) *Extraterritorial jurisdiction in theory and practice* (1996) 64, 78 suggests that jurisdiction is a matter of degree and ought to be regarded as a unitary phenomenon characterized by different stages of exercise of power; similarly Brownlie (n 24 above) 309–10.

[72] Terms borrowed from article III, § 2 of the United States Constitution.

[73] Cf Cameron (n 23 above) 563: '[I]t can be argued that the exercise of adjudicative or enforcement jurisdiction is necessary before a law making an unlawful claim to extraterritorial jurisdiction could be said to be in breach of international law'. A D'Amato, *The Concept of Custom in International Law* (1971) 88 points out that a mere claim has little value as a prediction of what a State will actually do.

law.[74] What matters is that there is exercise of State power, whatever the branch of government.[75] The Court in the *Lotus* case did not consider whether the Turkish statute on which the prosecution was based accords with international law (legislative jurisdiction) or whether the Turkish court was competent under international law to hear the case (judicial jurisdiction). It confined itself to the question of whether jurisdiction did or did not exist.

H. JURISDICTION AND GLOBALIZATION

People around the globe are more connected to each other than ever before. Information and money flow more quickly than ever. Goods and services produced in one part of the world are increasingly available in all parts of the world. International travel is more frequent. This phenomenon has been called 'globalization'. Because jurisdiction over crime is traditionally linked with territory and nationality it is opportune to conclude this chapter with some brief reflections on the effects of globalization on jurisdiction.[76]

The first point to be made is that mass migration and high mobility erode the concept of nationality.[77] Millions of individuals reside temporarily or permanently outside the State of their nationality, many more are transiently on foreign soil, and more people than ever hold citizenship in more than one nation. From a State's perspective the numbers of nationals outside its territory and non-nationals or dual nationals within it increase continuously.

A second remark concerns the other important basis for State jurisdiction: territoriality. Technological advances, the more sophisticated structure of commercial organizations, and the growth of enterprises with transnational links erode the concept of territoriality.[78] As a result it becomes increasingly difficult to determine when and where offences of any complexity take place.[79] The progressive erosion of both nationality and territoriality poses

[74] This turned out to be the case in *Arrest Warrant of 11 April* 2000. After the ICJ judgment a Belgian appeals court ruled that the proceedings in Belgium against the accused violated Belgian law. See the Belgium country study in Part II below.

[75] The Inter-American Court of Human Rights in *Velásquez-Rodríguez* articulated this rule: 'Under international law a State is responsible for the acts of its agents undertaken in their official capacity and for their omissions, even when those agents act outside the sphere of their authority or violate internal law' (ser. C no 4, para 170), reprinted in (1989) 28 *Int'l L Materials* 291.

[76] See generally PS Berman, 'The Globalization of Jurisdiction', (2002) 151 *University of Pennsylvania LR* 311.

[77] A commentator speaks in this regard of the 'postnational transformation of citizenship': L Bosniak, 'Multiple Nationality and Postnational Transformation of Citizenship' (2002) 42 *Virginia J Int'l L* 979, 980.

[78] Home Office (UK), Steering Committee Report, *Review of Extra-Territorial Jurisdiction* (1996) p 4 para 1.10.

[79] Ibid.

immense challenges to 'ordinary' law enforcement and compels us to rethink the traditional concept of jurisdiction. A case in point is the United Kingdom where a 1996 Home Office report acknowledges that the sacrosanct rule of territoriality may not be tenable in the future.[80]

Finally, as noted above, transnational advocacy networks, themselves to some degree a product of globalization, increasingly demand the use of extraterritorial jurisdiction by States as a method to further common interests of the international community.[81] In a time when forum and *locus delicti* can be linked by global communication and information networks it becomes more and more difficult for States to dismiss these demands under the pretext that prosecuting extraterritorial offences is unfeasible.

SUMMARY

To summarize is to simplify, but it may be instructive to end this chapter with a synopsis. Currently there is no global convention with respect to criminal jurisdiction. International law leaves States a wide measure of discretion in the matter, yet postulates the existence of limits. One of them is the non-interference principle, a corollary of the sovereign equality of States. Through a growing body of multilateral and bilateral treaties virtually all States have pledged to co-operate in the suppression of international crimes and serious common offences. An individual defendant cannot challenge the jurisdiction of the forum State on the international plane, due to lack of standing. Instead, excessive exercise of jurisdiction may result in inter-State responsibility. The so-called principles of jurisdiction are useful as 'signposts'. Their application to a specific dispute requires further balancing of interests of the States concerned and of the requirements of justice. The globalization phenomenon has repercussions on jurisdiction as it erodes the traditional links of territoriality and nationality. Moreover, pressure is building in the international legal system to 'denationalize' the administration of criminal justice in order to further the common interests of the international community.

[80] Ibid 11.

[81] See N Roht-Arriaza, *Transnational Justice* (University of Pennsylvania Press; forthcoming 2004).

2

Doctrine

This chapter presents the principal scholarly views on universal jurisdiction, including drafts, reports, and resolutions of international learned bodies and conferences. The overview is limited to sources whose primary focus is (universal) jurisdiction, rather than with works that treat it tangentially in the context of other concerns. Scholarly comments on recent cases are considered in Part II below.

It should be kept in mind that teachings of publicists are only a subsidiary means for determining rules of international law.[1] As noted by a commentator highly critical of universal jurisdiction, the authority in the international legal order lies with States and not in the opinion of publicists.[2]

Nonetheless, there are good reasons to begin with a focus on doctrine. Until fairly recently there was little significant State practice on the subject; theory thus provides a longer historical background than practice. Second, this chapter is meant to lay the theoretical groundwork for the empirical part of this study, and to anticipate some of the critical issues arising in practice.

Nearly all contemporary authors recognize the existence of a universality principle.[3] The issue is therefore not its existence, but its content or scope. Without overlooking the fact that categorization runs the risk of oversimplification and rigidity, this study has identified three doctrinal versions of the universality principle. To capture the crucial distinctions among them, and again at the risk of generalization, the following working notions are proposed: co-operative general universality principle, co-operative limited universality principle, and unilateral limited universality principle. General versus limited refers to the offences subject to universal jurisdiction, and co-operative versus unilateral to the international sphere or context in which universal jurisdiction is exercised. The order in which the different versions are discussed corresponds more or less to the chronological order in which they were developed.

A. THE CO-OPERATIVE GENERAL UNIVERSALITY PRINCIPLE

The term 'general' means that the principle applies to all serious offences, ie conduct punishable by a severe sentence in most legal systems. No explicit distinction is made between international crimes and common domestic

[1] Cf article 38 ICJ Statute.

[2] This is one of the main themes of AP Rubin, *Ethics and Authority in International Law* (1998).

[3] A rare exception is Rubin, ibid.

crimes, but the former are obviously included. 'Co-operative' refers to the international sphere or context in which jurisdiction is exercised: the *judex loci deprehensionis* steps in to avoid an impasse which would otherwise result from the impossibility of extraditing a foreign suspect. The ensuing prosecution can be seen as a form of bilateral co-operation in penal criminal matters.

The origin of the co-operative general universality principle can be traced back to the sixteenth-century Spanish author Covarruvias. The medieval Italian city-states generally recognized the jurisdiction of the criminal courts of both the *locus delicti* and, at a time when the concept of nationality was unknown, of the place of domicile of the offender.[4] In case of *vagabundi*, persons without a permanent residence, only the courts of the *locus delicti* were competent. To close a possible loophole, the *judex deprehensionis* was exceptionally given jurisdiction, which scholars justified by the concept of fictitious domicile.[5]

The category of offenders subject to the jurisdiction of the *judex deprehensionis* was later expanded to include also *assassini* (murderers), *banniti* (exiles), and *latrones* (thieves or robbers).[6] Italian commentators likened *assassini* and *banniti* to *vagabundi*, while they justified universal jurisdiction over theft by the theory of the continued offence: a thief continues his offence wherever he takes the stolen object. Thus, medieval Italian scholarship accepted the competence of the *judex loci deprehensionis* for a limited category of criminals only.

Covarruvias found it arbitrary to subject only fugitive *vagabundi, assassini, banniti*, and *latrones* to the jurisdiction of the place of arrest. Referring to a natural law common to all nations he defended the proposition that the *judex deprehensionis* had a duty either to punish or extradite *all* dangerous criminals—'*judex requisitus vel remittere tenetur, vel delinquentem ipsum punire*'[7]—thus originating the famous formula 'extradite or try'.[8]

The nineteenth and early twentieth centuries saw a period of intense codification of municipal law in the nation States of continental Europe and in the former Spanish and Portuguese colonies in America. At the international level States concluded what can be called the first 'international criminal law treaties', ie multilateral treaties in which they engage themselves to outlaw and repress conduct which they consider to be of international concern.[9] In addition, international learned bodies and conferences adopted resolutions, reports, and drafts on criminal jurisdiction.

[4] G Guillaume, 'La compétence universelle, formes anciennes et nouvelles' in *Mélanges offerts à Georges Levasseur: Droit pénal, droit européen* (1992) 23, 24.

[5] J Kohler, *Internationales Strafrecht* (1917) 37.

[6] G Solna, *Das Weltrechtsprinzip im internationalen Strafrecht* (1925) 13; Guillaume (n 4 above) 25.

[7] D Covarruvias, *Practicorum quaestionum*, chapter 11, no 7 (cited in Guillaume, ibid, 27). *Remittere* being a synonym for *dedere*, Guillaume points out that the paternity of the maxim *aut dedere aut judicare* (extradite or try) comes to Covarruvias and not to Grotius as the common opinion holds.

[8] Later versions of this adage substitute *punire* (to punish) with *judicare* (to adjudicate) or with *persequi* (to prosecute) and *remittere* (send back) with *dedere* (hand over).

[9] See ch 3 s A below.

At its Munich Session of 1883, the prestigious Institute of International Law adopted a resolution that strongly influenced the codification process. Inspired by provisions in the Austrian penal codes of 1803[10] and 1852,[11] the Institute resolved:

> Article 10. Every Christian State (or recognizing the legal principles of Christian States), which has custody over an offender may try and punish him when, notwithstanding *prima facie* evidence of a serious crime and culpability, the *locus delicti* cannot be determined, or when the extradition of the culprit, even to his home State, is not granted (*n'est pas admise)* or is considered dangerous.
>
> In this case, the court will apply the most favourable law to the accused, taking into account the probable place of the crime, the nationality of the accused, and the law of the forum State.[12]

The Institute clearly considered the competence of the *judex deprehensionis* as complementary and subsidiary to the jurisdiction of the territorial State (spelled out in article 1 of the Resolution) and the State of nationality of the offender (spelled out in article 7). Only when extradition is impossible, eg the territorial State is 'not civilized' or is 'in state of revolution',[13] may prosecution take place in the custodial State. The subsidiary competence applies to all extraditable offences, ie offences of a certain gravity that are punishable in both the territorial and custodial States.

The opinions of members of the Institute differed regarding the justification of what was dubbed the 'universality principle'. Von Bar relied on the natural law ideas of universal justice and solidarity among nations as propagated by the founders of modern international law.[14] Brusa, by contrast, grounded the competence of the *judex loci deprehensionis* on the territoriality principle,

[10] The relevant provisions of the 1803 penal code are reprinted in F Meili, *Lehrbuch des internationalen Strafrechts und Strafprozeßrechts* (1910) 64–5.

[11] The relevant provisions of the 1852 penal code read: 'Art. 39. Again, if a foreigner has committed abroad an offence other than those indicated in the preceding paragraph, he shall always be arrested upon entering the country; arrangement shall be made forthwith for his extradition to the State where the offence was committed.

Art. 40. Should the foreign State refuse to receive him, the foreign offender will generally be prosecuted in accordance with the provisions of the present penal code. If, however, more lenient treatment is prescribed by the criminal law of the place where he committed the act, he shall be treated according to this more lenient law. Expulsion shall also be included in the penal sentence in addition to the infliction of the usual penalty': translation from Harvard Research in International Law, 'Jurisdiction with Respect to Crime' (1935) 29 *Am J Int'l L* 435, 574–5.

[12] The resolution is reprinted in French in (1883–5) 7 *Annuaire de l'Institut de Droit International* 148. The official comment on article 10 by von Bar and Brusa is quoted in M Travers, *Le droit pénal international et sa mise en oeuvre en temps de paix et en temps de guerre. Tome I. Principes.—Règles générales de compétence des lois répressives* (1920) 130.

[13] The report of von Bar and Brusa cites these examples. In the first case the offender could not be extradited without exposing him to 'barbaric' justice, whereas extradition in the second case would be 'dangerous' (Travers, ibid, 130).

[14] A Mercier, 'Le conflit des lois pénales en matière de compétence' [1931] *Annuaire de l'Institut de Droit International*, I, 87, 134.

arguing that the right to punish follows from the right of every State to defend its public order. 'The culpable act travels with the offender' (*l'action coupable voyage avec le délinquent*), and the mere presence of an unpunished criminal threatens the domestic moral and legal order, and justifies a 'territorial jurisdiction'.[15] Brusa thus provided universal jurisdiction with a positivist basis: it is the expression of a State's internal sovereignty.[16]

By the late nineteenth and early twentieth centuries many a municipal criminal code had incorporated the universality principle as proposed by the Institute, namely universal jurisdiction over all extraditable offences if extradition of the foreign suspect is impossible for reasons unrelated to the offence.[17]

One of the earliest and most comprehensive studies of the principles of jurisdiction that crystallized in the codification processes is Donnedieu de Vabres' classic *Les principes modernes du droit pénal international* (1928). In order to reconcile society's interest in efficient repression of criminality and the individual's fundamental rights, the author advocated a strict jurisdictional hierarchy for all crimes: (1) *judex loci delicti*, (2) *judex loci domicilii* (the place where the offender resided when he committed the crime), and (3) *judex loci deprehensionis*.

Donnedieu de Vabres' hierarchy allows the *judex loci deprehensionis* to intervene only when the foreign offender cannot be extradited to a more competent State, for whatever reason. Universal jurisdiction is thus an *ultimum subsidum*, but should be exercised generally and consistently (*de façon générale et constante*).[18]

A State, which in these circumstances prosecutes a foreigner, does not revendicate a sovereign right of its own [...]. It does not act to defend its own interests. It steps in, in default of any other State, to prevent in the interest of humanity an outrageous impunity (*Il intervient, à défaut de tout autre État, pour éviter, dans un intérêt humain, une impunité scandaleuse*). Therefore, its intervention has a very subsidiary character and cannot take place unless the State has physical custody over the offender.[19]

The exercise of universal jurisdiction is, just like the practice of extradition, the negation of the right of asylum (*L'exercise de la compétence universelle est, au même titre que la pratique de l'extradition, le négation du droit d'asile*).[20]

[15] Ibid 134.

[16] On the distinction between internal and external sovereignty, see B Simma (ed) *Kommentar zur Charta der Vereinten Nationen* (1991) 39–48.

[17] For a compilation of these code provisions, see Meili (n 10 above) 184–95; Solna (n 6 above) 29–43; Mercier (n 14 above) 574–6; H Donnedieu de Vabres, *Les principes modernes du droit pénal international* (1928) 153–60.

[18] Ibid 169.

[19] Ibid 135. Donnedieu de Vabres further stresses that a suspect must be voluntarily present in the forum State: 'It is out of the question that he be tried in absentia or that his extradition is requested' (ibid 160).

[20] Ibid 137.

A similar view on universal jurisdiction is expressed in authoritative international resolutions and drafts of that period: the resolution of the 1927 Warsaw Conference for the Unification of Penal Law,[21] the resolution of the 1932 Hague International Congress of Comparative Law,[22] and the 1935 Draft Convention on Jurisdiction with Respect to Crime by Harvard Research in International Law.[23]

Concurrently, two scholars introduced a distinction that foreshadowed the current academic distinction between the principles of universality and representation.[24] The first was Travers, author of the *magnum opus, Le droit pénal international* (1920), whose volume I is entirely devoted to jurisdiction. Starting from the notion that penal law is 'a right of social defence proper to a group' (*un droit de défense sociale propre à un groupement*),[25] Travers rejected the 'theory of universality':

> The basis of this system is the existence of a moral and juridical solidarity among States. Because of this solidarity, an offence should no longer be considered a violation of the positive laws of a specific country, but as compromising the conditions necessary to the existence, or at least [to] the prosperity, of society. Hence the consequence that the right to punish does not belong to a particular country but to all nations whose positive laws criminalize the conduct.
>
> Formulated so broadly, this theory has to be rejected. It goes against the nature of the penal law and against the very conception of State. Every State has, in principle, no other mission than to defend its own interests. Because its sovereignty is limited, it cannot act on behalf of all humanity; it only represents the Society of nations *parte in qua*. The nature of the State determines the scope of its criminal law. The goal of criminal law is to protect the group and only the group. Its origin, its basis are in contradiction with the idea itself of universality. Moreover, this idea can only be justified by the notion of natural laws (*droits naturels*) or by morality. But the existence of natural laws, which is postulated and cannot be proven, is contradicted by the facts. [...]

[21] Reprinted in French in Harvard Research in International Law (n 11 above) 641–2. In addition to universal jurisdiction over certain international offences (article 6), the resolution provides in article 7 that all offences committed abroad by a foreigner may be punished if the foreign individual is present, if extradition has not been requested or could not been granted, and if the minister of justice orders the prosecution.

[22] Reprinted in French in Harvard Research in International Law (n 11 above) 644–5. Besides universal jurisdiction over 'serious offences directed against general interests of humanity', article 4 of the resolution provides the right for every State to punish acts committed abroad by a foreigner, even against a foreigner, if these acts constitute a criminal offence under the penal law of the offender, if the suspect is present on the territory and cannot be extradited, and if there is a complaint by the victim or an official denunciation by the foreign authority, as well as an initiative by the national authority.

[23] Reprinted in Harvard Research in International Law (n 11 above) 439–42. Other than universal jurisdiction over piracy (article 9), the resolution provides in article 10(a) ('Universality: other crimes') for universal jurisdiction with respect to any crime, 'if the act or omission which constitutes the crime is also an offence by the law of the place where it was committed, if surrender of the alien for prosecution has been offered to such other State or States and the offer remains unaccepted, and if prosecution is not barred by lapse of time under the law of the place where the crime was committed'.

[24] See ch 1 s F above.

[25] Travers (n 12 above) 11.

Morality is only universal if one considers peoples with an identical degree of civilization and at the same time. [. . .] Penal law and morality may correspond but they are clearly distinct.[26]

Nonetheless, Travers accepted the subsidiary jurisdiction of the *judex loci deprehensionis* (the future representation principle) because the presence of an unpunished wrongdoer harms the interests of the State of refuge, in a double way:

The example of an offender peacefully enjoying the benefits of his misdeed encourages criminality and the possibility of an offender taking refuge in a State with the certainty that its penal law will not be applied would attract riffraff to hospitable countries, necessarily impacting their social order. . . . Extradition and expulsion are inadequate remedies for this double danger because the first is not always feasible and the latter does not produce a sufficiently moralizing effect.[27]

The second author was Mikliszanski, who further articulated the theoretical distinction between 'the subsidiary penal law' (*le droit pénal subsidiaire*) and 'the system of universality of the right to punish' (*le système de l'universalité du droit de punir*):

The subsidiary penal law is the penal law of a State, which in a given case, takes the place of the penal law of another State, which in principle has priority, but for whatever reason, cannot be applied. Priority is given to the territorial or national law, but from the moment that neither can be applied, a third law, namely from the place where the accused has been found, is applicable.

The idea is simple. An offence should never remain unpunished; the possibility to cross borders should not shield the common criminal from punishment. He has to be aware that wherever he goes he will be held responsible. It is thus the duty of the custodial State to supply an inadequacy of the territorial State and the State of nationality of the offender, which by hypothesis cannot act. To defeat the eventual calculations of the offender, that is the master idea of the subsidiary penalization.

What then is the principle of universality of the right to punish? It is the principle according to which every penal norm, far from being limited to a certain territory, is eminently international (*interétatique*), or rather supranational (*supraétatique*). In the administration of justice, the nationality of the perpetrator or the victim and the place of commission are irrelevant. . . .

Extension of the validity of the penal norm to all countries and individuals is the basic idea behind the universalist repressive system.

. . . While the subsidiary penal law places itself at the purely practical level—prevent offenders from fleeing justice—the universalist theory, in contrast, places itself at the

[26] Ibid 75–6.

[27] Ibid 106. Travers did not justify jurisdiction based on the idea that an offender who enters a foreign country accepts its laws, for two reasons. First, it would require making a distinction between offenders who voluntarily entered the *forum deprehensionis* and those who are present independently from their own will. Second, penal laws are applied because of considerations proper to the State whereby the will or consent of the individual does not have to be taken into consideration.

philosophical level, at the level of the very nature of the penal norm: stripping the latter of the statist-territorial character (*caractère étatico-territorial*) which has been wrongly attributed to it, and retaining only its true and unique value which is to be fundamentally and uniquely human. It follows that jurisdiction based on the universal principle is not subsidiary at all, does not supply an inadequacy of another more competent jurisdiction to avoid impunity, but is an independent and primary right.[28]

Unlike Travers, Mikliszanski accepted the universalist theory, at least for the then emerging category of *delicta juris gentium*.

For the repression of those crimes, it is not about to assign to the State a simple auxiliary role, an international courtesy. It really is about giving to the penal norm a universally valid expression of human justice, doing away with every consideration of a statist and national order (*supprimer… toute considération d'ordre étatique et nationale*) to rally exclusively behind the idea of combating the offence. Thus, the competence attributed to the *judex deprehensionis* in respect of *delicta juris gentium* cannot have a simple subsidiary or facultative character. This competence must be primary and obligatory, so that it is exercised in the name of the whole international community. Indeed, in the system of universal repression, and here it differs from the system of subsidiary penal law, the criminal judges of the entire world all represent the same and only justice (*tous ils représentent la même et seule justice*). It follows that the *judex deprenhensionis*, although he applies his own law, does not act solely for his own State, but also for all the other States. This is one of the most interesting practical aspects of the universality theory: the perpetration of the offence triggers the equal competence of all criminal courts, but only the judge of the place of arrest may actually exercise jurisdiction (*la perpétration de l'acte punissable entraîne la compétence égale de toutes les lois qui le prévoient, mais l'exercise n'en est donné qu'à une seule, à savoir à celle qui est en vigueur au lieu où le délinquant a été saisi*).[29]

After World War II the content of international criminal law as an academic discipline widened. The Nuremberg judgment[30] and Principles[31] recognized that individuals may be criminally responsible under international law, causing a shift from the study of (municipal) rules of jurisdiction to the study of substantive rules of international criminal law. The distinction between common crimes and international crimes found final acceptance.

In a world without a standing international criminal court, universal jurisdiction became a distinctive feature of the new category of crimes. As a result, common crimes were no longer subject to the 'universal' jurisdiction of the

[28] K Mikliszanski, 'Le système de l'universalité du droit de punir et le droit pénal subsidiaire' [1936] *Revue de science criminelle et de droit pénal comparé* 331–3.

[29] Ibid 338–9.

[30] Trial of the Major War Criminals before the International Military Tribunal sitting at Nuremberg (Germany), judgment of 1 October 1946.

[31] Principles of International Law Recognized in the Charter of the Nuremberg Tribunal and in the Judgment of the Tribunal, adopted by the ILC at its second session, in 1950, and submitted to the General Assembly as a part of the Commission's report covering the work of that session. The report, which also contains commentaries on the principles, appears in [1950] *Ybk Int'l L Commision*, vol II, 374.

custodial State, but to its 'representation' jurisdiction. A switch of labels occurred: the universality principle, as it was known before World War II, became the representation principle[32] or 'vicarious administration of justice',[33] although in some publications the 'old' universality principle occasionally surfaced.[34]

Whichever the label, scholars have subsequently defended the idea that a State may exercise jurisdiction over serious common crimes committed abroad when extradition of the foreign offender is not possible for reasons unrelated to the offence. Justifications for the exceptional competence of the *judex loci deprehensionis* are sought in natural law (the existence of a criminal law common to all nations), in positivism (universal jurisdiction is a mere expression of a State's internal sovereignty), and in pragmatism (closing any possible jurisdictional loophole).

B. THE CO-OPERATIVE LIMITED UNIVERSALITY PRINCIPLE

The co-operative limited universality principle differs from the one just discussed in that it only applies to international offences. Common yet serious domestic offences are thus excluded. Its origin dates from the writings of two of the founders of modern international law, Grotius and de Vattel. Both men developed and codified legal rules that bound the sovereign States of Europe, then just emerging from medieval society, in their relations with one another. Though often cited by legal scholars and practitioners as 'evidence' in support of universal jurisdiction, their views on the subject are limited to a few paragraphs in general works on international law.

In his classic *De Jure Belli ac Pacis Libri Tres* (1625),[35] Grotius argued that ordinarily crimes 'should be left to the States themselves and their rulers, to be punished or condoned at their discretion'.[36] However, 'kings . . . have the right of demanding punishments not only on account of injuries committed against themselves or their subjects, but also on account of injuries which do not directly affect them but excessively violate the law of nature or of nations in regard of any persons whatsoever'.[37]

[32] Eg D Oehler, *Internationales Strafrecht. Geltungsbereich des Strafrechts. Internationales Rechtshilferecht. Recht der Gemeinschaften, Völkerstrafrecht* (2nd edn, 1983) ch 13; SZ Feller, 'Jurisdiction over Offenses with a Foreign Element' in MC Bassiouni and VP Nanda (eds) *A Treatise on International Criminal Law, II* (1973) 5, 34–7.

[33] Eg J Meyer, 'The Vicarious Administration of Justice: An Overlooked Basis of Jurisdiction' (1990) 31 *Harvard Int'l LJ* 108.

[34] Eg Consultative Assembly of the Council of Europe, 'Report on the Settlement of Conflicts in Criminal Matters' (1965) Doc. 1873, Explanatory Memorandum by Mr de Grailly, para 34.

[35] Translated by FW Kelsey, *The Law of War and Peace* (1925).

[36] Ibid book II, chapter XXI, §III, 1.

[37] Ibid book II, chapter XX, §XL, 1.

To assure chastisement of a fugitive offender against the law of nature or of nations, Grotius advocated the following practical solution:

Since as a matter of fact States are not accustomed to permit other States to cross their borders with an armed force for the purpose of exacting punishment, and since such a course is inexpedient, it follows that the State in which he who has been found guilty (For the judicial investigation should precede the surrender; it is not fitting 'to give up those who have not been tried,' says Plutarch, *Romulus* [vii = 21 C](original note).) dwells ought to do one of two things. When appealed to it should either punish the guilty person as he deserves, or it should entrust him to the discretion of the party making the appeal.[38]

It is noteworthy that the asylum State has an obligation to extradite or *punish*, and that this obligation does not arise until another State has made an appeal and the individual has been found guilty by the asylum State's courts.

De Vattel followed the lines of Grotius in his work *Le droit des gens ou les principes de la loi naturelle appliqués à la conduite et aux affaires des Nations et des Souverains* (1758).[39] As a rule, only the territorial State is competent '[f]or, nature does not give to men or to nations any right to inflict punishment, except for their own defence and safety...; whence it follows that we cannot punish any but those by whom we have been injured'.[40] However:

[We] ought to except from this rule those villains, who, by the nature and habitual frequency of their crimes, violate all public security, and declare themselves the enemies of the human race (*ennemis du Genre-humain*). Poisoners, assassins, and incendiaries by profession may be exterminated wherever they are seized; for they attack and injure all nations, by trampling underfoot the foundations of their common safety. Thus, pirates are sent to the gibbet by the first into whose hands they fall. If the sovereign of the country where the crimes of that nature have been committed, reclaims the perpetrators of them, in order to bring them to punishment, they ought to be surrendered to him, as being the person who is principally interested in punishing them in an exemplary manner.[41]

These views are elementary, but Grotius and de Vattel clearly coupled universal jurisdiction and extradition. When an appeal has been made, the custodial State should co-operate either by extraditing the suspect or by prosecuting him before its own courts. The accent is therefore more on the *negative obligation*

[38] Translated by FW Kelsey, *The Law of War and Peace* (1925), book II, chapter XXI, §IV, 1. The original Latin version of the last sentence reads '*Alterum facere debeat, aut ut ipsa interpellata pro merito puniat nocentem, aut ut eum permittat arbitrario interpellantis*'.

[39] Translated by J Chitty, *The Law of Nations or Principles of Natural Law Applied to the Conduct and Affairs of Nations and Sovereigns* (1839).

[40] Ibid book I, chapter XIX, para 232: 'If an exiled or banished man has been driven from his country for any crime, it does not belong to the nation in which he has taken refuge to punish him for the fault committed in a foreign country. For, nature does not give to men or to nations any right to inflict punishment, except for their own defence and safety (§ 169); whence it follows that we cannot punish any but those by whom we have been injured.'

[41] Ibid book I, chapter XIX, para 233.

not to shield a fugitive from prosecution by granting asylum[42] than on a *positive right* to exercise universal jurisdiction. The right is primarily a corollary of the obligation.

The rights and obligations thus created are *bilateral* between the custodial State and the State(s) directly linked to the offence. Grotius' and de Vattel's policy proposals do not sanction a third country's right to punish an offender. As in the writings of Covarruvias, *aut dedere aut judicare* stands for the duty of the *judex loci deprehensionis* either to extradite or to punish.

The universality principle thus envisaged is endorsed by a number of international resolutions. At its Cambridge session in 1931, the Institute of International Law adopted a new resolution on criminal jurisdiction. The relevant provision reads:

> Article 5. Every State has the right to punish acts committed abroad by a foreigner who is found on its territory, provided these acts violate general interests protected by international law (such as piracy, trade in negroes, trade in white women, propagation of contagious diseases, attacks on international communication means and destruction of undersea cables, counterfeiting of currency and securities, etc.), if extradition of the accused is not requested or if the territorial State or the State of nationality of the offender do not accept an extradition offer.[43]

A similar provision was adopted by the International Congress of Comparative Law in 1932.[44] In these texts the link between extradition and universal jurisdiction is present, but has been attenuated.

Aut dedere aut judicare subsequently developed into an independent or primary right of the custodial State to prosecute *delicta juris gentium*. The disconnection of extradition and universal jurisdiction can be found in the

[42] Cf Donnedieu de Vabres (n 17 above) 137: 'The exercise of universal jurisdiction is, just like the practice of extradition, the negation of the right of asylum.'

[43] The resolution is reprinted in French in [1931] *Annuaire de l'Institut de Droit International*, II, 235.

[44] The resolution is reprinted in French in Harvard Research in International Law (n 11 above) 644. Article 4 provides: 'Every State has the right to punish acts committed abroad by a foreigner, even against a foreigner, provided these acts constitute a criminal offence under the penal law of the offender, if the suspect is present of the territory and if he cannot be extradited. The exercise of this right must be limited to the prosecution of serious offences directed against general interests of humanity, namely:

A. Piracy
B. Slave trade
C. Trade in women and children
D. Trade in controlled substances
D. Trade in obscene publications
E. Counterfeiting of currencies, securities and bonds
F. Propagation of contagious diseases
H. Attacks on international communication means, canals, and undersea cables
I. Other offences subject of international conventions

For all other offences, the exercise of this right must be conditional upon the request of the injured person or the denunciation of the foreign authority, and upon the initiative of the national authority.'

writings of Mikliszanski,[45] Feller,[46] and Oehler, author of one of the most comprehensive and analytical post-World War II studies on criminal jurisdiction.[47] According to Oehler, the universality principle (*Weltrechtspflegeprinzip*) provides for an independent right of the *judex loci deprehensionis* to prosecute offences that 'pose an equal threat to all nations'.[48] The only required link with the forum State is the voluntary presence of the offender.[49]

Under this system, the perpetrator of an international offence knows that wherever he decides to go or to hide, he may be put on trial.[50] This could, in theory, result in 'forum shopping', but the choices of a fugitive offender are usually severely limited by geographical constraints and visa regulations. Moreover, the intent of the person fleeing is generally to avoid any trial, not to choose the most favourable forum.

Admittedly, the co-operative character of universal jurisdiction exercised without considering extradition to a more competent State is hardly in evidence. As stated in the introduction to this chapter, categorization and labelling are inherently somewhat arbitrary, leading to results that may not be fully satisfactory. 'Co-operative', however, was chosen to contrast with 'unilateral' in the third version of the universality principle, which is discussed next.

C. THE UNILATERAL LIMITED UNIVERSALITY PRINCIPLE

The unilateral limited universality principle no longer requires any link with the forum State. The only criterion is the international legal character of the offence. Jurisdiction is truly 'universal' because *any* State may unilaterally launch an investigation, even *in absentia*. Extradition of the suspect is perfectly acceptable to secure personal jurisdiction for trial.

This seems to be the view taken by KC Randall in his leading article *Universal Jurisdiction Under International Law* (1988).[51] The universality principle 'provides every State with jurisdiction over a limited category of offences generally recognized as of universal concern, regardless of the situs of the offence and the nationality of the offender and the offended'.[52] Once an offence rises to the level

[45] Mikliszanksi (n 28 above) 338–9 defended for the category of *delicta juris gentium* a 'system of universality of the right to punish' in which 'the perpetration of the offence triggers the equal competence of all criminal courts, but only the judge of the place of arrest may actually exercise jurisdiction'.

[46] Feller (n 32 above) 32–3.

[47] Oehler (n 32 above) ch 14.

[48] Ibid 541.

[49] Cf C Lombois, 'De la compassion territoriale' [1995] *Revue de science criminelle et de droit pénal comparé* 399, 403: 'the judge exercising [universal jurisdiction] can only be the *judex deprehensionis*. This is implied in the writings of all publicists. Without this condition, the system would become even more unrealistic than it is (and it is already quite unrealistic).'

[50] Cf the Latin adage *ubi te invenero, ibi te judicabo* ('where I find you, there I will put you on trial').

[51] 66 *Texas LR* 785.

[52] Ibid 788, quoting O Schachter, *International Law in Theory and Practice* (1985) 262.

of an international crime it is *ipso facto* subject to universal jurisdiction,[53] which is no longer the negation of the right to grant asylum but the positive right of any State to prosecute the offender without regard to his whereabouts.

Randall introduces the *erga omnes*[54] and *jus cogens*[55] concepts in his discussion on individual criminal responsibility under international law and universal jurisdiction:

> Violations of obligations *erga omnes* and *jus cogens* norms offend all States, whether committed by State actors or individuals. Indeed, domestic jurisdiction over those violations may draw support from the *Barcelona Traction* case dictum, which, although not without ambiguity, may support a type of *actio popularis*, enabling any State to vindicate rights common to all. If that dictum supports judicial remedies against State offenders, it logically supports judicial remedies against individual offenders, thus complementing the universality principle. In this way, the *erga omnes* and *jus cogens* doctrines may buttress the universal jurisdiction of all States.[56]

The use of the *Barcelona Traction* dictum as authority for universal jurisdiction has been criticized by Higgins:[57]

> It is spoken of as if it provides guidance for the contemporary application of the principle of universality of jurisdiction—as if the Court was affirming universal jurisdiction in respect of each of these offences. Of course, the Court was doing nothing of that kind. Its dictum was made in the context not of asserting jurisdiction but of an examination of the law relating to diplomatic protection....

[53] Ibid 788, citing L Henkin, R Pugh, O Schachter, and H Smit, *International Law* (1987) 823. For a different view, see R Higgins, *Problems and Process: International Law and How We Use It* (1994) 62.

[54] The concept of *erga omnes* first appeared in a dictum in *Barcelona Traction, Light and Power Company Ltd* ICJ Reports 1970, 3, paras 33 and 34: '[A]n essential difference should be drawn between the obligations of a State towards the international community as a whole, and those arising *vis-à-vis* another State in the field of diplomatic protection. By their very nature the former are the concern of all States. In view of the importance of the rights involved, all States can be held to have a legal interest in their protection; they are obligations *erga omnes*. Such obligations derive, for example, in contemporary international law, from the outlawing of acts of aggression, and of genocide, as also from the principles and rules concerning the basic rights of the human person, including protection from slavery and racial discrimination. Some of the corresponding rights of protection have entered into the body of general international law (*Reservations to the Convention on Genocide, Advisory Opinion*: ICJ Reports 1951, 23); others are conferred by international instruments of a universal or quasi-universal character.' On the concept of obligations *erga omnes*, see A De Hoogh, *Obligations erga omnes and international crimes: A theoretical inquiry into the implementation and enforcement of the international responsibility of states* (1996); M Ragazzi, *The Concept of International Obligations Erga Omnes* (1997).

[55] *Jus cogens* is a peremptory norm of general international law, which article 53 of Vienna Convention on the Law of Treaties defines as 'a norm accepted and recognized by the international community of States as a whole as a norm from which no derogation is permitted and which can be modified only by a subsequent norm of general international law having the same character'. On the concept of *jus cogens*, see FA Mann, 'The Doctrine of Jus Cogens in International Law' in FA Mann *Further Studies in International Law* (1990) 84.

[56] Randall (n 51 above) 831.

[57] Higgins (n 53 above) 57; even more critical is AP Rubin, 'Actio Popularis, Jus Cogens and Offenses Erga Omnes' 35 *New England LR* (2001) 265, 277–8.

> Further the nationality-of-claims rule concerns diplomatic representation in civil claims. This is true of the stated exception to the rule, where obligations are owed *erga omnes*. The universality principle, by contrast, is concerned with the application of criminal jurisdiction.[58]

The passage in *Barcelona Traction* should be read against a (much criticized) dictum of the Court some years earlier in the *South West Africa* cases, according to which *locus standi* is not constituted by the fact that all States have an interest in humanitarian matters.[59] *Barcelona Traction* arguably overrules *South West Africa* on this point but, as Higgins points out, standing in the context of diplomatic protection and State responsibility is quite a different matter from standing to punish an individual.

Under the system proposed by Randall there is no basis for the offender to predict where he will be tried. Prosecution takes complete precedence over the place of trial in this policy-oriented approach. Donnedieu de Vabres and Oehler both categorically reject the exercise of universal jurisdiction through extradition; the former because it tramples on the fundamental rights of the individual,[60] the latter because the forum State abuses a right, interferes in the domestic affairs of the States who are otherwise competent, and acts like a 'world policeman' at the risk of unhinging international criminal law as a whole.[61]

The unilateral limited universality principle also raises the question of compatibility with the International Criminal Court.[62] As first conceived, this notion of the universality principle was a substitute for a non-existing international criminal court, an idealistic solution to the incomplete structure of the international legal order.[63] Now that the ICC is established, it would seem illogical to hold on to it and attribute similar, if not broader, powers to a single State than to a treaty-based court.

Only one resolution by an international learned body seems to endorse so broad a right.[64] Article 8 of the 1993 draft Resolution on the Extraterritorial

[58] See ch 1 s B above.

[59] *South West Africa*, ICJ Reports 1966, 6, para 50: 'Humanitarian considerations may constitute the inspirational basis for rules of law . . . Such considerations do not, however, in themselves amount to rules of law. All States are interested—have an interest—in such matters. But the existence of an "interest" does not of itself entail that this interest is specifically juridical in character.'

[60] H Donnedieu de Vabres 'Les Leçons de l'histoire et le progrès de droit pénal international' [July–September 1951] *Revue de Science Criminelle et de Droit Pénal Comparé* 1, 5.

[61] D Oehler, 'Auslieferungsersuchen, Einlieferung und der Geltungsbereich des Strafrechts' in *Festschrift der Rechtswissenschaftlichen Fakultät zur 600-Jahr-Feier der Universität zu Köln* (1988) 489, 497–500.

[62] On this issue see, although somewhat outdated, B Graefrath, 'Universal Criminal Jurisdiction and an International Criminal Court' (1990) 1 *Eur J Int'l L* 67. See also the conclusions of this book.

[63] This is understood in most (early) writings on the subject; some are explicit, eg S Glaser, *Infraction internationale: Ses éléments constitutifs et ses aspects juridiques* (1957) 31: 'International crimes are subject to the system of universal repression or universal jurisdiction, *as long as there is no international criminal court*' (emphasis added).

[64] But see, recently, the Princeton University Program in Law and Public Affairs, *The Princeton Principles on Universal Jurisdiction* (2001), Principle 1(3): 'A state may rely on

Jurisdiction of States by the Institute of International Law provides:

1. Under the principle of universality, jurisdiction may be exercised in order to protect certain interests of the international community as a whole.
2. Jurisdiction under the principle of universality extends to persons regardless of their nationality and the place where they committed their acts.
3. The principle of universality shall apply to offences as defined under conventional and customary international law, such as piracy, the hijacking of aircraft, terrorism, and the trade of narcotics.
4. Jurisdiction under the previous paragraph may be exercised irrespective of signature or ratification of any international convention by the State of the nationality of the accused.[65]

As in the Institute's previous resolution of 1931,[66] universal jurisdiction is limited to *delicta juris gentium*. On the other hand, no longer present are the conditions that (1) the accused is found on the forum State's territory, that (2) his extradition is not requested, or that (3) the territorial State or the State of nationality of the accused do not accept an extradition offer. New tempering provisions couched in terms of 'reasonableness' and 'non-interference' are instead introduced in article 4:

1. Extraterritorial jurisdiction, whatever the specific title under which it is claimed, shall be exercised reasonably, while balancing the interests of the States concerned.
2. Nothing in this Resolution is to be construed as an entitlement for one State to interfere with the internal affairs of other States.

The Restatement (Third) of the Foreign Relations Law of the United States as promulgated by the American Law Institute in 1987[67] clearly influenced the Institute of International Law in its preparation of the above quoted draft Resolution. Sections 404 and 423 of the Restatement recognize that international law permits any State to apply its laws to punish 'certain offenses recognized by the community of nations as of universal concern', without making any reference to the whereabouts of the accused. Section 403(1), however, prohibits the exercise of extraterritorial jurisdiction 'when the exercise of such jurisdiction is unreasonable'.

Neither text excludes *a priori* the possibility of exercising universal jurisdiction over a suspect who is not present. Moreover both recognize that the

universal jurisdiction as a basis for seeking the extradition of a person accused or convicted of committing a serious crime under international law as specified in Principle 2(1) provided that it has established a *prima facie* case of the person's guilt and that the person sought to be extradited will be tried or the punishment carried out in accordance with international norms and standards on the protection of human rights in the context of criminal proceedings.'

[65] Reprinted in (1993) 65 *Ybk Institute Int'l L*, II, 174.

[66] See s B above.

[67] American Law Institute, *Restatement of the Law (Third), The Foreign Relations Law of the United States* (1987).

question whether the forum State is acting within the perimeters of reasonableness and non-interference, even when a suspect is present, can only be determined on a case-by-case basis, taking into consideration all the facts.

With these provisions and remarks the discussion has come to full circle: an exercise of jurisdiction by any State other than the territorial State violates *prima facie* the non-interference principle;[68] the forum State must therefore be prepared to show that its proceedings are nevertheless justified under some principle of jurisdiction; the universality principle allows, in theory, any State to punish 'universal offenses';[69] in practice, every form of extraterritorial jurisdiction must be exercised reasonably and without interfering with the internal affairs of other States.

SUMMARY

This chapter has provided a brief overview of the theories for universal jurisdiction. The universality principle encompasses three different concepts: (1) the secondary or subsidiary jurisdiction of the *custodial State* over *all serious offences* if extradition of the suspect is impracticable; (2) the jurisdiction, whether primary or subsidiary, of the *custodial State* over *international offences only*; (3) the primary right of *any State* to try *international offences*, without regard to the offender's whereabouts. Clearly, these versions overlap to some extent. The first and the third versions include the second because the greater includes the lesser. As it represents the common ground, only the co-operative limited universality principle seems to qualify at this point as a 'signpost'.[70] An evolution in the course of time can be seen from the first version of the universality principle, through the second, and towards the third. Illustrative of this evolution are the three resolutions by the Institute of International Law, respectively adopted in 1887, 1931, and 1993. All three versions co-exist in current doctrine. The co-operative limited universality principle, however, is now better known as the representation principle, especially in the Germanic legal culture.

[68] See ch 1 s F above.

[69] Term used by the American Law Institute in § 423 of the *Restatement (Third) of the Foreign Relations Law of the United States* (n 67 above).

[70] Cf the discussion in ch 1 s F above.

3

International texts

This chapter examines universal jurisdiction in international texts. A distinction is made between multilateral conventions, resolutions from intergovernmental bodies, and official drafts and studies. Conventions constitute a direct source of international law for the immediate parties. A secondary effect of conventions is that generalizable provisions may be considered expressions of *opinio juris* for the purpose of ascertaining international custom.[1] The second and third groupings do not constitute true sources of law; nonetheless, resolutions may indicate *opinio juris* and drafts and official reports exhibit contemporary trends and may lay the groundwork for future resolutions, declarations of principles, or conventions. Besides searching for provisions on universal jurisdiction in multilateral conventions and for indications of an *opinio juris* among States in non-legally binding international texts, this chapter lays further groundwork for the discussion of municipal legislation and case-law in Part II below.

A. MULTILATERAL CONVENTIONS

Over the years States have entered into a considerable number of multilateral conventions with penal characteristics.[2] One of those characteristics is the establishment of a basis for criminal jurisdiction. Some conventions put in place a system of universal repression. A commentator[3] has observed that the use of the term 'universal' is misleading in this context, that unless the jurisdiction clause in a treaty is declaratory of customary international law or acquires customary law status through generalized ratification and implementation, jurisdiction is not truly 'universal' until all States of the world have ratified the treaty.[4]

[1] Cf the discussion in ch 1 s D above.

[2] This part of my study has greatly benefited from the following works: RS Clark, 'Offenses of International Concern: Multilateral State Practice in the Forty Years Since Nuremberg' (1988) 57 *Nordic J Int'l L* 49; G Guillaume, 'Terrorisme et droit international' (1989) 215 *Receuil des cours de l'académie de droit international*, I, 287; G Guillaume, 'La compétence universelle, formes anciennes et nouvelles' in *Mélanges offerts à Georges Levasseur: Droit pénal, droit européen* (1992) 23; MC Bassiouni and EM Wise, *Aut Dedere Aut Judicare: The Duty to Extradite or Prosecute in International Law* (1995). MC Bassiouni, *International Criminal Law Conventions and their Penal Provisions* (1997) is particularly useful, offering an historical record of the evolution of conventional international criminal law.

[3] I Cameron, *The Protective Principle of International Criminal Jurisdiction* (1994) 80.

[4] Article 34 of the Vienna Convention on the Law of Treaties provides: 'A treaty does not create either obligations or rights for a third State without its consent'. Article 38 of the

This raises the question whether jurisdiction clauses in treaties are of a permitting or an obligatory nature, and revives the more general question whether international law is constitutive or regulative of State rights.[5] Some argue that criminal law conventions are minimalist frameworks whose goal is not to create additional rights for the signatories, but to oblige them to establish jurisdiction to avoid possible lacunae.[6] Most authors implicitly take the opposite view.[7] The empirical approach taken here carefully examines the texts of conventions and their implementation by States.

The analysis goes beyond purely jurisdictional issues to ask the following questions: what is the interest or value protected by the convention, and who are the typical perpetrators? Conventions adopted before and after World War II are distinguished for analytical reasons and because of the great significance of the Nuremberg trial and judgment[8] on international law.

Pre-World War II conventions

A comprehensive compilation of international instruments with penal characteristics contains some one hundred conventions drafted before World War II.[9] They concern matters such as slave trade, slavery, and forced labour; laws and customs of war; protection of submarine cables; 'white slave' traffic; circulation of obscene materials; drugs; terrorism; and counterfeiting currency. For the most part, States commit themselves in these conventions to criminalize certain conduct; the term 'international crime' or 'crime under international law' does not yet appear. Only four conventions establish an extraterritorial jurisdictional basis; three call for universal repression; they are discussed below in chronologic order.

International Convention for the Suppression of Counterfeiting Currency

The International Convention for the Suppression of Counterfeiting Currency[10] appears to be the very first convention to contain an *aut dedere aut judicare*

Convention states: 'Nothing in articles 34 and 37 precludes a rule set forth in a treaty from becoming binding upon a third State as a customary rule of international law, recognized as such'. MP Scharf, 'Application of Treaty-Based Universal Jurisdiction to Nationals of Non-Party States' (2001) 35 *New England LR* 363 specifically deals with the issue here considered.

[5] Cf the discussion in ch 1 s A above.

[6] Eg L Gardocki, 'The Principle of Universality' in N Jareborg (ed) *Double Criminality: Studies in International Criminal Law* (1989) 57, 58.

[7] Eg D Oehler, *Internationales Strafrecht. Geltungsbereich des Strafrechts. Internationales Rechtshilferecht. Recht der Gemeinschaften, Völkerstrafrecht* (2nd edn, 1983) 522, 524.

[8] Trial of the Major War Criminals before the International Military Tribunal sitting at Nuremberg (Germany), judgment of 1 October 1946.

[9] Bassiouni 1997 (n 2 above).

[10] Geneva, 20 April 1929; 112 LNTS 371; partially reprinted in Bassiouni 1997 (n 2 above) 1171.

clause. Article 9 provides:

> Foreigners who have committed abroad any offence referred to in article 3, and who are in the territory of a country whose internal legislation recognizes as a general rule the principle of the prosecution of offences committed abroad, should be punishable in the same way as if the offence had been committed in the territory of that country.
>
> The obligation to take proceedings is subject to the condition that extradition has been requested and that the country to which application is made cannot hand over the person accused for some reason which has no connection with the offence.

Article 9 as a whole is addressed only to countries whose internal legislation recognizes in principle the prosecution of offences committed abroad. As noted in chapter 2 above, a considerable number of countries had adopted this rule by the early twentieth century. The goal of article 9 is clearly not to create additional rights for these States but to make the exercise of universal jurisdiction mandatory with respect to counterfeiting currency. That obligation arises when a request for extradition has been received and denied. Absent such a request, the custodial State may, but does not have to, initiate proceedings against the foreign offender. The protected right, security of national currency, is a pre-eminent State interest to which there is a clear parallel interest in the repression of counterfeiting. Offenders are typically private persons acting for personal gain.

Convention for the Suppression of the Illicit Traffic in Dangerous Drugs

The second treaty providing for universal jurisdiction is the Convention for the Suppression of the Illicit Traffic in Dangerous Drugs.[11] Article 8 provides:

> Foreigners who are in the territory of a High Contracting Party and who have committed abroad any of the offences set out in article 2 shall be prosecuted and punished as though the offence had been committed in that territory if the following conditions are realized—namely, that:
>
> (a) extradition has been requested and could not be granted for a reason independent of the offence itself;
> (b) the law of the country of refuge considers prosecution for offences committed abroad by foreigners admissible as a general rule.

The goal seems once more to make the exercise of universal jurisdiction mandatory for those countries whose internal law allows the prosecution of foreigners for offences committed abroad, rather than to create additional rights for the signatories. The obligation to initiate proceedings is subject to a prior request for extradition which has been denied. Absent such a request, the custodial State presumably still may unilaterally initiate proceedings against

[11] Geneva, 26 June 1936; 198 LNTS 299; partially reprinted in Bassiouni 1997 (n 2 above) 920.

the foreign offender. It will be remembered that around the time of the adoption of this convention, two international conferences listed trade in controlled substances among the *delicta juris gentium* subject to universal jurisdiction.[12] The protected interests are public morals and health. Offenders are typically private persons acting for personal gain. The offence often involves a transnational element: the transportation of drugs from producer to consumer countries or from one consumer country to another because of differing drug laws and policies.

Convention for the Prevention and Punishment of Terrorism

The universal jurisdiction provision in the Convention for the Prevention and Punishment of Terrorism[13] (which never entered into force) resembles the provisions just discussed. Article 10 provides:

> Foreigners who are on the territory of a High Contracting Party and who have committed abroad any of the offences set out in articles 2 and 3 shall be prosecuted and punished as though the offence had been committed in the territory of that High Contracting Party, if the following conditions are fulfilled—namely, that:
>
> (a) extradition has been demanded and could not be granted for a reason not connected with the offence itself;
> (b) the law of the country of refuge recognizes the jurisdiction of its own courts in respect of offences committed abroad by foreigners;
> (c) the foreigner is a national of a country which recognizes the jurisdiction of its own courts in respect of offences committed abroad by foreigners.

The peremptory language 'shall be prosecuted' suggests again that the goal is not to create additional rights for the signatories but to oblige those States whose internal law allows the prosecution of extraterritorial offences by foreigners to do so actively. New and unique is the introduction of a reciprocity condition in subsection (c). Article 1(2) defines terrorism as 'criminal acts *against a State* [emphasis added] and intended or calculated to create a state of terror in the minds of particular persons, or a group of persons, or the general public'. Thus the rights protected are pre-eminently State interests and the offenders are typically non-State agents.

The three conventions discussed incorporate the first version of an international *aut dedere aut judicare* formula. They defer to the municipal laws of the States parties with respect to extraterritorial offences. Signatories are not required to amend their rules of jurisdiction. An obligation to institute proceedings arises only for those countries whose internal legislation recognizes

[12] The 1927 Warsaw Conference for the Unification of Penal Law and the 1932 Hague International Congress of Comparative Law (see ch 2 s A above).

[13] Geneva, 16 November 1937; C.546.M.383.1937.V., série de publications de la Société des Nations, Questions Juridiques, 1937, V.10; partially reprinted in Bassiouni 1997 (n 2 above) 791.

as a general rule the principle of the prosecution of offences committed abroad *and* who have received and rejected an extradition request. It may be concluded that these first conventions are minimalist frameworks.

Three common characteristics of the conventions might help explain their broad jurisdictional base. First, all three concern State interests, the protection of which are perceived by signatories as of parallel interest. In this respect, it is noticeable that the conventions against slavery and related practices,[14] which protect what are now called human rights, fail to provide for universal jurisdiction. Second, State agents are not within the purview of the typical class of offenders. And third, the offences in question often involve a transnational element.

Post-World War II conventions

After World War II global and regional intergovernmental organizations became the driving forces behind an intensified treaty-making process. Some two dozen treaties thus adopted to criminalize certain conduct and establish a form of universal repression, the following of which are discussed below: the Geneva Conventions and Protocol Additional Relating to the Protection of Victims of International Armed Conflicts, the Convention for the Protection of Cultural Property in the Event of Armed Conflict, the Convention on the Law of the Sea, the International Convention for the Suppression of the Crime of Apartheid, the Convention for the Suppression of Unlawful Seizure of Aircraft, and the Convention against Torture and Cruel, Inhuman, or Degrading Treatment or Punishment. The discussion commences, however, by reviewing a convention that noticeably does *not* provide for universal jurisdiction.

Convention on the Prevention and Punishment of the Crime of Genocide

The Convention on the Prevention and Punishment of the Crime of Genocide[15] (hereinafter 'Genocide Convention') was the first human rights convention adopted by the United Nations and was an immediate response to Nuremberg, which had dealt with genocide not as a separate crime but as a crime against humanity in connection with war. As noted in chapter 2, pre-World War II doctrine was quasi-unanimous on the existence of universal jurisdiction over *delicta juris gentium*. The adoption of a convention on genocide offered a unique opportunity to see whether States were willing to follow doctrine. The drafting history of the Convention's jurisdiction clause will therefore be reviewed.[16]

[14] For a list of these treaties and their penal and jurisdictional provisions, see Bassiouni 1997 (n 2 above) 683–710 and Oehler (n 7 above) 521–2.

[15] New York, 9 December 1948; 78 UNTS 277.

[16] This section draws heavily on WA Schabas, *Genocide in International Law* (2000) which supersedes earlier authoritative comments such as PN Drost, *Genocide: United Nations Legislation on International Criminal Law* (1959), N Robinson, *The Genocide Convention: A*

Following its affirmation of the Principles of International Law recognized by the Charter of the Nuremberg Tribunal,[17] the UN General Assembly adopted on 11 December 1946 resolution 96(I) on the crime of genocide.[18] The resolution affirms that genocide is a crime under international law, invites the Member States to enact the necessary legislation for the prevention and punishment of genocide, recommends international co-operation with a view to facilitating the prevention and punishment of the crime, and requests the Economic and Social Council to undertake studies with a view to drawing up a draft convention on the crime of genocide. The drafting was completed within two years. Three principal drafts (including the final text) were produced during this process, each with a different jurisdiction clause.

The first draft by the Secretariat[19] set out the rule of universal punishment in article VII: 'The High Contracting Parties pledge themselves to punish any offender under this Convention within any territory under their jurisdiction, irrespective of the nationality of the offender or of the place where the offence has been committed'. Moreover, States parties vowed to commit persons suspected of genocide for trial by an international court in cases where they were themselves unwilling to try the offenders or grant extradition, or where the acts were committed by individuals acting as organs of the State or with its support or tolerance (article IX). It was the opinion of the Secretary-General and the experts involved that inasmuch as genocide is by its nature an offence under international law the Convention would fail its purpose if acts of genocide could not be prosecuted outside the territories of the Parties of the Convention.[20] They also noted that universality of repression seemed to have been the intention of General Assembly Resolution 96(I).[21]

Of the twelve countries that replied to the Secretary-General's appeal for comments four commented on article VII specifically.[22] The United States of America proposed prosecution for crimes committed outside the territory of a State only with the consent of the States upon whose territory genocide was committed.[23] The Soviet Union was equally negative about universal jurisdiction.[24] Views in support of confining the Convention to territorial jurisdiction

Commentary (1960) and M Lippman, 'The Drafting of the 1948 Convention for the Prevention and Punishment of Genocide' (1985) 3 *Boston University Int'l LJ* 1; for a summary in French of the drafting history of the jurisdiction clause, see J Graven, 'Les crimes contre l'humanité' (1950) 76 *Receuil des cours de l'académie de droit international* 427, 516–22.

[17] UNGA Res 95(I) (1946); 188 UN Doc A/64/Add.1(1946).

[18] Reprinted in Robinson (n 16 above) 121–2 and in Schabas (n 16 above) 45.

[19] Draft prepared by the Secretariat's Human Rights Division with the expert advice of R Lemkin, author of *Axis Rule in Occupied Europe* (1944) who coined the word 'genocide', and Professors H Donnedieu de Vabres and V Pella. The draft is reprinted in Robinson (n 16 above) 122–30 and in Schabas (n 16 above) 552–9.

[20] Robinson (n 16 above) 31.

[21] Schabas (n 16 above) 355 points out that this is an exaggerated reading. The initial draft of the resolution recommended universal jurisdiction, but any reference to it was eliminated in the final version.

[22] Schabas (n 16 above) 56–7.

[23] Ibid 355.

[24] Ibid.

were also expressed by the Netherlands.[25] In comments on the Secretariat draft, only Siam (Thailand) endorsed universal jurisdiction.[26] The Secretariat's draft, together with the comments, was submitted to an Ad Hoc drafting committee composed of China, France, Lebanon, Poland, the Soviet Union, the United States of America, and Venezuela.

The Ad Hoc Committee abandoned the principle of universal repression. The new draft provided: 'Persons charged with genocide or any of the other acts enumerated in Article IV shall be tried by a competent tribunal of the State in the territory of which the act was committed or by a competent international tribunal'.[27] The Report of the Ad Hoc Committee summarizes the discussions among its members on the question of universal jurisdiction as follows:

> Those in favor of universal repression held that genocide would be mostly committed by the State authorities themselves or that these authorities would have aided and abetted the crime. Obviously in this case the national courts of that State would not enforce repression of genocide. Therefore, whenever the authorities of another State had occasion to arrest the offenders they should turn them over to their own courts. The supporters of the principle of universal repression added that, since genocide was a crime in international law, it was natural to apply the principle of universal repression. They quoted conventions on the repression of international offences such as traffic in women and children, counterfeiting currency, etc.
>
> The opposite view held that universal repression was against the traditional principles of international law and that permitting the courts of one State to punish crimes committed abroad by foreigners was against the sovereignty of the State. They added that, as genocide generally implied the responsibility of the State, on the territory of which it was committed, the principle of universal repression would lead national courts to judge the acts of foreign governments. Dangerous international tension might result.
>
> A member of the Committee, while he agreed that the right to prosecute should not be left exclusively to the courts of the country where genocide had been committed, declared himself opposed to the principle of universal repression in the case of genocide. It is a fact, he said, that the courts of the various countries of the world do not offer the same guarantee. Moreover, genocide is distinguished from other crimes under international conventions (traffic in women, traffic in narcotic drugs, counterfeiting currency) by the fact that, though in itself it is not a political crime, as stated in Article IX of the draft Convention, it nevertheless has or may have political implications. Therefore, there is a danger that the principle of universal repression might lead national courts to exercise a biased and arbitrary authority over foreigners. This representative therefore proposes that jurisdiction be given to an international court to which States would surrender the authors of genocide committed abroad whom they had arrested and whom they would be unwilling to extradite.[28]

[25] Ibid. [26] Ibid.

[27] The Ad Hoc Committee draft is reprinted in Robinson (n 16 above) 131–7 and in Schabas (n 16 above) 559–64.

[28] Quoted in Study on the Question of the Prevention and Punishment of the Crime of Genocide, Mr N Ruhashyankiko, Special Rapporteur, UN Doc E/CN.4/Sub.2/416 (1978).

The Ad Hoc Committee draft was then referred to the Sixth Committee of the General Assembly for an article-by-article consideration.[29] Various amendments were submitted.[30] Iran proposed incorporating the concept of universal jurisdiction in article VII by adding the following paragraph: 'They [persons charged with genocide or any of the other acts enumerated in Article IV] may also be tried by tribunals other than those of the States in the territories of which the act was committed, if they have been arrested by the authorities of such States, and provided no request has been made for their extradition'.[31] The sponsor stressed that the application of universal punishment was envisaged only as a subsidiary measure, according to the principle *aut dedere aut punire*.[32] The premise was that any offence against international law involves subsidiary universal punishment.[33] Subsidiary universal jurisdiction, according to the delegate, had to be distinguished from primary universal jurisdiction which applies to offences such as piracy and allows the State of arrest to try an offender whether or not a request for extradition from the territorial State has been received.[34] By contrast, under the principle of subsidiary universal jurisdiction, the State was bound to extradite offenders and not to put them on trial unless extradition was not requested or was impossible.[35]

Australia, Brazil, Denmark, Haiti, India, the Philippines, and Venezuela endorsed the premise and the substance of the Iranian amendment.[36] They argued that the amendment would make it possible to ensure the punishment of the guilty party when he took refuge in a country other than that in which he committed the offence. In such cases, under the principle of territorial competence, the criminal would not be punished where his extradition was not requested by the country in which the crime had been committed, or where extradition was impossible for reasons of *force majeure*, or because States are not obliged to extradite their own nationals. Supporters of the Iranian amendment also maintained that even if the courts of the various countries in the world did not all offer the same guarantees, the offender had only himself to blame if he fled from the place where he had committed his offence and proceeded to a State where the laws were more severe or whose courts offered him fewer guarantees. They further argued that the application of the principle of universal

[29] Official Records of the General Assembly, Third Session, Sixth Committee, Part I, 97th, 98th, and 100th Meetings. The discussion of the jurisdiction clause can be found at 360–407.

[30] See extensively Robinson (n 16 above) 80–6; Schabas (n 16 above) 357–60.

[31] UN Doc A/C.6/218.

[32] Study on the Question of the Prevention and Punishment of the Crime of Genocide (n 28 above) 194.

[33] Official Records of the General Assembly (n 29 above) 395.

[34] Ibid 394–5.

[35] Ibid.

[36] Some delegations proposed modifications to the wording. India, for example, suggested the following text: 'They may also be tried by the tribunals of any other State, party to the present Convention, in whose territory they may be found, provided no request for their extradition has been duly made, either by the State of which they are nationals or by the State in which the act was committed' (ibid 396–7).

punishment was not inconsistent with the sovereignty of States because if the State on whose territory the offence had been committed wished to try the offender itself, it would request his extradition; but if it expressed no such desire, it thereby tacitly renounced its right to try him.

The great Powers, however, opposed the Iranian amendment. The delegate of the United States of America called the principle of universal punishment 'one of the most dangerous and unacceptable of principles', adding that the United States government, which had also wished to limit the jurisdiction of the proposed international tribunal, 'would *a fortiori* vigorously oppose the adoption of the principle of universal repression'.[37] The representative of the Soviet Union stated that:

> it was wrong to automatically apply to the crime of genocide a penal system accepted in dealing with other crimes which also violated international law but were altogether different in character. Universal punishment was justified in the cases of traffic in women or piracy by the fact that it was often extremely hard, if not impossible, to determine the place where the crime had been committed. In the case of genocide, however, if judicial proceedings were to be instituted by the courts of the State in which the offender had been arrested, documents and witnesses would have to be asked for from the State on whose territory the crime had been committed; and it was to be expected that the latter State, jealous of its sovereignty, would not consent to surrender its penal jurisdiction to another State, since the principal of universal punishment was even more incompatible with the sovereignty of States than international punishment.[38]

France was hardly keener about universal jurisdiction.[39] The United Kingdom delegate cited municipal law reasons against universal jurisdiction.[40] Some representatives observed that article VII of the Ad Hoc Committee draft does not rule out the jurisdiction of the courts other than those of the territorial State.[41] The Iranian amendment was decisively rejected by 29 votes to 6, with 10 abstentions.[42] Article VII of the Ad Hoc Committee draft became article VI in the final draft.

The Convention was adopted unanimously and without abstention by the General Assembly on 9 December 1948.[43] Article VI provides that '[p]ersons

[37] Ibid 399. [38] Ibid 403. [39] Schabas (n 16 above) 356.

[40] The delegate considered the Iranian amendment to be 'incompatible with the principle of territoriality on which the jurisdiction of penal courts in the United Kingdom is based. Criminal courts in the United Kingdom did not punish British citizens for crimes committed abroad and, except in time of war, those courts could not punish aliens for crimes which they had committed outside the territory of the United Kingdom' (Official Records of the General Assembly (n 29 above) 402).

[41] The Greek delegate opined that '[i]t was possible, in theory, that some States would adopt the principle of universal punishment; there was nothing in Art. VII to prevent that' (ibid 405). A number of countries, however, made declarations and reservations to the effect that the provision excludes universal jurisdiction (Study on the Question of the Prevention and Punishment of the Crime of Genocide, n 28 above, 197).

[42] Official Records of the General Assembly (n 29 above) 406.

[43] UNGA Res 260A (III) (1948). As of April 2001, 132 States had ratified the Convention.

charged with genocide or any of the other acts enumerated in Article III shall be tried by a competent tribunal of the State in the territory of which the act was committed, or by such international penal tribunal as may have jurisdiction with respect to those Contracting Parties which shall have accepted its jurisdiction'. To give effect to the second option provided for in article VI the General Assembly, immediately after the adoption of the Convention, invited the International Law Commission to study the desirability of establishing an international judicial organ for the trial of persons charged with genocide and other crimes.[44] The court envisaged was established on 1 July 2002 when the ICC Statute[45] entered into force.

The controversy over universal jurisdiction continues today. The issue was briefly addressed by the two *ad hoc* judges in *Application of the Convention on the Prevention and Punishment of the Crime of Genocide*[46] before the International Court of Justice. Judge Kreca recalled that the Convention 'does not contain the principle of universal repression. It has firmly opted for the territorial principle of the obligation of prevention.'[47] His colleague Judge Lauterpacht took a diametrically opposed view; the purpose of article I of the Convention, which states that genocide is a crime under international law, is 'to permit parties, within the domestic legislation that they adopt, to assume universal jurisdiction over the crime of genocide'.[48] As noted by a commentator, Judge Lauterpacht did not refer to article VI in his discussion on the universal jurisdiction issue.[49]

As will be seen below in Part II, domestic courts also remain divided. *Expressio unius est exclusio alterius* is a well established principle of statutory construction. The better view, therefore, is that the Convention rejects the concept.[50] On the other hand, it is noteworthy that the Genocide Convention, unlike contemporary *aut dedere aut judicare* conventions, does *not* contain a clause to the effect that jurisdiction in accordance with national law beyond the terms of the treaty is permissible.[51] Anyway, the universal jurisdiction contemplated during the drafting of the Convention was the (subsidiary) jurisdiction of the *judex loci deprehensionis*, not the virtual right of *any* State to prosecute a suspect.

Why is the first convention to use the term 'crime under international law' negative on universal jurisdiction? One can see several reasons. History shows that genocide usually implies the responsibility of the territorial State.

[44] UNGA Res 260B (III) (1948), reprinted in Robinson (n 16 above) 145–6.

[45] Rome Statute of the International Criminal Court (Rome, 17 July 1998; UN Doc A/CONF.183/10; reprinted in (1998) 37 *Int'l L Materials* 999).

[46] *Application of the Convention on the Prevention and Punishment of the Crime of Genocide*, ICJ Reports 1993, 325.

[47] Ibid 464.

[48] Ibid 443.

[49] Schabas (n 16 above) 364.

[50] Schabas (n 16 above) 367; Drost (n 16 above) 102–3.

[51] See the discussion below of the Convention for the Suppression of Unlawful Seizure of Aircraft, and the Convention against Torture and Cruel, Inhuman, or Degrading Treatment or Punishment.

The Convention obliges parties to punish all persons having committed genocide, 'whether they are constitutionally responsible rulers, public officials or private individuals' (article IV). Exclusion of State immunity—a novelty—*and* universal jurisdiction in one and the same instrument probably went too far. Genocide is typically committed against a State's own citizens. The lack of an international element may have contributed to the apprehension to allow other States to become involved. Perhaps most importantly of all, the great Powers did not want to know about universal jurisdiction.

Geneva Conventions Relating to the Protection of Victims of Armed Conflicts

Less than a year after the Genocide Convention four other important post-Nuremberg instruments came into being: the Convention for the Amelioration of the Condition of the Wounded and Sick in Armed Forces in the Field,[52] the Convention for the Amelioration of the Condition of the Wounded, Sick, and Shipwrecked Members of the Armed Forces at Sea,[53] the Convention Relative to the Treatment of Prisoners of War,[54] and the Convention Relative to the Protection of Civilian Persons in Time of War[55] (hereinafter referred to as the '1949 Geneva Conventions'). The Conventions were supplemented in 1977 by two Additional Protocols.[56] Together they make up the core of international humanitarian law.

The Conventions and Additional Protocol I apply in *international* armed conflict.[57] Conversely, Additional Protocol II governs the protection of victims of *non-international* armed conflict. A jurisdiction clause common to the Conventions[58] and Additional Protocol I[59] provides, in part, as follows:

> The High Contracting Parties undertake to enact any legislation necessary to provide effective penal sanctions for persons committing, or ordering to be committed, any of the grave breaches of the present Convention defined in the following Article.

[52] Geneva, 12 August 1949; 75 UNTS 970 ('Geneva Convention I').
[53] Geneva, 12 August 1949; 75 UNTS 971 ('Geneva Convention II').
[54] Geneva, 12 August 1949; 75 UNTS 972 ('Geneva Convention III').
[55] Geneva, 12 August 1949; 75 UNTS 973 ('Geneva Convention IV').
[56] Additional Protocol Relating to the Geneva Conventions of 12 August 1949, and Relating to the Protection of Victims of International Armed Conflicts (Geneva, 8 June 1977; 1125 UNTS) ('Additional Protocol I') and Additional Protocol Relating to the Geneva Conventions of 12 August 1949, and Relating to the Protection of Victims of Non-international Armed Conflicts (Geneva, 8 June 1977; 1125 UNTS 17513) ('Additional Protocol II').
[57] An exception is article 3, common to the 1949 Geneva Conventions, which applies 'in the case of an armed conflict not of an international character'.
[58] Articles 49, 50, 129, and 146 of respectively Geneva Conventions I, II, III, and IV.
[59] Article 85(1) of Additional Protocol I makes the common jurisdiction clause of the Conventions also applicable to the repression of grave breaches of the Protocol.

Each High Contracting Party shall be under an obligation to search for persons alleged to have committed, or to have ordered to be committed, such grave breaches, and shall bring such persons, regardless of their nationality, before its own courts. It may also, if it prefers, and in accordance with the provisions of its own legislation, hand such persons over for trial to another High Contracting Party concerned, provided such High Contracting Party has made out a *prima facie* case.

The expression 'regardless of their nationality' suggests universal jurisdiction. Is that so? This question may seem superfluous but for a while there was discussion whether the right to try non-nationals was limited to belligerent States parties or extended also to neutral States parties. It should be noted here that an influential 1945 publication[60] was only concerned with the question whether, under international law, a *belligerent* State has jurisdiction to punish an enemy war criminal in its custody when the victim of the war crimes was a national of another State and the offence took place outside of territory under control of the punishing State.[61] Röling, the Dutch professor and former judge of the International Military Tribunal for the Far East, has emphatically defended a narrow reading of the jurisdiction clause.[62] Other commentators[63] have likewise suggested that only belligerent States parties may exercise 'universal' jurisdiction under the Conventions. The view has been persuasively rebutted by one of the principal architects of the penal provisions in the Conventions[64] and by others[65] on the basis of a careful examination of the *travaux préparatoires*. Furthermore, nearly all countries surveyed in Part II below have extended their jurisdiction over grave breaches independently of their involvement in the conflict, the place of commission, and the nationality of the victims.[66] In light of article 31(3)(b) of Vienna Convention on the Law of Treaties,[67] which provides that any subsequent practice in the application of the treaty may help establish the agreement of the parties regarding its application, it is safe to say that the broad interpretation

[60] WB Cowles, 'Universality of Jurisdiction Over War Crimes' (1945) 33 *California LR* 177–218.

[61] Ibid 178.

[62] BVA Röling, 'Enkele volkenrechtelijke aantekeningen bij de wet oorlogsstrafrecht' [1959] *Nederlands Tijdschrift voor Internationaal Recht* (special issue) 263, 268–70.

[63] Oehler (n 7 above) 847 points out that the text is not clear about the place of commission and the nationality of the victim: it does not say 'wherever committed' or 'against whomever committed'. DW Bowett, 'Jurisdiction. Changing Patterns of Authority over Activities and Resources' (1982) 53 *British Ybk Int'l L* 1, 12 cites Röling with approval.

[64] MW Mouton, 'De wet oorlogsstrafrecht en het internationale recht' [1960] *Nederlands Tijdschrift voor Internationaal Recht* 59, 61–4 observes, *inter alia*, that the clause mentions 'the *contracting* parties', and not 'the parties to the conflict'.

[65] AR Carnegie, 'Jurisdiction over Violations of the Laws and Customs of War' (1963) 39 *British Ybk Int'l L* 402, 408; R van Elst, 'Implementing Universal Jurisdiction Over Grave Breaches of the Geneva Conventions' (2000) 13 *Leiden J Int'l L* 815, 821–2.

[66] A recent comprehensive survey found 55 countries that have established universal jurisdiction over all or some of the grave breaches (van Elst, ibid 828–36).

[67] Vienna, 23 May 1969; 1155 UNTS 331.

is correct. The common jurisdiction clause of the 1949 Geneva Conventions and Additional Protocol I is thus rightly considered an example of universal jurisdiction.[68]

Then the question arises: what form of universal jurisdiction?[69] A textual analysis yields the following. The first paragraph of the jurisdiction clause addresses itself to the High Contracting Parties; all are obliged to enact any legislation necessary to provide effective penal sanctions to repress grave breaches. The first sentence of the second paragraph, despite the wording, is only addressed to the custodial State because a State can only search on its own the territory and can only bring before its courts suspects who are present there. The obligation to search and prosecute is complemented by an alternative obligation in the second sentence of the paragraph: 'It may also, if it prefers, and in accordance with the provisions of its own legislation, hand such persons over for trial to another High Contracting Party concerned, provided such High Contracting Party has made out a *prima facie* case'.

Can third States, without any link to the offence or offender, draw an argument from this sentence to ask for a suspect's extradition with a view to prosecuting him before its courts, ie exercise universal jurisdiction *in absentia*? The semi-official commentaries of the Conventions are silent on the issue, which may be indicative.[70] The text speaks of handing a suspect over for trial to another High Contracting Party *concerned*,[71] which suggests that a link or interest is required.[72] Any other interpretation would hardly be reconcilable with the above-mentioned discussion on belligerent versus neutral States parties. If there was even uncertainty about the right of a neutral State with custody over the offender, how then could such a right extend to neutral States without custody? Furthermore, one would not expect States at the Geneva Diplomatic Conference to hold a substantially different view on universal jurisdiction from that which they held just a year earlier during the drafting of the Genocide Convention.

[68] G Dahm, *Zur Problematik des Völkerstrafrechts* (1956) 34 describes the jurisdiction clause of the Geneva Conventions as a case of unqualified universal jurisdiction (*uneingeschränkte Weltrechtsprinzip*). See also Y Sandoz, 'Penal Aspects of International Humanitarian Law', in MC Bassiouni (ed) *International Criminal Law* (2nd edn, 1998) I, 393, 414; Carnegie (n 65 above) 408; van Elst (n 65 above) 819–20. *Contra*: AP Rubin, 'Actio Popularis, Jus Cogens and Offenses Erga Omnes?' (2001) 35 *New England LR* 265, 269–71.

[69] Cf the different doctrinal notions of the universality principle discussed in ch 2 above.

[70] J Pictet, *The Geneva Conventions of 12 August 1949: Commentary published under the general editorship of Jean S. Pictet. I. Geneva Convention for the Amelioration of the Condition of the Wounded and Sick in Armed Forces in the Field* (1952) 362–6. According to WM Mouton, 'La protection pénales des conventions internationals humanitaires' [1953] *Revue internationale de droit pénal* 851, 855–6 the Conventions incorporate the system of the jurisdiction of the *judex deprehensionis*.

[71] 'To another a High Contracting Party concerned' reads in the French version '*à une autre Partie Contractante, interessée à la poursuite*'.

[72] Cf AP Rubin (n 68 above) 270. On the other hand, proposals that the Contracting Party requesting extradition should prove its interest in the prosecution were rejected. See, Final Record of the Diplomatic Conference of Geneva of 1949, vol. II-B, 177; P de La Pradelle, *La Conférence Diplomatique et les Nouvelles Conventions de Genève du 12 Août 1949* (1951) 256–7.

This leads to a third question: why was universal jurisdiction accepted more readily for grave breaches than for genocide, which are both typically perpetrated by State agents? A possible explanation is that grave breaches necessarily imply an international element: diversity of nationality between victim and perpetrator is a constitutive element of a grave breach.[73] Genocide, by contrast, is mostly committed against a State's own nationals. Another reason may be that the issue received less attention during the drafting of the Geneva Conventions, which together comprise more than two hundred substantive provisions, than during the drafting of the Genocide Convention where jurisdiction was just one of only eight substantive provisions. The fact that the 1949 Geneva Conventions were drafted shortly after a conflict in which so many countries were involved has also been advanced as an explanation.[74]

To conclude, the grave breaches repression regime of the 1949 Geneva Conventions and Additional Protocol I is imperative, whereby *judicare* comes before *dedere*[75] and is based on actual custody over the offender. Contrary to *aut dedere aut judicare* in the three pre-World War II conventions discussed earlier, the competence of the *judex loci deprehensionis* over grave breaches is primary *and* mandatory for all States parties, not just for those whose internal legislation recognizes as a general rule the principle of prosecution of extraterritorial offences.

Convention for the Protection of Cultural Property in the Event of Armed Conflict

The Convention for the Protection of Cultural Property in the Event of Armed Conflict[76] is yet another humanitarian law treaty with penal provisions. Article 28 provides that '[t]he High Contracting Parties undertake, within the framework of their ordinary criminal jurisdiction, all necessary steps to prosecute and impose penal or disciplinary sanctions upon those persons, of whatever nationality, who commit or order to commit a breach of the present Convention'.

The expression 'of whatever nationality' could be read as creating universal jurisdiction,[77] but a narrower interpretation has also been advanced.[78]

[73] The grave breaches universal repression regime does not apply to violations of common article 3 of the 1949 Geneva Conventions and of Additional Protocol II, which govern internal armed conflicts (cf nn 58, 59 above).

[74] Röling (n 62 above) 266. On the question why universal jurisdiction was included in the 1949 Geneva Conventions, see van Elst (n 65 above) 823–5.

[75] van Elst (n 65 above) 819 therefore suggests that we refer to *aut judicare aut dedere* instead of *aut dedere aut judicare*, because the obligation to initiate criminal proceedings comes first and exists independently of the question whether a request for extradition has been received.

[76] The Hague, 14 May 1954; 249 UNTS 215.

[77] Eg Carnegie (n 65 above) 409 and Y Dinstein, 'International Criminal Law' (1985) 20 *Israel LR* 206, 214 (citing Carnegie with approval).

[78] Clark (n 2 above) 57 says that article 28 can also be read as an expression of the territorial principle, extending it to include occupied territory.

The clause is definitely less imperative than the jurisdiction clause in the 1949 Geneva Conventions; States parties are not required to amend their municipal law in order to establish any extraterritorial jurisdiction over violations of the Convention; the imposition of disciplinary sanctions (which can only apply to members of their own armed forces) is sufficient. Like the 1949 Geneva Conventions and Additional Protocol I, this Convention applies only to international armed conflicts (article 18); breaches thus necessarily imply an international element. Offenders are typically members of the military and other State agents associated with the war effort.

Convention on the Law of the Sea

Long one of the most elaborate international legal regimes is that of the sea. Two conventions are relevant: the Convention on the High Seas[79] and the Convention on the Law of the Sea.[80] Only the latter is considered here because the provisions of interest to this study are identical in the two conventions.

The widely accepted fundamental principle that the high seas should be open to ships of all States is codified in article 89: 'No State may validly purport to subject any part of the high seas to its sovereignty'. In criminal law terms, no State may police the high seas, ie search foreign ships and carry out arrests. An exception is made for piracy,[81] which article 101(1) defines as:

> Any illegal act of violence, detention or any act of depredation committed for private ends by the crew or the passengers of a private ship or a private aircraft, and directed:
>
> (a) on the high seas against another ship or aircraft, or against persons or property on board such ship or aircraft or in a place outside the jurisdiction of any State;
> (b) against a ship, aircraft, persons or property in a place outside the jurisdiction of any State.

The jurisdictional aspects of piracy are spelled out in article 105, which reads:

> On the high seas, or in any other place outside the jurisdiction of any State, every State may seize a pirate ship or aircraft, or a ship taken by piracy and under control of pirates, and arrest the persons and seize the property on board. The courts of the State which carried out the seizure may decide upon the penalties to be imposed, and may also determine the action to be taken with regard to the ships, aircraft or property, subject to the rights of third parties acting in good faith.

[79] Geneva, 29 April 1958; 450 UNTS 82.

[80] Montego Bay, 10 December 1982; 516 UNTS 205. The Convention replaces for the States parties since its entry into force on 16 November 1994 the Convention on the High Seas.

[81] Piracy is the subject of extensive literature. See eg the magisterial work V Pella, 'La répression de la piratérie' (1926) 15 *Receuil des cours de l'académie de droit international* 149–275, and more recently AP Rubin, *The Law of Piracy* (2nd edn, 1997).

It is generally accepted that these provisions are declaratory of customary international law.[82] To constitute an act of piracy *iure gentium* subject to universal jurisdiction the *locus delicti* must be the high sea or a place outside the jurisdiction of any State. Furthermore, only acts of violence committed for private ends by crews or passengers of private craft can constitute piracy *iure gentium*. State agents, State craft, and official acts are excluded from the purview of the definition,[83] making it the only convention which applies exclusively to private actors.

These two particular constitutive elements, the *locus delicti* and the private act(or) requirement, explain why universal jurisdiction over piracy is undisputed.[84] Such jurisdiction cannot possibly infringe on another State's sovereignty. They also make piracy inappropriate for analogies;[85] yet some jurists bracket together pirates, war criminals, criminals against humanity, and torturers as *hostis humanis generis*, ie enemies of all humankind. A pointed example is the *Filartiga* case in which Judge Kaufmann wrote that 'the torturer has become—like the pirate and slave trader before him—*hostis humani generis*, an enemy of all mankind'.[86]

One of the explanations offered for the labelling of piracy as an offence against the law of nations is a provision in the United States Constitution which gives Congress the power 'to define and punish Piracies and Felonies on the High Seas, and Offenses against the Law of Nations'.[87] The text, however, does not speak of piracy and *other* offences against the law of nations; this close conjunction of piracy and international offences in the text is apparently a fortuitous result of a last-minute change.[88] As Judge Moore put it in his dissenting opinion in the *Lotus* case, piracy in its jurisdictional aspects is truly *sui generis*.[89]

[82] As for the international customary law status of piracy and its jurisdictional regime before international codification, see Harvard Research in International Law, 'Piracy' (1932) 26 *Am J Int'l L* 739; see also more recently KC Randall, 'Universal Jurisdiction under International Law' (1988) 66 *Texas LR* 785, 792 (with references).

[83] Article 102 contains an exception which strengthens the rule: 'The acts of piracy, as defined in article 101, committed by a warship or government ship or government aircraft whose crew has mutinied and taken control of the ship or aircraft are assimilated to acts committed by a private ship or aircraft'.

[84] For a discussion of authorities, municipal statutes and cases, see Pella (n 81 above); Harvard Research in International Law (n 82 above) 563–73; TH Sponsler, 'The Universality Principle of Jurisdiction and the Threatened Trials of American Airmen' (1968–1969) 15 *Loyola LR* 43, 44–7; Randall (n 82 above) 791–8.

[85] The modern offence of aircraft hijacking ('air piracy') is an exception. On piracy by analogy, see Rubin (n 81 above) 313–31 (critical).

[86] *Filartiga* v *Peña-Irala* 630 F.2d 876 (2d Cir. 1980) at 890, reprinted in (1980) 19 *Int'l Legal Materials* 966.

[87] EM Wise, 'Note on International Standards of Criminal Law and Administration', in Mueller and Wise (eds) *International Criminal Law* (1965) 135, 162.

[88] Ibid.

[89] 1927 PCIJ Reports, ser. A, no 10, 4, para 70.

International Convention for the Suppression and Punishment of the Crime of Apartheid

Apartheid is the practice of racial segregation and discrimination as an official State policy. Because it has some common elements with genocide[90] it should not come as a surprise that the International Convention for the Suppression and Punishment of the Crime of Apartheid[91] (hereinafter 'Apartheid Convention') is modelled after the Genocide Convention.

Article I(1) of the Convention declares[92] that apartheid is 'a crime against humanity and that inhuman acts resulting from the policies and practices of *apartheid*... are crimes violating the principles of international law...' Article III adds that 'international criminal responsibility shall apply, irrespective of the motive involved, to individuals, members of organizations and institutions and representatives of the State, whether residing in the territory of the State in which the acts are perpetrated or in some other State...' Unlike the Genocide Convention, however, the Apartheid Convention provides in article V for universal jurisdiction: 'Persons charged with the acts enumerated in article II of the present Convention may be tried by a competent tribunal of any State Party to the Convention which may acquire jurisdiction over the person of the accused or by an international penal tribunal having jurisdiction with respect to those States Parties which shall have accepted its jurisdiction'.

Why was what failed to gain support in the drafting process of the Genocide Convention acceptable twenty-five years later?[93] The prospect of establishing an international criminal court which both conventions envisage was much bleaker in 1973 than in 1948 and the prospect of the target countries (the territorial States) adhering to the Convention was *nihil*. More importantly, the Apartheid Convention is clearly drafted with three countries in mind, or more accurately three regimes, namely the white minority regimes in the former Rhodesia, Namibia, and the Republic of South Africa. The Convention is in fact tailored to the officials of regimes that were the last vestige of colonialism in Africa. Therefore, States parties have little reason to fear reciprocity.

[90] Apartheid is directed against a racial group, one of the 4 groups protected by the Genocide Convention, involves the State, and is typically committed against a State's own citizens.

[91] New York, 30 November 1973; 1015 UNTS 243. For an excellent analytical comment on the Apartheid Convention and its historical and contemporary significance, see RS Clark, 'Apartheid', in MC Bassiouni (ed) *International Criminal Law* (2nd edn, 1998) I, 643.

[92] The term 'declare' (instead of 'confirm') is significant. Indeed, there are few grounds, if any, for saying that apartheid was a crime under international law before the Convention. However, by April 2001 101 States had ratified the Apartheid Convention. Despite the conspicuous failure by West European and American States to ratify, the (unexpected) high number of ratifications indicates that the prohibition of apartheid is gaining or has already gained customary international law status. Note also that apartheid can be a grave breach of Additional Protocol I (article 85(3)(c)) and, under certain conditions, a crime against humanity under article 7(1)(j) ICC Statute.

[93] Clark (n 91 above) 653–9 devotes considerable attention to the issue of universal jurisdiction in the Apartheid Convention.

The position of the Soviet Union illustrates this. During the drafting of the Apartheid Convention, it pushed for universal jurisdiction and argued that the Convention applies to nationals of non-party States.[94] In contrast, during the drafting of the Genocide Convention, the Soviet Union had argued that 'the principle of universal punishment was even more incompatible with the sovereignty of States than international punishment'.[95] Since it was obvious that the target regimes would never sign the Convention the States parties' claim of universal jurisdiction extends necessarily to nationals of a non-party State, and in fact *only* to nationals of a non-party State.[96] Because of this, the Apartheid Convention, more than any other of the conventions under discussion here, raises the question of the effect of treaties on third States.[97]

It will be noted that article V is drafted in permissive terms ('may be tried'). No (former) apartheid official has ever been prosecuted in a third State. With the abolition of apartheid in the target countries the Convention will probably become obsolete. The historical importance of the Convention and its relevance for the present subject should not be underestimated. It turned out to be an important step between the Genocide Convention and the Convention against Torture and Other Cruel, Inhuman, or Degrading Treatment or Punishment, which is discussed later. A commentator assesses the significance of the Apartheid Convention as follows:

> States which are not necessarily sympathetic to international penal law in general or universal jurisdiction in particular found it possible to accept those concepts in dealing with the South African issue. Many States which otherwise would not talk seriously about creating an international criminal court have done so in the South African context. The Western States, however, treated the drafting of the Convention as something of a Soviet plot and played little part in shaping its language. They seem to have believed that few States would put their ratifications where their rhetoric was and that the treaty would, in the fullness of time, die a natural death. As it turned out, they were

[94] According to Soviet Union delegate, '[t]he obligation to prevent crimes against international law and to punish such crimes was binding on South Africa, whether or not it had adhered to the Convention. Since apartheid was recognized as a crime against humanity in international law, the provisions of the Convention could also be made binding on South Africa' (quoted in Clark ibid 655).

[95] N 38 above.

[96] I leave aside the real possibility that a number of apartheid officials had dual citizenship. Apparently, this was a real concern to the United Kingdom. Its representative cited the universal jurisdiction clause as one of the reasons for voting against the adoption of the Convention and made reservations regarding the application of the Convention against British nationals: 'There are a number of features of the Convention which we find entirely unsatisfactory and unacceptable. One of the most important is that it contains provisions which could violate the principles of international law concerning the proper exercise of criminal jurisdiction, principles to which we attach the highest importance. The provisions in question purport to authorize contracting States to exercise criminal jurisdiction by persons who are not their nationals. That assertion of jurisdiction would be totally inadmissible as far as my Government is concerned, and if this Convention should enter into force, my Government would reserve its rights in relation to any attempt to assert jurisdiction over United Kingdom nationals' (quoted in Clark (n 91 above) 657).

[97] On the effect of international criminal law treaties on third States see Scharf (n 4 above).

wrong. The Convention has obtained a respectable number of parties, and has had an impact on the shaping of contemporary international criminal law.[98]

Convention for the Suppression of Unlawful Seizure of Aircraft

The Convention for the Suppression of Unlawful Seizure of Aircraft[99] (hereinafter 'Hague Hijacking Convention') is the first of some twenty global and regional treaties concluded since 1970 that contain an *aut dedere aut judicare* provisions.[100] It may be noted that in the *Lockerbie* case[101] some judges took the view that 'in general international law there is no obligation to prosecute in default of extradition'.[102] *Aut dedere aut judicare* in the Hague Hijacking Convention reads as follows.

Article IV [Obligation to establish jurisdiction]

1. Each Contracting Party shall take such measures as may be necessary to establish its jurisdiction over the offence and any other act of violence against passengers or crew committed by the alleged offender in connection with the offence, in the following cases:
   (a) when the offence is committed on board an aircraft registered in that State;
   (b) when the aircraft on board which the offence is committed lands in its territory with the alleged offender still on board;
   (c) when the offence is committed on board an aircraft leased without crew to a lessee who has his principal place of business or, if the lessee has no such place of business, his permanent residence, in that State.
2. Each State Party shall likewise take such measures as may be necessary to establish its jurisdiction over the offence in the case where the alleged offender is present in its territory and it does not extradite him pursuant to Art. VIII to any of the States mentioned in Paragraph 1 of this article.
3. This Convention does not exclude any criminal jurisdiction exercised in accordance with national law.

Article VII [Obligation to extradite or prosecute]

The Contracting State in the territory of which an alleged offender is found shall, if it does not extradite him, be obliged without exception whatsoever and whether or not

[98] Clark (n 91 above) 661. [99] The Hague, 16 December 1970; 860 UNTS 105.

[100] On the incorporation of *aut dedere aut judicare* in post-WW II multilateral treaties, see D Costello, 'International Terrorism and the Development of the Principle *Aut Dedere Aut Judicare*' (1975) 10 *J Int'l L & Economics* 483; J Bigay, 'Extrader ou punir' [1980] *Revue de droit pénal et de criminologie* 113; JJE Schutte, 'Enforcement measures in international criminal law' (1981) 52 *Revue internationale de droit pénal* 441; Clark (n 91 above); Guillaume 1989 and 1992 (n 2 above); Bassiouni and Wise (n 2 above).

[101] *Questions of Interpretation and Application of the 1971 Montreal Convention arising from the Aerial Incident at Lockerbie*, ICJ Reports 1992, 3.

[102] Joint declaration of Judges Evensen, Tarassov, Guillaume, and Aguilar Mawdsley (ibid 24). For a similar opinion see A Huet and R Koering-Joulin, *Droit pénal international* (1994) 317 and C Shachor-Landau, 'Extra-Territorial Penal Jurisdiction and Extradition' (1980) 29 *Int'l & Comparative LQ* 274, 278. Conversely, Bassiouni and Wise (n 2 above) 68 contend that *aut dedere aut judicare* has international customary law status, or stronger, that it is a rule of *jus cogens*.

the offence was committed in its territory, to submit the case to its competent authorities for the purpose of prosecution. Those authorities shall take their decision in the same manner as in the case of any ordinary offence of a serious nature under the law of that State.

Article VIII [Extradition]

1. The offence shall be deemed to be included as an extraditable offence in any extradition treaty between Contracting States. Contracting States undertake to include the offence as an extraditable offence in every treaty to be concluded between them.
2. If a Contracting State which makes extradition conditional on the existence of a treaty receives a request for extradition from another Contracting State with which it has no extradition treaty, it may at its option consider this Convention as the legal basis for extradition in respect of the offence. Extradition shall be subject to the other conditions provided by the law of the requested State.
3. Contracting States which do not make extradition conditional on the existence of a treaty shall recognize the offence as an extraditable offence between themselves subject to the conditions provided by the law of the registered State.
4. The offence shall be treated, for the purpose of extradition between Contracting States, as if it had been committed not only in the place in which it occurred but also in the territories of the States required to establish their jurisdiction in accordance with Art. IV, paragraph 1.

These provisions, which have been copied textually or with minor changes[103] into more than a dozen multilateral conventions,[104] create a two-tier system

[103] The wording in some conventions is less imperative. For example, article 4(2)(b) of the Convention Against Illicit Traffic in Narcotic Drugs and Psychotropic Substances states that '[e]ach Party *may* also take such measures as may be necessary to establish its jurisdiction over the offences it has established in accordance with article 3, paragraph 1, when the alleged offender is present in its territory and it does not extradite him to another Party' (emphasis added).

[104] These include: Convention for the Suppression of Unlawful Acts against the Safety of Civil Aviation (Montreal, 23 September 1971; 974 UNTS 177), Convention on the Prevention and Punishment of Crimes against Internationally Protected Persons, including Diplomatic Agents (New York, 14 December 1973; 1035 UNTS 167), International Convention against the Taking of Hostages (New York, 18 December 1979; 1316 UNTS 21931), Convention on the Physical Protection of Nuclear Material (Vienna, 3 March 1980; 1456 UNTS 24631), Inter-American Convention to Prevent and Punish Torture (Cartegena de Indias, 9 December 1985; OAS Treaty Series No 67), Protocol on the Suppression of Unlawful Acts of Violence at Airports Serving International Civil Aviation, supplementary to the Convention for the Suppression of Unlawful Acts against the Safety of Civil Aviation (Montreal, 24 February 1988; 1589 UNTS 14118), Convention for the Suppression of Unlawful Acts against the Safety of Maritime Navigation (Rome, 10 March 1988; 1678 UNTS 29004), United Nations Convention against Illicit Traffic in Narcotic Drugs and Psychotropic Substances (Vienna, 20 December 1988; UN Doc E/CONF.82/15), International Convention against the Recruitment, Use, Financing, and Training of Mercenaries (New York, 4 December 1989; UN Doc A/Res/44/34), Convention on the Safety of United Nations and Associated Personnel (New York, 9 December 1994; UN Doc A/49/742 (1994)); Inter-American Convention on Forced Disappearance of Persons (Belem do Para, 6 September 1994), International Convention for the Suppression of Terrorist Bombings (New York, 15 December 1997; UN Doc A/RES/52/164), International Convention for the Suppression of the Financing of Terrorism, adopted by the General Assembly of the United Nations (New York, 9 December 1999; UN Doc A/RES/54/109).

for the establishment of jurisdiction. The first tier requires each Party to establish its jurisdiction over offences in a number of specified situations. The second tier is based on *aut dedere aut judicare*, which is embedded in a three-part structure.

The core is the obligation for a State party in whose territory an alleged offender is found to submit the case to its competent authorities for the purpose of prosecution if it does not extradite him (article VII). Two corollary provisions intend to secure the possibility for the custodial State to fulfil the obligation; article VIII creates the necessary legal basis for the custodial State to grant extradition requests; article IV(2) obliges States parties to take such measures as are necessary to establish jurisdiction *ratione materiae* and *ratione loci* under municipal criminal law in case an alleged offender is present in its territory and it does not extradite him. Article IV(3) allows States to establish jurisdiction beyond the situations specified in article IV(1), eg on the basis of the nationality of the offender or the victim.

It is not clear from the parenthetic clause whether an obligation to submit a case to the competent authorities for the purpose of prosecution arises only after a request for extradition has been received and denied by the custodial State, or whether this obligation exists also without any extradition request having been made.[105] Judge Guillaume of the ICJ, who as a French delegate was involved in the drafting of the Hague Hijacking Convention and later became the chairman of the Legal Committee of the International Civil Aviation Organization under whose auspices the Convention was drafted, has suggested that the vague clause 'if it does not extradite him' was a deliberate choice on the part of the States.[106] National implementation practice is inconclusive.[107]

However, the pre-World War II version of *aut dedere aut judicare*, which makes the obligation to institute proceedings subject to the explicit condition that extradition was requested but could not be granted, is still used in the current multilateral treaties.[108] Is it then possible to maintain that two quite different formulas mean exactly the same? On the other hand, one of the pernicious

[105] Schutte (n 100 above) 447.

[106] Guillaume 1992 (n 2 above) 35; likewise Bigay (n 100 above) 118.

[107] Austria, for example, has copied the provision 'if it does not extradite him' into its implementing statute, leaving the final interpretation to the judge if a case arises. The Netherlands, on the other hand, has made a reservation to the effect that it will submit the case only if it has received and rejected a request for extradition from another State party. See the Austria and Netherlands country studies in Part II below.

[108] See eg the Convention on Psychotropic Substances (Vienna, 21 February 1971; 1019 UNTS 175); Protocol Amending the Single Convention on Narcotic Drugs, 1961 (Geneva, 25 March 1972; 976 UNTS 3); Convention to Prevent and Punish the Acts of Terrorism Taking the Form of Crimes Against Persons and Related Extortion that are of International Significance (Washington DC, 2 February 1971; OAS Treaty Series No 37); European Convention on the Suppression of Terrorism (Strasbourg, 10 November 1976; ETS No 90); SAARC Regional Convention on Suppression of Terrorism (Kathmandu, 4 November 1987); and European Convention for the Protection of the Environment through Criminal Law (Strasbourg, 4 November 1998; ETS No 172).

consequences of the interpretation that the obligation 'to submit'[109] exists independently from an extradition request would be that States with a strong link to the offence or offender could by their inaction shift their treaty obligations onto the custodial State.

Besides problems of interpretation, *aut dedere aut judicare* is also susceptible to severe criticism in practical terms. The Dutch government lawyer and publicist Schutte has listed no less than ten points of criticism, one of which is that the provision fully disregards the fact that many common grounds for refusal to extradite constitute at the same time impediments for the requested State itself to institute proceedings for the same offence.[110]

It might be asked why a formula that was not acceptable for the drafters of the Genocide Convention is now blindly and automatically copied into most international criminal law conventions. One explanation is that the modern *aut dedere aut judicare* conventions are for the most part 'law and order' conventions[111] aimed at protecting State interests. More than half of the conventions mentioned[112] could be denominated as anti-terrorism instruments. The suppression of the conduct in question presumably serves parallel State interests.[113] The perpetrators are typically, but not necessarily,[114] non-State or para-State actors, and most of the offences in question are committed in an international context[115] or require an international constitutive element.[116] State sovereignty is therefore less of an issue. Another explanation is a change of *opinio juris* on the part of States, and of the great Powers in particular, which is illustrated by the drafting history of the convention discussed next.

Convention against Torture and Other Cruel, Inhuman, or Degrading Treatment or Punishment

The Convention against Torture and Other Cruel, Inhuman, or Degrading Treatment or Punishment[117] (hereinafter 'UN Torture Convention') outlaws

[109] On the obligation 'to submit' in *aut dedere aut judicare* formulas, see Bigay (n 100 above) 118–19; Guillaume 1989 (n 2 above) 369–70.

[110] JJE Schutte, 'Enforcement measures in international criminal law' (1981) 52 *Revue internationale de droit pénal* 441, 445–53 sums up 17 grounds for refusal to extradite, of which only 3 really warrant and make practicable a system of *aut dedere aut judicare*. See also Bigay (n 100 above) 116.

[111] Cf Clark (n 91 above) 86.

[112] Nn 104 and 108 above.

[113] Cf Schutte (n 100 above) 442.

[114] For example, an agent of Libya was convicted for the bombing on 21 December 1988 of Pan Am flight 103 above Lockerbie, Scotland: Scottish High Court of Justiciary at Camp Zeist (The Netherlands): *Her Majesty's Advocate* v *Al Megrahi*, reprinted in (2001) 40 *Int'l L Materials* 581 (upheld on appeal).

[115] The offence of aircraft hijacking, for example, is likely to show one or more international elements, eg international flight, international airspace, diversity of nationality between the hijackers and the crew, the passengers, the State of registration of the craft, or the 'target State'.

[116] Some of the offences referred to have an international constitutive element, eg crimes against internationally protected persons and against United Nations and associated personnel.

[117] New York, 10 December 1984; 1465 UNTS 85. My comments are for the most part based on JH Burgers and H Danelius, *The United Nations Convention against Torture: A Handbook*

the intentional infliction of severe pain and suffering 'by or at the instigation of or with the consent or acquiescence of a public official or other person acting in an official capacity' (article 1). Because no international element is required the Convention basically protects the right of citizens to be free from torture by their own public authorities. From a sovereign's perspective the situation differs totally from piracy and 'law and order' conventions. Nonetheless, the UN Torture Convention copies with minor differences the *aut dedere aut judicare* formula as it appeared first in the Hague Hijacking Convention. The relevant provisions read as follows:

Article 5 [Obligation to establish jurisdiction]

1. Each State Party shall take such measures as may be necessary to establish its jurisdiction over the offences referred to in Art. 4 in the following cases:
   1. When the offences are committed in any territory under its jurisdiction or on board a ship or aircraft registered in that State;
   2. When the alleged offender is a national of that State;
   3. When the victim is a national of that State if that State considers it appropriate.
2. Each State Party shall likewise take such measures as may be necessary to establish its jurisdiction over such offences in cases where the alleged offender is present in any territory under its jurisdiction and it does not extradite him pursuant to Art. 8 to any of the States mentioned in Paragraph 1 of this Article.
3. This Convention does not exclude any criminal jurisdiction exercised in accordance with internal law.[118]

Article 7 [Obligation to extradite or prosecute]

1. The State Party in territory under whose jurisdiction a person alleged to have committed any offence referred to in Art. 4 is found, shall in the cases contemplated in Art. 5, if it does not extradite him, submit the case to its competent authorities for the purpose of prosecution.
2. These authorities shall take their decision in the same manner as in the case of any ordinary offence of a serious nature under the law of that State. In the cases referred to in Art. 5, paragraph 2, the standards of evidence required for prosecution and conviction shall in no way be less stringent than those which apply in the cases referred to in Art. 5, paragraph 1.

on the Convention against Torture and Other Cruel, Inhuman, or Degrading Treatment or Punishment (1988). The authors were involved as diplomats in the drafting of the Convention. Burgers, then member of the Netherlands delegation to the UN Commission on Human Rights, served in 1982–84 as the Chairman-Rapporteur of the working groups set up by the Commission to draw up the text of the Convention. Danelius, then Under-Secretary for Legal and Consular Affairs of the Swedish Ministry of Foreign Affairs, wrote the initial draft of the Convention and played a central role in all sessions of the working group.

[118] This provision seems less helpful here than in the Hague Hijacking Convention because article 5(1) already specifically includes most bases of jurisdiction. It leaves open the possibility of establishing jurisdiction based on eg the residence of the victim or the perpetrator.

3. Any person regarding whom proceedings are brought in connection with any of the offences referred to in Art. 4 shall be guaranteed fair treatment at all stages of the proceedings.

Article 8 [Extradition]

1. The offences referred to in Art. 4 shall be deemed to be included as extraditable offences in any extradition treaty existing between States Parties. States Parties undertake to include such offences as extraditable offences in every extradition treaty to be concluded between them.
2. If a State Party which makes extradition conditional on the existence of a treaty receives a request for extradition from another State Party with which it has no extradition treaty, it may consider this Convention as the legal basis for extradition in respect of such offences. Extradition shall be subject to the other conditions provided by the law of the requested State.
3. States Parties which do not make extradition conditional on the existence of a treaty shall recognize such offences as extraditable offences between themselves subject to the conditions provided by the law of the requested State.
4. Such offences shall be treated, for the purpose of extradition between States Parties, as if they had been committed not only in the place in which they occurred but also in the territories of the States required to establish their jurisdiction in accordance with Art. 5, paragraph 1.

According to authoritative commentators, these jurisdiction provisions constitute 'a cornerstone of the Convention'.[119] The proposal to insert an *aut dedere aut judicare* formula came from Sweden.[120] The assumption was that the territorial State would prosecute and punish equivalent acts committed by non-State actors under its criminal law, but would probably not prosecute acts of torture committed by itself or its officials.[121] Opposition to the Swedish proposal came from a number of Latin American countries (then under military dictatorship), in particular Argentina and Uruguay.[122]

Of the superpowers, the United Kingdom stood by its view taken during the drafting of the Genocide Convention, 'that it would find it difficult to breach the territorial principle normally applied in its criminal law'.[123] The United States, however, in a complete change from its position during the drafting of the Genocide Convention, advocated the inclusion of a universal jurisdiction clause in the Convention.[124] China, which until then had considered universal

[119] Burgers and Danelius (n 117 above) 131.

[120] The text of the original Swedish draft and revised Swedish draft is reprinted in Burgers and Danelius (n 117 above) 57–8.

[121] Ibid 45.

[122] Ibid 78. At the deliberations of the Working Goup in 1984 the new Argentine government supported universal jurisdiction (ibid 94).

[123] N 40 above.

[124] Replying to the Argentine delegation the US delegate stated that: 'such jurisdiction was intended primarily to deal with situations where torture is a State policy and, therefore, the State in question does not, by definition, prosecute its officials who conduct torture. For the international community to leave enforcement of the convention to such a State would be essentially

jurisdiction 'a product of theory of limited sovereignty' and 'an instrument of Western imperialism of the Super Powers',[125] accepted the Swedish proposal.[126] So did the Soviet Union[127] which had already dropped its opposition against universal jurisdiction during the drafting of the Apartheid Convention.[128]

Some delegations considered that the obligation to submit a case to the competent authorities for the purpose of prosecution jurisdiction should be dependent on an extradition request having been made but refused.[129] The predominant opinion and the opinion reflected in the Convention, however, is that jurisdiction must be established also for cases where no extradition request is made by any other State.[130]

As with the 1949 Geneva Conventions, it can be asked whether *aut dedere aut judicare* in the UN Torture Convention sanctions a third country's right to exercise jurisdiction *in absentia*? Can a State not mentioned in either article 5(1) or 5(2) ask for a suspect's extradition with a view to prosecuting him before its courts? The last part of article 5(2) only considers extradition 'to any of the States mentioned in Paragraph 1 of this Article'. Furthermore, exhaustive commentaries on *aut dedere aut judicare* in the UN Torture Convention[131] and in the International Convention Against the Taking of Hostages[132] do not suggest such a competence. Therefore, the question must be answered negatively.

a formula for doing nothing. Therefore in such cases universal jurisdiction would be the most effective weapon against torture which could be brought to bear. It could be utilized against official torturers who travel to other States, a situation which was not at all hypothetical. It could also be used against torturers fleeing from a change of government in their States if, for legal or other reasons, extradition was not possible' (quoted in Burgers and Danelius (n 117 above) 78–9).

[125] H Li, *Die Prinzipien des internationalen Strafrechts: Eine vergleichende Untersuchung zwischen dem internationalen Strafrecht der Volksrepublik China und dem der Bundesrepublik Deutschland* (1991) 202. In 1987 the Standing Committee of the People's National Congress of China officially recognized the universality principle as part of Chinese law (ibid).

[126] Burgers and Danelius (n 117 above) 94–5. [127] Ibid 59.

[128] Cf the discussion of the Apartheid Convention above.

[129] A Brazilian amendment which proposed a system of subsidiary universal jurisdiction, namely only if the States of territorial or national jurisdiction did not request extradition within a set period or if such a request were denied, was rejected: Burgers and Danelius (n 117 above) 85.

[130] Ibid 132–3. In this respect, Burgers and Danelius note 'that during the *travaux préparatoires* it was suggested that jurisdiction should exist after a certain time had elapsed without extradition having been requested, but no such time-limit appears in the text of the Convention. Each State is therefore free to determine, within reasonable limits, at what stage it is justified to conclude that no extradition request will be made' (ibid 133).

[131] Burgers and Danelius (n 117 above); A Boulesbaa, *The UN Convention on Torture and the Prospects for Enforcement* (1999) 204–5, is explicit: 'The term "universal jurisdiction" as used in the *travaux préparatoires* [...] does not connote the same technical meaning as "universal jurisdiction" over piracy in which any State may prosecute the pirate if it obtains personal jurisdiction over him regardless of whether it has any connection with the crime or the pirate.'

[132] JJ Lambert, *Terrorism and hostages in international law: A commentary on the Hostages Convention 1979* (1990) 133 observes that the drafters considered the 'primary' jurisdiction of the countries mentioned in article 5(1) and the 'secondary' or 'subsidiary' jurisdiction of the custodial State. However, Lambert does not mention the possibility of 'tertiary' jurisdiction of other countries.

This review of post-World War II multilateral treaty practice showed that nearly thirty conventions put in place a system of universal repression for specific offences. The 1949 Geneva Conventions, the Convention for the Protection of Cultural Property in the event of Armed Conflict, the Convention on the Law of the Sea, and the Apartheid Convention each have their own provision on universal jurisdiction. The contemporary trend, however, is to use an *aut dedere aut judicare* clause.

Introduced in 1970 and since then copied into some two dozen other conventions, the modern version of *aut dedere aut judicare* is far more elaborated and imperative than the pre-World War II version, but neither sanctions the exercise of universal jurisdiction *in absentia*. Initially limited to 'law and order' conventions aimed at protecting State interests against offences by non-State agents, *aut dedere aut judicare* is now also included in 'human rights' conventions. In the latter case, national courts might be called upon to judge acts of foreign State agents. The drafting histories of the conventions discussed showed a fundamental change of attitude of the great Powers *vis-à-vis* universal jurisdiction.

B. RESOLUTIONS OF INTERGOVERNMENTAL BODIES

A resolution is a formal expression of the will or opinion of an official body or a public assembly, adopted by vote.[133] As already stated, it is not a source of law,[134] but resolutions of such bodies as, for instance, the UN General Assembly may indicate an *opinio juris* of States and may constitute starting points for the development of customary law in the event that State practice locks on.[135] This section searches for *opinio juris* in resolutions adopted in response to specific events: World War II, the 1994 genocide in Rwanda, and atrocities in Chile during the *Pinochet* regime.

[133] Black's Law Dictionary (4th edn, 1968) 1474.

[134] Exceptions are resolutions by the United Nations Security Council acting under Chapter VII of the UN Charter.

[135] *Legality of the Threat or Use of Nuclear Weapons*, ICJ Reports 1996, 66, para 70: '... General Assembly resolutions, even if they are not binding, may sometimes have normative value. They can, in certain circumstances, provide evidence important for establishing the existence of a rule or the emergence of an *opinio juris*. To establish whether this is true in a given General Assembly Resolution, it is necessary to look at its content and the conditions of its adoption; it is also necessary to see whether an *opinio juris* exists as to its normative character. Or a series of resolutions may show the gradual evolution of the *opinio* juris required for the establishment of a new rule.' See also R Higgins, 'The Role of Resolutions of International Organizations in the Process of Creating Norms in the International System' in W Butler (ed) *International Law and the International System* (1987) 21–30; I Brownlie, *Principles of Public International Law* (4th edn, 1990) 11; B Simma (ed) *Charta der Vereinten Nationen* (1991) 218.

Principles of International Co-Operation in the Detection, Arrest, Extradition, and Punishment of Persons Guilty of War Crimes and Crimes Against Humanity

The UN General Assembly adopted in 1973 the Principles of International Co-Operation in the Detection, Arrest, Extradition, and Punishment of Persons Guilty of War Crimes and Crimes Against Humanity (hereinafter 'Principles of International Co-Operation').[136] Prior to that the General Assembly had adopted a number of simple resolutions on the same subject;[137] while these resolutions were aimed primarily at war criminals of the European Axis the scope of the Principles of International Co-Operation is no longer confined to World War II.

Before discussing the Principles of International Co-Operation a few remarks about the views of States on universal jurisdiction in the immediate aftermath of World War II are appropriate. Some argue that the jurisdiction of the International Military Tribunals of Nuremberg and Tokyo was at least partly based on the universality principle.[138] They draw support from a passage in the Nuremberg judgment that '[t]he Signatory Powers created this Tribunal, defined the law it was to administer, and made regulations for the proper conduct of the Trial. In doing so, *they have done together what any of them might have done singly*'[139] (emphasis added). This opinion has been criticized[140] and can readily be juxtaposed with a passage from the Tokyo Judgment:

> In our opinion the law of the Charter is decisive and binding on the Tribunal. This is a special tribunal set up by the Supreme Commander under authority conferred on him by the Allied Powers. It derives its jurisdiction from the Charter. [...] In the result, *the members of the Tribunal, being otherwise wholly without power in respect to the trial of the Accused*, have been empowered by the documents, which constituted the Tribunal and appointed them as members, to try the Accused but subject always to the duty and responsibility of applying to the trial the law set forth in the Charter[141] (emphasis added).

After Nuremberg and Tokyo the International Law Commission formulated the Principles of International Law Recognized in the Charter of the

[136] GA Res 3074 (XXVIII) of 3 December 1973, UN Doc A/9030/Add.1 (1973).

[137] Under the heading Question of the Punishment of War Criminals and of Persons Who Have Committed Crimes Against Humanity, the General Assembly adopted Resolutions 2338 (XXII) of 18 December 1967, 2583 (XXIV) of 15 December 1969, and 2712 (XXV) of 15 December 1970.

[138] Eg Carnegie (n 65 above) 415; HT King, 'Universal Jurisdiction: Myths, Realities, Prospects, War Crimes and Crimes Against Humanity: The Nuremberg Precedent' (2001) 35 *New England LR* 281, 281–4.

[139] Judgment (n 8 above) section 'The Law of the Charter'.

[140] Sponsler (n 84 above) 43, 49–51; Randall (n 82 above) 785, 804–10; E Zoller, 'Territorial Effect of the Norm on Responsibility', in G Ginsburgs and VN Kudriavtsev (eds) *The Nuremberg Trial and International Law* (1990) 106, 109.

[141] International Military Tribunal for the Far East, Tokyo (Japan), judgment of 12 November 1948, section 'Jurisdiction of the Tribunal'.

Nuremberg Tribunal and in the Judgment of the Tribunal,[142] which in effect codify the main legal characteristics and consequences of a crime under international law. Any reference to universal jurisdiction is absent. It may be concluded therefore that immediately after World War II there was little evidence of any *opinio juris* among States that crimes under international law were subject to universal jurisdiction.[143]

The Principles of International Co-Operation, adopted in 1973, provide as follows.

1. War crimes and crimes against humanity, wherever they are committed, shall be subject to investigation and the persons against whom there is evidence that they have committed such crimes shall be subject to tracing, arrest, trial and, if found guilty, to punishment.
2. Every State has the right to try its own nationals for war crimes and crimes against humanity.
3. [...]
4. States shall assist each other in detecting, arresting and bringing to trial persons suspected of having committed such crimes and, if they are found guilty, in punishing them.
5. Persons against whom there is evidence that they have committed war crimes and crimes against humanity shall be subject to trial and, if found guilty, to punishment, as a general rule in the countries in which they committed those crimes. In that connection, States shall co-operate on questions of extraditing such persons.

6–9 [...]

The proclamation stops conspicuously short of urging the custodial States to exercise universal jurisdiction. If anything, principles 2 and 5 seem to confirm the principle of territoriality of jurisdiction, although the wording 'as a general rule' does not exclude the jurisdiction of other States. On the whole, World War II-inspired resolutions from the 1960s and 1970s furnish extremely little indication of an *opinio juris* that what they refer to as 'the gravest crimes in international law' would be subject to universal jurisdiction. However, the resolutions should be interpreted in the light of the specific circumstances of World War II criminals left in peace by unwilling authorities (of asylum countries) or protected by municipal statutes of limitation. So the issue was not whether the custodial, or better, asylum States had a right to prosecute them, but whether they could shield them from prosecution by refusing their extradition.

UN Security Council Resolution 978 (1994) on Rwanda

In 1994 Rwanda was the scene of genocide and massacres of civilians, and of a simultaneous non-international armed conflict between the government

[142] UN Doc A/CN.4/SER.A/1950/Add; reprinted in [1950] *Ybk Int'l L Commission*, vol II, 374.

[143] Cf the discussion of the drafting of the Genocide Convention above.

forces and a rebel army. The violence caused the wholesale collapse of the Rwandan criminal justice system and a mass exodus of Rwandans. Among these refugees were former public officials and members of the militia who bear responsibility for the killings.

Acting under Chapter VII of the UN Charter, the Security Council established the International Criminal Tribunal for Rwanda[144] with concurrent but primary jurisdiction.[145] Because of the presence of many culprits outside Rwandan territory, foreign governments were forced to play a role either by providing refuge to them, facilitating their extradition to Rwanda or the ICTR, or prosecuting them before their own courts on the basis of universal jurisdiction. The latter scenario is endorsed by the UN Special Rapporteur on Rwanda[146] and arguably also by the Security Council which urged States:

> [t]o arrest and detain, in accordance with their national law and relevant standards of international law, *pending prosecution* by the International Tribunal for Rwanda or *by the appropriate national authorities*, persons found within their territory against whom there is sufficient evidence that they were responsible for acts within the jurisdiction of the International Tribunal for Rwanda'[147] (emphasis added).

The resolution arguably envisages *prosecution* in third countries; otherwise it would have said '...*extradition* to the appropriate national authorities'. One could thus take the view that the resolution implies recognition by no less than the UN Security Council, where the great Powers have veto power, of universal jurisdiction under general international law over the offences within the subject-matter jurisdiction of the ICTR. One could also minimize the importance of the resolution by arguing that it is a response to very specific circumstances: the great number of perpetrators, their presence abroad, and the wholesale collapse of the Rwandan judicial system; it is noteworthy that no such resolution was apparently adopted with respect to the former Yugoslavia.[148]

Resolutions regarding the arrest of former Chilean President Augusto Pinochet

The arrest in 1998 in the United Kingdom at the request of Spain of former Chilean President Pinochet on charges of gross human rights violations allegedly committed in Chile during his presidency[149] provoked some rare

[144] Resolution 955 of 8 November 1994. [145] Article 8 ICTR Statute.

[146] Report on the situation of human rights in Rwanda submitted by Mr René Degni-Ségui, Special Rapporteur of the Commission on Human Rights, under para 20 of resolution S-3/1 of 25 May 1994; UN Doc E/CN.4/1996/7, 28 June 1995, para 49: '[T]he national courts of Rwanda and other countries will be called on to deal with the cases referred to them'.

[147] Resolution 978 of 27 February 1995.

[148] I refer to the International Criminal Tribunal for the former Yugoslavia established by UN Security Council Resolution 827 on 25 May 1993.

[149] See the Spain and United Kingdom country studies in Part II below.

official public statements on the issue of extraterritorial criminal jurisdiction. The Parliament of the European Union congratulated the Spanish and British authorities for their co-operation in the arrest and reaffirmed 'its commitment to the principle of universal justice to protect human rights';[150] some other European countries thereafter instituted their own criminal proceedings against Pinochet, although mostly for crimes allegedly committed in Chile against their nationals.[151] Conversely, the heads of State of the Mercosur countries, Bolivia, and Chile condemned in a joint statement 'the unilateral and extraterritorial enforcement of national laws'[152] and denounced the Spanish and British actions as 'violations of the principles of legal equality among States and of the non-intervention in the domestic affairs of other countries'.[153]

The Inter-American Commission on Human Rights, for its part, took note of 'one of the greatest advances in recent international public law: establishment of the principle of individual criminal responsibility within the international legal order' and recommended that 'the member States of the Organization of American States adopt such legislative and other measures as may be necessary to invoke and exercise universal jurisdiction in respect of individuals in matters of genocide, crimes against humanity, and war crimes'.[154] The UN Subcommission on Promotion and Protection of Human Rights likewise noted with approval that 'recent initiatives taken by victims in bringing legal actions in the framework of extraterritorial competence as provided for by national legislation—with due respect to the right to a fair trial—have interrupted the process of impunity from which General Augusto Pinochet benefited [...]'. It invited 'all Governments to cooperate in a reciprocal manner even when there is no treaty to facilitate the task of legal authorities dealing with proceedings initiated by victims acting either within the framework of the principle of universal competence as recognized in international law or under a domestic law which establishes an extraterritorial legal competence, in particular because of the nationality of the victim or of the perpetrator'.[155]

With the exception of the declaration of the Mercosur heads of State, the above resolutions all endorse the Spanish proceedings against Pinochet. The Mercosur statement is plainly negative on universal jurisdiction but an important political factor should not be overlooked. Many of these heads of State

[150] Resolution of the European Union Parliament of 21 October 1998 (ref: B-0975/98).

[151] See the Belgium, France, Germany, and Switzerland country studies in Part II below.

[152] Joint declaration of the Mercosur countries (Brazil, Argentina, Paraguay, Uruguay) and Bolivia and Chili, Rio de Janeiro, 9 December 1998 (available in English from FBIS-LAT-98-343).

[153] Ibid.

[154] Inter-American Commission on Human Rights, Recommendations on Universal Jurisdiction and the International Criminal Court, 101st special session, Annual Report 1998, ch VII.

[155] UN Subcommission on Promotion and Protection of Human Rights, 27th meeting 18 August 2000, resolution 2000/24 'Role of universal or extraterritorial competence in preventive action against impunity' (adopted without a vote).

represent governments that have chosen not to prosecute human rights abuses by the former regime to facilitate the transfer of power; indeed, the declaration stresses 'the importance of those domestic agreements that have been democratically achieved'. However, the issue of the compatibility of universal jurisdiction and national amnesty measures falls outside the scope of the present study.[156]

C. OFFICIAL DRAFTS AND STUDIES

Drafts and official reports exhibit contemporary trends and may lay the groundwork for future resolutions, declarations of principles, or conventions. This section considers the Draft European Convention on Conflicts of Jurisdiction in Criminal Matters, the Draft Code of Crimes Against the Peace and Security of Mankind, and the reports of UN Special Rapporteurs and experts Van Boven, Bassiouni, and Joinet.

Draft European Convention on Conflicts of Jurisdiction in Criminal Matters

In 1965 the Legal Committee of the Consultative Assembly of the Council of Europe prepared the Draft European Convention on Conflicts of Jurisdiction in Criminal Matters.[157] Although never proposed for adoption, the draft Convention is significant because it reflects the philosophy underlying the municipal rules of jurisdiction of most Western European countries. Because nine of the countries studied in Part II below are from that part of the world, a brief discussion of the draft Convention is appropriate.

The draft Convention is based on the recognition of concurrent jurisdiction in cases with an international element. Its goal is to establish an order among competing claims; accordingly, the draft envisions the following hierarchy: the territorial State (article 3), the State of which the offender is a national or in which he is domiciled (article 4), and as a last resort the custodial State (article 5).

Article 5 provides that '[t]he State in whose territory is found the perpetrator of a grave offence committed abroad against life, limb, freedom, morality or property, or an offence against common interests protected by international law, may prosecute and try him if the States competent under articles 3 and 4

[156] On this subject see JE Méndez and G Meintjes, 'Reconciling Amnesties with Universal Jurisdiction' (2000) 2 *Int'l L Forum* 76.

[157] Consultative Assembly of the Council of Europe, *Report on the settlement of conflicts of jurisdiction in criminal matters*, Doc 1873 of 27 January 1965, Rapporteur: Mr de Grailly. See also the very informative preparatory report by H Grützner, *Le champ d'application du droit pénal: Aperçu comparatif élaboré en vue de la préparation d'une Convention européenne portant unification des dispositions relatives au champ d'application du droit pénal* (1964).

fail to prosecute, refrain from requesting or refuse an offer of extradition'. The comment on article 5 explains:

> The universality principle is, of course, the principle whereby the court of the place in which the offender is located (*judex deprehensionis*) is competent to hear the case, irrespective of the place of commission and of the nationality of the offender or his victim. The principle arose from a need to ensure the safety of certain basic values in which every State has an equal concern. These are either fundamental values such as life, sexual morality, family morality or property, which are protected by all penal codes or interests protected by international conventions and *jus gentium*.
>
> [...]
>
> The universality principle, following the concept on which it is based, implies a subordination of jurisdictions. That is to say, the *judex deprehensionis* may only intervene if other courts (those of the place of commission or those of the country of nationality of the offender) with primary jurisdiction fail to do so.[158]

Article 5 combines the co-operative general and the co-operative limited universality principle as identified in chapter 2 above. The *judex deprehensionis* may prosecute serious offences (whether common or international) if the more competent States fail to prosecute, refrain from requesting or refuse an offer of extradition. A system for the relaying of information and the communication of requests and notifications is spelled out in article 8 of the draft Convention. Thus, the spirit of the draft Convention lies in the principle of respect of sovereignty and collaboration between States in the exercise of their criminal jurisdiction; there is no place for an exercise of universal jurisdiction *in absentia*.

Draft Code of Crimes against the Peace and Security of Mankind

Pursuant to a General Assembly resolution[159] the International Law Commission adopted in 1950 the Principles of International Law Recognized in the Charter of the Nuremberg Tribunal and in the Judgment of the Tribunal[160] and in 1954 the Draft Code of Offences against the Peace and Security of Mankind.[161] Both instruments are completely silent on the issue of jurisdiction, be it of an international tribunal or of national courts. The Draft Code foundered in the General Assembly due to lack of agreement on a definition of aggression. In 1981, however, the General Assembly invited the ILC to resume its work on the Draft Code, 'taking duly into account the results achieved by the process of progressive development in international law'.[162] This instruction suggests, as noted by a commentator, that the ILC

[158] Article-by-article comment by Rapporteur de Grailly at paras 34, 36 (ibid).

[159] Resolution 177 (II) of 21 November 1947.

[160] N 142 above.

[161] Reprinted in [1954] *Ybk Int'l L Commission*, vol II, 150.

[162] Resolution 36/106 of 10 December 1981.

was to take into account changes that might have occurred in the law since 1954, changes that the General Assembly seems to have assumed have occurred.[163]

The ILC completed its work in 1996. The new Draft Code of Crimes against the Peace and Security of Mankind[164] incorporates the three-part *aut dedere aut judicare* formula introduced by the Hague Hijacking Convention:

Article 8—Establishment of jurisdiction

Without prejudice to the jurisdiction of an international criminal court, each State Party shall take such measures as may be necessary to establish its jurisdiction over the crimes set out in articles 17 [genocide], 18 [crimes against humanity], 19 [crimes against United Nations and associated personnel] and 20 [war crimes], *irrespective of where or by whom those crimes were committed*. Jurisdiction over the crime set out in article 16 [aggression] shall rest with an international criminal court. However, a State referred to in article 16 is not precluded from trying its nationals for the crime set out in that article [emphasis added].

Article 9—Obligation to extradite or prosecute

Without prejudice to the jurisdiction of an international criminal court, the State Party in the territory of which an individual alleged to have committed a crime set out in articles 17 [genocide], 18 [crimes against humanity], 19 [crimes against United Nations and associated personnel] or 20 [war crimes] is found shall extradite or prosecute that individual.

Article 10—Extradition of alleged offenders

1. To the extent that the crimes set out in articles 17, 18, 19 and 20 are not extraditable offences in any extradition treaty existing between States Parties, they shall be deemed to be included as such therein. States Parties undertake to include those crimes as extraditable offences in every extradition treaty to be concluded between them.
2. If a State Party which makes extradition conditional on the existence of a treaty receives a request for extradition from another State Party with which it has no extradition treaty, it may at its option consider the present Code as the legal basis for extradition in respect of those crimes. Extradition shall be subject to the conditions provided in the law of the requested State.

[163] R Rayfuse, 'The Draft Code of Offences Against the Peace and Security of Mankind: Eating Disorders at the International Law Commission' (1997) 8 *Crim L Forum* 43, 46.

[164] Published with an article-by-article commentary in [1996] *Ybk Int'l L Commission*, vol II(2), 15. Prior to that, in 1994 the ILC had completed the Draft Statute for an International Criminal Court, which became the basis for the ICC Statute. The substantive provisions (the crimes) of the Draft Code and the subject-matter jurisdiction of the ICC essentially overlap. The Draft Code lists five crimes: aggression (article 16), genocide (article 17), crimes against humanity (article 18), crimes against United Nations and associated personnel (article 19), and war crimes (article 20). Under article 5 of its Statute the ICC has jurisdiction over these offences except crimes against United Nations and associated personnel.

3. States Parties which do not make extradition conditional on the existence of a treaty shall recognize those crimes as extraditable offences between themselves subject to the conditions provided in the law of the requested State.
4. Each of those crimes shall be treated, for the purpose of extradition between States Parties, as if it had been committed not only in the place in which it occurred but also in the territory of any other State Party.

The commentary explains that:

Jurisdiction over the crimes covered by the Code is determined in the first case by international law and in the second case by national law. As regards international law, any State party is entitled to exercise jurisdiction over an individual allegedly responsible for a crime under international law set out in articles 17 to 20 *who is present in its territory* under the principle of 'universal jurisdiction' set forth in article 9[165] [emphasis added].

In respect of genocide, the commentary notes that article VI of the Genocide Convention restricts national court jurisdiction to the territorial State, but considers that universal jurisdiction over genocide is fully justified 'in view of the character of the crime of genocide as a crime under international law for which universal jurisdiction existed as a matter of customary law for those States that were not parties to the Convention and therefore not subject to the restriction contained therein'.[166]

The commentary also addresses the question whether an obligation to prosecute a foreign offender arises only after a request for extradition has been received and denied by the custodial State, or whether this obligation exists also without any extradition request having been made. The fundamental purpose of *aut dedere aut judicare* 'is to ensure that individuals who are responsible for particularly serious crimes are brought to justice by providing for the effective prosecution and punishment of such individuals by a competent jurisdiction',[167] and the commentary therefore concludes that 'in the absence of a request for extradition, the custodial State would have no choice but to submit the case to its national authorities for prosecution'.[168]

The ILC takes the view that crimes under international law are *ipso facto* subject to universal jurisdiction of the custodial State and that establishment of an international criminal court will not change that. To the contrary, the ILC envisages a division of labour between an international tribunal and national courts exercising territorial or universal jurisdiction.[169] Compared with earlier ILC texts (the Nuremberg Principles of 1950 and the 1954 Draft Code) this Draft Code represents a remarkable change. It should be noted, however, that

[165] Comment on article 8 at (7).
[166] Comment on article 8 at (8).
[167] Comment on article 9 at (2).
[168] Comment on article 9 at (7).
[169] See on this issue B Graefrath, 'Universal Jurisdiction and an International Criminal Court' (1990) 1 *Eur J Int'l L* 67.

neither the Draft Code nor the lengthy commentary suggest a virtual right of any State to exercise universal jurisdiction *in absentia*.

Reports of UN Special Rapporteurs and Experts

The UN Commission on Human Rights has entrusted a number of Special Rapporteurs and experts with a mandate to develop principles and guidelines regarding the questions of impunity of perpetrators of gross human rights violations and of the right of victims to restitution, compensation, and rehabilitation. The reports by Special Rapporteurs van Boven[170] and his successor Bassiouni[171] lead to the adoption by the Commission of Basic Principles and Guidelines on the Right to a Remedy and Reparation for Victims of Violations of International Human Rights and Humanitarian Law.[172] Principles 4 and 5 provide:

4. Violations of international human rights and humanitarian law norms that constitute crimes under international law carry the duty to prosecute persons alleged to have committed these violations, to punish perpetrators adjudged to have committed these violations, and to cooperate with and assist States and appropriate international judicial organs in the investigation and prosecution of these violations.
5. To that end, States shall incorporate within their domestic law appropriate provisions providing for universal jurisdiction over crimes under international law and appropriate legislation to facilitate extradition or surrender of offenders to other States and to international judicial bodies and to provide judicial assistance and other forms of cooperation in the pursuit of international justice, including assistance to and protection of victims and witnesses.

The 'van Boven-Bassiouni Principles' urge States to establish and exercise universal jurisdiction over violations of international human rights and humanitarian law norms that constitute crimes under international law. The fact they do not copy the popular *aut dedere aut judicare* formula, which links the exercise of such jurisdiction to the voluntary presence of the foreign suspect,[173] may be significant.

Unlinking universal jurisdiction and the presence of the offender is clearly the viewpoint of expert Joinet, whose Set of Principles for the Protection and

[170] Study concerning the right to restitution, compensation and rehabilitation for victims of gross violations of human rights and fundamental freedoms. Final Report submitted by Mr Theo van Boven, Special Rapporteur, UN Doc E/CN.4/Sub.2/1993/8, 2 July 1993.

[171] The right to restitution, compensation, and rehabilitation for victims of gross violations of human rights and fundamental freedoms. Final report of the Special Rapporteur, Mr M Cherif Bassiouni, submitted in accordance with Commission resolution 1999/33, E/CN.4/2000/62, 18 January 2000.

[172] The 'van Boven-Bassiouni Principles' were adopted by the Commission at its 56th session in January 2000.

[173] Cf the discussion of the Hague Hijacking Convention and the UN Torture Convention above in this chapter.

Promotion of Human Rights through Action to Combat Impunity[174] propound:

Principle 21. Jurisdiction of national courts

As a rule, the national courts shall have jurisdiction. However, the subsidiary jurisdiction of a foreign court or concurrent jurisdiction of an international court may be accepted when, in view of the circumstances, the national courts are not yet in a position to respond satisfactorily to the justice requirements of a constitutional State or are physically unable to function.

Principle 22. Jurisdiction of foreign courts

The subsidiary jurisdiction of foreign courts shall be exercised by virtue of either a provision on universal jurisdiction set forth in a treaty in force or of a provision of internal law establishing a rule of extraterritorial jurisdiction for serious crimes under international law.

Principle 23. Measures to strengthen the effectiveness of treaty provisions on universal jurisdiction

(A) A provision on universal jurisdiction applicable to serious crimes under international law should be included in all international human rights instruments dealing with such crimes;

(B) By ratifying such instruments, States pledge, pursuant to such a provision, to seek and prosecute the perpetrators of the crimes mentioned above when there are serious reasons to believe that such persons are in their territory, with a view to trying or extraditing them. They are consequently bound to take legislative or other measures under internal law to ensure the implementation of the provision on universal jurisdiction.

Principle 24. Measures to determine extraterritorial jurisdiction in internal law

In the absence of a ratification making it possible to apply such a provision to the country where the crime was committed, and notwithstanding the principle of sovereignty according to which States have recourse to criminal legislation [*sic*] only when there is a direct link—territorial or personnel—between the State and the crime, States shall take measures in their internal legislation to establish extraterritorial jurisdiction over serious crimes under international law which have been committed outside their territory, whatever the nationality of the perpetrator or the victim, and which by their nature are within the purview not only of the internal criminal law but also of a system of international jurisdiction to which the concept of frontiers is alien.

Expert Joinet speaks of the subsidiary jurisdiction rather than the universal jurisdiction of foreign courts. *Subsidiary* jurisdiction here no longer stands

[174] The administration of justice and the human rights of detainees. Question of impunity of violations of human rights (civil and political rights): final report prepared by Mr L Joinet, pursuant to Subcommission resolution 1995/35, UN Doc E/CN.4/Sub.2/1996/18, 29 June 1996.

for the competence of the *judex loci deprehensionis* when extradition is impossible[175] but refers instead to the *complementary* jurisdiction of any foreign court over an offender left in peace in and by the territorial State. When the courts of the latter 'are not yet in a position to respond satisfactorily to the justice requirements of a constitutional State or are physically unable to function' (Principle 21) any State may launch criminal proceedings. This proposal strongly resembles the jurisdiction of the International Criminal Court[176] which depends on the 'unwillingness' or 'inability' of the territorial State to prosecute.[177]

SUMMARY

This chapter has examined universal jurisdiction in international texts. The goal was threefold: to look for provisions on universal jurisdiction in multilateral conventions, to find indications of a common *opinio juris* on universal jurisdiction among States, and to lay the further groundwork for the discussion of legislation and case-law in Part II below.

Little pertinent data could be found in the period before World War II. Only three out of some one hundred multilateral conventions with penal characteristics establish a form of universal repression. These three conventions have in common that they defer to the municipal laws of the States parties in respect to extraterritorial offences, that they protect State interests against attacks by non-State agents, and that the offences in question often involve a transnational element.

The period after World War II presents a very different picture. Nearly thirty treaties, the majority adopted in the last two decades, establish a form of universal repression. The protected interests now include fundamental rights of individuals and groups against gross abuses by public authorities. States have thus recognized that under certain circumstances a third State may prosecute and punish not only foreign citizens but also foreign State agents, even when the offence in question involves no international or transnational element.

Rejected for the Genocide Convention and contested not so long ago during the drafting of the UN Torture Convention, *aut dedere aut judicare* now seems to be the obvious formula for international criminal law treaties. In contradistinction to the pre-World War II conventions, *all* States parties must now bring criminal proceedings when a person, whatever his nationality, suspected of

[175] Cf the discussion of the co-operative general and co-operative limited universality principles in ch 2 above.

[176] The preamble and article 1 ICC Statute provide that the jurisdiction of the Court 'shall be complementary to national criminal jurisdictions'. See also the conclusions of this book.

[177] Cf article 17 ICC Statute.

having committed an offence falling under the treaty is present on its territory and it does not extradite him. A textual analysis and a review of authoritative commentaries showed that *aut dedere aut judicare* does not sanction a third country's right to launch proceedings *in absentia. Aut dedere aut judicare* jurisdiction is thus 'universal' in the sense that the custodial State is competent *wherever* the crime was committed, not in the sense that *whoever* may prosecute. Further evidence of *opinio juris* on the part of States that international crimes can under certain circumstances be subject to universal jurisdiction was found in resolutions by intergovernmental bodies and in official drafts and studies.

PART II

Universal Jurisdiction in Municipal Law

Introduction

The previous chapter considered States' discursive and normative positions on universal jurisdiction expressed in the multilateral diplomatic process. This part deals with legislative and judicial practice at the municipal level. It brings together, and makes accessible in English, detailed accounts of universal jurisdiction in fourteen countries: Australia, Austria, Belgium, Canada, Denmark, France, Germany, Israel, the Netherlands, Senegal, Spain, Switzerland, the United Kingdom (England and Wales), and the United States of America.

The choice of these countries is not accidental. They were selected from an initial survey of more than fifty countries. The main criterion for choosing the fourteen was the existence of either criminal statutes with universal application or cases of universal jurisdiction.[1] Other criteria were representativeness of the major legal systems and the dominant role some countries play in shaping international law and policy.

Admittedly, fourteen countries represent only a small fraction of the nearly two hundred sovereign States. Because the main criterion of selection was the availability of legislative or judicial practice, it follows that in the great majority of States there are presumably few hard facts on universal jurisdiction. Thus, at this point we know already that the countries discussed are not statistically representative and that we will not find general and consistent State practice, one of the two elements of international custom.[2] But, as Lord Denning MR stated, '[w]henever a change is made, someone some time has to make the first move. One country alone may start the process. Others may follow. At first a trickle, then a stream, last a flood.'[3]

Many of the countries discussed carry great weight in international affairs and exercise a significant influence on the law and practice in other States. Decisions on questions of international law by federal courts in Canada, Germany, or the United States, or by the British House of Lords, or the French Court of Cassation are given great authority by courts in other countries and by international tribunals. One of the great public international lawyers of the twentieth century stated in this regard:

> The slow growth of international custom has been compared with the gradual formation of a road across vacant land. To begin with, the tracks are many and uncertain, scarcely visible on the ground. Then, most users, for some reason of common utility,

[1] Piracy cases are not considered because jurisdiction over piracy is *sui generis* (cf the discussion of the Convention of the Law of the Sea in ch 3 above). For a discussion of piracy cases, see AP Rubin, *The Law of Piracy* (2nd edn, 1997).

[2] Cf the discussion of international custom in the Introduction, s D above.

[3] *Trendtex Trading Corporation* v *Central Bank of Nigeria* [1977] QB 529, 556.

> follow the same line; a single path becomes clear, which in turn gives place to a road henceforth recognized as the only regular way, though it is impossible to say at what precise moment the latter change took place. Among the users are always some who mark the soil more deeply with their footprints than others, either because of their great weight, which is to say their power in this world, or because their interests bring them more frequently this way. Thus it happens that the great Powers, after imprinting a definite direction upon usage, make themselves the guarantors and defenders. Their role, which was always decisive in the formation of customary international law, is to confer upon usages that degree of effectiveness without which the legal conviction, condition of general assent, would find no sufficient basis in social reality. Many customs owe their origin wholly to decisions or acts of great Powers which by their repetition or sequence, and above all by the idea of order that finally grows out of them, have little by little lost their personal, contingent, in a word political character and taken on that of a custom in process of formation.[4]

As far as possible the same matrix has been used for each country to facilitate comparison. The point of departure was always the need for a context-sensitive analysis. A country study consists of three sections. Section A presents a *tour d'horizon* of the ambit of a country's criminal law. The goal here is to demonstrate the great diversity of municipal rules of jurisdiction. A sketch of a country's attitude towards extraterritorial jurisdiction, mainly by exploring the relevant codes, is followed by a presentation of and commentary on laws that endow the courts with universal jurisdiction. One way to discover and understand a State's legal position on a topic important to international law is by examining municipal laws.[5]

Section A also considers for each country the standing of victims in criminal proceedings and the application of the principles of double criminality, *lex mitior*, and *ne bis in idem*. 'Double criminality' points to the requirement that criminal law be predictable. It implies that the conduct the forum State seeks to punish must also be considered a crime where it occurred.[6] When there is double criminality the *lex mitior* rule (literally 'milder law') may operate. In this case, the criminal judge applies either his own substantive law or the law of the *locus delicti*, whichever is more favourable to the defendant.[7] *Ne bis in idem* (literally 'not twice in the same') means that an accused cannot be tried twice for the same facts. In an international context *ne bis in idem* refers to recognition of foreign criminal judgments.[8] When a country study does not mention these principles, it only means they are not codified.

4 C de Visscher, *Theory and Reality in Public International Law* (1968) 154–5.

5 *Anglo-Iranian Oil Company* ICJ Reports 1952, 89, 93.

6 On double criminality in an international context, see C Van den Wyngaert, 'Double Criminality as a Requirement to Jurisdiction' in N Jareborg (ed) *Double Criminality: Studies in International Criminal Law* (1989) 43.

7 See K Cornils, 'The use of foreign law in domestic adjudication', in N Jareborg (ed) *Double Criminality: Studies in International Criminal Law* (1989) 70.

8 On *ne bis in idem* in an international context, see H Jung, 'Zur Internationalisierung des Grundsatzes ne bis in idem' in PA Albrecht *et al.* (eds) *Festschrift für Horst Schüler-Springorum*

Section B of each country study deals with cases of universal jurisdiction or with judicial decisions in which the issue was raised. Each case report pays detailed attention to the factual and legal context of the proceedings. A context-sensitive analysis is necessary to avoid hasty conclusions and improper analogies. The goal is to offer an accurate analysis of universal jurisdiction as it is practised. Section C for each country is a brief summary.

The length and depth of the country studies vary considerably. Obviously, the broader the rules of jurisdiction, the more there is to say about a country. As a result, most elaborate are the reports on the continental European countries because they traditionally claim more extensive extraterritorial jurisdiction than common law countries. No attempt has been made to provide a complete picture of any particular country. The countries are discussed in alphabetical order but the chronology and interplay of legislative initiatives and judicial decisions in the respective countries should not be overlooked.

(1993) 493; P Baauw, 'Ne bis in idem' in B Swart and A Klip (eds) *International Criminal Law in the Netherlands* (1997) 75; G Stessens and C Van den Wyngaert, 'The International Non Bis In Idem Principle: Resolving Some of the Unanswered Questions' (1999) 48 *Int'l & Comparative LQ* 779.

4

Australia

A. AMBIT OF THE CRIMINAL LAW

Jurisdiction over crime has long been governed by the common law rule that 'all crime is local',[1] a rule now codified in the Criminal Code Act of 1995, Part 2.7 'Geographical jurisdiction'. The Constitution gives Parliament the authority to enact criminal statutes with extraterritorial application, a power that has been little used.[2] This study reviews the War Crimes Act 1945, the War Crimes Amendment Act 1988, the Geneva Conventions Act 1957, the International Criminal Court Act 2002, and the Crimes (Torture) Act 1988.

War Crimes Act 1945

The War Crimes Act 1945[3] provided for the trial and punishment of violations of the laws and usages of war committed during World War II at any place whatsoever 'against any persons who were at any time resident in Australia or against certain other persons' (Preamble). Section 12 defined the latter category as 'British subjects or citizens of any power allied or associated with His Majesty in any war'. Some thousand individuals were reportedly tried under the Act immediately after World War II.[4] In 1961 Australia closed the chapter on such trials, until...

War Crimes Amendment Act 1988

...Media reports in the 1980s suggested that among the many post-World War II immigrants from Europe were Nazi war criminals. The government appointed ACC Menzies to report on these allegations and to make recommendations. The 'Menzies Report'[5] concluded that serious war criminals

[1] For the rationales of the rule which originated in England, see the United Kingdom country study below.

[2] Section 51(xxix) of the Constitution confers plenary legislative power on Parliament with respect to 'external affairs'; see the discussion of the *Polyukhovitch* case below.

[3] Act No 48, 1945.

[4] For a discussion of the Australian WWII war crimes legislation and prosecutions see, extensively, G Triggs, 'Australia's War Crimes Trials: All Pity Choked' in TLH McCormack and GJ Simpson (eds) *The Law of War Crimes: National and International Approaches* (1997) 121 and GT Blewitt, 'National Prosecutions for International Crimes: The Australian Experience' in MC Bassiouni (ed) *International Criminal Law* (2nd edn, 1998) III, 301.

[5] A Menzies, *Review of Material Relating to the Entry of Suspected War Criminals into Australia* (1987).

from World War II had probably entered, and were probably presently residents of, Australia. In order to allow their prosecution Parliament passed the War Crimes Amendment Act 1988,[6] which almost entirely repeals and replaces the original legislation.

Section 5 of the Act defines 'war' to mean a war 'in so far as it occurred in Europe in the period beginning on 1 September 1939 and ending on 8 May 1945'. The effect of this definition is to limit the scope of the Act to Nazi war crimes, excluding Japanese war crimes committed during World War II. Section 11 provides that a person 'shall not be charged with an offence against the Act unless he or she is an Australian citizen or a resident of Australia or of an external Territory'. Insofar as the Act applies to crimes committed abroad by persons who, at the time of commission, had no relevant connection with Australia, it could be considered an assertion of universal jurisdiction. However, the Act requires a strong link at the time of prosecution: the accused must be either an Australian citizen or a permanent resident. Furthermore, Australia's belligerency in World War II creates a constructive link with any war crime committed during that conflict.

Three prosecutions have been initiated under the amended Act, each failing during the early stages.[7] Nearly half a century after World War II, this purely retrospective statute has no more practical relevance.[8]

Geneva Conventions Act 1957

As the title indicates, the Geneva Conventions Act[9] implements the 1949 Geneva Conventions. Part II, section 7, provides in part:

> (1) A person who, *in Australia or elsewhere*, commits, or aids, abets or procures the commission by another person of, a grave breach of any of the Conventions or of Protocol I is guilty of an indictable offence.
>
> (2) [...]
>
> (3) This section applies to persons *regardless of their nationality or citizenship* [emphasis added].
>
> (4) [...]
>
> (5) [...]
>
> (6) An offence against this section shall not be prosecuted in a court except by indictment in the name of the Attorney-General.
>
> (7) [...]

[6] Act No. 3, 1989, as amended by the Geneva Conventions Amendment Act 1991, Act No. 27, 1991.

[7] Triggs (n 4 above) 129–34.

[8] The special investigation unit was disbanded in 1992. More recently, in May 1998 the Prime Minister announced that there was insufficient evidence to prosecute an alleged war criminal who had been deported by both the United States and Canada.

[9] Act No 103, 1957.

Grave breaches of the Geneva Conventions and of Additional Protocol I are subject to universal jurisdiction without many conditions. It is, for instance, not required that Australia was at any time a party in the armed conflict, that extradition is impracticable, or that the alleged offender is 'present' or can be 'found' in Australia. Barring a link requirement in the law of criminal procedure a foreigner could be prosecuted after being extradited to Australia. Subsection 6 ensures that the federal government retains absolute discretion over prosecutions under the Act. All provisions relating to the punishment of breaches of the Geneva Conventions were repealed by the statute next discussed, the International Criminal Court Act 2002.

International Criminal Court Act 2002

The International Criminal Court Act 2002[10] creates the offences of genocide, crimes against humanity, war crimes, and crimes against the administration of justice of the ICC. The intention is to make the jurisdiction of the ICC 'complementary to the jurisdiction of Australia with respect to offences in this division that are also crimes within the jurisdiction of that Court'.[11] As for the geographical ambit, division 268.123 of the Act provides that section 15.4 of the Criminal Code Act 1995 applies, which reads:

> If a law of the Commonwealth provides that this section applies to a particular offence, the offence applies:
>
> (a) whether or not the conduct constituting the alleged offence occurs in Australia; and
> (b) whether or not a result of the conduct constituting the alleged offence occurs in Australia.

Division 268.123 of the International Criminal Court Act in combination with section 15.4 of the Criminal Code Act thus provides for universal jurisdiction over the core ICC crimes. The establishment of universal jurisdiction over genocide, crimes against humanity, and war crimes committed in a non-international armed conflict is not the fulfilment of any treaty obligation[12] yet conforms to the 'division of labor' envisaged by the Draft Code of Crimes against the Peace and Security of Mankind and the Joinet report. As will be seen, several other countries have taken this approach.

Under the Act the mere presence (as opposed to residence) of a foreigner is a sufficient basis for jurisdiction over offences committed abroad. There is no indication in the Act of an intent on the part of the legislature that universal jurisdiction can be exercised over a foreigner who is not present. Whether any rule of criminal procedure would stand in the way of an exercise of universal

[10] Act No. 42, 2002, assent 27 June 2002.
[11] Division 268.1 of the Act.
[12] Cf the discussion of these documents in ch 3 s C above.

jurisdiction *in absentia* could not be ascertained. As under the Geneva Conventions Act 'proceedings must not be commenced without the Attorney-General's written consent'.[13]

Crimes (Torture) Act 1988

The Crimes (Torture) Act 1988[14] implements the UN Torture Convention. During the drafting of the Convention Australia had opposed the use of *aut dedere aut judicare*.[15] The relevant sections of the Crimes (Torture) Act provide as follows.

4. This Act extends to all external Territories and has *extra-territorial operation* according to its tenor.
5. (1) Except as provided by this section, this Act is not intended to exclude or limit the operation of any other law of the Commonwealth or any law of a State or Territory.
   (2) Where any conduct by a person is both an offence against this Act and an offence against any other law referred to in subsection (1) and the person is convicted or acquitted of either of those offences, that person is not liable to be convicted of the other of those offences.
   (3) Where a person has been convicted or acquitted in a country outside Australia of an offence against the law of that country in respect of any conduct, that person is not liable to be convicted of an offence against this Act in respect of that conduct.
6. (1) Where:
   (a) at any time after the commencement of this Act, a person who:
      (i) is a public official or is acting in an official capacity; or
      (ii) is acting at the instigation, or with the consent or acquiescence, of a public official or person acting in an official capacity; does *outside Australia* an act that is an act of torture; and
   (b) that act, if done by the person at that time in a part of Australia, would constitute an offence against the law then in force in that part of Australia; the person is guilty of an offence against this Act, punishable, upon conviction, by the same penalty as would be applicable if the person were found guilty of the offence referred to in paragraph (b).
   (2) In determining for the purposes of subsection (1) whether or not an act is or was, under the law in force at a particular time in a part of Australia, an offence of a particular kind, regard shall be had to any defence under that law that can be or could have been established in a proceeding for the offence.
7. A person shall not be charged with an offence against this Act unless the person:
   (a) is an Australian citizen; or
   (b) is *present* in Australia.

[13] Division 268.127 of the Act. [14] Act No 148, 1988.

[15] JH Burgers and H Danelius, *The United Nations Convention against Torture: A Handbook on the Convention against Torture and Other Cruel, Inhuman or Degrading Treatment or Punishment* (1988) 78.

8. (1) Proceedings for an offence against this Act shall not take place except with the consent in writing of the Attorney-General [emphases added].
(2) [...]
(3) [...]

The Act makes extraterritorial torture punishable in Australia (section 6) without requiring double criminality, but a foreigner cannot be charged unless he is present (section 7); a preceding request for extradition by another State does not seem to be necessary. Section 5 protects an offender against double jeopardy after a foreign judicial decision. Section 8 assures that the federal government retains absolute control over prosecutions.

B. CASE-LAW

Polyukhovitch v *The Commonwealth*

No cases of universal jurisdiction have been reported, but in *Polyukhovitch* v *The Commonwealth*[16] the Australian government took an outspoken position on the issue. The accused was a naturalized immigrant from the Ukraine. He was the first person to be charged under the War Crimes Amendment Act 1988. The central charge was alleged involvement in a mass killing in the Ukraine between 1941 and 1943. Before his trial, which ended in acquittal, he challenged the constitutionality of the War Crimes Amendment Act 1988 before the High Court. He argued that the Act is beyond the external affairs power of the federal parliament[17] and violates the *ex post facto* prohibition of the Constitution.[18]

The government contended that both issues had to be seen in an international legal context.[19] With regard to the extraterritorial application of the Act it argued that Australia has at least an international right, if not an obligation to prosecute, and punish persons alleged to be guilty of war crimes and crimes against humanity, irrespective of the place where the crime was committed or where the alleged offender is found and irrespective of the citizenship or residence of the alleged offender or the victim.

The High Court upheld the constitutionality of the Act. The opinions of Justices Brennan and Toohey expand upon the notions of universal jurisdiction, international crimes, and the relationship between them. Both dismiss the contention that customary international law *obliges* Australia to try and

[16] *Polyukhovitch* v *The Commonwealth* (1991) 172 CLR 501. For a narrative history of the case, see D Bevan, *A Case to Answer: The story of Australia's first European war crimes prosecution* (1994).

[17] See n 2 above.

[18] In this regard see also ES Kobrick, 'The Ex Post Facto Prohibition and the Exercise of Universal Jurisdiction Over International Crimes' (1987) 87 *Columbia L Rev* 1515.

[19] Arguments adapted from the opinion of Justice Brennan para 22.

punish foreign perpetrators of war crimes and crimes against humanity. Regarding the existence of a *right* Justice Brennan opines that 'Australia's international personality would be incomplete if it were unable to exercise a jurisdiction to try and to punish offenders against the law of nations whose crimes are such that their subjection to universal jurisdiction is conducive to international peace and order'.[20] The analysis of Justice Toohey focuses on the relationship between international crimes and universality of jurisdiction.

> [T]he two questions—whether a crime exists and the scope of jurisdiction to prosecute—are inextricably linked. An international crime is constituted, precisely, where conduct is identified which offends all humanity, not only those in a particular locality; the nature of the conduct creates the need for international accountability. Where conduct, because of its magnitude, affects the moral interests of humanity and thus assumes the status of a crime in international law, the principle of universality must, almost inevitably, prevail. This is particularly true of crimes against humanity since they comprise, by definition, conduct abhorrent to all the world.[21]
>
> Therefore, while the question whether war crimes and crimes against humanity were subject to universal jurisdiction during World War II remains theoretically distinct, the question whether the crimes existed as such at that time is basic. If such conduct amounted, then, to customary international crimes, their very nature leads to the conclusion that they were the subject of universal jurisdiction.[22]

Although the proceedings against Polyukhovitch were *not* an exercise of universal jurisdiction, the Australian government expressed a strong and unequivocal *opinio juris* on the matter. It took the view, and the High Court concurred, that prosecuting and punishing war crimes and crimes against humanity, wherever and by whomever committed, is a legitimate exercise of State sovereignty, a position which is reflected in the International Criminal Court Act 2002.

C. SUMMARY

Australia adheres to the common law doctrine that all crime is local. Parliament only enacts criminal statutes with extraterritorial application when *obliged* to do so by treaty. However, in *Polyukhovitch* the government and the High Court recognized that the *right* to exercise universal jurisdiction over crimes under (customary) international law exists independently from a treaty. The International Criminal Court Act further evidences that view.

[20] Ibid para 33 (references omitted).
[21] Opinion of Justice Toohey para 34 (references omitted).
[22] Ibid para 35.

The presence in Australia of a foreign offender is a prerequisite for laying charges under the Crimes (Torture) Act. The Geneva Conventions Act and the International Criminal Court Act, on the other hand, are silent on the issue but contain no indication of an intent to enforce the law *in absentia*. Prosecution of offences under any of the Acts discussed is the prerogative of the federal executive.

5

Austria

A. AMBIT OF THE CRIMINAL LAW

The ambit of the Austrian penal code (*Strafgesetzbuch*, or StGB) is spelled out in §§62–67, which constitute so to speak the 'international criminal law'[1] of Austria. Together with their German counterparts,[2] they form one of the most comprehensive and elaborate sets of rules of criminal jurisdiction. Such explicit provisions are, as will be seen, typical for continental European penal codes and codes thereon modelled.

The basic principle is expressed in §62: 'Austrian criminal law is applicable to acts committed within the country'. It may be noted that before the adoption of the current code in 1975 the basic principle was nationality, not territoriality. So the starting point was the opposite of the common law tenet that criminal law is territorial.[3] StGB §63 extends Austria's territorial jurisdiction to offences on board Austrian aircraft and ships.

The code's extraterritorial application is defined in §§64–65. Because Austria is the first continental European country discussed in this book it is thought to be instructive, particularly for readers from a common law country, to reproduce §§64–65 in their entirety, with their headings.

Criminal offences committed abroad which shall be punished regardless of the law of the State where they were committed

§64. (1) The following offences committed abroad shall be punished according to the Austrian penal statutes, irrespective of the penal law of the State where the offence was committed:

1. industrial espionage for a foreign country (§124), high treason (§242), preparations for high treason (§244), subversive associations (§246), assaults on supreme organs

I warmly thank Dr Friedrich Hauptmann for his suggestions and critical comments.

[1] 'International criminal law' is translated in the German legal language into two different terms with different content. *Internationales Strafrecht* stands for the set of municipal, mostly codified rules determining the scope of application of a State's substantive criminal law; *Völkerstrafrecht* (literary 'criminal law of the nations') refers to substantive international criminal law.

[2] Austria and Germany worked together in the preparation of their current penal codes. One of the results is a quasi-identical ambit (*räumlicher Geltungsbereich*). Compare §§62–65 of the Austrian code and §§2–7 of the German code. For comments on the ambit of the Austrian code see V Liebscher, 'Die neue Struktur des Internationalen Strafrechtes (§§62 bis 67 StGB)' (1974) 94 *Juristische Blätter* 393; R Linke,'Grenzen der Strafgerichtsbarkeit: Zugleich Besprechung der zweiten Auflage von Oehler, Internationales Strafrecht' (1984) 39 *Österreichische Juristenzeitung* 487; K Schwaighofer, 'Kommentierung der §§62–66 StGB' in *StGB-Kommentar: System und Praxis* (1997); E Foregger and G Kodek, *Strafgesetzbuch. Kurzkommentar* (6th edn, 1997).

[3] Jurisdiction over nationals was, under the previous code, always based on the nationality principle, even when the offence was committed in Austria. The territoriality principle applied only to offences committed within the country by foreigners.

of the State (§§249–251), treason (§§252–258) and criminal offences against the federal armed forces (§§259–260);

2. criminal offences committed by any person against an Austrian civil servant (§74, paragraph 4) during or because of the performance of his duties, and criminal offences committed by a person in his capacity as Austrian civil servant;
3. false testimony at court (§288) and false testimony before an administrative authority, if in the latter case the testimony was duly sworn or corroborated by oath (§289), in proceedings pending at an Austrian court or before an Austrian administrative authority;
4. kidnapping for the purpose of extortion (§102), abandonment of a person to a foreign power (§103), slave traffic (§104), exploitative procurement (§104a), traffic in persons (§217), counterfeiting (§232), forgery of particular protected bonds as punishable under §232 (§237), criminal organizations (§278a para 1) and criminal offences under §§28 paras 2 to 5, 31 para. 2, and 32 para 2 of the Narcotics Act, if either Austrian interests were violated by the offence or if the offender is not extradited;
   4a. serious sexual abuse of minors (§206), sexual abuse of minors (§207), and pornography with minors (§207a, subsections 1 and 2), if the offender is an Austrian citizen with residence in Austria;
   4b. development and proliferation of weapons of mass destruction if the offender is an Austrian citizen, and with regard to the development of nuclear weapons only if the act is not committed pursuant to an order or under the responsibility of a nuclear weapon State party to the Treaty on the Non-Proliferation of Nuclear Weapons (§177a);
5. hijacking (§185), criminal offences against life and limb or against liberty, which were committed in connection with hijacking, and intentional imperilment of the safety of aviation (§186), if:
   a—the offence is directed against an Austrian aircraft;
   b—the aircraft lands in Austria with the offender still on board;
   c—the aircraft is leased without crew to a lessee who has his principal place of business or, in the absence of such place, his permanent residence in Austria; or if
   d—the offender is present in Austria and will not be extradited;
6. other criminal offences, if Austria is under an obligation to prosecute them—even if committed abroad—irrespective of the penal law of the State where they were committed;
7. criminal offences committed by an Austrian citizen against an Austrian citizen, if both have their domicile or permanent residence in this country;
8. complicity (§12) in an offence committed by the principal in Austria, and also receiving (§164) and money laundering (§§165, 278a paragraph 2) in connection with an offence committed in Austria.

[...]

(2) Where the penal statutes referred to in paragraph 1 are inapplicable solely on the grounds that the act constitutes an offence punishable by a severer penalty, the offence committed abroad shall nonetheless be punished according to the Austrian penal statutes, irrespective of the penal law of the State where the offence was committed.

Criminal offences committed abroad which shall be punished only if they are punishable under the law of the State where they were committed.

§65. (1) For other offences committed abroad than those referred to in §§63 and 64, Austrian penal statutes apply under the proviso that these offences are also punishable under the law of the State where they were committed:

1. if the offender was an Austrian at the time when he committed the offence, or if he acquired the Austrian citizenship later on and is still holding it when the criminal proceedings are instituted against him;
2. if the offender, though he was a foreigner at the time when he committed the offence, was found in this country and if, due to reasons different from the nature and characteristics of the offence, he is not extradited to a foreign State.

(2) The sentence shall be determined in such way that its total effects do not put the offender into a position less favourable than under the law of the State where the offence was committed.

(3) If there is no penal jurisdiction at the place where the offence was committed, it is sufficient that the offence is punishable under Austrian law.

(4) However, the offence ceases to be punishable:

1. if the punishability has lapsed according to the law of the State where the offence was committed;
2. if the offender has been acquitted or if his prosecution has otherwise been dropped by final decision of a court in the State where the offence was committed;
3. if the offender was lawfully convicted by a foreign court and he has served his sentence, or if he has not served his sentence, was pardoned or execution of the sentence has become proscribed; [ie by becoming time-barred];
4. as long as the execution of the sentence imposed by a foreign court is totally or partially suspended.

(5) Preventive measures provided for under Austrian laws may, if the respective conditions are fulfilled, be ordered against an Austrian national even if he or she can not be punished in Austria for one of the reasons specified in the preceding paragraph.[4]

As can readily be observed, the ambit of the Austrian penal code is far reaching. StGB §64(1) subparagraphs 1–5 enumerate *specific* offences over which Austria has extraterritorial jurisdiction. In contrast, §§64(1) subparagraph 6 and 65(1) subparagraphs 1–2 are *general* clauses: §65(1) subparagraph 1 provides for wholesale active personality jurisdiction; §64(1) subparagraph 6 and §65(1) subparagraph 2, for their part, provide for universal jurisdiction. The latter two are discussed in the chronological order in which they were introduced into Austrian law.

Strafgesetzbuch §65(1) subparagraph 2

StGB §65(1) subparagraph 2 provides for Austrian jurisdiction 'if the offender, though he was a foreigner at the time when he committed the offence, was

[4] Translation based on H Epp, 'Austria' (1989) 60 *Revue internationale de droit pénal* 115, 124–6; updated with the kind help of Dr Friedrich Hauptmann and Dr Claus Kreß.

found in this country and if, due to reasons different from the nature and characteristics of the offence (*aus einem anderen Grund als wegen der Art oder Eigenschaft seiner Tat*) is not extradited to a foreign State (*nicht an das Ausland ausgeliefert werden kann*)'.

This municipal *aut dedere aut judicare* clause is a manifestation of what was called in chapter 2 above the co-operative general universality principle, namely the secondary or subsidiary jurisdiction of the custodial State over all serious offences if extradition of a suspect is impracticable. As noted in that chapter, this form of the universality principle became better known after World War II as the representation principle or vicarious administration of justice, especially in the Germanic legal culture. The earliest version of what is now StGB §65(1) subparagraph 2 appeared in the penal code of 1803 under §§30 to 34[5] and was justified by reference to 'a duty on the part of the civilized world to combat international crime'.[6] The code of 1852 (*Strafgesetz*, or StG) contained provisions to the same effect under §§39 and 40.[7]

StGB §65 explicitly states that the principles of *lex mitior* and double criminality apply. Any bar to the prosecution of the offence in the territorial State is a bar to prosecution in Austria. The requirement that the foreign offender cannot be extradited 'due to reasons different from the nature and characteristics of the offence' constitutes a further limit: the offence must be extraditable *per se*. Prosecution of political, military, and fiscal offences is thus excluded, as well as that of all minor offences, because under Austrian extradition law an offence is only extraditable if it carries a prison sentence of more than one year in Austria and in the requesting State.[8] 'Reasons different from the nature and characteristics of the offence' means that extradition is not possible either because there is no request from the territorial State even though Austria has offered extradition, or because there is no co-operation at all in criminal matters between Austria and the territorial State.[9] A qualified system of mandatory prosecution applies. The prosecutor can renounce to investigate if this is not against the public interest[10] or when

[5] In fact, the Austrian code of 1803 was the very first penal code that contained the *aut dedere aut judicare* principle. See C Pappas, *Stellvertretende Strafrechtspflege* (1996) 47 and H Grützner, *Le champ d'application du droit pénal: Aperçu comparatif élaboré en vue de la préparation d'une Convention européenne portant unification des dispositions relatives au champ d'application du droit pénal* (1964) 47.

[6] Grützner, ibid.

[7] StG §§39 and 40 provided that when the territorial State refuses to undertake the prosecution of the offender, the punishment of the criminal must, as a general rule, take place in accordance with the provisions of Austrian criminal law. For the text (in English) of §§39 and 40, see Harvard Research in International Law, 'Jurisdiction with Respect to Crime' (1935) 29 *Am J Int'l L* 435, 574–5.

[8] Section 11(1) of the Statute on Extradition and Mutual Assistance in Criminal Matters.

[9] Foregger and Kodek (n 2 above) 197; Schwaighofer (n 2 above) commentary on §65(7).

[10] Section 9(3) of the Statute on Extradition and Mutual Assistance in Criminal Matters reads: 'The public prosecutor may refrain from prosecuting an offence if Austrian criminal jurisdiction is based only on §65(1) subpara 2 StGB, and public interests do not oppose the refrainment from

a thorough investigation is impossible because the territorial State does not co-operate.[11]

Strafgesetzbuch §64(1) subparagraph 6

StGB §64(1) subparagraph 6, introduced with the current code in 1975, endows Austrian courts with jurisdiction over 'criminal offences, if Austria is under an obligation to prosecute them—even if committed abroad—irrespective of the penal law of the State where they were committed'. This is a prototypical example of a general domestic 'enabling clause'. As will be seen, general enabling clauses are commonly used in continental Europe. The purpose is to avoid amending the penal code each time the country in question becomes a party to a convention that requires the establishment of extraterritorial jurisdiction over a specific offence.

The term 'obligation' in §64(1) subparagraph 6 refers to a treaty obligation.[12] The foreign offender's presence is not expressly required but Austrian commentators agree that subparagraph 6 should be read in conjunction with the *aut dedere aut judicare* clause of the relevant treaties.[13] In addition, they argue that a teleological interpretation of subparagraph 6 commands that the conditions of §64(1) subparagraphs 4 and 5, on violation of Austrian interests or non-extradition of the offender, be read into subparagraph 6.[14] StGB §64(1) subparagraph 6 represents what in chapter 2 above was called the co-operative limited universality principle. Prosecution under §64(1) subparagraph 6 is mandatory[15] and not dependent on the consent or initiative of the highest prosecutorial or executive authorities. Application of the principles of double criminality and *lex mitior* is explicitly excluded.

The question arises: what is the relationship between §64(1) subparagraph 6 and §65(1) subparagraph 2? For example, a foreigner found in Austria is suspected of torture abroad. Torture is a felony under StGB §312 and Austria is a party to the UN Torture Convention. Under which provision can the suspect be charged? Has the prosecutor an option between §64(1) subparagraph 6 (no double criminality, mandatory prosecution) and §65(1) subparagraph 2 (double criminality, *lex mitior*, qualified mandatory prosecution)? Austrian scholars consider §65 to be subsidiary to §64. A prosecution can only be based on the former if the latter is inapplicable.[16]

prosecution, in particular, when punishment is not indicated to deter the commission of offences by others'.

[11] Schwaighofer (n 2 above) commentary on §65.

[12] C Mayerhofer, 'Können Kriegverbrechen auf dem Gebiet des ehemaligen Jugoslowien von österreichischen Gerichten verfolgt werden?' (1994) 116 *Juristische Blätter* 567, 568.

[13] Epp (n 4 above) 122; Schwaighofer (n 2 above) commentary on §64; Foregger and Kodek (n 2 above) 194.

[14] Ibid.

[15] Schwaighofer (n 2 above) criticizes this rigid rule and formulates proposals *de lege ferenda*.

[16] Ibid, commentary on §65; Foregger and Kodek (n 2 above) 197.

B. CASE-LAW

This author came across two prosecutions on the basis of the municipal *aut dedere aut judicare* clause, both involving citizens from the neighbouring State of Yugoslavia.

Public Prosecutor v *Milan T*

Public Prosecutor v *Milan T*[17] appears to be the earliest internationally reported case of universal jurisdiction anywhere in the world. The accused left Yugoslavia in 1952 in order to escape prosecution for property crimes (fraud). After his arrival in Austria he committed further offences there, but before he could be arrested he fled to Germany. The German authorities handed him back to Austria, where he was duly convicted for the offences he had committed in Austria. While serving his sentence, his extradition was requested by Yugoslavia for the offences committed there. Austria refused on the ground that while in Germany the accused had established contact with a Yugoslav refugee organization opposed to the Yugoslav government, and was therefore in danger of political persecution in Yugoslavia. Instead, Austria instituted its own criminal proceedings for the offences committed in Yugoslavia. The accused contended that StG §40 provides for jurisdiction only when the territorial State is unwilling to prosecute. On appeal, the Supreme Court rejected the argument:

> [T]he principle of universal criminal jurisdiction (*Weltstrafrechtsprinzip*) is based on the concept that the fight against crime is a common task of all civilized States. In accordance with this principle of universal criminal jurisdiction, StG §40 provides that where the home State of a criminal offender, or the State in the territory of which a criminal offence has been committed, refuses to undertake the prosecution of the offender, the punishment of the criminal must, as a general rule, take place in accordance with the provisions of Austrian criminal law. The introductory words of StG §40, however, were not intended to convey that criminal proceedings against foreign nationals who have committed a criminal offence in a foreign country may be taken in accordance with Austrian criminal law only where the home State of the offender or the State in the territory of which the criminal offence has been committed has refused to exercise extradition, but were also intended to cover the case where a criminal prosecution by either of those States is not possible. The provision contained in the first sentence of StG §40 is preponderantly of a procedural character and concerns jurisdictional competence, but its purpose is not to provide for freedom from prosecution of common crimes (*gemeinen Verbrechen*) which are punishable in accordance with Austrian law.
>
> [. . .]

[17] Oberste Gerichtshof, 29 May 1958, reprinted in Oberste Gerichtshof, Serie Strafsachen, XXIX, No 32; edited version (in English) published in (1963) 28 *Int'l LR* 341.

In the case before the Court the extradition of Milan T, having regard to the facts which are charged against him, would have been permissible as the facts charged constitute common crimes. The refusal of the request for extradition, however, was based on grounds—as is evident from the reasons given by the lower Court—which, although not connected with the nature of the offence, had nevertheless to be taken into account in view of the analogous application of the provisions of article 33(I) of the Convention of the Status of Refugees (1951). It is a requirement of the proper administration of justice of a State which, the greater its generosity in granting asylum to political refugees (and not only politically persecuted persons), the less must be its inclination to waive its subsidiary right to institute criminal proceedings in respect of common crimes committed by such refugees in the territory of a foreign State. This subsidiary right to institute criminal proceedings must be exercised in particular where the extradition of an offender might violate the internationally recognized rights of refugees.[18]

In *Public Prosecutor* v *Milan T* the forum State prosecuted a foreigner for a common offence committed abroad after declining an extradition request on human rights grounds.[19] The Supreme Court convincingly stated that the greater a country's generosity in granting asylum, the less must be its inclination to waive its subsidiary right to institute proceedings for crimes committed abroad by persons whom it admits to its territory and affords protection. The Court's reference to StG §40 as universal jurisdiction (instead of representation jurisdiction) illustrates how even in the Germanic legal culture the two concepts are not clearly distinguished.[20]

Public Prosecutor v *Cvjetkovic*

The second reported case of universal jurisdiction is *Public Prosecutor* v *Cvjetkovic*.[21] The war and ethnic violence in the former Yugoslavia in the first half of the 1990s caused an influx into Austria of tens of thousands of refugees, including Cvjetkovic. When Austrian authorities received information from other refugees and from Interpol Sarajevo that he was listed as a war criminal they launched an investigation. Austria notified the Bosnian authorities of the arrest of the suspect. The latter did not react due to the ongoing war. The International Criminal Tribunal for the former Yugoslavia did not take over the proceedings.[22]

[18] Translation based on (1963) 28 *Int'l LR* 341.

[19] Cf the discussion on jurisdiction, extradition, and human rights in ch1 s D above.

[20] See also Liebscher (n 2 above) 394.

[21] Landesgericht Salzburg, 31 May 1995 (trial judgment); Oberste Gerichtshof, 13 July 1994 (appeals judgment) (copies on file with author). The case is briefly discussed in A Marschik 'The Politics of Prosecution: European National Approaches to War Crimes' in TLH McCormack and GJ Simpson (eds) *The Law of War Crimes: National and International Approaches* (1997) 65, 77–82.

[22] This summary of the factual background is adapted from the indictment (copy on file with author). The ICTY was at the time of the arrest of Cvjetkovic in its start-up phase.

According to the indictment, the accused, as commander of a Serbian military unit, was responsible for the 'ethnic cleansing' of the Muslim part of the village of Kucice in April 1992. He was charged with genocide[23] (killing a member of the Muslim group and deliberately inflicting on the Muslim group conditions of life likely to bring about its physical destruction in whole or in part), complicity in genocide (killing a member of the Muslim group), murder and complicity in murder (for the same killings), and complicity in arson. A jury acquitted him of all charges.[24] This appears to have been the first ever trial for genocide anywhere in the world.

On a motion for interlocutory appeal on jurisdiction, the Supreme Court held that Austria is competent under domestic and international law.[25] StGB §65(1) paragraph 2 provides a *domestic* legal basis because there is double criminality[26] and the suspect is not extradited. The decision notes in this respect that genocide is not a political offence for the purpose of extradition under article III of the Genocide Convention and that co-operation in criminal matters with Bosnia and Herzegovina is impossible due to the ongoing war. A teleological interpretation of the Genocide Convention justifies Austria's *international* capacity:

> Article VI of the Genocide Convention, which provides that persons charged with genocide or any of the acts enumerated in Article III shall be tried by a competent tribunal of the State where the act was committed, or by such international penal tribunal as may have jurisdiction with respect to those Contracting Parties which shall have accepted its jurisdiction, is based on the fundamental assumption that there is a functioning criminal justice system in the *locus delicti* (which would make the extradition of a suspect legally possible). Otherwise—since at the time of the adoption of the Genocide Convention there was no international criminal court—the outcome would be diametrically opposed to the intention of its drafters and a person suspected of genocide or any of the acts enumerated in Article III could not be prosecuted because the criminal justice in the *locus delicti* is not functioning and the international criminal court is not in place (or its jurisdiction has not been accepted by the State concerned).[27]

Public Prosecutor v *Cvjetkovic* was the first trial by a municipal court exercising universal jurisdiction with respect to the ethnic violence in the Balkan in the first half of the 1990s. It can be asked why Austria did not prosecute the accused, a military commander, on the basis of StGB §64(1) subparagraph 6 in conjunction with the 1949 Geneva Conventions. This would have been preferable from a prosecutorial point of view since grave breaches are easier to

[23] Genocide (*Völkermord*) is a criminal offence under StGB §321.

[24] Landesgericht Salzburg (n 21 above). [25] Appeals judgment (n 21 above) 7.

[26] The Yugoslav penal code of 1951, which is applicable in Bosnia and Herzegovina, sanctions genocide (article 124), intentional homicide (article 135), and arson (article 268).

[27] Appeals decision (n 21 above) 7.

establish than genocide.[28] The answer is the principle of mandatory prosecution (*Legalitätsprinzip*), which does not allow a prosecutor to choose a lesser charge if he believes there is sufficient evidence to secure a conviction for a more serious offence.[29] Some Austrian scholars also take the view that the enabling clause, which was enacted in 1975, cannot retroactively apply to treaties that became binding on Austria before 1975, such as the 1949 Geneva Conventions and the Genocide Convention.[30] The Supreme Court's decision is noteworthy in that it finds universal jurisdiction compatible, not with the text, but with the purpose of the Genocide Convention. As will be seen, courts in Germany, Israel, and Spain have adopted a similar view.

C. SUMMARY

The ambit of Austrian criminal law is broad. A municipal *aut dedere aut judicare* clause, the very first of its kind, provides for universal jurisdiction over all extraditable offences if the foreign defendant cannot be extradited. A general enabling clause also establishes jurisdiction over treaty offences. Despite broad provisions, only two cases of universal jurisdiction have been reported. The defendants in both cases were refugees from a neighbouring country seeking protection by Austria. Prosecution by the forum State was a last resort when extradition was impossible because of an insurmountable legal or factual obstacle. The forum State acted in a spirit of international solidarity and collaboration, with due respect for the interests of other States and of the defendants (application of the principles of double criminality and *lex mitior*). *Milan T* and *Cvjetkovic* may therefore be considered textbook illustrations of, respectively, the co-operative general and the co-operative limited universality principle.

[28] Genocide requires proof of an 'intent to destroy, in whole or in part, a national, ethnical, racial or religious group, as such' (cf article II of the Genocide Convention).

[29] I thank Dr Friedrich Hauptmann for pointing this out.

[30] The question whether StGB §64(1) subpara 6 in conjunction with the Genocide Convention provides a basis for universal jurisdiction over genocide was not brought before the Court. In this respect Mayerhofer (n 12 above) 567, 568 argues that StGB §64(1) subpara 6 does not apply because the Genocide Convention does not *oblige* States parties to try or to extradite a suspect.

6

Belgium

A. AMBIT OF THE CRIMINAL LAW

Belgian jurisdictional rules are scattered throughout the penal code (*Code pénal*, or CP), the code of penal procedure (*Code de procédure pénale*, or CPP), and special statutes.[1] The basic principles are expressed in CP articles 3 and 4. The former provides that the offence committed on Belgian territory by Belgians or foreigners will be punished according to Belgian law. The latter, for its part, states that extraterritorial offences by Belgians or foreigners cannot be punished in Belgium unless provided for by statute.

Most exceptions to the territoriality rule can be found in the preliminary title of the code of penal procedure (*Titre préliminaire du Code de procédure pénale*, or CPP TP) under chapter II, entitled: 'Prosecution of felonies and misdemeanours committed outside the Kingdom' (*De l'exercice de l'action publique à raison des crimes ou des délits commis hors du territoire du royaume*). The protective principle is embodied in article 6(1) and (2) (in respect of Belgian offenders) and article 10(1) and (2) (in respect of foreign offenders). Article 7(1) is a general active personality clause.[2] General passive personality jurisdiction is provided for in article 10(5).[3] General active and general passive personality jurisdiction cannot be exercised unless there is double criminality. Moreover, prosecution is subject to a number of procedural and other conditions which do not apply to offences committed on Belgian

An earlier version of this country study appeared as 'Universal Criminal Jurisdiction: The Belgian State of Affairs' in (2000) 11 *Crim L Forum* 183–216. The permission of Kluwer Academic Publishers to republish is acknowledged.

[1] The following chronology of commentaries gives an idea of the expansion of the ambit of Belgian criminal law: PE Trousse, 'La compétence extraterritoriale des jurisdictions répressives belges', in *Rapports belges au VIIe Congrès international de droit comparé* (1966) 511–38; Van den Wyngaert, 'De toepassing van de strafwet in de ruimte: Enkele beschouwingen', in *Liber Amicorum Frédéric Dumon* (1983) 501; F Thomas, 'De internationale gelding van de strafwet in de ruimte', in A De Nauw *et al.* (eds) *Actuele problemen van strafrecht* (1988) 195–214; HD Bosly and D Vandermeersch, *Droit de procédure pénale* (1999) 53–67; T Vander Beken, *Forumkeuze in het internationaal strafrecht: Verdeling van misdrijven met aanknopingspunten in meerdere staten* (1999) 54–6, 92–3, 112–15, 134–8, 158–64, 215–16.

[2] CPP TP article 7(1), introduced in 1964, reads: 'Any Belgian who commits outside the territory of the Kingdom an act that is a felony (*crime*) or misdemeanour (*délit*) under Belgian law may be prosecuted in Belgium if the act is also punishable under the law of the country where the offence is committed'.

[3] CPP TP article 10(5), introduced in 1984, states: 'A foreigner who has committed outside the territory of the Kingdom a felony (*crime*) against a Belgian citizen may be prosecuted in Belgium if the conduct is punishable by imprisonment of more than five years under the law of the country where it occurred'.

territory, such as a formal complaint by the foreign authorities or by the foreign victim or his relatives.[4]

The universality principle can be found in CPP TP articles 10.3, 10ter, 10quater, and 12bis, and in the Act Concerning the Punishment of Grave Breaches of International Humanitarian Law. Except for CPP TP article 10.3 they are all the result of recent legislative initiatives.

Code de procédure pénale, titre préliminaire, article 10.3

CPP TP article 10.3 makes punishable the offence of counterfeiting foreign currency by foreigners abroad but prosecution is subject to official denunciation (*avis officiel*) by the authorities of the country whose currency is counterfeited. The provision was introduced in 1932 to implement the International Convention for the Suppression of Counterfeiting Currency.[5]

Code de procédure pénale, titre préliminaire, article 10ter

The 1995 Act for the Suppression of Trade in Humans and of Child Pornography[6] introduced CPP TP article 10ter, which provides:

> Belgian citizens, or foreigners found in Belgium, may be prosecuted in Belgium, even without official denunciation by foreign authorities, if they have committed outside the Kingdom any of the offences defined in articles 372, 373, 375, 376 and 377 [indecent assault and rape] of the penal code if the victim is younger than 16 years of age, [any of the offences defined] in articles 379 [depravity of youth], 380bis [trade in humans], 381bis and 383bis, §§1 and 3 [child pornography] of the penal code, [any of the offences defined] in article 77bis, §§2 and 3 [immigrant smuggling] of the law of 15 December 1980 regarding the entry into the Kingdom, the stay, the residence, and the expulsion of foreigners, and [any of the offences defined] in articles 10, 11, 12 and 13 of the law of 9 March 1993 regarding the regulation and control of the activities of matrimonial agencies.

The Act for the Suppression of Trade in Humans and of Child Pornography does not create any new offences under Belgian law. Its only purpose is to allow the prosecution in Belgium of Belgians[7] and foreigners who commit abroad any of the enumerated crimes, irrespective of the nationality of the

[4] For an overview of the procedural conditions governing the prosecution of extraterritorial offences, see 'De l'exercise de l'action publique à raison des crimes ou des délits commis hors du territoire du Royaume' in *Les Novelles: Corpus Juris Belgici, Procédure Pénale vol. I* (1946) 213; Van den Wyngaert (n 1 above) 508.

[5] For a discussion of this convention see ch 3 s A above.

[6] Loi contenant des dispositions en vue de la répression de la traite des êtres humains et de pornographie enfantine, Moniteur Belge 25 April 1995. For an analysis and comment, see O Vandemeulebroeke and F Gazan, 'Traite des êtres humains: exploitation et abus sexuels. Les nouvelles lois des 27 mars et 13 avril 1995' (1995) 75 *Revue de Droit Pénal et de Criminologie* 973.

[7] As regards the prosecution of Belgian citizens under the law, article 10ter overlaps to some degree with the general active personality clause in article 7(1).

victim. The offences subject to universal jurisdiction under this law are of a diverse nature. While some are the subject of international conventions, such as trade in humans[8] and (child) pornography,[9] others, like indecent assault and rape of minors, are not. However, even in the former case, the jurisdiction clauses in the relevant conventions only mention the territorial State and the State of the nationality of the offender. In other words, universal jurisdiction over all the offences enumerated in article 10ter finds no basis in conventional international law.

It should be observed, however, that the unilateral establishment of some form of extraterritorial jurisdiction over 'child sex tourism' is a recent phenomenon in the 'consumer countries' of the Western world.[10] But unlike, for example, the United States legislation,[11] which applies to nationals and resident aliens who travel abroad with intent to engage in a sexual act with a juvenile, thus literally sex *tourists*, the Belgian Act, although also drafted with the sex tourist in mind, applies to *any* child sexual abuse, wherever and by whomever committed, whether it is an act of sex tourism or not. The only textual condition of article 10ter is that the foreign offender be found in Belgium, but some commentators argue on the basis of the parliamentary records that double criminality is also required.[12]

The timing of the law presents a bitter irony. A year after its adoption in 1995 Belgium was rocked by the *Dutroux* affair, a case of confinement, prolonged sexual abuse, and murder of several children who had been kidnapped some years before. The parliamentary commission of inquiry into the justice department's handling of the investigation revealed serious individual failures, incompetence, and structural problems.[13] Unfortunately, the actual prosecution of the case, which has no international or extraterritorial elements, is not faring much better. At the time of writing none of the suspects had been tried (although some have been in custody since 1996).

[8] Trade in humans, especially in women and children, is the subject of several international conventions. For a list of these treaties and their penal and jurisdictional provisions, see MC Bassiouni, *International Criminal Law Conventions and their Penal Provisions* (1997) 683.

[9] International traffic in obscene materials is also the subject of several international conventions. For a list of these treaties and their penal and jurisdictional provisions, see Bassiouni (ibid) 1145–68.

[10] On the prosecution of child sex tourism in Germany, see G Bertram, 'Sextourismus und Strafverfolgung' (1996) 49 *Neue Juristische Wochenschrift* 436. Even common law countries like Australia, Canada, Ireland, New Zealand, the United Kingdom, and the United States have enacted, or are considering enacting, legislation to tackle the problem of sex tourism by their nationals or residents. Note that article 4 of the Optional Protocol to the Convention on the Rights of the Child (New York, 25 May 2000) now provides broad permissive extraterritorial jurisdiction for States parties.

[11] Child Sexual Abuse Prevention Act, Pub L No 103-322 (1994), codified as 18 USC §2423.

[12] Vandemeulebroeke and Gazan (n 6 above) 1064–6 also argue that the double criminality requirement of article 7(1) also applies to extraterritorial offences by Belgians under article 10ter.

[13] Report of the Dutroux Commission (April 1997) chapter 3.

Code de procédure pénale, titre préliminaire, article 10quater

The 1999 Act Concerning the Repression of Corruption[14] introduced article 10quater into the Preliminary title CPP. Article 10quater endows Belgian courts with extraterritorial jurisdiction over corruption by whomever of an official of a foreign State or an international governmental organization if the offender is found in Belgium and if the Belgian authorities have received an official complaint (*avis officiel*) from the competent authorities of the State or organization in question. If the corruption involves an official of the European Union a complaint is not required.

Code de procédure pénale, titre préliminaire, article 12bis

CPP TP article 12bis, introduced in 2001,[15] is a general domestic enabling clause. It reads: 'The Belgian courts are competent to take cognizance of offences committed outside the territory of the Kingdom that are the object of an international convention binding on Belgium (*visées par une convention internationale liant la Belgique*) if the convention obliges in any way (*de quelque manière que ce soit*) to submit the case to the competent authorities for the purpose of prosecution'.

Prior to its enactment, the legislature, when implementing international criminal law conventions, followed three lines of approach:[16] the adoption of a special statute (not incorporated in a code), the amendment of the domestic rules on extraterritorial jurisdiction, or no action at all. In the second case, the adaptation of domestic criminal law was achieved by one of two courses: the amendment of Chapter II of the Preliminary title CPP, or the adoption of a jurisdiction clause in the act of parliament approving the international convention and authorizing ratification by the government. In the third case, the judicial authorities drew their competence from the convention itself if it was self-executing. The adoption of a blanket enabling clause finally brings uniformity and clarity.

Code de procédure pénale, titre préliminaire, articles 12–14

CPP TP articles 12–14 contain the general rules governing the admissibility of criminal proceedings regarding crimes and misdemeanours committed abroad. Article 12 provides that prosecution in Belgium can only take place if the suspect is found in Belgium (*si l'inculpé est trouvé en Belgique*).[17]

[14] Loi du 10 février 1999 relative à la répression de la corruption, Moniteur Belge 23 March 1999.

[15] Loi du 18 juillet 2001 portant modification de l'article 12bis de la loi du 17 avril 1878 contenant le Titre préliminaire du Code de procédure pénale, Moniteur Belge 1 September 2001.

[16] On this point I take Van den Wyngaert's analysis a step further: C Van den Wyngaert, 'Belgium' (1989) 60 *Revue internationale de droit pénal* 153, 157.

[17] An exception is made for protective jurisdiction and for crimes committed abroad by persons subject to Belgian military law. On the interpretation of the expression 'found in Belgium' in Belgian penal statutes, see *Les Novelles* (n 4 above) 219–21.

Proceedings *in absentia* or after the suspect's presence has been secured through extradition are excluded.[18] Article 13 bars prosecution after foreign *res judicata*, including a foreign pardon or amnesty.[19] Finally, article 14 states that in all cases arising under Chapter II CPP TP, the suspect will be prosecuted and sentenced according to Belgian law.

Loi relative à la répression des violations graves du droit international humanitaire

In 1993 the Belgian legislature adopted the Act to implement the Geneva Conventions and Additional Protocols (hereinafter 'War Crimes Act').[20] This statute lists twenty acts that constitute grave breaches of the Conventions and Protocols and declares them crimes under international law (*crimes de droit international*). The original Act was substantially amended in 1999. Its new title is Act Concerning the Punishment of Grave Breaches of International Humanitarian Law (*Loi relative à la répression des violations graves du droit international humanitaire*).[21] Genocide and crimes against humanity, whether committed in time of peace or in time of war, are added to the list of crimes under international law.

Article 7 contains a jurisdiction clause, which reads, in part, as follows: 'Belgian courts[22] are competent to take cognizance of offences stipulated in the present law irrespective of the place where they have been committed (*Les juridictions belges sont compétentes pour connaître des infractions prévues à la présente loi, indépendamment du lieu où celles-ci auront été commises*)'.

Article 9(3) recognizes the right of any person who claims to be the victim (*toute personne qui se prétendra lésée*) of any of the enumerated offences to initiate a criminal investigation.[23] The situation is thus the exact opposite of

[18] Bosly and Vandermeersch (n 1 above) 65.

[19] On *ne bis in idem* in Belgian law, see Vander Beken (n 1 above) 256–60.

[20] Loi du 16 juin 1993 relative à la répression des infractions graves aux Conventions internationales de Genève du 12 août 1949 et aux Protocols I et II du 8 juin 1977, Additionnels à ces Conventions, Moniteur Belge 5 August 1993. For a detailed commentary, see A Andries, C Van den Wyngaert, E David, and J Verhaegen, 'Commentaire de la loi du 16 juin 1993 relative à la répression des infractions graves au droit international humanitaire' (1994) 74 *Revue de Droit Pénal et de Criminologie* 1114.

[21] Moniteur Belge 23 March 1999. An English translation is published in (1999) 38 *Int'l L Materials* 918 with introductory note by S Smis and K Van der Borght. For a commentary, see P d'Argent, 'La loi du 10 février 1999 relative à la répression des violations graves du droit international humanitaire' (1999) 118 *Journal des Tribunaux* 549. H Panken and J Wouters (eds) *De Genocidewet in Internationaal Perspectief* (2002). For the drafting history, see Documents du Sénat 1-749—1997/1998 and 1-749—1998/1999.

[22] Ordinarily the civilian courts are competent, but when Belgium is in a state of war military courts have jurisdiction (article 9(1)).

[23] This provision implements a recommendation of the XIVth Congress of the International Association of Penal Law that victims of international offences be given the right to initiate criminal proceedings. The resolution is reprinted in (1990) 61 *Revue internationale de droit pénal* 131.

that in some other countries here examined,[24] where in cases of alleged violations of international humanitarian law only the highest (federal) prosecutorial authorities are competent.

Article 5(3) provides that the Act shall apply equally to all persons without any distinction based on official capacity. Strangely enough, this would only apply to foreign heads of State and ministers; under the Belgian Constitution the King enjoys absolute immunity (article 88) and ministers cannot be prosecuted for opinions expressed in the exercise of their functions (article 101).[25]

Ratione temporis, it was the drafters' intent that the Act should also apply to acts of genocide and crimes against humanity committed *before* its adoption 'because crimes against humanity and genocide were already crimes under customary and conventional international law. Any other interpretation would be contrary to the *ratio legis* of the present bill.'[26] However, some commentators argue convincingly that absent an explicit derogation in the Act the general prohibition on retroactive action of criminal statutes, as provided for in article 2 of the penal code, applies.[27]

From a subject-matter point of view the Act has several original features. The domestic criminalization of crimes against humanity, let alone the establishment of universal jurisdiction over such crimes, is not the fulfilment of a treaty obligation.[28] The domestic criminalization of genocide, on the other hand, is the tardy implementation of an international treaty-based duty.[29] As for war crimes, the Act applies also to armed conflicts not of an international character, whereas the treaty obligation is limited to international armed conflicts.[30] By including Additional Protocol II, which applies to non-international armed conflicts, in the original title and the body of the law, the legislature decided to criminalize acts which are not 'grave breaches' but are merely 'prohibited' under the 1949 Geneva Conventions and Protocols. The extension to non-international armed conflicts is significant in view of the fact that the Act provides for universal jurisdiction without a basis in conventional international law.

[24] Namely Australia, Canada, and Germany.

[25] Cf d'Argent (note 21 above) 552.

[26] Justice Committee of the Senate, Doc. parl., Senate, S.O. 1-749/3, 18–19.

[27] L De Smet and F Naert, 'De wet betreffende de bestraffing van ernstige schendingen van het internationaal humanitair recht: een internationaal rechtelijk perspectief' (2001) Katholieke Universiteit Leuven Instituut voor Internationaal Recht, Working Paper #13, 15. The retrospective operation of the Act can be compared with the Israeli Nazi and Nazi Collaborators (Punishment) Law, with the Australian War Crimes Amendment Act 1988, with the British War Crimes Act 1991, with the French laws governing co-operation with the International Tribunals for the former Yugoslavia and for Rwanda, and with the Canadian Crimes Against Humanity and War Crimes Act. See the respective country studies in this book. More generally, see ES Kobrick, 'The Ex Post Facto Prohibition and the Exercise of Universal Jurisdiction Over International Crimes' (1987) 87 *Columbia L Rev* 1515.

[28] There is no specialized international convention on crimes against humanity.

[29] Article V of the Genocide Convention obliges States parties to enact the necessary legislation to provide for effective penalties for persons guilty of genocide. The Convention became binding upon Belgium in 1952.

[30] Cf the discussion in ch 3 s A above.

Before turning to case-law it is necessary to consider briefly the role crime victims can play in criminal proceedings[31] and Belgian extradition law. While victims are not entitled to bring prosecutions before the courts in Belgium—this is the exclusive right of the public prosecutor—they may initiate a criminal investigation. If the public prosecutor, in the exercise of his discretion, decides not to prosecute, or is still considering his position, the victim may, by making himself a civil party (*constitution de partie civile*), seize an examining magistrate (*juge d'instruction*). This is fundamentally different from the victim's mere complaint, which is little more than a denunciation of the crime: a complaint does not have any procedural consequences, it does not seize a court of law, and the public prosecutor is free not to proceed with the case. An examining magistrate thus seized is bound to start a criminal investigation if he establishes jurisdiction. Not even the Minister of Justice can prevent or end an investigation initiated by a civil party. A court will ultimately determine whether the results of the investigation warrant a trial. The criminal trial court is also competent to adjudicate the civil claim.

The mechanism of *constitution de partie civile* thus allows the victim to circumvent the principle of prosecutorial discretion, which is important precisely in cases of extraterritorial crimes[32] where the public prosecutor might hesitate to follow up on a complaint for reasons of political expediency. However, an investigation into (international) crimes committed abroad requires extraordinary resources, eg investigators, translators, and a budget for rogatory missions. What and how many resources will be made available to the investigating magistrate is very much a discretionary decision by the public prosecutor. Consequently, without his significant support, the examining magistrate's investigation will be futile.

Only the actual victim or a relative of the victim, not persons indirectly damaged by the offence, may constitute themselves civil parties.[33] The latter is required to deposit at the time of his *constitution de partie civile* the anticipated cost of the proceedings. If the case is subsequently dismissed or if the trial results in an acquittal the civil party must bear all costs.

As for extradition, the Belgian Extradition Act of 15 March 1874 provides that a person can only be extradited if there is an extradition treaty with the requesting state (article 1, §1), that extradition shall be refused if the requesting State

[31] For an account in English of the law of criminal procedure in Belgium, see C Van den Wyngaert, 'Belgium' in C Van den Wyngaert (ed) *Criminal Procedure Systems in the European Community* (1993) 1.

[32] On the legal position in Belgian law of victims of offences with an international element, see G Vermeulen, T Vander Beken, P Zanders, and B De Ruyver, *Internationale samenwerking in strafzaken en rechtsbescherming: Pleidooi voor een geïntegreerde nationale en internationale benadering* (1995) chapter 11. On the adjudication in Belgium of the civil claim arising from an extraterritorial offence, see F Thomas, 'De burgerlijke vordering wegens misdrijven met een buitenlands element' (1982) 19 *Tijdschrift voor Privaatrecht* 13.

[33] But see the discussion above of article 9(3) of the War Crimes Act.

does not give formal assurances that the death penalty, if imposed, will not be carried out (article 1, §2, al. 3) and that extradition shall be refused if there is reason to believe that extradition is sought to prosecute a person because of his race, religion, nationality, or political opinions (article 2bis). The human rights obstacles to extradition follow from Belgium's obligations under human rights treaties.[34]

B. CASE-LAW

The issue of universal jurisdiction over serious violations of international humanitarian law has developed into a veritable juridical soap opera which was still going on at the time of writing. There follows a review of the current state of affairs.

Public Prosecutor v *Higaniro* et al.

The first case, *Public Prosecutor* v *Higaniro* et al.[35] arose out of the genocide of the Tutsi and the massacres of moderate Hutu in Rwanda during the armed conflict between government forces and the rebel army of the Rwandan Patriotic Front from April to July 1994.[36] There are several links between Belgium and the events in Rwanda. First, during the early days of the massacres, certain public media in Rwanda launched an anti-Belgian campaign. Ten Belgian members of the United Nations peace-keeping force, three Belgian aid development workers, and a dozen Belgian civilians were murdered *because* of their nationality.[37] Second, one of the individuals behind the radio station which incited the genocide and the killing of Belgians is himself a Belgian citizen.[38] Third, during the height of the genocidal campaign, Belgian forces conducted a humanitarian operation to evacuate nationals and the Belgian government decided to withdraw unilaterally from the United Nations peace-keeping force. Fourth, one way or another, survivors as well as instigators of the violence found refuge in Belgium.[39] Fifth, as the former colonial ruler, Belgium maintained many and important (semi-)official contacts with Rwanda. Extradition of a suspect to Rwanda was *a priori* excluded absent

[34] See the discussion on jurisdiction, extradition, and human rights in ch 1 s D above.

[35] There were 4 defendants: Alphonse Higaniro, Vincent Ntezimana, Consolata Mukangango, and Julienne Mukabutera. Assize Court of Brussels 8 June 2001 (copy on file with author). For a comment on the actual trial see L Reydams, 'Belgium's First Judicial Application of Universal Jurisdiction: the *Butare Four* Case' (2003) 1 *J Int'l Crim Justice* (forthcoming in issue 2).

[36] See the discussion of UN Security Council Resolution 978 (1994) in ch 3 s B above.

[37] Human Rights Watch and International Federation of Human Rights Leagues, *Leave None to Tell the Story: Genocide in Rwanda* (1999) 187–92.

[38] The case of *Georges Ruggiu*, in which Belgium later deferred to the ICTR (see n 48 below).

[39] Between April 1994 and the end of 1997, 1,730 Rwandans applied for political asylum in Belgium, of whom 979 were granted refugee status (source: Commissariat-Général pour les réfugiés et apatrides, 1997).

an extradition treaty between the two countries. Because of the numerous links the Rwandan tragedy constituted an important test case for the extraterritorial application of the War Crimes Act.

Private parties took a series of initiatives and used all possible avenues to set the Belgian criminal justice process in motion. As early as July 1994, just weeks after the facts, relatives of Rwandan and Belgian victims of the massacres filed complaints with the office of the public prosecutor in several jurisdictions. They asked for the application of the 1993 War Crimes Act against a number of Rwandans, some of whom were residing at known addresses in Belgium. Family members of the ten murdered peace-keepers filed a criminal complaint with an examining magistrate against unidentified individuals. At the end of 1995, Rwandan, Zairian, as well as Belgian injured parties filed a complaint with the president of the Lower House of Parliament against the Belgian ministers of defence and foreign affairs at the time of the conflict.[40] Finally, under relentless pressure from the relatives of the murdered peace-keepers, in 1997 the Belgian Senate established the Parliamentary Commission of Inquiry into the Events in Rwanda.[41] Although these initiatives are distinct and technically very different, they are interrelated in a catalytic process.

The office of the prosecutor in Brussels gave an assurance that the alleged offences would be investigated like any serious offence committed within the territory. Logically, this implies the immediate appointment of an examining magistrate. However, the judicial authorities were hesitant to act on these first complaints based on the War Crimes Act. Such an attitude had been accurately predicted by commentators.[42] Meanwhile, the evidence that genocide had been committed started mounting.[43] In November 1994 the International Criminal Tribunal for Rwanda was established and a new series of complaints followed. In February 1995 the United Nations Security Council adopted Resolution 978.[44] Finally, in March 1995 the Minister of Justice exceptionally made use of his right to set in motion criminal proceedings (*droit d'injonction positive*) by enjoining the head of the office of the prosecutor in Brussels, who in turn appointed an examining magistrate for all the Rwandan cases.[45]

[40] The basis was article 4 *in fine* of the 1993 War Crimes Act stating that a person who knows of a plan to commit any of the offences under the Act and who has the means to prevent or stop their execution but who fails to do so is criminally responsible.

[41] A parliamentary commission of inquiry has all the investigative powers of an examining magistrate and is required to inform the highest prosecutorial authorities if in the course of an investigation it finds reasonable grounds to believe that criminal offences have been committed. The Rwanda Commission's voluminous final report was made public in December 1997.

[42] Andries *et al.* (n 20 above) 1122: 'There may be questions of interpretation of the Act. The judicial authorities will use such technical snags as excuses but in reality their abstentionist attitude is determined by psychological barriers to act independently from politico-military considerations of the Nation or from the *raison d'État*'.

[43] Reports from the UN Commission of Experts and from the Special Rapporteur for Rwanda of the UN Commission of Human Rights.

[44] See ch 3 s B above.

[45] The military authorities, for their part, instituted court-martial proceedings against a senior Belgian field commander on charges of lack of caution or precaution in relation to the death

Between May and December 1995 the magistrate and five investigators worked full time on the Rwandan cases. Their sweeping investigation focused on, but was not limited to, incidents and suspects with a link to Belgium.[46] Rwanda and several other countries lent their support by allowing rogatory commissions on their territory.[47] At the request of the ICTR Belgium deferred its proceedings against a number of suspects[48] and arrested several others.[49] After much procrastination Belgian authorities decided to join the remaining cases for the purpose of trial.[50] The Brussels assize court found the four defendants guilty of violations of the 1949 Geneva Conventions (common article 3) and Additional Protocol II (article 4(2)(a));[51] the sentences ranged from twelve to twenty years' imprisonment.[52]

Belgium's first war crimes prosecution on the basis of universal jurisdiction ended with an expeditious trial and a clear conviction. However, the fact remains that after a swift and sweeping investigation by an examining magistrate it took the prosecutorial authorities as much as five years to commit the suspects for trial. Such a delay is hardly reconcilable with the right to be tried within a reasonable time. Then again, the delays at the ICTR are even longer. The trial there of the 'Butare Six', which includes two suspects transferred from Belgium to the ICTR in 1996,[53] opened shortly *after* the Brussels trial (and was still going on in early 2003).

The defendants did not challenge Belgium's jurisdiction under international law. The mandatory 'try or extradite' regime of the 1949 Geneva Conventions does not apply to violations of common article 3 and Additional Protocol II.[54] Belgium was therefore under no *obligation* to prosecute the suspects.

of the Belgian peace-keepers. The accused was acquitted of all charges: Military court Brussels, 4 July 1996, summarized in English in (1998) 1 *Ybk Int'l Humanitarian L* 413 (case note by M Coggen).

[46] In total, 10 files (*dossiers*) were opened, involving 21 individuals; see 2 publications by the magistrate who led the investigations: D Vandermeersch, 'La répression en droit belge des crimes de droit international' (1997) 68 *Revue Internationale de droit pénal* 1093, 1121–33 and D Vandermeersch, 'Les poursuites et le jugement des infractions de droit humanitaire en droit belge' in *Actualité du droit international humanitaire* (Brussels, 2001) 123, 127–8.

[47] Belgian rogatory commissions went to Rwanda, Ghana, Togo, Tanzania, and France.

[48] Belgium deferred its proceedings against Ferdinand Nahimana (ICTR-96-11), Georges Ruggiu (ICTR-97-32), Théoneste Bagosora (ICTR-96-7), Bernard Ntuyahaga (ICTR-98-40), Elie Ndayambaje (ICTR-96-8), and Joseph Kanyabashi (ICTR-96-15). Only the latter 2 had been present in Belgium at any time after the events.

[49] Belgium arrested at the ICTR's request Augustin Ndindiliyimana (ICTR-2000-56), Protais Zigiranyirazo (ICTR-01-73-I), and Emmanuel Ndindabahizi (ICTR-01-71-I).

[50] In October 2002 another Rwandan suspect was arrested in Belgium (*Le Soir*, 7 November 2002). Barring a request for deferral by the ICTR there is a possibility of a second Rwandan war crimes trial in Belgium.

[51] The defendants were not charged with genocide or crimes against humanity, perhaps to avoid a possibly controversial retroactive application of the War Crimes Act as amended. For a commentary on the actual trial, see Reydams (n 35 above).

[52] A cassation appeal was rejected.

[53] Namely Elie Ndayambaje and Joseph Kanyabashi; see n 48 above.

[54] See the discussion of the 1949 Geneva Conventions in ch 3 s A above.

Conversely, several facts militate strongly for a *right* to prosecute. Some pioneering decisions of the tribunals for the former Yugoslavia and for Rwanda have recognized certain 'internal atrocities'[55] as crimes under customary international law.[56] As noted above, there were strong links between the armed conflict and Belgium, and extradition to the territorial State was legally impossible. The ICTR with primary jurisdiction declined to take over the proceedings. Belgium was thus faced with the dilemma of whether to grant asylum to persons suspected of the most serious crimes under international law, or to prosecute them. In any event, Rwanda waived its right to protest by fully collaborating with the proceedings.

Prosecution in Belgium also was reasonable from the defendants' point of view. Rwanda and Belgium were at the relevant time party to the 1949 Geneva Conventions and Additional Protocol II, the Belgian implementing statute predated the events, and the defendants had come voluntarily to Belgium. Three of them even had strong ties with Belgium long before 1994.[57] Thus the determination of the forum was not arbitrary, and in retrospect the venue probably was to their advantage. Compared with the sentencing practice of the ICTR and the Rwandan courts, they got off lightly.

Aguilar Diaz et al. v *Pinochet*

Aguilar Diaz et al. v *Pinochet*,[58] a second case of universal jurisdiction, involved former Chilean President Augusto Pinochet. On 1 November 1998 Aguilar Diaz and other Chilean exiles living in Belgium filed a criminal complaint with an examining magistrate against Pinochet, then under arrest in Britain pending the outcome of a Spanish extradition request. The presence in Belgium of a Chilean exile community is the only link between Belgium, Pinochet, and his alleged crimes. The plaintiffs alleged that Pinochet had during his presidency committed, in Chile, crimes under international law as defined in the War Crimes Act.[59] They could not rely on the UN Torture Convention which Belgium had not ratified at that time.[60]

[55] The term is borrowed from the title of Professor Theodor Meron's seminal article 'The International Criminalization of Internal Atrocities' (1994) 89 *Am J Int'l L* 554.

[56] The ICTY Appeals Chamber in the *Prosecutor* v *Tadic* (IT-94-1-AR72), Decision on Jurisdiction, 2 October 1995, reprinted in (1996) 35 *Int'l L Materials* 32, para 132, and the ICTR in *Prosecutor* v *Akayesu* (ICTR-96-4T), 2 September 1998, reprinted in (1998) 37 *Int'l L Materials* 1411, paras 601–17 have held that some violations of common article 3 to the 1949 Geneva Conventions, which provides minimum protection to victims of an armed conflict not of an international character, as well as some violations of Additional Protocol II, are crimes under customary international law which entail individual criminal responsibility.

[57] The indictment notes that 3 of the 4 defendants received a college education in Belgium.

[58] Tribunal of first instance of Brussels (examining magistrate), order of 6 November 1998, reprinted in 118 *Journal des Tribunaux* (1999) 308 with critical note by J Verhoeven; also reprinted in *Revue de Droit Pénal et de Criminologie* (1999) 278 with concurring note by J Burneo Labrin and HD Bosly; references in this book to the order refer to the page numbers in *Revue de Droit Pénal et de Criminologie*.

[59] The complaints were filed before the amendment of the Act in 1999.

[60] Belgium ratified the UN Torture Convention on 25 June 1999.

In order to determine whether he had jurisdiction,[61] the magistrate addressed several important issues of international law: the immunity of a (former) head of State; universality of jurisdiction over crimes under international law (grave breaches of the 1949 Geneva Conventions and Additional Protocols and crimes against humanity); and prescription (statute of limitations).

With regard to the first issue, the magistrate concluded that Pinochet was not immune from personal jurisdiction in this matter.[62] On the second issue, the magistrate observed that the 1993 War Crimes Act endows the Belgian judicial authorities with universal jurisdiction and that it was the legislature's unambiguous intent that the law should apply even when the alleged perpetrator is not present on Belgian territory. However, the crimes were allegedly committed before the enactment of the statute on 16 June 1993. Determining that rules of jurisdiction, like any other procedural rules, apply immediately, the magistrate concluded that they may be applied to offences committed before their entry into force, if this would not violate the principle of legality:

> [T]o the extent that the acts defined in the law of 16 June 1993 were already punishable in the Belgian legal order as common crimes such as murder, manslaughter, assault, hostage taking, and torture, the legality principle as embodied in article 2 of the Belgian penal code does not seem to oppose the initiation of criminal proceedings regarding such acts as crimes under international law as long as the sanctions are those which were applicable to the underlying common offence at the time of commission, or possibly the milder current sanctions (principles of legality of sanctions and of retroactivity of the milder criminal law).[63]

The magistrate concluded, however, on the basis of the information available regarding the situation in Chile at the time of the alleged offences, that there was no internal armed conflict as defined in article 1 (paragraphs 1 and 2) of Additional Protocol II and accordingly held the 1993 War Crimes Act to be inapplicable. He then examined *ex officio*, as required by law, whether the facts alleged by the plaintiffs constituted other crimes under international law, namely crimes against humanity. Referring to the statutes and case-law of the Nuremberg, former Yugoslavia, and Rwanda tribunals, and to municipal statutes and judicial decisions, he found *prima facie* evidence that the alleged facts constituted crimes against humanity as defined by customary international law.

In view of the fact that Belgian criminal statutes made no express mention of crimes against humanity at that time, the magistrate's analysis of whether such crimes are governed by Belgian criminal law merits quotation at length (citations omitted).

> Is the notion of crime against humanity, as defined by international law, directly applicable in our domestic legal order?

[61] Under Belgian law an examining magistrate is obliged to determine prior to performing any acts of investigation whether he has jurisdiction over the offences alleged in a complaint. The plaintiff's characterization of the offences is not binding on the magistrate.

[62] Order (n 58 above) 280–1.

[63] Ibid 282.

Although our law does not contain the concept of crime against humanity, certain acts within the definition of crime against humanity are covered by our common criminal law (for instance murder, manslaughter, assault and battery, confinement with torture, hostage taking, . . .)

[T]he concept of crime against humanity has been incorporated in several international documents but these texts codify only a customary law crime. This is proven by the fact that several of these documents were drafted after the commission of the acts. If the latter were not pre-existing crimes under customary law, they could not have been punished because of the principle of the non-retroactivity of penal laws.

The Belgian legislature has recognized the existence of the international *ad hoc* tribunals and has incorporated their statutes in our internal legal order [. . .]

Consequently, we find that before being codified in a treaty or statute, the prohibition on crimes against humanity was part of customary international law and of international *jus cogens*, and this norm imposes itself imperatively and *erga omnes* on our domestic legal order.

Customary international law is equivalent to conventional international law and can be applied directly in the Belgian legal order.

[. . .]

National judicial authorities often give the impression that they are trying to evade prosecution of crimes against humanity instead of ascertaining whether they can prosecute them under international and national law [. . .]

Concerning the enforcement of international humanitarian law, too, the risk is not that States may overstep their competence but rather that by looking for excuses to justify their alleged incompetence, they condone the impunity of the most serious crimes (which certainly goes against the *raison d'être* of international law).

The general principle of international law *aut dedere aut judicare* (the obligation to try or extradite) imports the necessity of combating impunity of crimes under international law and the responsibility of State authorities to ensure punishment of such crimes irrespective of the place of commission.

Only one of the following two alternatives can hold: *either* crimes against humanity are ordinary crimes which do not transcend national boundaries and their punishment is left to the discretion of the States *or* crimes against humanity are of an unspeakable and unacceptable nature and their punishment is a common responsibility of all States.

In the latter case, all States and all humankind have a legal interest in the punishment of such crimes. Hence, it follows that, even in the absence of a treaty, national authorities have the right—and in some circumstances the obligation—to prosecute the perpetrators independently of the place where they hide.

The struggle against impunity of persons responsible for crimes under international law is, therefore, a responsibility of all States. National authorities have, at least, the right to take such measures as are necessary for the prosecution and punishment of crimes against humanity.[64]

[64] Order (n 58 above) 285–8 (citations omitted).

The decision then refers to the terms of the United Nations General Assembly's Principles of International Co-operation in the Detection, Arrest, Extradition, and Punishment of Persons Guilty of War Crimes and Crimes Against Humanity (which are silent on universal jurisdiction)[65] and concludes: 'For these reasons we find that, as a matter of customary international law, or even more strongly as a matter of *jus cogens*, universal jurisdiction over crimes against humanity exists, authorizing national judicial authorities to prosecute and punish the perpetrators in all circumstances'.[66]

With regard to the third issue, the magistrate found that, as a matter of customary international law, crimes against humanity cannot become prescribed and that this principle is directly applicable in the domestic legal order.[67]

Having established his jurisdiction, the magistrate issued a warrant for the arrest of Pinochet alleging crimes against humanity and the Belgian government requested his extradition from the United Kingdom. British authorities ultimately released Pinochet on medical grounds. He returned promptly to Chile.

The case of *Aguilar Diaz* et al. v *Pinochet* and the ensuing extradition request prompt several thoughts. The magistrate referred to *aut dedere aut judicare* and to an international custom as the international legal bases for his decision to declare himself competent. It is, however, far from established that *aut dedere aut judicare* is a general principle of international law as the magistrate alleged, or a rule of customary international law.[68] As seen in chapters 2 and 3 above, universal jurisdiction is generally regarded as the competence of the *judex* (*loci*) *deprehensionis*, ie the State in whose territory a foreign offender 'is present' or 'is found', and therefore can be arrested. True, Pinochet would have been 'present' in Belgium, but only *because* of his extradition. This scenario seems to distort the meaning of *aut dedere aut judicare* which, assuming it is a rule of international law, does not establish a third country's right to punish but only creates bilateral rights and obligations between the State where an offender 'is present' and the State(s) directly linked to the offence.

In addition to *aut dedere aut judicare*, the magistrate resorted to international custom as a basis for his universal competence but without elaborating how he reached that view. This author has identified only two cases prior to 1998 that bear resemblance to the case presented to the magistrate.[69] Therefore, no general and consistent practice appears to have existed at the time of the decision.[70]

Then there is the problem of institutional capacity. In *Public Prosecutor* v *Higaniro* et al. it took five years, after the completion of the investigation,

[65] See the discussion in ch 3 s B above.
[66] Order (n 58 above) 288.
[67] Ibid 289–90 (citations omitted).
[68] See chapter 3 n 102 above.
[69] Namely the *Yunis* case in the United States and the *Pinochet* case in Spain (see the respective country studies below).
[70] Cf Verhoeven (n 58 above) 5956.

to commit the suspects for trial. The suspects in the above mentioned *Dutroux* affair have been awaiting their trial since 1996. Against that background, how reasonable was it to request the extradition of an octogenarian against whom an investigation for crimes against humanity had barely started? Establishing crimes against humanity requires, given their constitutive elements, extraordinary investigative capacity, especially when they were committed in a distant country.

After this decision and the subsequent amendment of the War Crimes Act matters took their own course. Victims of human rights violations from all over the world flooded the Belgian authorities with complaints. Hardly a month went by without some international outcast being indicted on the basis of the War Crimes Act.[71] Two cases are discussed below.

Public Prosecutor v *Ndombasi* et al.

An arrest warrant issued by a Brussels magistrate against Yerodia Abdoulaye Ndombasi, then acting Minister of Foreign Affairs of the Democratic Republic of Congo, led to the case concerning the *Arrest Warrant of 11 April 2000*, which is the subject of a postscript to this book. *Public Prosecutor* v *Ndombasi* et al.[72] is the result of an application by the Brussels public prosecutor and of *constitutions de partie civile*.[73] The facts of the case arise from the ongoing war in the eastern Congo. The warrant asserts that televized statements by the accused in August 1998 provoked massacres of Tutsi civilians[74] and charges him with crimes under the Belgian War Crimes Act. The warrant was issued *in absentia*. There is no link between Belgium and the alleged facts other than the presence in Brussels of a relatively large Congolese community.

After the International Court of Justice ruled in favour of the Congo two things happened. First, Belgium rescinded the illegal arrest warrant. Second, and this came as a *coup de théâtre*, the *chambre de mises en accusation* in Brussels, a pre-trial appeals court, ruled that the proceedings (*poursuites*) against Ndombasi were inadmissible (*irrecevables*) from the beginning because the accused was not present in Belgium as required by CPP TP article 12.

The appeals decision in *Public Prosecutor* v *Ndombasi* et al. limits the exercise of universal jurisdiction under the War Crimes Act to cases where the foreign suspect is voluntarily present in Belgium. The court based itself on a provision in the domestic code of penal procedure; it did not consider international law. As for the timing of the decision, it is bizarre for a country to

[71] *New York Times*, 27 December 2001, A8. See also Vandermeersch (2001) (n 46 above) 128–9.

[72] Chambre de mises en accusation of Brussels, 16 April 2002 (copy on file with author).

[73] The complaint names three other defendants, including the then acting President of the Congo, Laurent-Désiré Kabila (copies on file with author).

[74] Taken from Congo's application instituting proceedings before the ICJ at 5.

issue an international arrest warrant and insist on its international legality before the ICJ, only to have a domestic court decide two years later that the warrant contravenes municipal law. The ruling also implies that the proceedings against Pinochet were ill founded under domestic law.

Abbas Hijazi et al. v *Sharon* et al.

Abbas Hijazi et al. v *Sharon* et al.[75] was the result of a complaint (*plainte avec constitution de partie civile*)[76] by survivors of the massacre of Palestinian refugees in the camps of Sabra and Chatila (Lebanon). The massacre took place in 1982 during a massive Israeli invasion of Lebanon when Ariel Sharon was defence minister of Israel. The UN General Assembly condemned the killings as 'an act of genocide';[77] an official Israeli commission of inquiry into the massacres concluded that Sharon 'bears personal responsibility'.[78] At the time of the complaint (June 2001) Sharon was prime minister of Israel. Other than the fact that the plaintiffs were briefly in Belgium to file the complaint there is no link between the forum and the events.

Understandably the case led to diplomatic friction. Both Sharon and the State of Israel intervened in the proceedings. It may be noted that Israel of all countries has a genocide law that excludes immunity based on official capacity and provides for universal jurisdiction.[79] The *chambre de mises en accusation* in Brussels (differently composed than in *Ndombasi*) declared the proceedings inadmissible because the defendant was not present as required by CPP TP article 12. The court opined, moreover, that the exercise of universal jurisdiction *in absentia* is contrary to the Genocide Convention, the Geneva Conventions, the European Convention for the Protection of Fundamental Rights and Freedoms, and the principle of sovereign equality of States.[80]

The appeal decision in *Abbas Hijazi* et al. v *Sharon* et al. confirms the *Ndombasi* ruling that a suspect's presence is a condition precedent for universal jurisdiction under domestic law; the court added, however, that proceedings *in absentia* are also incompatible with international law and with the principle of sovereign equality of States in particular. The court did not get as far as dealing with other issues, such as State immunity, the questionable retroactive application of the War Crimes Act,[81] or the effects of a Lebanese amnesty.

[75] *Chambre de mises en accusation* of Brussels, 26 June 2002 (copy on file with author).
[76] The complaint is directed against Ariel Sharon, Amos Yaron (the commander of an Israeli army unit at Sabra and Chatila), and X (copy on file with author).
[77] Ibid 9.
[78] *The Beirut Massacre: The Complete Kahan Commission Report*, Princeton, Karz Cohl (1983) 104 (quoted in the complaint at 6).
[79] See the Israel country study below.
[80] Judgment (n 75 above), section A, paragraph 9. The same court declared inadmissible the proceedings against the President of Ivory Coast Laurent Gbagbo, his predecessor Robert Gueï, and two of his ministers for the violent suppression of demonstrations in October and December 2000 (*De Standaard*, 27 June 2002, 3).
[81] See n 27 above.

Unless the cassation appeals are granted the rulings obviously affect the dozen or so other (former) foreign officials indicted *in absentia*.[82] It may be noted in this regard that some lawmakers have announced legislation to 'safe' the War Crimes Act before the highest court hears the case.[83] (Meanwhile several protagonists of the Rwandan genocide live undisturbed in Belgium.)[84]

C. SUMMARY

Universal jurisdiction over serious violations of international humanitarian law has become one big tangle in Belgium, which makes summarizing difficult. Drawing conclusions when the last word has not yet been spoken is even trickier. One cannot fail to notice the gap between the aim of the Belgian legislature (the establishment of universal jurisdiction far beyond treaty obligations) and the apparent lack of institutional capacity of the domestic criminal justice system. The presence in Belgium of suspected Rwandan *génocidaires* illustrates this: four were tried after an unjustifiable delay, a dozen or more are left in peace. This situation fuels the criticism that the proceedings *in absentia* against the world's villains are window-dressing. Such proceedings were possible because of a concurrence of legal circumstances: unlimited and retrospective application of the War Crimes Act, exclusion of immunity based on official capacity, and an unrestricted right for victims to initiate proceedings before any district court. The result was absurd: a tiny country (with a none too efficient criminal justice system) assumed broader powers than the ICC. Long overdue appeals decisions have now halted these *in absentia* proceedings, but legislation has been announced to make them possible again, thereby ignoring the appeals ruling that universal jurisdiction without a material and objective link violates the principle of sovereign equality of States.

[82] One of them is Hissène Habré, the former leader of Chad. The case against him in Belgium is the continuation of the *Habré* case in Senegal (see below, Senegal country study). After the decision of the Senegalese court of cassation that the former leader could not be prosecuted in Senegal (his current country of residence) for human rights violations allegedly committed in Chad during his presidency plaintiffs took their case to Belgium. Their *constitution de partie civile* was declared admissible and a team of Belgian investigators went on a rogatory mission to Chad to hear witnesses and inspect the sites of mass graves (*De Standaard*, 27 February 2002).

[83] The amendment (copy on file with author) proposes a new elaborate article 7 modelled after §153f of the German code of penal procedure (see the Germany country study below).

[84] According to *De Standaard*, 26 April 2002 the ICTR Prosecutor met with Belgian officials to express her concern about the presence in Belgium of 15 senior officials of the ousted Rwandan regime. In October 2002 one of them was reportedly arrested (see n 50 above).

7

Canada

A. AMBIT OF THE CRIMINAL LAW

Jurisdiction over crime in Canada is still largely governed by the common law rule that 'all crime is local'.[1] The territoriality principle is not stated expressly but is implicit in the way in which offence-creating sections of the Criminal Code and of other criminal enactments are drafted; that is, no mention is made in an offence-creating section as to the *locus* of the conduct unless the section is to be applicable to conduct outside Canada, and in that event the section expressly says so.[2] If criminal conduct outside Canada is to be punishable by a court in Canada both the 'applicability of law' and 'jurisdiction of courts' must be explicitly provided for in federal legislation.[3]

The Constitution specifically allows Parliament to make laws with extra-territorial operation.[4] Such laws can be found in section 7 of the Criminal Code, titled 'Offences outside Canada', and in offence-creating sections of other acts of parliament. A reading of section 7 reveals immediately that, in principle, Canada does not exercise active and passive personality jurisdiction.[5]

Section 7 does, however, list a number of offences under international treaties[6] which, when committed outside Canada, are punishable in Canada if the alleged offender, whatever his nationality, after the commission of the offence, is 'present' in Canada. These provisions have in common the legal fiction that the act or omission committed outside Canada shall be deemed to

[1] For the rationales of the rule which originated in England, see the United Kingdom country study below. For studies on the scope of application of Canadian criminal law, see SA Williams and JG Castel, *Canadian Criminal Law: International and Transnational Aspects* (1981) and Law Reform Commission of Canada, *Extraterritorial Jurisdiction: Working Paper 37* (1984).

[2] Law Reform Commission of Canada (ibid) 13.

[3] Ibid 3–4. Canada differs in this respect from most other countries where either is a sufficient basis for prosecution of an extraterritorial offence. France is another exception (see below).

[4] The Canadian Constitution incorporates s 3 of the Statute of Westminster 1931 (United Kingdom), c 4, as a constitutional instrument in the schedule to the Constitution Act 1982.

[5] Exceptions include active personality jurisdiction over treasonable acts (s 46(3)) and bigamy (s 254(1)(b)).

[6] The offences listed are: offences committed on aircraft, offences against fixed platforms or international maritime navigation, offences against fixed platforms or navigation in the internal waters or territorial sea of another State, offences against internationally protected persons, the offence of hostage taking, offences involving nuclear material, torture, war crimes, and crimes against humanity. On the implementation of international criminal law treaties in Canadian law see L Kos-Rabcewicz-Zubkowski, 'Canada' (1989) 60 *Revue internationale de droit pénal* 195 and J Terry 'The Canadian Criminal Code, Universal Jurisdiction, and the Prosecution of Foreign Human Rights Offenders in Canadian Courts' (1989) (unpublished LLM thesis, Harvard Law School).

have been committed in Canada. The initiation of proceedings is not dependent on any request or initiative by the authorities of the *locus delicti*. Like in Australia, the federal government retains absolute discretion over the prosecution of extraterritorial offences.[7] The pleas of *autrefois acquit, autrefois convict*, and pardon apply to foreign decisions,[8] but double criminality is not required.

Three statutes in the area of international humanitarian law provide for universal jurisdiction, the Geneva Conventions Act, the Criminal Code section 7(3.71)–(3.77), and the Crimes Against Humanity and War Crimes Act, which are discussed next.

Geneva Conventions Act

As its name suggests, the Geneva Conventions Act[9] implements the 1949 Geneva Conventions and Additional Protocols. Section 3 reads as follows.

> (1) Every person who, *whether within or outside Canada*, commits a grave breach referred to in Article 50 of Schedule I, Article 51 of Schedule II, Article 130 of Schedule III, Article 147 of Schedule IV, or Article 11 or 85 of Schedule V is guilty of an indictable offence, and
> (a) if the grave breach causes the death of any person, is liable to imprisonment for life; and
> (b) in any other case, is liable to imprisonment for a term not exceeding fourteen years.
>
> (2) Where a person is alleged to have committed an offence referred to in subsection (1), proceedings in respect of that offence may, *whether or not the person is in Canada*, be commenced in any territorial division in Canada and that person may be tried and punished in respect of that offence in the same manner as if the offence had been committed in that territorial division.
>
> (3) [...]
>
> (4) Proceedings with respect to an offence referred to in subsection (1), other than proceedings before a service tribunal as defined in section 2 of the National Defence Act, may only be commenced with the personal consent in writing of the Attorney General of Canada or the Deputy Attorney General of Canada and be conducted by the Attorney General of Canada, or counsel acting on behalf thereof (emphases added).

[7] S 7(7): 'No proceedings shall be instituted under this section without the consent of the Attorney General of Canada if the accused is not a Canadian citizen'.

[8] S 7(6): 'Where a person is alleged to have committed an act or omission that is an offence by virtue of this section and that person has been tried and dealt with outside Canada in respect of the offence in such a manner that, if that person had been tried and dealt with in Canada, he would be able to plead *autrefois acquit, autrefois convict* or pardon, that person shall be deemed to have been so tried and dealt with in Canada'. On *ne bis in idem* in respect of extraterritorial offences and foreign decisions, see Williams and Castel (n 1 above) ch 26. For a succinct overview of the Canadian law of criminal procedure, see K Roach, 'Canada' in CM Bradley (ed) *Criminal Procedure: A Worldwide Study* (1999) 53.

[9] Revised Statutes 1985, ch G-3.

Section 3 is remarkable for its detail and scope. It appears to be one of the most carefully drafted jurisdiction provisions in any Geneva Conventions implementation statute reviewed in this book. Section 3 is also a rare example of unlimited interpretation of the jurisdiction clause of the Conventions since proceedings may be commenced for extraterritorial offences 'whether or not the person is in Canada'. This permits Canadian authorities to seek extradition, assuming of course that bilateral co-operation exists. The Geneva Conventions Act is, however, *de facto* repealed by the comprehensive Crimes Against Humanity and War Crimes Act. The true universal jurisdiction clause of the Geneva Conventions Act will thus probably remain an academic curiosity that was never put into practice.

Criminal Code, section 7(3.71–3.77)

Section 7(3.71–3.77) of the Criminal Code was entirely repealed in 2000 by the Crimes Against Humanity and War Crimes Act, but is relevant because of its historical significance. In 1986 the Commission of Inquiry on War Criminals[10] found that Nazi war criminals were probably living in Canada. The Commission was of the opinion that no prosecution could successfully be launched under the existing war crimes legislation and recommended a number of statutory revisions. As a consequence, the federal parliament enacted in 1987 the Act to amend the Criminal Code, the Immigration Act, and the Citizenship Act.[11] By virtue of that legislation subsections 3.71–3.77 were introduced into section 7 of the Criminal Code; subsection 3.71 provided for extraterritorial jurisdiction; it read as follows.

> Notwithstanding anything in this Act or any other Act, *every person* who, either before or after the coming into force of this subsection, commits an act or omission *outside Canada* that constitutes a war crime or a crime against humanity and that, if committed in Canada, would constitute an offence against the laws of Canada in force at the time of the act or omission shall be deemed to commit that act or omission in Canada at that time if,
>
> (a) at the time of the act or omission,
>   (i) that person is a Canadian citizen or is employed by Canada in a civilian or military capacity,
>   (ii) that person is a citizen of, or is employed in civilian or military capacity by, a state that is engaged in an armed conflict against Canada, or
>   (iii) the victim of the act or omission is a Canadian citizen or a citizen of a state that is allied with Canada in an armed conflict; or

[10] Commission of Inquiry on War Criminals, *Report, Part I: Public* (1986).

[11] Statutes of Canada 1987, ch 37. See extensively SA Williams, 'Laudable Principles Lacking Application: The Prosecution of War Criminals in Canada' in TLH McCormack and GJ Simpson (eds) *The Law of War Crimes: National and International Approaches* (1997) 151.

(b) at the time of the act or omission, Canada could, in conformity with international law, exercise *jurisdiction* over the person with respect to the act or omission *on the basis of the person's presence in Canada* and, subsequent to the time of the act or omission, *the person is present in Canada* (emphases added).

Subsection 3.71(a) deals with crimes committed outside Canada by a Canadian citizen or employee of Canada, or by a citizen of a State engaged in an armed conflict against Canada, or a crime of which the victim was a citizen of Canada or one of its allies. In such cases, Canadian courts have jurisdiction even if the offender is not present in Canada. Subsection 3.71(b) provides for universal jurisdiction, provided that the foreign offender is present in Canada.

Four naturalized Canadians were prosecuted for Nazi war crimes in occupied Europe on the basis of section 7(3.71).[12] As in Australia, all those prosecutions failed. Since then the Canadian government proceeds against such suspects with administrative procedures only, especially by denaturalizing and deporting foreign war criminals.[13] In a constitutional challenge against the retroactivity of the Act the Ontario High Court of Justice opined that the universality principle:

recognizes that with respect to certain types of international crimes a country has the right to prosecute an offender irrespective of the fact that the offence was not committed on its territory. The *condition precedent* to the exercise of jurisdiction with respect to such international crimes *is that the accused person must be found within the territory of the country asserting jurisdiction*[14] (emphases added).

Crimes Against Humanity and War Crimes Act

The Crimes Against Humanity and War Crimes Act[15] incorporates the provisions of the ICC Statute into Canadian legislation. Its twofold objective is to allow full co-operation with the ICC in matters of investigation and prosecution and to increase national capacity and punish alleged perpetrators of genocide, crimes against humanity, and war crimes, including on the basis of (retroactive) universal jurisdiction.[16] The Act's jurisdiction provisions are in

[12] For details and strategy, see R Provost, 'Canada' (2000) 3 *Ybk Int'l Humanitarian L* 440, 442–4.

[13] Among the cases of deportation for crimes against humanity committed abroad in the recent past are *Sivakumar* v *Canada*, Minister of Employment and Immigration, Federal Court of Canada (Court of Appeal), 4 November 1993, 1 FC 433, 163 NR 197, 44 ACWS (3d) 563, and *Mugesera* v *Minister of Citizenship and Immigration*, Immigration and Refugee Board (Appeal Division) of Canada, 6 November 1998, summarized in 93 *Am J Int'l L* 529 (1999) (case note by William Schabas).

[14] *Regina* v *Finta*, Ontario High Court of Justice, 61 DLR (4th) 85, 106.

[15] The full title of this act is An Act respecting genocide, crimes against humanity and war crimes and to implement the Rome Statute of the International Criminal Court, and to make consequential amendments to other Acts, 2000, ch 4. The Act entered into force on 23 October 2000. See WA Schabas, 'Canadian Implementing Legislation for the Rome Statute' (2000) 3 *Ybk Int'l Humanitarian L* 337–46.

[16] Provost (n 12 above) 440, 441.

essence identical to section 7(3.71–3.77) of the Criminal Code, which are repealed. They read, in part, as follows.

6. (1) *Every person* who, either before or after the coming into force of this section, commits *outside Canada*

    (a) genocide,
    (b) a crime against humanity, or
    (c) a war crime,

    is guilty of an indictable offence and may be prosecuted for that offence in accordance with section 8.

7. [...]
8. A person who is alleged to have committed an offence under section 6 or 7 may be prosecuted for that offence if
    (a) at the time the offence is alleged to have been committed,
        (i) the person was a Canadian citizen or was employed by Canada in a civilian or military capacity,
        (ii) the person was a citizen of a state that was engaged in an armed conflict against Canada, or was employed in a civilian or military capacity by such a state,
        (iii) the victim of the alleged offence was a Canadian citizen, or
        (iv) the victim of the alleged offence was a citizen of a state that was allied with Canada in an armed conflict; or
    (b) *after the time the offence is alleged to have been committed, the person is present in Canada.*[17]
9. [...]
    (3) No proceedings for an offence under any of sections 4 to 7, 27 and 28 may be commenced without the personal consent in writing of the Attorney General or Deputy Attorney General of Canada, and those proceedings may be conducted only by the Attorney General of Canada or counsel acting on their behalf (emphases added).

Prosecution of extraterritorial offences under the Act always requires a link with Canada; *either* the crime must be committed by a Canadian citizen or employee of Canada, or by a citizen of a State engaged in an armed conflict against Canada, or against a citizen of Canada or of one of its allies (s 8(a)(ii) to (iv)), in which cases Canadian courts are competent even if the offender is not present in Canada, *or* alternatively, Canadian courts may exercise jurisdiction over any person if after the crime the offender is present in Canada (section 8(b)).[18] That the presence in the latter case must be voluntary follows *a contrario* from section 8(a); any other interpretation would make that section superfluous.

[17] Draft s 8(b) originally provided: 'at the time of the act or omission, Canada could, in conformity with international law, exercise jurisdiction over the person with respect to the act or omission on the basis of the person's presence in Canada and, subsequent to the time of the act or omission, the person is present in Canada'.

[18] Schabas (n 15 above) 343.

The Act repeals the provisions on crimes against humanity and war crimes in the Criminal Code but not the above-mentioned Geneva Conventions Act, despite substantial overlap. By virtue of the principle *lex posterior derogat priori* it can be argued that universal jurisdiction over grave breaches of the Conventions is now conditional upon the foreign suspect's voluntary presence in Canada.

As with all other extraterritorial offences proceedings may not be commenced without the personal consent in writing of the Attorney General or Deputy Attorney General of Canada, and those proceedings may be conducted only by the Attorney General of Canada or counsel acting on their behalf (section 9(3)).

Section 12 of the Act provides that the pleas of *autrefois acquit, autrefois convict*, and pardon apply, unless the proceedings in the foreign court were for the purpose of shielding the person from criminal responsibility or were not otherwise conducted independently or impartially in accordance with the norms of due process recognized by international law, and were conducted in a manner that, in the circumstances, was inconsistent with an intent to bring the person to justice.[19]

It also may be noted that the Act no longer distinguishes between international and non-international armed conflicts for purposes of jurisdiction. Canadian courts are competent independently of the nature of the conflict.

For the rest, the remarks made above about the substantive provisions of similar Australian and Belgian laws apply. The establishment of universal jurisdiction over crimes against humanity, genocide, and war crimes committed in a non-international armed conflict is not the fulfilment of any treaty obligation yet conforms to the 'division of labour' envisaged by the Draft Code of Crimes against the Peace and Security of Mankind and by the Joinet report.[20]

No cases of universal jurisdiction under any of the Acts discussed here have been reported.

B. SUMMARY

As a rule, Canada only establishes extraterritorial jurisdiction in the execution of a treaty obligation. The comprehensive Crimes Against Humanity and War Crimes Act, however, provides for universal jurisdiction over genocide, crimes against humanity, and war crimes even though, except for grave breaches of the Geneva Conventions, no treaty obligation exists or, in the case of genocide, even despite a contrary jurisdiction clause in a relevant convention. Universal jurisdiction requires the voluntary presence in Canada of the foreign

[19] Cf almost *verbatim* article 17(2) of the ICC Statute.

[20] See ch 3 s C above.

offender. The Geneva Conventions Act arguably constitutes an exception but has been *de facto* repealed by the Crimes Against Humanity and War Crimes Act. As in Australia, the federal executive has exclusive control over criminal proceedings regarding extraterritorial offences, with no possibility for victims to intervene. Immigration law allows an alternative course of action against foreigners suspected of crimes against humanity and war crimes outside Canada: deportation.

8

Denmark

A. AMBIT OF THE CRIMINAL LAW

Denmark is a member of the Nordic Council, a regional co-operation framework of the Scandinavian countries. The 'international criminal law' of these countries has three common characteristics. From the beginning of the twentieth century, they have claimed extensive extraterritorial jurisdiction, more extensive than many other European countries.[1] The Scandinavian States are representative of a philosophy of co-operation in criminal matters, expressed in a number of agreements *inter se* and with other European countries in the framework of the Council of Europe, the European Union, and in general within the United Nations. Their criminal codes also require the municipal authorities to exercise jurisdiction in accordance with the rules of public international law.[2]

The ambit of the Danish penal code (*Straffeloven*, or Strfl.)[3] is spelled out in §§6–12. Strfl. §6(1)(1) expresses the basic principle: 'Acts committed [...] within the territory of the Danish State [...] shall be subject to Danish criminal jurisdiction'. Strfl. §7(1)(2) contains a general active personality clause. Jurisdiction on this basis is limited by the double criminality requirement but extends to resident aliens, and to citizens and resident aliens of Finland, Iceland, Norway, or Sweden, provided they are 'present' in Denmark.[4] Jurisdiction is not conditional on a complaint by the foreign authorities or the victim. The protective principle is expressed in Strfl. §8(1)(1), which vests Danish authorities with jurisdiction over acts committed abroad, irrespective of the nationality of the perpetrator, 'where the act violates the independence,

I warmly thank Mr Lars Plum for suggestions and critical comments.

[1] I Cameron, *The Protective Principle of International Criminal Jurisdiction* (1994) 23 speaks in this regard about the 'universalism' of the jurisdictional system of the Scandinavian countries. On the ambit of Finnish penal law, see AHJ Swart, 'Jurisdiction in Criminal Law: Some Reflections on the Finnish Code from a Comparative Perspective' in R Lahti and K Nuotio (eds) *Criminal Law Theory in Transition* (1992) 527 and K Cornils, 'Zur Regelung des raümlichen Geltungsbereichs im finnishen Strafgesetzentwurf' in ibid 571. On the ambit of Swedish penal law, see A Nelson, 'Swedish and Foreign Crimes in the Swedish Criminal Justice System' in N Jareborg (ed) *Double Criminality: Studies in International Criminal Law* (1989) 11 and Cameron (this n) 103–15.

[2] Strfl. §12: 'The application of the provisions of sections 6–8 of this Act shall be subject to the applicable rules of international law'.

[3] An English version of the code is available in G Høyer, M Spencer, and V Greve, *The Danish Criminal Code* (1997). All translations of the code are taken from that work.

[4] According to Cameron (n 1 above) 169 the principle applies prospectively, ie the important date is when the prosecution is brought, not when the crime is committed.

security, Constitution or public authorities of the Danish State, official duties towards the State or such interests, the legal protection of which depends on a personal connection with the Danish State'.[5] Danish criminal law does not recognize the passive personality principle, except when an offence of a certain severity is committed against a Dane or a person resident in the Danish State outside the territory of any State (Strfl. §8(1)(3)). Universal jurisdiction is provided for in Strfl. §8(1)(5) and Strfl. §8(1)(6), which are discussed next.[6]

Straffeloven §8(1) subparagraph 5

Strfl. §8(1)(5), introduced in 1986, is an enabling clause which replaces numerous previous changes in an enumerative list of conventions for which Danish authorities had to establish jurisdiction.[7] Strfl. §8(1)(5) reads: 'Acts committed outside the territory of the Danish State, shall also come within Danish criminal jurisdiction, irrespective of the nationality of the perpetrator where the act is covered by an international convention in pursuance of which Denmark is under an obligation to start legal proceedings'.

The text does not mention that the foreign offender should be 'found' in Denmark, but in *Lee Urzua* et al. v *Pinochet* (see below) the Director of Public Prosecution held that Danish jurisdiction only exists if the suspect is voluntarily present. Like most other domestic enabling clauses, ratification of the convention in question by the State of nationality of the offender or by the territorial State is not a condition. Whether jurisdiction under Strfl. §8(1)(5) is subsidiary depends on the wording and construction of the relevant convention. The authority to bring a prosecution under this section lies with the Minister of Justice.[8]

Straffeloven §8(1) subparagraph 6

Strfl. §8(1)(6) is a municipal *aut dedere aut judicare* clause,[9] which reads:

> Acts committed outside the territory of the Danish State, shall also come within Danish criminal jurisdiction, irrespective of the nationality of the perpetrator *where*

[5] For a commentary on the protective principle in Danish law, see I Cameron, 'The Protective Principle of Criminal Jurisdiction in Nordic Criminal Law' in R Lahti and K Nuotio (eds) *Criminal Law theory in transition: Finnish and comparative perspectives* (1992) 544, 556–8 and Cameron (n 1 above) 171–9.

[6] In addition to Strfl. §8(1)(5) and Strfl. §8(1)(6), Strfl. §8(1)(4) provides for universal jurisdiction over aircraft hijacking or crimes of violence against a person committed in connection with hijacking. The Military Criminal Code also provides for something akin to universal jurisdiction, namely jurisdiction over violations of humanitarian law wherever committed against military personnel of allies when Denmark is at war; see M Holdgaard Bukh, 'Prosecution Before Danish Courts of Foreigners Suspected of Serious Violations of Human Rights or Humanitarian Law' (1994) 6 *Eur Rev Public L* 339, 347–8.

[7] For comments, see ibid 341–5.

[8] Rigsadvokatens Meddelelse 7/1992 (circular letter of the Director of Public Prosecution).

[9] For comments on Strfl. §8(1)(6), see Holdgaard Bukh (n 6 above) 341–5.

transfer of the accused for legal proceedings in another country is rejected, and the act, provided it is committed within the territory recognized by international law as belonging to a foreign State, is punishable according to the law of this State, and provided that according to Danish law the act is punishable with a sentence more severe than one year of imprisonment (emphasis added).

The term 'rejected' implies that an extradition request must have been received and refused by Denmark.[10] Jurisdiction under this subsection is thus always subsidiary and only the Minister of Justice has the authority to bring a prosecution.[11]

As for criminal procedure, in Denmark the principle of opportunity of prosecution applies. The victim has no right to be a party to the proceedings under the penal aspects of the case; if dissatisfied with the prosecution, he may complain up through the prosecutorial system.[12]

B. CASE-LAW

Public Prosecutor v *Saric*

The case of *Public Prosecutor* v *Saric*[13] arose out of the war and ethnic violence in the former Yugoslavia in the first half of the 1990s.[14] The accused, a citizen from Bosnia-Herzegovina, came as a refugee to Denmark. Other Bosnian refugees pointed him out as a guard at a camp where they had been detained and physically abused. Danish judicial authorities asserted jurisdiction on the basis of Strfl. §8(1)(5) in conjunction with articles 129–30 and 146–7 of respectively the Third and Fourth 1949 Geneva Conventions,[15] which both Denmark and Bosnia-Herzegovina have ratified. In the absence of specific criminal code provisions on violations of the 1949 Geneva Conventions the accused was charged under the corresponding municipal offences of violence against persons. The International Criminal Tribunal for the former Yugoslavia declined a Danish offer to take over the proceedings. A jury found the accused guilty on fourteen of the twenty-five charges.

[10] For comments on Strfl. §8(1)(6), see Holdgaard Bukh (n 6 above) 346.

[11] Rigsadvokatens Meddelelse 7/1992.

[12] For an account in English of Danish criminal procedure, see V Greve 'Denmark' in C Van den Wyngaert (ed) *Criminal procedure systems in the European Community* (1993) 51–72.

[13] Østre Landsret, 25 November 1994 (Trial judgment); Højesteret, 15 August 1995 (Appeals judgment), reprinted in *Ugeskrift for Retsvæsen* 1995, 838H, English translation published in (1998) 1 *Ybk Int'l Humanitarian L* 431.

[14] Information from E Merlung, 'National Implementation: The Universal Jurisdiction. The Saric Case' in *The Punishment of War Crimes: International Legal Perspectives* (1996) 12.

[15] The Danish Ministry of Foreign Affairs had characterized the war in the former Yugoslavia as an international armed conflict.

Public Prosecutor v *Saric* appears to have been the first conviction for grave breaches of the 1949 Geneva Conventions by a court in a third State. The accused had come voluntarily to and established significant links with the forum State, which exercised jurisdiction after the competent international tribunal declined to take over the proceedings and after co-operation with the authorities of the territorial State failed because of the war. Prosecution was the fulfilment of an obligation under the Geneva Conventions. Paraphrasing Donnedieu de Vabres, one can say that Denmark stepped in 'in default of any other State, to prevent, in the interest of humanity, an outrageous impunity'.[16]

Lee Urzua et al. v *Pinochet*

The case of *Lee Urzua* et al. v *Pinochet*[17] was an attempt by Chilean exiles to launch criminal proceedings in Denmark against former Chilean President Augusto Pinochet at the time he was under arrest in England.[18] Plaintiffs, nine of whom had obtained Danish citizenship, alleged persecution and torture in Chile during Pinochet's rule.

The Director of Public Prosecution declined to prosecute the case for lack of jurisdiction. After careful analysis of the object, purpose, and jurisdiction clauses of all international conventions that could possibly apply (the UN Torture Convention in particular) and thorough examination of the drafting history of Strfl. §8(1)(5) and of scholarly comments thereon, he concluded that Danish jurisdiction under Strfl. §8(1)(5) only exists if the suspect is present in Denmark.[19] Hence, he rejected the scenario of bringing about the suspect's presence through extradition because otherwise 'there would be no limit on Danish jurisdiction over crimes that are the subject of an international convention'.[20] The Director furthermore opined that article VI of the Genocide Convention (which he doubted applied in the instant case) only provides for the jurisdiction of the territorial State or an international tribunal.[21]

C. SUMMARY

The ambit of Danish penal law is broad. A domestic *aut dedere aut judicare* clause and a general enabling clause endow Danish courts with universal

[16] H Donnedieu de Vabres, *Les principes modernes du droit pénal international* (1928) 135.

[17] Opinion of the Director of Public Prosecution of 3 December 1998, case no. 555/98 (copy on file with author). I am indebted to Mr Lars Plum for an English translation. The case is reported in (2000) 3 *Ybk Int'l Humanitarian L* 469.

[18] See Spain and United Kingdom country studies below.

[19] Opinion of the Director of Public Prosecution (n 17 above) 26–9.

[20] Ibid 29.

[21] Ibid 26.

jurisdiction over all serious common offences and treaty offences. Prosecution of common offences on the basis of universal jurisdiction is only possible after a request for extradition has been received and rejected. Universal jurisdiction over treaty offences, on the other hand, is not dependent on any request by another State; it suffices that the foreign suspect is voluntarily present in Denmark. Accordingly, a Bosnian refugee was tried and convicted for grave breaches of the Geneva Conventions committed in the former Yugoslavia while proceedings against former Chilean President Pinochet *in absentia* were dismissed for lack of jurisdiction.

9

France

A. AMBIT OF THE CRIMINAL LAW

The ambit of French criminal law[1] is spelled out in articles 113-1 to 113-10 of Book I, Title I, Chapter III (*De l'application de la loi pénale dans l'espace*) of the penal code (*Code pénal*, or CP). Article 113-2 expresses the basic principle: 'French criminal law is applicable to offences committed on the territory of the Republic'. General active personality jurisdiction is provided for in article 113-6, and protective jurisdiction in article 113-10. Passive personality jurisdiction is also well established in French law but this has not always been so. It will be remembered that in the *Lotus* case the French government had contested its international legality.[2] Earlier, in 1873, the Court of Cassation held in the *Fornage* case[3] that French jurisdiction:

> cannot extend to offences committed outside the territory by foreigners who, by reason of such acts, are not justiciable by the French tribunals; seeing that, indeed, the right to punish emanates from the right of sovereignty, which does not extend beyond the limits of territory; that, except in cases specified in article 7 of the Code of Criminal Instruction, the provision of which is founded on the right of legitimate self defense, the French tribunals are without power to judge foreigners for acts committed by them in a foreign country; that their incompetence in this regard is absolute and permanent; that it can be waived neither by the silence nor by the consent of the accused; that it exists always the same at every stage of the proceedings.[4]

This view has been abandoned with the introduction of general passive jurisdiction, first only for felonies (*crimes*) and since 1994 also for misdemeanours (*délits*) (article 113-6).[5] Prosecution on the basis of the active or passive personality principle is subsidiary to the jurisdiction of the territorial State[6] and is barred by a final foreign decision, except a pardon (article 113-9).[7] The presence of the

[1] See, extensively, F Desportes and F Le Gunehec, *Le nouveau droit pénal* (1995) 275–301; R Koering-Joulin and A Huet, 'Compétence des tribunaux répressifs français et de la loi pénale française: Infractions commises à l'étranger' (1991) *Editions Techniques—Juris-Classeurs, Fascicule 20, procédure pénale, articles 689 à 696*. For a comparative study of the ambit of French and United States criminal law, see CL Blakesley, 'A Conceptual Framework for Extradition and Jurisdiction Over Extraterritorial Crimes' [1984] *Utah L Rev* 685.

[2] See the discussion of the *Lotus* case in ch 1 s A above.

[3] Reprinted in 84 *Journal du Palais* 229 (1873) (cited in Blakesley, n 1 above, 702).

[4] Quotation and translation taken from Blakesley (ibid) 702–3.

[5] Blakesley (ibid) 713–15 explains the French rationales for passive personality jurisdiction.

[6] Ibid 709, 714.

[7] A foreign pardon was an obstacle to prosecution under the previous code. With the new law, the legislature wanted to exclude the possibility of a purely opportunistic pardon. See Desportes

offender in France is not required, and a trial in his absence is possible:[8] the *Astiz* case is an example. In 1990 the *Cour d'assises* of Paris tried and convicted *in absentia* Captain Alfredo Astiz, a member of the Argentine military junta, for the kidnapping and disappearance in Argentina of two French nuns.[9] In the French component of the *Pinochet* case,[10] an examining magistrate in Paris issued an international warrant against the former head of State for false imprisonment accompanied by torture of French citizens in Chile.[11]

The provisions on the ambit of the penal code are complemented by a provision in the code of penal procedure (*Code de procédure pénale*, or CPP) on jurisdiction of the courts. Article 689 CPP states: 'The perpetrators or accomplices of offences committed abroad may be prosecuted and tried before French courts when French law applies to the offence by virtue of a provision in book I of the penal code or in any other legislative text, or when an international treaty gives French courts the right to take cognizance of the offence'.

In the latter case ('when an international treaty gives French courts the right to take cognizance of the offence') the application of French substantive law follows from the jurisdiction of the courts because of the 'solidarity between jurisdictional and legislative competence'.[12] The universality principle can be found in articles 689-1 to 689-10 CPP and in the laws governing the co-operation with the international tribunals for the former Yugoslavia and Rwanda.

Code de procédure pénale, articles 689-1 to 689-10

Articles 689-1 to 689-10 are an unusual combination of a domestic enabling clause (article 689-1) and an enumeration of international conventions providing for universal jurisdiction (articles 689-2 to 689-10). (It should be noted that the 1949 Geneva Conventions are not listed.) Article 689-1 reads, in part, as follows.

By virtue of the international conventions mentioned in the following articles (*en application des conventions internationals visées aux articles suivants*) may be

and Le Gunehec (n 1 above) 295. On *ne bis in idem* in French law, see T Vander Beken, *Forumkeuze in het internationaal strafrecht: Verdeling van misdrijven met aanknopingspunten in meerdere staten* (1999) 265–8.

[8] On the procedure where a defendant is tried in his absence (known as '*contumace*'), the consequences and the remedies, see R Vogler, 'Criminal Procedure in France' in J Hatchard, B Huber, and R Vogler (eds) *Comparative Criminal Procedure* (1996) 14, 83 and J Pradel, 'France' in C Van den Wyngaert (ed) *Criminal Procedure Systems in the European Community* (1993) 105, 133.

[9] *Public Prosecutor* v *Astiz*, Cour d'assises of Paris, 16 March 1990. For the antecedents of the *Astiz* case see NS Rodley, 'Torture, Extra-Legal Execution and "Disappearance" as Crimes under International Law' in PR David, *Crime and Criminal Policy: Papers in Honour of Manuel López-Rey Y Arrojo* (1985) 587, 595–7.

[10] See the Spain and United Kingdom country studies below.

[11] Cour d'appel de Paris. Tribunal de Grande Instance de Paris (examining magistrate), orders of 2 and 12 November 1998 (case note by B Stern in (1999) 93 *Am J Int'l L* 696).

[12] Desportes and Le Gunehec (n 1 above) 298.

prosecuted and tried by the French courts (*peut être poursuivie et jugée par les juridictions françaises*), if found in France (*si elle se trouve en France*), any person who has committed outside the territory of the Republic one of the offences enumerated in these articles (*toute personne qui s'est rendue coupable hors du territoire de la République de l'une des infractions énumérées par ces articles*).

French courts can base their competence on the enabling clause, provided the treaty is self-executing.[13] The enumeration in articles 689-2 to 689-10 is a mere 'mnemonic for the judges'.[14] Article 692 confirms the validity in the French legal order of foreign *res judicata*. Double criminality or ratification of the convention in question by the State of nationality of the offender or by the territorial State is not required.

ICTY/ICTR implementation and co-operation laws

Common article 2 of the laws governing the co-operation with the ICTY[15] and the ICTR[16] provide for jurisdiction over all offences falling within the competence *ratione materiae, loci*, and *temporis* of the *ad hoc* tribunals, if the perpetrators are found in France (*si les auteurs sont trouvés en France*).[17] The tribunals' statutes only require States to co-operate in the investigation and prosecution of suspects and to defer, if requested, to the competence of the tribunals. The French Minister of Justice explained that 'the establishment of universal jurisdiction, which is not required by the UN Security Council Resolution, is an important new development which expresses the willingness of France to collaborate as efficiently as possible in the prosecution of such crimes'.[18] Surprisingly, the later ICC collaboration law[19] does not provide for universal jurisdiction.

That special laws providing for retroactive universal jurisdiction were adopted suggests that atrocities committed in the former Yugoslavia or Rwanda

[13] C Lombois, 'De la compassion territoriale' [1995] *Revue de science criminelle et de droit pénal comparé* 399, 401.

[14] Ibid.

[15] Loi no 95-1 du 2 janvier 1995 portant adaptation de la législation française aux disposition de la résolution 827 du Conseil de Sécurité des Nations Unies instituant un tribunal international en vue de juger les personnes présumées responsables de violations graves du droit international humanitaire commises sur le territoire de l'ex-Yougoslavie depuis 1991, Journal Officiel de la République Française 3 January 1995.

[16] Loi no 96-432 du 22 mai 1996 portant adaptation de la législation française aux disposition de la résolution 955 du Conseil de Sécurité des Nations Unies instituant un tribunal international en vue de juger les personnes présumées responsables d'actes de génocide ou d'autres violations graves du droit international humanitaire commis en 1994 sur le territoire du Rwanda et, s'agissant des citoyens rwandais, sur le territoire d'Etats voisins, Journal Officiel de la République Française 23 May 1996.

[17] Common article 2, para 1.

[18] Circulaire du 10 février 1995 commentant la loi no 95-1 du 2 janvier 1995, Journal Officiel de la République Française 21 February 1995, and Circulaire du 22 juillet 1996 prise pour l'application de la loi no 96-432 du 22 mai 1996, Journal Officiel de la République Française 26 August 1996.

[19] Loi no 2002-268 du 26 février 2002 relative à la coopération avec la Cour pénale internationale, Journal Officiel de la République Française 27 February 2002.

could ordinarily not be prosecuted in France. Furthermore, extradition of a suspected *génocidaire* to Rwanda would be equally impossible because the Rwandan special genocide law[20] prescribes the death penalty for certain categories of *génocidaires*. Since France is a party to Protocol No 6 to the European Convention for the Protection of Human Rights and Fundamental Freedoms concerning the Abolition of the Death Penalty[21] it cannot extradite a suspect for a capital offence unless the requesting State gives an assurance that the death penalty will not be imposed, or if imposed, would not be executed.[22]

During the drafting of the laws a debate took place on whether, for French courts to be competent, there should be a link with the forum State. Human rights organizations opposed the condition that the suspect must be found in France.[23] The government contended that the elimination of this condition would be tantamount to endowing the French judiciary, not with a universal *competence*, but with a universal *vocation*.[24] An amendment that the victim's presence would be sufficient was rejected. The debate elicited some pertinent comments by Lombois:

> Universal jurisdiction—in the *current* state of criminal law in all countries, where legislative and judicial competence are linked—unfortunately makes the applicable law dependent—*retroactively*, against all principles—on the coincidental place of arrest. At least one can pretend to be convinced by the argument that the offender chooses his law, by choosing his refuge. But doesn't it go much too far to leave to a *private* party—motivated by revenge—the power to determine the applicable law? [...] If there are indeed cases where the criminal judge should apply foreign penal law, it is here, in the hypotheses of universal competence, that it is most urgent to start doing so. One should start *there*, before innovating conditions for its exercise[25] (emphasis in original).

Before turning to the case-law a few words are needed about the role victims can play in criminal proceedings.[26] The principle of prosecutorial discretion applies for territorial as well as extraterritorial offences. However, the victim of a crime may trigger proceedings himself by the mechanism of *constitution de partie civile* with an examining magistrate. The ICTY/ICTR implementation and co-operation laws explicitly affirm this right.[27] Civil

[20] Loi organique no 8196 du 30/8/96 sur l'organisation des poursuites des infractions constitutives du crime de génocide ou de crimes contre l'humanité, commises à partir du 1er octobre 1990, Journal Officiel de la République Rwandaise No 17 of 1 September 1996.

[21] Strasbourg, 23 April 1983; ETS 114.

[22] Affaire *Aylor*, Conseil d'État, 15 October 1993, reprinted in *Journal du droit international* (1994) 413 with case note by J Chappez. See also the discussion on jurisdiction, extradition, and human rights in ch 1 s D above.

[23] Lombois (n 13 above) 402–3; B Stern, 'La compétence universelle en France: Le cas des crimes commis en ex-Yougoslavie et au Rwanda' (1997) *German Ybk Int'l L* 280, 296–7.

[24] Lombois (n 13 above); Stern (n 23 above).

[25] Lombois (n 13 above) 403; Stern (n 23 above) 296–7, on the other hand, criticizes the law, arguing that universal jurisdiction properly understood does not require any link with the forum State.

[26] See Vogler (n 8 above) 25, 42–3, 72–3 and Pradel (n 8 above) 115.

[27] Common article 2 reads: 'Any person who claims to have suffered harm from an offence may initiate a criminal investigation (*peut se constituer partie civile*) under the ordinary rules of the code of penal procedure if French courts are competent'.

party status extends only to those who have suffered 'actual, personal and direct' injuries arising from the commission of a misdemeanour or felony.[28]

Although it is the responsibility of the prosecution to represent the public interest in conducting prosecutions, nevertheless certain organizations are authorized to intervene in particular cases. For example, civil party status in relevant cases is permissible for established organizations formed to combat racism (article 2-1 CPP), sexual violence (article 2-2 CPP), child abuse (article 2-3 CPP), war crimes (article 2-4 CPP), and discrimination (article 2-5 CPP). An examining magistrate who is seized by a civil party has an obligation to determine prior to opening an investigation whether he is competent. The magistrate's decision can be appealed by the civil party and by the prosecution before the *Chambre d'Accusation*, a division of the Court of Appeal. The appeal decision can be appealed before the *Cour de Cassation*. In each instance the civil party and the prosecution are heard.

B. CASE-LAW

Victims of the wars and ethnic violence in the former Yugoslavia and Rwanda or their relatives have tried to set in motion the French criminal justice system. Before dealing with some decisions in these cases it is appropriate to mention the remarkable view of the *Cour de Cassation* on the spatial dimension of crimes against humanity. In the famous *Barbie* case[29] the court held: '[B]y reason of their nature, the crimes against humanity with which Klaus Barbie, who claims German nationality, is charged in France where those crimes were committed, do not simply fall within the scope of French municipal law but *are subject of an international criminal order to which the notions of frontiers and extradition rules arising therefrom are completely foreign*'[30] (emphasis added). In these unambiguous terms France's highest court recognized that crimes against humanity transcend State sovereignty, and that notions of frontiers are therefore inapplicable.

Javor et al. v *X*

The case of *Javor* et al. v *X*[31] is the result of a complaint (*constitution de partie civile*) by Bosnian refugees in July 1993, thus *before* the adoption by

[28] Vogler (n 8 above) 26.

[29] *Fédération Nationale des Déportés et Internés Résistants et Patriotes and Others* v *Barbie*, 6 October 1983, reprinted in *Journal du droit international* (1983) 779 with case note by B Edelman; English translation published in 78 *Int'l L Reports* 125.

[30] Quotation taken from the English translation in 78 *Int'l L Reports* 128. For an extensive comment on this passage see Edelman (ibid) 790–5.

[31] Tribunal de Grande Instance de Paris (examining magistrate), 6 May 1994; Cour d'Appel de Paris, 24 October 1994; Cour de Cassation (chambre criminelle), 26 March 1994 (copies on

the French parliament of the ICTY co-operation law. The plaintiffs alleged that acts of torture, grave breaches, crimes against humanity, and genocide were committed upon them in a Serbian detention camp in the former Yugoslavia. The complaint did not name perpetrators or suggest that a perpetrator might be present on French territory.

It should be noted that crimes against humanity and genocide were only introduced in the French penal code on 1 March 1994.[32] At the relevant time France and Bosnia and Herzegovina were parties to the Genocide Convention, the 1949 Geneva Conventions and Additional Protocols, and the UN Torture Convention.[33]

The examining magistrate[34] held that absent an explicit provision on universal jurisdiction in the Genocide Convention he lacked jurisdiction over genocide. He also found he had no jurisdiction over crimes against humanity because in the French legal order the concept of crimes against humanity was at that time confined to World War II.[35] On the other hand, he declared himself competent to investigate the torture and grave breaches allegations.

The Paris Court of Appeal confirmed the decision with regard to genocide and crimes against humanity but reversed it in respect of torture and grave breaches. The Court stated that by virtue of articles 5 and 7 of the UN Torture Convention and article 689-2 CPP, 'universal jurisdiction of French courts over torture results from an objective and material link (*un élément objectif et matériel de rattachement*) consisting of the presence of the presumed culprit on French territory'.[36] In the absence of any indications of such presence, French judicial authorities have no jurisdiction. Regarding grave breaches the Court ruled that article 689 CPP is not a sufficient basis because the 1949 Geneva Conventions are not self-executing.

The extremely succinct decision of the Court of Cassation[37] states that the interpretation of the Court of Appeal is correct, that the ICTY implementation

file with author). For comments see, extensively, R Maison, 'Les premiers cas d'applications des dispositions pénales des Conventions de Genève par les jurisdictions internes' (1995) 6 *Eur J Int'l L* 260–73 and Stern (n 23 above).

[32] The current penal code, which criminalizes crimes against humanity (article 212-1) and genocide (article 211-1), came into effect on 1 March 1994 and therefore applies only partially to the conflict in Bosnia, which started in 1991.

[33] Yugoslavia became a party to the UN Torture Convention on 10 September 1991, Bosnia and Herzegovina (by succession) on 1 September 1993.

[34] N 31 above.

[35] Before 1 March 1994 crimes against humanity were incorporated in the French legal order by reference to the Nuremberg Principles (Law of 26 December 1964). However, French jurisprudence had restricted crimes against humanity to crimes committed in the context of World War II by or on behalf of the Axis powers. See C Grynfogel, 'Le concept de crime contre l'humanité: Hier, aujourd'hui et demain' (1994) 74 *Revue de Droit Pénal et de Criminologie* 13; L Sadat Wexler, 'The interpretation of the Nuremberg Principles by the French Court of Cassation: From Touvier to Barbie and Back Again' (1994) 32 *Columbia J Transn'l L* 289.

[36] N 31 above 7–8.

[37] N 31 above.

and co-operation law of 2 January 1995—adopted *after* the decision of the Court of Appeal—endows French courts with jurisdiction if the perpetrators 'are found in France', and that the sole presence in France of *victims* is not a sufficient basis for universal jurisdiction.

In *Javor* et al. v *X*, positivism and dualism prevailed over the radical cosmopolitan view on international criminal justice that had emerged in the *Barbie* case.[38] That the 1949 Geneva Conventions are not self-executing is contrary to French doctrine which had considered them to be directly applicable since their ratification by France in 1951[39] and contrasts with judicial decisions in Denmark, Germany, and Switzerland.[40] The narrow (yet correct) interpretation of article VI of the Genocide Convention stands out against decisions of the highest courts in Austria, Germany, Israel, and Spain.[41] On the other hand, the requirement that the suspect be present is consonant with decisions in Belgium, Denmark, Germany, and the Netherlands.[42] *Javor* set the stage for the Rwandan litigation which was already well under way.

Dupaquier et al. v *Munyeshyaka*

The case of *Dupaquier* et al. v *Munyeshyaka*[43] is one of several cases[44] that arose out of the presence in France of alleged *génocidaires* from Rwanda.[45] These cases differ from the Bosnian case in four respects. First, the complaints named names and hiding places in France and the alleged offences had taken place after the introduction of the new penal code, which, as noted above, criminalizes genocide and crimes against humanity. Second, one cannot overlook the many connections between France and the dramatic events in Rwanda: France had a strong foothold in Rwanda before the

[38] The decision was strongly criticized by some French scholars. Maison (n 31 above) 272–3 argues that the sole presence of the victim justifies the exercise of jurisdiction under the 1949 Geneva Conventions. Also critical are Stern (n 23 above) and M Massé, 'Ex-Yugoslavie, Rwanda: Une compétence "virtuelle" des juridictions françaises?' (1997) *Revue de science criminelle et de droit pénal comparé* 893–8.

[39] See Lombois (n 13 above) 401.

[40] See the respective country studies in this book. See also a 1996 decision of the Hungarian Constitutional Court (Decision No 36/1996 (IX. 4) AB of the Constitutional Court (Official Journal: 1996/75 pp 4673–5)) which held the Geneva Conventions to be directly applicable (discussed in (1998) 1 *Ybk Int'l Humanitarian L* 451). Whether an international convention can be directly applicable in the domestic legal order is, however, purely a matter of national law.

[41] See the respective country studies in this book.

[42] Ibid.

[43] Tribunal de Grande Instance de Privas (examining magistrate), 9 January 1996; Cour d'Appel de Nimes, 20 March 1996; Cour de Cassation (chambre criminelle), 6 January 1998 (copies on file with author). The text of the latter decision is reprinted in 102 *Revue Générale de Droit International Public* 1998, 825–32; an English translation is published in (1998) 1 *Ybk Int'l Humanitarian L* 598.

[44] The other cases include *Biziyaremye* et al. v *Munyemana*, and *Reporters sans Frontières* v *Radio-Télévision Libre des Milles Collines* (copies on file with author). Apparently these cases were not pursued after the decision of the examining magistrate not to open an instruction for lack of jurisdiction.

[45] The Rwanda context is discussed in ch 3 s B above.

conflict,[46] had intervened during the conflict,[47] and had assisted at the end of the conflict with the controversial 'evacuation' of some four hundred Rwandans closely linked to the defeated regime.[48] Third, the UN Security Council, of which France is a permanent member, had urged States 'to arrest and detain [...] persons found within their territory against whom there is sufficient evidence that they were responsible for acts within the jurisdiction of the International Criminal Tribunal for Rwanda',[49] whereas apparently no such resolution was adopted with regard to the former Yugoslavia. Finally, extradition of a suspected *génocidaire* to Rwanda would be difficult for the reasons set out above.

Wenceslas Munyeshyaka, the accused, fled to France shortly after the dramatic events in Rwanda in 1994. In July 1995, thus *before* the adoption by the French parliament of the ICTR Co-operation law, some individuals acting on behalf of victims[50] filed a complaint against him for his alleged role in the events. The public prosecutor entrusted an examining magistrate with a brief to investigate (*réquisitoire afin d'informer*) the conduct of the accused in Rwanda during the time of the armed conflict there, citing articles 689, 689-1, and 689-2 CPP and the UN Torture Convention as a basis for jurisdiction, and articles 211-1 (genocide) and 212-1 (crimes against humanity) CP. The magistrate ruled that he was competent for the torture charges only.[51]

The Court of Appeal reversed that ruling.[52] Jurisdiction can only be established on the basis of the most serious and most specific offence. Since the acts committed by the suspect, if proven, constituted genocide, jurisdiction must be established on that basis. Since neither the Genocide Convention nor the French penal code provide for universal jurisdiction over genocide, French courts have no jurisdiction over the events in Rwanda.

The Court of Cassation quashed the appeals decision on two grounds.[53] First, the alleged acts fall under the definition of the torture (as defined in article 1 of the UN Torture Convention) and therefore can be prosecuted in France. Second, the ICTR co-operation law, which had meanwhile been adopted, applies to the case. After more than two years of litigation there was a final decision on jurisdiction and investigation of the allegations could begin.

[46] A report of the French parliament on the tragic events in Rwanda acknowledges that the French government had erred in supporting a government bent on genocide. See Assemblée Nationale, Rapport d'information déposé en application de l'article 145 du règlement par la mission d'information de la commission de la défense nationale et des forces armées et de la commission des affaires étrangères, sur les opérations militaires menées par la France, d'autres pays et l'ONU au Rwanda entre 1990 et 1994 (15 December 1998).

[47] Opération Turquoise, carried out with a UN mandate, was officially a humanitarian intervention, but see the very critical Human Rights Watch and International Federation of Human Rights Leagues, *Leave None to Tell the Story: Genocide in Rwanda* (1999) 668–90.

[48] Ibid 613.

[49] See ch 3 s B above.

[50] It is not clear from the available documents what the relationship was between the plaintiffs and the victims on whose behalf the complaint was filed.

[51] N 43 above.

[52] Ibid.

[53] Ibid.

The three decisions in *Dupaquier* et al. v *Munyeshyaka* are extremely concise and pay hardly any attention to international law or the recent developments in international criminal law. Two substantive comments can be made, however. Given the strict positivist reasoning, it is surprising that the French judiciary was willing to assert jurisdiction on the basis of the UN Torture Convention even though Rwanda was not party to that Convention. The issue was apparently never raised; perhaps it was simply overlooked. Second, the Court of Cassation's decision that the alleged acts fall under the definition of torture (as defined in article 1 of the UN Torture Convention) contrasts with a decision of the highest court of the Netherlands that the killing of a person without first torturing him does not constitute torture.[54] Since the final decision on jurisdiction little seems to have been accomplished. What is more, eight years after the Rwandan genocide several protagonists reportedly reside unchallenged in France.[55]

Fédération Internationale des Ligues des Droits de l'Homme et al. v *Ould Dah*

After *Javor* and *Munyeshyaka*, human rights organizations[56] initiated proceedings against several foreign visitors and residents on the basis of the UN Torture Convention in conjunction with the relevant CPP and CP provisions.[57] One such case is *Fédération Internationale des Ligues des Droits de l'Homme* et al. v *Ould Dah*,[58] which concerned a Mauritanian army captain at a training camp in France. The plaintiffs, former Mauritanian army officers now living in France, alleged brutalities upon them in Mauritania in 1990/91.

A debate ensued before the examining magistrate over the competence of French courts because torture as such was not a crime under French law until the entry into force of article 222-1 CP on 1 March 1994 and because the facts complained of fell under a Mauritanian amnesty law.[59] (The fact that Mauritania is not a party to the UN Torture Convention was not raised.)

With regard to the first issue, the magistrate noted that under French law before 1994 torture constituted an aggravating circumstance of offences

[54] See the *Bouterse* case in the Netherlands country study below.

[55] *De Standaard*, 26 April 2002, reports that the ICTR prosecutor has taken up the issue with French authorities.

[56] As noted above, civil party status is permissible for established organizations formed to combat *inter alia* racism, war crimes, and discrimination.

[57] See *Le Monde*, 4 March 2002: '*Les ONG cherchent à faire appliquer en France la "compétence universelle"*'.

[58] *Fédération Internationale des Ligues des Droits de l'Homme* et al. v *Ould Dah*, Cour d'Appel de Montpellier (examining magistrate), 25 May 2001 (copy on file with author).

[59] Article 1 of law no 93-23 of 14 June 1993 provides that 'full and total amnesty is given to the members of the armed forces and the security forces responsible for offences committed between 1 January 1989 and 18 April 1992 in respect of the events which took place within these forces and which led to armed actions and violent acts'.

against the life, physical integrity, or freedom of a person. With regard to the amnesty law, the judge took the view that 'whatever the legitimacy of an amnesty in the context of a local policy of reconciliation, this law has effect only in the territory of the State concerned and is not opposable to third countries in the context of the application of international law'. Having thus established his jurisdiction, the magistrate issued an indictment on charges of torture and ordered a trial.

The decision in *Fédération Internationale des Ligues des Droits de l'Homme* et al. v *Ould Dah* conforms with French law and the UN Torture Convention, which was drafted with a scenario such as the instant case in mind. The trial could have been the very first by a municipal court on the basis of universal jurisdiction over torture, had the accused not managed to sneak out of France despite judicial control measures.

C. SUMMARY

France, the plaintiff in *Lotus*, now claims itself to have general passive personality jurisdiction. When French nationals were victimized abroad, judicial authorities have been willing to prosecute and convict the foreign perpetrator, even in his absence. Universal jurisdiction, on the other hand, is only established if a treaty obliges it to do so. Exceptions are the ICTY/ICTR co-operation laws which provide for retrospective universal jurisdiction over offences within the jurisdiction of both tribunals, provided there is an 'objective and material link consisting of the presence of the presumed culprit on French territory'. Years of litigation have produced few concrete results. In one case the investigation has dragged on since 1995, in the other case the suspect managed to leave France before his trial. Trials on the basis of universal jurisdiction for violations of international humanitarian law are not to be expected because the ICC co-operation law does not provide such a basis and the 1949 Geneva Conventions, which have been held to be non-self executing, lack implementation.

10

Germany

A. AMBIT OF THE CRIMINAL LAW

The geographical scope of application (*räumlicher Geltungsbereich*) of the German penal code (*Strafgesetzbuch*, or StGB) is spelled out in its §§3–7.[1] StGB §3 expresses the basic principle: 'German penal law is applicable to acts committed within the country'.[2] Extraterritorial offences are subdivided into three categories: offences against nationally protected rights or interests (*Auslandstaten gegen inländische Rechtsgüter*) (§5), offences against internationally protected rights or interests (*Auslandstaten gegen international geschützte Rechtsgüter*) (§6), and 'other situations' (*Geltung für Auslandstaten in anderen Fällen*) (§7). The first category comprises fifteen crimes[3] that are punishable irrespective of the law of the *locus delicti*, provided there is a specific link with Germany at the time of commission. The category 'other situations' includes a general passive (§7(1))[4] and general active personality clause (§7(2)(1)),[5] both subject to double criminality. The universality principle can be found in StGB §6, StGB §7(2)(2), and in the Code of Crimes Against International Law.

I warmly thank Dr Claus Kreß for his many suggestions and critical comments.

[1] As noted in the Austria country study, Germany and Austria collaborated in the drafting of their current penal codes. One of the results is a quasi-identical geographical ambit: §§3–7 of the German and §§62–65 of the Austrian code are textually similar.

[2] From 1940 until 1975 the territoriality principle applied only to foreigners; crimes by Germans were governed by the active personality principle, even when committed in Germany. See D Oehler, *Internationales Strafrecht. Geltungsbereich des Strafrechts. Internationales Rechtshilferecht. Recht der Gemeinschaften, Völkerstrafrecht* (2nd ed, 1983) 122 and C Pappas, *Stellvertretende Strafrechtspflege* (1996) 53–4.

[3] This category includes a mixture of offences such as high treason, industrial espionage, abortion, and traffic in human organs.

[4] StGB §7(1) reads: 'German criminal law applies to offences committed abroad against a German national, if the act is punishable under the law of the *locus delicti* or if the *locus delicti* is not subject to any criminal jurisdiction'. A Henrich, *Das passive Personalitätsprinzip im deutschen Strafrecht* (1994) 118 reports only three cases of passive personality jurisdiction. Recently the Federal Supreme Court ruled that Germany has jurisdiction over offences in Chile during the Pinochet dictatorship against German nationals: Bundesgerichtshof, 18 November 1998, partially reprinted in H Ahlbrecht and K Ambos (eds) *Der Fall Pinochet(s): Auslieferung wegen staatsverstärkter Kriminalität?* (1999) 100; see also K Thun, 'Zur Strafverfolgung Pinochets in der Bundesrepublik Deutschland' in ibid 19.

[5] StGB §7(2)(1) reads: 'German criminal law applies to offences committed abroad by a German national or by a person who became a German national after the offence, if the offence is punishable under the law of the *locus delicti* or if the *locus delicti* is not subject to any criminal jurisdiction'. It should be noted that extradition of nationals is constitutionally forbidden but a December 2000 amendment allows for exceptions to the International Criminal Court and to European Union countries.

Strafgesetzbuch §6 'Offences Against Internationally Protected Interests or Rights'

German doctrine unanimously considers StGB §6 to be an expression of the universality principle (*Weltrechtsprinzip*).[6] It provides as follows.

German criminal law applies, irrespective of the law of the *locus delicti*, to the following acts committed abroad:

(1) genocide (§220a);[7]
(2) crimes involving atomic energy, explosives, and radiation in cases under §§307, 308 (I) to (IV), 309(II), and 310;
(3) attacks on air and sea traffic (§316c);
(4) traffic in human beings (§180b) and aggravated traffic in human beings (§181);
(5) unauthorized distribution of narcotics;
(6) dissemination of pornography in cases under §184(III) & (IV);
(7) forgery of currency and securities (§§146, 151, and 152), forgery of credit cards and forms for eurocheques (§152a(I) to (IV)), as well as their preparation (§§149, 151, 152, and 152a(V));
(8) economic subsidy fraud (§264);
(9) acts that are to be prosecuted by the terms of an international treaty binding on the Federal Republic of Germany even if they are committed outside the country.

All but one[8] of the offences on this heterogeneous list are the subject of a treaty, but in several cases the German legislature has gone further than the treaty terms. For instance, there is no basis for universal jurisdiction in the International Convention for the Suppression of White Slave Traffic,[9] in the International Convention for the Suppression of the Circulation of and Traffic in Obscene Materials,[10] or in the Genocide Convention.[11]

The final paragraph of StGB §6 is a domestic enabling clause similar to those found in Austrian, Belgian, Danish, French, Israeli, and Spanish law.[12] StGB §6(9) offers the basis for universal jurisdiction over *inter alia* grave breaches of the 1949 Geneva Conventions,[13] terrorism, hostage taking, and

[6] For a comprehensive and rigorous analysis of StGB §6 see K Ambos in *Münchener Kommentar zum StGB*, vol 1, 97–112.

[7] This provision was repealed on 30 June 2002 when the Code of Crimes Against International Law entered into force (see below).

[8] An exception is detonating explosives (StGB §6(2) and §308).

[9] Paris, 4 May 1910; 1 LNTS 83.

[10] Geneva, 12 September 1923; 27 LNTS 213. This convention was even renounced by Germany in 1974. See P Wilkitzki, 'Federal Republic of Germany' (1989) 60 *Revue internationale de droit pénal* 263, 274.

[11] See the discussion of the Genocide Convention in ch 3 above.

[12] For comments on StGB §6(9) see Ambos (n 6 above) 107–12 and *StGB Leipziger Kommentar: Großkommentar* (1997) 146–50; on the implementation of international criminal law (conventions) in the German legal order, see Wilkitzki (n 10 above) 270–7.

[13] Germany has not otherwise implemented the penal aspects of the 1949 Geneva Conventions. The terms 'war crimes' and 'grave breaches' do not appear in the penal code. See, extensively, SR Lüder, 'National Repression of Violations of International Humanitarian Law

torture, because Germany has ratified the relevant conventions.[14] Nothing in the text of StGB §6 requires a link with Germany. As will be seen, the issue has generated debate as a result of recent jurisprudence.

Strafgesetzbuch §7(2) subparagraph 2

StGB §7(2)(2) is a domestic *aut dedere aut judicare* clause and represents what was called in chapter 2 above the co-operative general universality principle, ie the secondary or subsidiary jurisdiction of the custodial State over all serious offences if extradition of the suspect is impracticable. As noted above, the earliest version of a municipal *aut dedere aut judicare* clause appeared in the Austrian penal code of 1803; its introduction into German law dates from 1940.[15] It should be noted that the German Extradition Act does *not* make extradition conditional on the existence of a treaty. But as shown in chapter 1, international human rights law *does* increasingly impact on extradition, which may explain the clause's growing practical relevance.[16] StGB §7(2)(2) provides:

> German criminal law also applies to any act committed abroad if the act is a criminal offence under the law of the *locus delicti*, or the *locus delicti* is not subject to any criminal jurisdiction, and if the offender was a foreigner at the time of commission of the offence, is found in Germany and is not extradited, although by the nature of the act he could be extradited under the German Extradition Act, because a request for extradition is not made or is rejected, or because extradition is not feasible.

This basis of jurisdiction is known in Germany as *stellvertretende Strafrechtspflege*,[17] and is distinguished from the universality principle in §6. The theoretical difference, according to German doctrine, is that the first is an exercise of criminal jurisdiction on behalf of another State, whereas jurisdiction on the basis of the latter is exercised on behalf of the world community.

StGB §7(2)(2) is a subsidiary basis for jurisdiction. Only if all other provisions are inapplicable can a prosecution be based on it[18] and three conditions must then be fulfilled. First, the act must be 'punishable' under the law of the

under German Domestic Law' (1997), unpublished paper presented at a Meeting of Experts on 'National Repression of Violations of International Humanitarian law', Geneva 23–5 September 1997, organized by the International Committee of the Red Cross.

[14] Respectively the European Convention on the Suppression of Terrorism, the International Convention Against the Taking of Hostages, and the UN Torture Convention; for an exhaustive list see Ambos (n 6 above) 108–12.

[15] Pappas (n 2 above) 45.

[16] For the increased practical relevance of StGB §7(2)(2) see R Schmitz, '§7 II Nr. 2 StGB und das Prinzip der stellvertretenden Strafrechtspflege' in E Samson (ed) *Festschrift für Gerald Grünwald* (1999) 619, 625–7.

[17] Translated in English as 'representation principle' or 'vicarious administration of justice'. See eg J Meyer, 'The Vicarious Administration of Justice: An Overlooked Basis of Jurisdiction' (1990) 31 *Harvard Int'l LJ* 108. For a thorough analysis of StGB §7(2)(2), see Pappas (n 2 above).

[18] Pappas (ibid) 14. As will be seen in the case-law section below, StGB §7(2)(2) has been used concurrently with StGB §6.

territorial State (*am Tatort mit Strafe bedroht*). This means that there must be a similar criminal norm[19] at the time of commission,[20] that prosecution is not barred by a statute of limitations,[21] and that no final decision has been rendered. Second, the suspect must be 'found in Germany' (*im Inland betroffen*), ie voluntarily present.[22] Third, he is not extradited because a request for extradition is not made or is rejected, or because extradition is for whatever reason 'not feasible' (*nicht ausführbar*). Non-feasibility presupposes, of course, that the offence is extraditable *per se*. However, no request or consent by the foreign authority is required and prosecution can even take place against its will. Arguably, this has little to do with administration of justice on behalf of another State, which is what *stellvertretende Strafrechtspflege* is supposed to be.[23]

Völkerstrafgesetzbuch

To bring domestic law into line with the ICC Statute, Germany has opted for a unique solution: a national Code of Crimes Against International Law (*Völkerstrafgesetzbuch*, or VStGB)[24] which makes the core ICC crimes offences under domestic law.[25] The Act introducing the Code distinguishes between applicability of the law and jurisdiction of the courts. The *applicability of the law* is defined in VStGB §1 under the heading *Anwendungsbereich*: 'This Act shall apply to all criminal offences against international law designated under this Act, to serious criminal offences (*Verbrechen*) designated therein even when the offence was committed abroad and bears no relation to Germany (*wenn die Tat im Ausland begangen wurde und keinen Bezug zum Inland aufweist*)'.

Like StGB §6, the Code provides for universal jurisdiction. One would not have expected otherwise. New, however, is the specification that the Code

[19] See A Eser, 'Grundlagen und Grenzen "stellvertretender Strafrechtspflege" (§7 Abs. 2 Nr. 2 StGB). Zur Problematik der "indentischen Tatortnorm" bei Auslandstaten, insbesondere bei Amnestierung am Tatort' [1993] *Juristenzeitung* 875.

[20] This is the prevailing view, but an important minority position holds that the act must still be punishable at the time of the German judgment. Eg Schmitz (n 16 above) 630–5.

[21] According to the traditional view (eg *Goltdammer's Archiv für Strafrecht* (1976) 242) it is irrelevant whether the foreign prosecution is barred by a statute of limitation; but a strong minority position holds the position stated in the text (eg O Lagodny and C Pappas, 'Urteilsanmerkung' [1994] *Juristenzeitung* 162.

[22] On the meaning of 'found in Germany' in StGB §7(2)(2) see D Oehler, 'Auslieferungsersuchen, Einlieferung und der Geltungsbereich des Strafrechts', in *Festschrift der Rechtswissenschaftlichen Fakultät zur 600-Jahr-Feier der Universität zu Köln* (1988) 489, 497–500.

[23] Pappas (n 2 above) 229 proposes therefore the amendment of StGB §7(2)(2) so that *stellvertretende Strafrechtspflege* can take place only at the request of the territorial State; Schmitz (n 16 above) 639 calls for its complete deletion.

[24] The Code of Crimes Against International Law is part of the Act of 26 June 2002 to Introduce the Code of Crimes Against International Law (*Gesetz zur Einführung des Völkerstrafgesetzbuches*), Bundesgesetzblatt Teil I, 2002 Nr 42, 2254. The Act, which is largely based on the preparatory work of a specialist working group established by the Federal Ministry of Justice, entered into force on 30 June 2002.

[25] The Act repeals all provisions on genocide in the StGB.

applies even when the offence bears no relation to Germany. As will be seen, the jurisprudence of the Federal Supreme Court, in the cases hitherto presented to it, attaches great importance to the existence of links. The explanatory memorandum to the Act[26] makes clear that the government does not share this view:

> The offences specified in this code always threaten the vital interests of the international community. The ICC Statute describes them as 'the most serious crimes of concern to the international community as a whole'. Therefore, they have a transnational (*grenzüberschreitenden*) character and are subject to the universality principle. Because of their particular impact, prosecution of extraterritorial offences, even those committed by foreigners, does not constitute an illegitimate interference with the sovereignty of other States. The application of German criminal law to extraterritorial acts that constitute an offence under the VStGB is therefore not dependent on the existence of a special domestic connection (*Inlandsbezug*). Because the federal Supreme Court has so far given a different interpretation to StGB §6, the unambiguous wording of VStGB §1 now makes it very clear that offences under the VStGB, in any event, do not require a special domestic link.[27]

The *jurisdiction of German courts* over extraterritorial offences under the VStGB is spelled out in a new §153f in the code of penal procedure (*Strafprozeßordnung*, or StPO). StPO §153f reads, in part, as follows.

> (1) In the cases referred to under §153c subsection (1), numbers 1 and 2, the public prosecution may dispense (*kann absehen*) with prosecuting an offence punishable pursuant to VStGB §§6 to 14, if the accused is not residing in Germany and such residence is not to be anticipated (*wenn sich der Beschuldigte nicht im Inland aufhält und ein solcher Aufenthalt auch nich zu erwarten ist.* [...]
>
> (2) In the cases referred to under §153c subsection (1), numbers 1 and 2, the public prosecution shall dispense (*soll absehen*) with prosecuting an offence punishable pursuant to VStGB §§6 to 14, if:
> 1. there is no suspicion of a German having committed such an offence,
> 2. such offence was not committed against a German,
> 3. no suspect in respect of such offence is residing in Germany and such residence is not to be anticipated (*kein Tatverdächtiger sich im Inland aufhält und ein solcher Aufenthalt auch nich zu erwarten ist*), and
> 4. the offence is being prosecuted before an international court or by a state on whose territory the offence was committed, whose national is suspected of its commission or whose national was harmed by the offence.
>
> The same shall apply if a foreigner accused of an offence committed abroad is residing in Germany but the requirements pursuant to the first sentence, numbers 2 and 4, have been fulfilled and transfer to an international court or extradition to the prosecuting State is permissible and considered.

[26] The explanatory memorandum (*Begründung*) of the government runs 91 pages (copy on file with author).

[27] Ibid 31 (citations omitted).

(3) If in the cases referred to under subsection (1) or (2) criminal proceedings have already been initiated, the public prosecution office may withdraw the charges at any stage of the proceedings and terminate the proceedings.

By virtue of StPO §153f(1) judicial authorities *may* decline to prosecute a foreigner suspected of having committed abroad an offence under the VStGB if he is not present in Germany and such presence is not to be anticipated. StPO §153f(2), for its part, provides the cumulative conditions that *bar* criminal proceedings in Germany in respect of extraterritorial offences by a foreigner under the VStGB: the victim is not German, the foreign suspect is not present in Germany, and the offence is being prosecuted before an international court or a municipal court in the territorial state, in the State of nationality of the suspect, or in the State of nationality of the victim. Prosecution is also barred if a foreign suspect is present in Germany, the victim was not a German, and transfer of the suspect to an international court or extradition to another State is permissible and considered (StPO §153 f(2) *in fine*). *A contrario*, prosecution in all other situations is mandatory. The explanatory memorandum adds that a journey (*Aufenthalt*) through Germany is considered a presence for purposes of StPO §153f.[28]

Summarizing, the Code of Crimes Against International Law applies irrespective of the *locus delicti* or the nationality of the offender (VStGB §1) but constraints of a procedural nature limit the jurisdiction of German courts (StPO §153f). The more likely a prosecution before an international tribunal or a national court with a link to the offence, the less German courts are competent; conversely, the less probable such a prosecution, the more 'universal' the jurisdiction of German courts.

Some constitutional and procedural issues need to be pointed out before reviewing the German cases. Article 25 of the Federal Constitution (*Grundgesetz*, or GG) provides that the general rules of public international law are part of the domestic legal order and have precedence over municipal laws. Thus, jurisdiction provisions have to be construed and applied in conformity with public international law. GG article 103(2) states that an act can only be punished if made punishable by law before its commission. *Ne bis in idem* is laid down in GG article 103(3), but a *foreign* judgment is no bar to a subsequent prosecution in Germany.[29]

With regard to procedure,[30] genocide and other serious offences (including hostage taking and attacks on air traffic), whether committed within or

[28] Ibid 88–9.

[29] HH Jescheck and T Weigend, *Lehrbuch des Strafrechts: Allgemeiner Teil* (5th edn, 1996) 176; Lüder (n 13 above) 13, citing a decision of the Federal Constitutional Court (Bundesverfassungsgericht, Official Records, vol 12, 66); T Vander Beken, *Forumkeuze in het internationaal strafrecht: Verdeling van misdrijven met aanknopingspunten in meerdere staten* (1999) 260–3.

[30] See generally: T Weigend, 'Germany' in CM Bradley (ed) *Criminal Procedure: A World Wide Study* (1999) 187; B Huber, 'Criminal Procedure in Germany' in J Hatchard, B Huber, and

without Germany, can only be prosecuted by federal authorities (*Generalbundesanwalt*).[31] Crime victims can participate in the criminal proceedings (StPO §§374–406h). Proceedings *in absentia* against an accused who is abroad are possible (StPO §276), but only for the purpose of preserving evidence for a possible future trial (StPO §285(1)).

B. CASE-LAW

By comparison with other countries, more foreigners have been prosecuted in Germany for crimes committed abroad against foreigners.[32] The present overview is limited to decisions that have significantly contributed to the jurisprudence on German extraterritorial jurisdiction.

Public Prosecutor v *Dost*

Public Prosecutor v *Dost*[33] is one of several cases before German courts involving foreigners who deal in soft drugs abroad. Typically, the dealer is a Dutch national who carries out his activities in the Netherlands near the German border.[34] The unlicensed sale or distribution of soft drugs is a criminal offence under both Dutch and German law, but the two countries have very different prosecutorial policies. The permissive attitude in the Netherlands attracts 'drug tourists' from countries with stricter policies, thereby frustrating those policies.[35]

In this case, Harm Dost, a Dutch national, worked in a crisis centre for drug addicts in a city near the German border. In that capacity he distributed hashish to young Germans who smuggled the drug into Germany and used or sold it there. Dost was arrested by the German authorities at a border crossing and was prosecuted and convicted for selling drugs in the Netherlands, in violation of the German Narcotic Drugs Law.[36] The Dutch authorities neither

R Vogler (eds) *Comparative Criminal Procedure* (1996) 96; HH Kühne, 'Germany' in C Van den Wyngaert (ed) *Criminal Procedure Systems in the European Community* (1993) 137.

[31] Gerichtsverfassungsgesetz §120(8) in combination with §142(a)(1).

[32] Pappas (n 2 above) 27–44 reports 11 prosecutions based on StGB §7(2)(2).

[33] Bundesgerichtshof, 20 October 1976, reprinted in 27 *Entscheidungen des Bundesgerichtshofs in Strafsachen* 30; English translation published in 74 *Int'l L Reports* 166.

[34] A Puttler, 'Extraterritorial Application of Criminal Law: Jurisdiction to Prosecute Drug Traffic Conducted by Aliens Abroad' in KM Meessen (ed) *Extraterritorial Jurisdiction in Theory and Practice* (1996) 103, 104. A Turkish national has reportedly also been convicted in Germany for dealing drugs in neighbouring Belgium; see A Krikke, 'De zaak-Dost: De rechtsmacht van de Bondsrepubliek bij de bestrijding van verdovende middelen' [1976] *Recht en Kritiek* 249, 250.

[35] Puttler (n 34 above) 104.

[36] Factual summary based on the judgment (n 33 above) and on Krikke (note 34 above) 249. The case seems to have generated more academic debate in the Netherlands than in Germany. See in addition to the works already cited: HD Cotterell 'Harm Dost en uitlevering' (1976) 51 *Nederlands Juristenblad* 830; AMM Orie, 'Internationaal strafrechtelijke aspecten van de Dost-affaire' (1976) 30 *Nederlands Juristenblad* 1045.

protested nor requested his extradition.[37] The trial court based its jurisdiction on StGB §6(5).

Dost appealed to the Federal Supreme Court (*Bundesgerichtshof*) claiming that §6(5) violates the non-interference principle (*Nichteinmischungsprinzip*) and therefore also GG article 25.[38] The Court held that StGB §6(5) is not incompatible with any general rule of international law within the meaning of GG article 25 and dismissed the appeal. The decision, which elaborates on the limits of State jurisdiction in general, merits quotation at length.

> Even if it is derived from [the non-interference principle] that it does not automatically follow from the sovereignty of States that they have the unrestricted right to extend their criminal jurisdiction to offences committed outside their territory, this would not lead to the conclusion that a general rule of international law existed with which StGB §6(5) was in conflict. *The very existence of such a rule is even today still disputed.* There appears to be even less consensus with regard to the extent of the restrictions placed by international law on the power of the national legislature to establish rules for the application of its criminal sanctions in such circumstances. *This Court is inclined to accept the proposition that any extension of State criminal jurisdiction to offences committed abroad by aliens requires the presence of some factor, connecting the case to the forum, which constitutes a justifiable basis for the exercise of jurisdiction.* There are, however, no clear criteria under international law for determining the weight to be given to such factors and the extent to which they may affect the national legislature's competence to establish such norms.
>
> In the struggle against criminality associated with drugs, the German legislature, in StGB §6(5), has resorted to the principle of the universal application of law. The decision to have recourse to this principle was not imperative, as the accused rightly points out in his grounds of appeal. The legislature could have chosen to adopt the principle of vicarious enforcement of criminal law (*stellvertretende Strafrechtspflege*), under which the liability of an offender to prosecution under German law is dependant upon the existence of corresponding provisions under the *lex loci* and the fact that the offender has not been extradited although his extradition would have been admissible in the circumstances (cf StGB §7(2)(2)). Contrary to the submissions contained in the grounds of appeal, however, this was not the only legally valid path which the legislature could have followed.
>
> The provisions of StGB §6(5) find their domestic justification in the Single Convention on Narcotic Drugs, 1961 [. . .] It is clear beyond any doubt from the provisions of the Agreement that the signatory States, which include the Netherlands, consider it necessary in the interests of health and the well-being of mankind to promote world-wide international co-operation in the fight against criminality associated

[37] Puttler (n 34 above) 116 quotes the Dutch government saying that 'if Germany let the Dutch national go, the Netherlands would consider the question of whether to prosecute him'. Krikke (n 34 above) 260–1 observes that the German—Dutch extradition agreement did not provide for the extradition of drug offences, and that the European Convention on Extradition was not yet in force between the two countries.

[38] GG article 25 provides that the general rules of public international law are part of the domestic legal order and have precedence over municipal laws.

with drugs. This aim, which is already mentioned in the preamble to the Convention, makes it clear that *the reference contained in StGB §6(5) to the principle of the universal application of law is at all events not an arbitrary course adopted by the German criminal authorities*. Relevant in this regard is article 36 of the Convention[39] which contains the obligation [for the signatory States] to ensure that every offence connected with drugs receives the appropriate punishment. [...]

The precise meaning of the relevant provisions of the Convention is not, however, decisive. There is in fact no general rule of international law prohibiting the application of the principle of universality of law in the absence of special provision by international convention. The decision of the German legislature expressed in the provisions of StGB §6(5) cannot therefore be denied legal effect (emphases added).[40]

Public Prosecutor v *Dost* unambiguously states that a country may exercise universal jurisdiction even when it cannot point to some specific treaty provision because no general rule of international law prohibits it from doing so.[41] The decision contradicts Oehler on this point,[42] showing the gap that often exists between doctrine, which insists on a positive permissive rule to establish extraterritorial (universal) jurisdiction, and practice, in which such jurisdiction is frequently claimed without looking for any international authorization. As long as the claim of universal jurisdiction is not purely arbitrary (the value protected must be international) and as long as there is some legitimizing link between forum and case the Federal Supreme Court sees no incompatibility with international law.

Public Prosecutor v *Tadic*

Public Prosecutor v *Tadic*[43] is the first of several cases that arose out of the war and ethnic violence in the former Yugoslavia in the first half of the 1990s.[44] Germany admitted hundreds of thousands of Bosnian refugees and participated in UN peace-keeping operations in the former Yugoslavia. At the

[39] Article 36 para 2 sub a, IV provides: 'Serious offences heretofore referred to committed either by nationals or by foreigners shall be prosecuted by the Party in whose territory the offence was committed, or by the Party in whose territory the offender is found if extradition is not acceptable in conformity with the law of the Party to which application is made, and if such offender has not already been prosecuted and judgment given'.

[40] Translation taken from 74 *Int'l L Reports* 166, 168 (citations omitted).

[41] Cf the discussion in ch 1 s A above.

[42] Oehler (n 2 above) 539 argues that the *judex loci deprehensionis* is only competent if explicitly provided for by international treaty or custom.

[43] Bundesgerichtshof (examining magistrate), 13 February 1994, partially reprinted in [1994] *Neue Zeitschrift für Strafrecht* 232; case note by D Oehler in [1994] *Neue Zeitschrift für Strafrecht* 485.

[44] Between 1993 and December 2000 124 investigations were opened involving 163 suspects. Eighty cases were dropped because of lack of evidence (source: Generalbundesanwalt beim Bundesgerichtshof). At the time of writing 4 trials had been reported and a fifth person was under pre-trial arrest (source: press release 3/2002 of 17 January 2002 of the Generalbundesanwalt beim Bundesgerichtshof). For a comprehensive analysis of the cases that have been tried, see K Ambos and S Wirth, 'Genocide and War Crimes in the Former Yugoslavia

relevant time an extradition treaty was in force between Germany and Bosnia[45] and both countries were parties to the Genocide Convention and 1949 Geneva Conventions.

One of the refugees was Tadic, whom other asylum seekers pointed out as a participant in brutalities against Muslim detainees at Serbian-run concentration camps in the summer of 1992. He was arrested on charges of aiding and abetting genocide in concurrence (*Tateinheit*) with murder and grievous bodily harm. The German proceedings came to an end with the transfer of the accused to the International Criminal Tribunal for the former Yugoslavia.[46] Earlier an examining magistrate of the Bundesgerichtshof issued a decision on German jurisdiction that paved the way for subsequent cases:

German penal law applies by virtue of StGB §6(1) to genocide committed abroad independently from the law of the territorial State (so-called universality principle). Prerequisites, however, are that international law does not forbid this and that there is a legitimate link (*ein legitimierender Anknüpfungspunkt*) in the concrete case; only then is the application of German penal law to extraterritorial conduct by foreigners justified. Absent such a link the forum State violates the non-interference principle which requires States to respect the sovereignty of other States. The significance of the legal values protected by StGB §6 or the general political interests of Germany alone do not justify the application of the universality principle.

The facts that the accused has resided voluntarily for several months in Germany, that he has established his centre of interests here (*Lebensmittelpunkt*), and that he was arrested here constitute a link. Whether such a connection with the forum State is always sufficient must not be decided because there are further legal and political considerations in this case which carry so much weight that Germany's exercise of universal jurisdiction seems not merely justified but even required.

The crime of aiding and abetting genocide coincides in the instant case with other serious offences which Germany is obliged to repress on the basis of international conventions. This circumstance also has an indirect legal effect with respect to the elements (*Tatbestand*) of StGB §220a, at least with respect to the applicability of the universality principle.

Furthermore, the prosecution of murders in Bosnia-Herzegovina by national courts fits in with numerous political, military, and humanitarian measures of the international community, including Germany, aimed at countering the expansion and dominance policies in the former Yugoslavia, in particular in Bosnia-Herzegovina, and at protecting the civilian Muslim population from persecution, decimation, and deportation. In those circumstances, there can be no question of an unlawful interference in the

Before German Criminal Courts' in H Fischer, C Kreß, and SR Lüder (eds) *International and National Prosecutions of Crimes under International Law: Current Developments* (2001) 769. Not discussed in the present study is *Public Prosecutor* v *Kuslic*: Bayerisches Oberstes Landesgericht, 15 December 1999; Bundesgerichtshof, 21 February 2001, partially reprinted in [2001] *Neue Juristische Wochenschrift* 2732. The case is not included because the decision does not add to the debate on German jurisdiction over genocide and war crimes abroad.

[45] Agreement of 26 November 1970.

[46] *Prosecutor* v *Tadic*, IT-94-1-AR72.

affairs of Bosnia-Herzegovina or of the present Republic of Yugoslavia. On the contrary, it would be inconceivable that Germany, in spite of the allegations and the provisions of StGB §6(1), would leave in peace a person who is suspected of having committed the worst possible crimes in the conflict in Bosnia-Herzegovina and who has come voluntarily to Germany.[47]

Public Prosecutor v *Djajic*

The second Bosnian case is that of *Public Prosecutor* v *Djajic*.[48] The accused came to Germany in 1993; he had lived there during his childhood and had maintained strong ties ever since. He was arrested and charged cumulatively, based on the same set of facts, with genocide, murder, and hostage-taking in Bosnia in 1992.[49] Upon notification, the ICTY and Bosnia declined to take over the proceedings.

The Bavarian Supreme Court found the accused guilty on fourteen counts of abetting murder and one count of attempted murder, but acquitted him of genocide because he lacked the necessary *mens rea*. The court based its jurisdiction over genocide on StGB §6(1) and over murder on §6(9) in conjunction with articles 3, 146, and 147 of the Fourth Geneva Convention, and on StGB §7(2)(2) because the Bosnian authorities had declined to request extradition. The decision follows the Federal Supreme Court's *Tadic* line of reasoning but adds the following point.

> Considerations of international law are important, but one should not overlook the fact that the prosecution of a foreigner for crimes committed abroad also serves an interest of the State of residence, namely not to become a refuge for offenders who have committed crimes under customary and conventional international law. Not to prosecute would undermine the trust (*Rechtsbewährungsprinzip*) of the German citizens in the national and international legal order. Furthermore, since the ICTY and the competent territorial State do not wish to take over the proceedings, Germany has an interest not to be perceived by the international community as a haven for international criminals.[50]

X v *SB and DB*

The case of *X* v *SB and DB*[51] tested the limits of German jurisdiction over genocide and grave breaches committed in the former Yugoslavia. Unidentified Bosnian refugees filed a complaint against SB and DB, without

[47] Judgment (n 43 above) at 4(a) (citations omitted).

[48] Bayerisches Oberstes Landesgericht, 23 May 1997 (copy on file with author), partially reprinted in [1998] *Neue Juristische Wochenschrift* 392; case notes by K Ambos in [1998] *Neue Zeitschrift für Strafrecht* 138 and by C Safferling in (1998) 92 *Am J Int'l L* 528.

[49] Indictment (copy on file with author).

[50] Decision as reprinted in [1998] *Neue Juristische Wochenschrift* 392, 395.

[51] Bundesgerichtshof, 11 December 1998, partially reprinted in [1999] *Neue Zeitschrift für Strafrecht* 236.

any indication of their presence in Germany. The Federal Supreme Court ruled that Germany has no jurisdiction over any of the offences for lack of a meaningful point of contact.

> Without meaningful point of contact respect for the sovereignty of other States (non-interference principle) can hardly be assured; if there were no other limitation than StPO §153c I Nr 1 [the principle of opportunity of prosecution] the municipal criminal justice system would be overloaded with 'worldwide' prosecutions.
>
> The only link with Germany is the plaintiff's presence. Even if he were the victim of any of the alleged crimes—which is doubtful—there would not be a sufficient connection. The presence of a victim of crime is not an appropriate basis for German jurisdiction because it is usually a matter of pure coincidence with no relation to the offence and offender. If it were an adequate criterion this would lead to an endless and internationally questionable extension of national jurisdiction. German courts would have to deal with cases when it is manifest from the start that there are very few chances properly to investigate and try them.
>
> It is quite another thing when the offender is present in Germany; in that case there is an internationally undisputed linking point for the exercise of jurisdiction.[52]

Public Prosecutor v *Jorgic*

Public Prosecutor v *Jorgic*[53] is a case of a long-time resident who returned to the former Yugoslavia during the midst of the war there in 1992. When in Germany he was arrested and charged with genocide of Bosnian Muslims. The ICTY and Bosnia declared they had no interest in taking over the proceedings.[54] The Supreme Court in Düsseldorf found the accused guilty of genocide. The trial court based its jurisdiction on StGB §6(1) and 6(9) and on the Federal Supreme Court's 'double link doctrine' of *Tadic*. The fact that, except while he joined the war in his homeland, the accused had maintained his centre of interests in Germany since 1969 constituted a sufficient personal link in the court's view.

The accused appealed to the Federal Supreme Court, contending *inter alia* that universal jurisdiction is incompatible with the Genocide Convention. The court rejected the argument in the following terms.

> The conviction of the accused by a German court on the basis of the universality principle is not forbidden under international law.

[52] Bundesgerichtshof, 11 December 1998, partially reprinted in [1999] *Neue Zeitschrift für Strafrecht* 236.

[53] Oberstes Landesgericht Düsseldorf, 26 September 1997 (copy on file with author); Bundesgerichtshof, 30 April 1999 (copy on file with author), partially reprinted in [1999] *Neue Zeitschrift für Strafrecht* 396, case notes by K Ambos in [1999] *Neue Zeitschrift für Strafrecht* 404, by G Werle in [1999] *Juristenzeitung* 1181, and by O Lagodny and C Nill-Theobald in [2000] *Juristische Rundschau* 205; Bundesverfassungsgericht, 12 December 2000 (copy on file with author), partially reprinted in [2001] *Neue Zeitschrift für Strafrecht* 240.

[54] This summary of the factual allegations is taken from the judgment of the Oberstes Landesgericht Düsseldorf (ibid).

Such a prohibition cannot be derived from article VI of the Genocide Convention. To be sure, the Convention does not incorporate the universality principle—whereas the draft did—but this is because a few countries were opposed to any international jurisdiction given the political character of the protected right. This did, however, not lead to the inclusion of a prohibition. The view that the provisions [of article VI] are not exhaustive is not only based on the drafting history; the opinion that genocide can only be punished by a court of the territorial State or by an international tribunal is irreconcilable with the obligation imposed by article I on all States to repress the international crime of genocide. Since genocide is most of the time condoned if not committed by the authorities effective repression by the territorial State cannot be expected. An international tribunal envisaged by the Genocide Convention did not exist until the creation of the ICTY in 1993, the ICTR in 1994, and the ICC by the not yet in force Rome Statute. The ICTY can at this moment dispose of a maximum of ten cases per year. Therefore, the repression of the many crimes committed in execution of the policy of 'ethnic cleansing' urges itself upon national courts.

This construction of the Genocide Convention is also supported by article 9(1) of the ICTY Statute which, independently of article VI of the Convention, provides for concurrent jurisdiction of national courts over genocide. The Prosecutor of the ICTY, who together with the trial chambers has authority to interpret the Statute, understands by 'national courts' not only courts of the territorial State but courts of all other States. This follows from the fact that the Prosecutor of the ICTY in this and other cases declined to take over the proceedings and applauded the prosecution by German authorities. If the international community of States was of the opinion that the provisions of article VI of the Genocide Convention were exhaustive, it would have made this clear in article 9 of the Statute by limiting concurrency of jurisdiction to the courts of Bosnia and Herzegovina, or better to the courts of the States of the former Yugoslavia. Further, the International Court of Justice in the *Case Concerning the Application of the Convention on the Prevention and Punishment of the Crime of Genocide* (*Bosnia and Herzegovina* v *Yugoslavia*) has held that the Convention's rights and obligations apply *erga omnes* and that the conventional obligation to prevent and repress genocide has no territorial limits.

From the absence of the universality principle in the Genocide Convention it follows only that States parties are not obliged to adopt this principle and prosecute a foreigner for acts of genocide committed abroad. When it comes to the repression of genocide, a crime under customary and conventional international law, no international norm prohibits States parties to do more than the conventional minimum.[55]

The accused appealed to the Constitutional Court,[56] arguing that Germany lacks jurisdiction under customary international law *and* under the Genocide Convention. Regarding the first contention, the Court acknowledged that parties to a convention can indeed also be bound by customary law and that conventional law does not necessarily take precedence over a derogating norm

[55] Bundesgerichtshof decision (n 53 above) s D, I (citations omitted).

[56] As noted earlier, by virtue of GG article 25 the general rules of public international law are part of the domestic legal order and have precedence over municipal laws.

of customary law.[57] In the case of the Genocide Convention, however, the Court took the view that a customary law prohibition on the exercise of universal jurisdiction would be diametrically opposed to the fulfilment of the obligations arising out of article I; such a derogation from article I is not permitted because the prohibition of genocide is part of international *jus cogens*.[58] With regard to the second contention, the decision stated as follows.

The universality principle applies to certain acts that endanger the legal interests of the international community of States. It differs from the representation principle codified in StGB §7(2)(2) in that it does not require double criminality and non-extradition.[59]

Whether the Genocide Convention contains a provision on universal jurisdiction has to be examined through interpretation. International conventions are to be interpreted from their text in accordance with their object and purpose with due regard to general international law. The lower courts' interpretation of StGB §6(1) in conjunction with article VI of the Genocide Convention regarding the scope of application of German law is in any event neither manifestly untenable, nor impossible to maintain under no imaginable circumstances and hence arbitrary.[60]

According to a textual interpretation the lower courts have constitutionally correctly determined that article VI of the Genocide Convention in any event does not contain a prohibition on German criminal jurisdiction. On the other hand, the Convention clearly does not regulate the question of jurisdiction exclusively, because, for example, the active or passive universality principle is not mentioned. The courts have thereupon interpreted article I of the Genocide Convention according to its object and purpose that the Convention intended effective punishment; consequently, the fact that there is no mention of the universality principle only means that the contracting Parties are not obliged to prosecute, although they are competent on the basis of this principle. It does not invite objections to prefer in some cases a 'systematic-teleological' interpretation above a textual interpretation of treaties. This applies in particular in the field of criminal jurisdiction over extraterritorial conduct on the basis of international conventions, because they are often vague on the issue of jurisdiction. Genocide, the gravest violation of human rights, is the classic example of the universality principle, whose function is precisely to close all loopholes in the prosecution of crimes against the fundamental legal interests of the community of States.[61]

[...]

Yet, the drafting history of the Genocide Convention indicates that [the universality principle] was deliberately not included. Article VII of the initial draft[62] contained the universality principle. In the draft of the Ad Hoc Committee, however, the universality principle was abandoned in favour of the territoriality principle. Sovereignty concerns and considerations of accession[63] influenced that decision. There are, however, no constitutional objections against the decision of the lower courts not to attribute

[57] Bundesverfassungsgericht (n 53 above) paras 14, 15 (citations omitted).
[58] Ibid para 16 (citations omitted). [59] Ibid para 37 (citations omitted).
[60] Ibid para 38. [61] Ibid para 39.
[62] See the discussion of the Genocide Convention in ch 3 s A above.
[63] Bundesverfassungsgericht (n 53 above) para 41 (citations omitted).

decisive importance to the drafting history. The preparatory work of a treaty is, according to article 32 of the Vienna Convention of the Law of Treaties, only a 'supplementary means of interpretation', to which recourse may only be had when the interpretation according to article 31 leaves the meaning ambiguous or obscure or leads to a result which is manifestly absurd or unreasonable. None of these alternatives apply in this case. The interpretation according to article 31 clearly leads the courts to the conclusion that the Convention allows prosecution on the basis of the universality principle. This result is not manifestly absurd or unreasonable.[64]

[...]

The question whether, as the appealed decisions state, another link is necessary because of the non-interference, does not have to be answered here. [The decision cites Ambos who argues that no link is necessary.] Because the claim that in this case the Federal Supreme Court's assertion of jurisdiction was *ultra vires* is unfounded, the question can be left open.[65]

Public Prosecutor v *Sokolovic*

Public Prosecutor v *Sokolovic*[66] is another case of a long-time resident returning to the former Yugoslavia and joining the war effort. The accused was found guilty of complicity in genocide in concurrence (*Tateinheit*) with confinement and grievous bodily harm. The trial court based its jurisdiction on StGB §6(1) and (9) in conjunction with the Fourth Geneva Convention. The Federal Supreme Court upheld the conviction but, more importantly, indicated a willingness to abandon its legitimizing link doctrine (in line with the last quoted paragraph of the *Jorgic* decision above).

In any case, the trial court has proven, in accordance with the until now prevailing jurisprudence which, over and above the wording of StGB §6 requires a legitimizing link in a specific case [...] that such links are present. It found a sufficient link in the fact that the accused had lived and worked in Germany continuously from 1969 until 1989, that he still had a house here, and that he returned regularly in the last couple of years to his house to collect his continuing allowance in Germany and to sign on with the Employment Office where he was still registered as a job-seeker. The Court is, however, inclined, at least for StGB §6(9), to consider that such additional legitimizing links are not necessary. Indeed, when Germany, in executing an internationally legally binding obligation—based on an international convention—prosecutes an extraterritorial offence by a foreigner against a foreigner and punishes according to German law, a violation of the non-interference principle can scarcely be alleged.[67]

[64] Ibid (citations omitted).
[65] Ibid para 43 (citations omitted).
[66] Oberstes Landesgericht Düsseldorf, 29 November 1999; Bundesgerichtshof, 21 February 2001, partially reprinted in [2001] *Neue Zeitschrift für Strafrecht* 658 and in [2001] *Neue Juristische Wochenschrift* 2728.
[67] Ibid at 4e (citations omitted).

The first Bosnian cases (*Tadic*, *Djajic*, *SB and DB*) built on the Dost ruling that a country may exercise universal jurisdiction under two conditions: the protected interest must be international and there must be some link between the case and the forum. In the Bosnian cases courts found a double link: an objective link consisting of the offender's presence in Germany, and a link between the conflict and Germany as a member of the international community. The latter link did not seem to be a *conditio sine qua non* for jurisdiction. Rather it was used as an argument for the proposition that German judicial authorities had an international *obligation* to act. The presence requirement, on the other hand, clearly was a necessary condition for jurisdiction under international law over both genocide and grave breaches of the 1949 Geneva Conventions.

The link doctrine provoked vigorous criticism by a new generation of German international criminal law scholars.[68] The old school, led by *éminence grise* Oehler, categorically rejects the exercise of universal jurisdiction *in absentia*.[69] The new school argues that an international offence cannot possibly be considered an internal affair; consequently, prosecution and punishment by a State without a link to the offence cannot constitute an unlawful interference with the domestic affairs of the territorial State.[70]

The Constitutional Court in *Jorgic* may have reserved its position on the issue, but in the drafting of the German Code of Crimes Against International Law the view of the new school has clearly prevailed.

C. SUMMARY

German penal law is unique among the countries here discussed in that it contains all three doctrinal versions of the universality principle. The ordinary penal code includes a domestic *aut dedere aut judicare* clause for common offences and a general enabling clause for treaty offences. The Code of Crimes Against International Law, for its part, provides for universal jurisdiction over genocide, crimes against humanity, and war crimes. The Code

[68] See the comments on *Jorgic* (Federal Supreme Court) by Ambos (n 6 above), by Werle (n 53 above), and by O Lagodny and C Nill-Theobald (n 53 above). See also Ambos and Wirth (n 44 above); SR Lüder, 'Eröffnung der deutschen Gerichtsbarkeit für den Völkermord im Kosovo?' (2000) 53 *Neue Juristische Wochenschrift* 269, 270; S van Heeck, 'Der aktuelle Fall: Die Anwendung deutschen Strafrechts auf Balkankriegsverbrechen' [2000] *Humanitäres Völkerrecht-Informationsschriften* 27, 32–3; C Kreß, 'Völkerstrafrecht in Deutschland' (2000) 20 *Neue Zeitschrift für Strafrecht* 617, 624–7.

[69] Oehler (n 22 above) 489, 497–500. The same author argues in [1994] *Neue Zeitschrift für Strafrecht* 485 that further links are necessary in addition to the presence of the accused.

[70] See the works cited in n 68 above.

distinguishes between applicability of the law and jurisdiction of the courts: the substantive provisions apply even when the offence bears no relation to Germany but the jurisdiction of German courts is limited by constraints of a procedural nature. As a result, the exercise of universal jurisdiction *in absentia* is possible, but only as a last resort. Germany was the first major power to claim such broad jurisdiction over the core ICC crimes. As many nations still have to adopt ICC implementing legislation it is not impossible that some will follow its example.

Overall, judicial authorities have diligently investigated and prosecuted citizens from the former Yugoslavia for atrocities committed during the recent Balkan wars. All the defendants, one way or another, had strong ties with Germany, often predating their crimes. The first judgments in these cases stressed the importance of links with the forum. Perhaps in anticipation of the Code of Crimes Against International Law, more recent decisions indicate a willingness to abandon the legitimizing link doctrine.

11

Israel

A. AMBIT OF THE CRIMINAL LAW

At the time of the establishment of Israel in 1948 the principal legislation in the area of criminal law was the Criminal Code Ordinance 1936, enacted by the British Mandatory Legislature and subsequently adopted by the Israeli legislature. As in the United Kingdom, the jurisdiction of the courts was limited to crimes committed within the territory.[1]

Ever since that time the ambit of the criminal law has been gradually broadened, to the point that in 1980 an Israeli commentator declared: 'Israel has deserted the Anglo-Saxon camp which adheres to the principle of territorial jurisdiction'.[2] The broadening legislation includes the Penal Law (Offences Committed Abroad) (Consolidated Version) 1973,[3] the Penal Law Amendment (Offences Committed Abroad) Law 1978,[4] and the New Penal Code of the State of Israel 1995.[5] The 1978 amendment constituted an additional departure from the Anglo-Saxon tradition in that extradition of a national is no longer allowed, save for an offence committed before he became an Israeli citizen.[6]

Articles 7–17 of the penal code spell out in great detail its scope of application *ratione loci*. Article 12 contains the basic principle: 'Israeli penal law shall apply to all domestic offences'. Article 13 endows Israeli courts with protective jurisdiction, which extends to offences against any Israeli national, resident, or Jew *as such*. Article 14 provides for general passive personality jurisdiction, including crimes against residents. By virtue of article 15 Israeli penal law applies to an extraterritorial offence 'by a person being—either at the time of or after committing the offence—an Israeli national or resident of Israel'.

To say that Israel has deserted the Anglo-Saxon camp is in fact an understatement. The extension of the protective, active personality, and passive personality

I thank Dr Itzhak Kugler for clarifications on Israeli law.

[1] M Kremnitzer, 'Criminal Law' in A Shapira and KC DeWitt-Arar (eds) *Introduction to the Law of Israel* (1995) 253. See also D Bein, 'Criminal Law' in I Zamir and S Colombo (eds) *The Law of Israel: General Surveys* (1995) 128, 139–42; A Bin-Nun, *The Law of the State of Israel: An Introduction* (1992) 104–11.

[2] C Shachor-Landau, 'Extra-Territorial Penal Jurisdiction and Extradition' (1980) 29 *Int'l & Comparative LQ* 274.

[3] English translation reprinted in 27 *Laws of the State of Israel* (1972–73) 32.

[4] English translation reprinted in 32 *Laws of the State of Israel* (1977–78) 63.

[5] English translation of the draft (which was adopted with minor changes) is reprinted in (1996) 30 *Israel L Rev* 5.

[6] Shachor-Landau (n 2 above) 274.

principles to offences against or by alien residents gives these principles a broader interpretation than in any of the other countries discussed. Prosecuting a foreigner for an extraterritorial offence against someone who is not a citizen or resident but a Jew (article 13), or for an extraterritorial offence committed before he became a resident (article 15) arguably constitutes an exercise of universal jurisdiction.

The penal code also contains a general enabling clause very similar to the ones in Austrian, Belgian, Danish, German, French, and Spanish law. Article 16(a) provides that 'Israeli penal law shall apply to foreign offences which Israel, by multilateral international conventions, has undertaken to punish even if they are committed by a person who is not an Israeli national or resident of Israel regardless of where they were committed'.[7] The use of such a clause is yet another sign of Israel's desertion of the Anglo-Saxon camp. Common law countries ordinarily enact an implementing statute for each convention. Article 16(a) says nothing about the whereabouts of the foreign offender but it would follow from the *aut dedere aut judicare* clauses in the conventions that he should be 'found' or 'present' in Israel before Israeli law can apply. On the basis of article 16(a) Israeli courts can exercise universal jurisdiction over torture and grave breaches of the Geneva Conventions because Israel has ratified the relevant conventions.

Article 9 of the penal code spells out a number of provisions applicable to extraterritorial offences generally.[8] A certain unilateralism in criminal matters transpires here. Foreign judgments are, in principle, not recognized and the application of the milder foreign law is explicitly excluded. In many countries examined in this book the situation is the exact opposite. No prosecution for an extraterritorial offence may be brought save by the Attorney General.[9]

Universal jurisdiction is also provided for in two special statutes which are discussed next: the Nazi and Nazi Collaborators (Punishment) Law 1950 and the Crime of Genocide (Prevention and Punishment) Law 1950.

[7] Translation taken from *Israel L Rev* (n 5 above).

[8] Article 9 reads:

(a) The incidence of Israeli penal law, including in the case of a foreign offence, is not restricted by any foreign law or foreign *res judicata* unless otherwise prescribed by law.
(b) There shall be no prosecution for a foreign offence save by the Attorney-General or with his written consent, upon his determination that such is in the public interest.
(c) Israeli penal law shall no longer apply to an offence if the person in question has been tried for it abroad at the request of the State of Israel and, if he has been convicted there, has also undergone his punishment for it.
(d) The incidence of Israeli penal law which is less restricted shall prevail over that of one which is more restricted, in respect to the same offence.

Translation taken from *Israel L Rev* (n 5 above).

[9] For other procedural matters, see E Harnon and A Stein, 'Israel' in CM Bradley (ed) *Criminal Procedure: A World Wide Study* (1999) 217–44.

Nazi and Nazi Collaborators (Punishment) Law 1950

The Nazi and Nazi Collaborators (Punishment) Law 1950[10] applies retroactively to certain offences committed 'in an enemy country' during the period of the Nazi regime or during World War II. The difference with similar laws in other countries[11] is that Israel was not engaged in World War II, it only being created thereafter. Its foundation, however, was a direct result of Nazi atrocities against Jews before and during the war. Israel became the new homeland of many Jewish survivors of the Holocaust. There are thus ample links between Israel and World War II crimes.

The principal offences under the law are 'crimes against the Jewish people', crimes against humanity, and war crimes (article 1); other offences include 'offences in places of confinement' (article 4), delivering up a persecuted person to enemy administration (article 5), and blackmailing a persecuted person (article 6). The law further provides that '[a] person who has committed an offence under this Law may be tried in Israel even if he has already been tried abroad, whether before an international tribunal or a tribunal of a foreign state, for the same offence' (article 9(a)).

Crime of Genocide (Prevention and Punishment) Law 1950

The Crime of Genocide (Prevention and Punishment) Law 1950[12] implements the Genocide Convention which, as shown in chapter 3 above, is negative on universal jurisdiction. Article 2 makes genocide punishable by death. Article 4 provides that '[a] person guilty of an offence under this law shall be punished whether he is a legally responsible ruler, a member of the legislative body, a public official or a private individual'.[13] Article 5 states that '[a] person who has committed outside Israel an act which is an offence under this law may be prosecuted and punished in Israel as if he had committed the act in Israel'. A link with Israel is not specifically required. This appears to have been the first municipal statute providing for universal jurisdiction over genocide, which makes it all the more remarkable that Israel voted against the ICC Statute at the United Nations Diplomatic Conference of Plenipotentiaries on the Establishment of an International Criminal Court in Rome in 1998.[14]

[10] English translation reprinted in J Badi (ed) *Fundamental Laws of the State of Israel* (1961) 162. For comments, see JM Wenig, 'Enforcing the Lessons of History: Israel Judges the Holocaust' in TLH McCormack and GJ Simpson (eds) *The Law of War Crimes: National and International Approaches* (1997) 103, 105–9.

[11] See the Australia, Canada, and United Kingdom country studies in this book.

[12] English translation reprinted in Badi (n 10 above) 152.

[13] Cf Article IV of the Genocide Convention.

[14] Israel eventually signed the ICC treaty, but in a communication received on 28 August 2002 the Israeli government informed the UN Secretary-General that 'Israel does not intend to become a party to the treaty. Accordingly, Israel has no legal obligations arising from its signature on 31 December 2000. Israel requests that its intention not to become a party, as expressed in this letter, be reflected in the depositary's status lists relating to this treaty' (source: UN Treaties website).

B. CASE-LAW

Two foreigners have been tried under the Nazi and Nazi Collaborators (Punishment) Law for their role in the Holocaust.[15]

Attorney General of Israel v *Eichmann*

For lack of other precedents, *Attorney General of Israel* v *Eichmann*[16] was for a long time at the centre of any discussion on universal jurisdiction. The accused, a former senior Nazi official, was abducted from Argentina[17] by members of the Israeli Secret Service and put on trial in Israel for his key role in the extermination of Jews during World War II. Germany, the State of nationality of the accused, did not protest against the trial by Israel. The indictment contained counts that related to crimes against Jews and non-Jewish groups. The Jewish victims were all nationals of European States. For the most part the facts were undisputed. However, the jurisdiction of the Court was challenged.[18] One of the arguments was that the alleged facts constituted 'genocide' and that the Genocide Convention only provides for the jurisdiction of the territorial State or an international tribunal.[19]

The District Court of Jerusalem (notwithstanding that neither the Genocide Convention nor the implementing Israeli law applied) considered the argument. It took the view that

> in the Convention for the Prevention and Punishment of Genocide the Members of the United Nations [...] contented themselves with the determination of territorial jurisdiction as a *compulsory minimum*. [...] It is clear that the reference in Article 6 to territorial jurisdiction, apart from the jurisdiction of the non-existent international tribunal, is not exhaustive. Every sovereign State may exercise its existing powers within the limits of customary international law, and accession of a State to the Convention does not involve the waiving of powers which are not mentioned in Article 6.[20]

The District Court then explained what these existing other powers are:

> The State of Israel's 'right to punish' the accused derives, in our view, from two cumulative sources: a universal source (pertaining to the whole of mankind), which

[15] Some Israeli citizens (Jewish collaborators or '*Kapos*') have also been prosecuted under the law: Wenig (n 10 above) 118–21.

[16] District Court of Jerusalem, 12 December 1961, reprinted (1968) 36 *Int'l L Reports* 5; Supreme Court of Israel, 29 May 1962, reprinted in ibid 277. For a thorough comment, see JES Fawcett, 'The Eichmann Case' (1962) 27 *British Ybk Int'l L* 181.

[17] Protesting against the violation of its territorial sovereignty, Argentina seized the UN Security Council. The latter condemned the abduction and requested Israel to make appropriate reparation.

[18] For a critical assessment of the jurisdictional issue, see Fawcett (n 16 above) 202–8.

[19] Cf the discussion of the Genocide Convention in ch 3 s A above.

[20] District Court judgment (n 16 above) para 25.

vests the right to prosecute and punish crimes of this order in every State within the family of nations; and a specific or national source, which gives the victim nation the right to try any who assault its existence.[21]

The Supreme Court, on appeal, put forward a slightly different reasoning. The Court found Israel's jurisdiction to accord with international law under a negative and a positive approach.[22] Relying on *Lotus*, the Court held that the law of 1950 upon which the proceedings were based was *not prohibited* by international law.[23] The positive approach concentrated on the international and universal character of the crimes, which *entitled* Israel to punish the accused. In an oft-quoted passage the Court took the view that:

Not only are all the crimes attributed to the Appellant of an international character, but they are crimes whose evil and murderous effects were so widespread as to shake the stability of the international community to its very foundations. The State of Israel, therefore, was entitled, pursuant to the principle of universal jurisdiction and acting in the capacity of guardian of international law and agent for its enforcement, to try the Appellant.[24]

The trial of Eichmann by Israel falls under what was called in chapter 2 above the unilateral limited universality principle. But as Fawcett rightly observes:

The *Eichmann* case is unique. There is no room for any view that there was a miscarriage of justice. But the exercise of jurisdiction by the Israeli courts rested upon a combination of extraordinary events, including both his own past actions and his condoned removal to Israel, the weakest point in that jurisdiction being its exercise over such of his crimes as constituted genocide; and the process in Israel would have served only to weaken the rule of law if it were to be invoked as a precedent for trials where such a combination was not present.[25]

The fact remains, however, that the District Court's construction of article VI of the Genocide Convention is flimsy.[26] *Expressio unius est exclusio alterius* is a well established principle of statutory construction and the suggestion that the parties to the Convention silently reserved to themselves the right to exercise universal jurisdiction is contradicted by the *travaux préparatoires*.[27]

Attorney General of Israel v *Demjanjuk*

Attorney General of Israel v *Demjanjuk*[28] was the second and last trial of a foreigner under the Nazi and Nazi Collaborators (Punishment) Law. The trial

[21] District Court judgment (n 16 above) para 30.

[22] Cf the discussion in ch 1 s A above.

[23] Supreme Court judgment (n 16 above) para 9.

[24] Ibid para 12.

[25] Fawcett (n 16 above) 215.

[26] Cf RR Baxter, 'Jurisdiction over War Crimes and Crimes Against Humanity: Individual and State Accountability' in MC Bassiouni and VP Nanda (eds) *A Treatise on International Criminal Law* (1973) 65, 85; WA Schabas, *Genocide in International Law* (2000) 360–1, 367.

[27] See ch 3 s A above.

[28] Demjanjuk's conviction was overturned by the Israeli Supreme Court: *Demjanjuk* v *Attorney General of Israel*, Supreme Court of Israel, 29 July 1993. For comments, see Wenig (n 10 above) 115–8.

posed the same jurisdiction issues as the *Eichmann* case and is therefore not discussed here. However, Israel's right under international law to try the accused was crucial in the extradition proceedings in the United States[29] where he had lived since World War II and had acquired citizenship.

C. SUMMARY

Once a common law country that adhered to the principle of territorial jurisdiction, Israel now claims extensive extraterritorial jurisdiction, in a more or less unilateral manner. The penal code and special statutes provide for universal jurisdiction over violent crimes against a Jew *as such*, over any serious common crime by a foreigner who subsequently becomes an Israeli resident, and over certain grave violations of international humanitarian law.

Two foreigners have been tried in Israel for offences committed in occupied Europe during World War II. They were forcibly brought to the forum State by abduction and extradition. The uniqueness of the constellation of facts in these cases, however, militates against their use as a precedent for trials where such circumstances are not present.

[29] See the United States country study below.

12

The Netherlands

A. AMBIT OF THE CRIMINAL LAW

In the Netherlands, the ambit of the criminal law (*strafmachtsrecht*) as a fundamental theoretical question is an academic discipline on its own.[1] Four concerns guide Dutch theory and practice in this regard: legal security (*rechtszekerheid*), proper administration of justice (*goede rechtsbedeling*), avoidance of conflicts of jurisdiction, and non-interference.[2] An important aspect of the proper administration of justice is the reasonable and responsible treatment of offenders, if possible within their own social environment. Thus, restoration rather than retribution is among the primary goals of criminal justice.

These considerations explain why the Netherlands is traditionally reticent in claiming extraterritorial jurisdiction[3] and why the penal code in article 68(2) bars prosecution in the Netherlands after foreign *res judicata*, including decisions not to prosecute.[4] However, it is important to note that this restraint is not prompted by international legal concerns alone but is to some degree self-imposed[5] by a country that holds particular, somewhat self-willed views on criminal law and criminal justice. This unilateral reserve also explains the criticism in Dutch academic circles of the German decision in the *Dost* case.[6]

I warmly thank Mr Bas van Riel for his suggestions and critical comments.

[1] For an illustration, see eg GAM Strijards, *Internationaal Strafrecht: Strafmachtsrecht* (1984).

[2] Council of Europe, European Committee on Crime Problems, Select Committee of Experts on extraterritorial jurisdiction, Working documents on the basis of which the report *Extraterritorial Criminal Jurisdiction* (1990) has been prepared. Dutch reply to question 26; MT Gerritsen, 'Jurisdiction' in B Swart and A Klip (eds) *International Criminal Law in the Netherlands* (1997) 49, 50; AMM Orie, CF Rüter, JJE Schutte, and AHJ Swart, 'Netherlands' (1989) 60 *Revue internationale de droit pénal* 395, 411. On the proper administration of justice and its role in the distribution of competence see, extensively, T Vander Beken, *Forumkeuze in het Internationaal Strafrecht: Verdeling van misdrijven met aanknopingspunten in meerdere staten* (1999) 276–80 who refers to AHJ Swart, 'Internationalisering van de strafrechtspleging', in C Kelk *et al.* (eds) *Grenzen en mogelijkheden: Opstellen over en rondom de strafrechtspleging* (1984) 112–29.

[3] AHJ Swart, 'De Nederlandse strafrechtspleging en het internationale recht' in *Internationalisering van het strafrecht. Ars Aequi Libri. Serie Strafrecht en criminologie, VI* (1986) 37, 47.

[4] For comments on article 68(2) see P Baauw, 'Ne bis in idem' in B Swart and A Klip (eds) *International Criminal Law in the Netherlands* (1997) 75–84 and Vander Beken (n 2 above) 268–71.

[5] Gerritsen (n 2 above) 50.

[6] See Germany country study above.

The rules of jurisdiction are spelled out in articles 2–8 of the penal code (*Wetboek van Strafrecht*).[7] These provisions apply not only to all offences under the code itself, but also to those defined in other statutes, unless the statute provides otherwise.[8] Territoriality of criminal law is the basic principle. Article 2 states: 'The criminal law of the Netherlands applies to anyone who commits any offence within the Netherlands'. Extraterritorial jurisdiction was traditionally limited to the protective (article 4) and active personality principles (article 5).[9] Dutch doctrine and practice have consistently been adverse to passive personality jurisdiction.[10] Only when an international convention binding on the Netherlands contains an unequivocal obligation to create passive personality jurisdiction have the Netherlands been willing, albeit reluctantly, to establish jurisdiction on that basis.[11] This opposition explains why the Netherlands waited until 1988 to become a party to the Convention on the Prevention and Punishment of Crimes against Internationally Protected Persons, including Diplomatic Agents.[12]

Dutch doctrine and practice have similar strong reservations about exercising universal jurisdiction.[13] It is only accepted if the obligation arises from customary or conventional international law.[14] The main objections are the risks of double jeopardy, conflicts of jurisdiction, the shifting of responsibilities,[15]

[7] For an English translation, see B Swart and A Klip (eds) *International Criminal Law in the Netherlands* (1997) 251–3; for comment, see MR Mok and RAA Duk, 'Toepassing van Nederlands strafrecht op buiten Nederland begane delicten' in *Handelingen der Nederlandse Juristen-Vereniging deel 1, tweede stuk* (1980) 2–149.

[8] Article 91 of penal code.

[9] Dutch nationals can be prosecuted in the Netherlands for all extraterritorial felonies (*misdrijven*), provided there is double criminality. Active personality jurisdiction can be explained by the fact that the 1967 Extradition Act forbids the extradition of Dutch citizens, unless the requesting State promises that the suspect, if convicted, can serve his sentence in the Netherlands (article 4). For a fuller account on active personality jurisdiction in the Netherlands, see Vander Beken (n 2 above) 103–5.

[10] Passive personality jurisdiction can be found though in special statutes on the punishment of offences committed in wartime; see Gerritsen (n 2 above) 58 and Vander Beken (n 2 above) 121–2.

[11] For example, the International Convention against the Taking of Hostages and the International Convention for the Suppression of Unlawful Acts against the Safety of Maritime Navigation leave discretion to the States parties in this matter. Hence, the Netherlands did not establish passive personality jurisdiction over the offences defined therein.

[12] New York, 14 December 1973; GA Res 3166 (XXVIII). Article 3 of the Convention requires each State party to establish its jurisdiction over crimes set forth in article 2, when the crime is committed against an internationally protected person who enjoys his status as such by virtue of functions which he exercises on behalf of that State. During the ratification process the Dutch government stated before parliament: 'We would like to set at rest the fear of parliament, that, through implementing the treaty provision into Dutch criminal law, we have abandoned our objections against the principle of passive personality, and that we might in future propose to give it a wider application. We therefore repeat loud and clear that we are not prepared to do so' (quoted in Council of Europe, European Committee on Crime Problems (n 2 above) Dutch reply to question 26).

[13] Orie *et al.* (n 2 above) 411–17. The Netherlands opposed universal jurisdiction for the Genocide Convention: WA Schabas, *Genocide in International Law* (2000) 355.

[14] Orie *et al.* (n 2 above).

[15] Gerritsen (n 2 above) 63. Indeed, if *all* States are virtually competent there is a serious risk that they shift responsibility and that, in the end, *no* State asserts jurisdiction.

and the obstruction of justice.[16] Moreover, the Dutch have fundamental conceptual and legal-theoretical criticisms of the *aut dedere aut judicare* formulas in modern international criminal law conventions.[17] The most important critiques are the absence of a hierarchy of jurisdictional principles[18] and the lack of clarity of the relationship between extradition and jurisdiction.[19]

It is standing practice to make a reservation to all international conventions containing an *aut dedere aut judicare* clause, to the effect that the Netherlands will only assert jurisdiction if a request for extradition from another State party has been received and refused.[20] These reservations are inspired by articles 6 and 7 of the 1977 European Convention on the Suppression of Terrorism[21] and are intended to ensure that international offences are in principle prosecuted by contracting parties with a strong jurisdictional claim.[22]

The reluctance to assert extraterritorial jurisdiction in general and the critique of *aut dedere aut judicare* clauses in international conventions have important effects on the way in which the latter are implemented. Usually ratification of such conventions does not lead to any extension of Dutch jurisdiction. Only when the convention itself contains an unequivocal *obligation* to assert universal jurisdiction will the legislature amend the penal code or enact a statute to establish the required jurisdiction.[23]

The penal code provides for universal jurisdiction over the crimes of piracy (article 4(5)) and counterfeiting currency (article 4(3) and 4(4)), where a basis lies in customary international law, the Convention on the High Seas, and the International Convention for the Suppression of Counterfeiting Currency. The presence of the foreign offender is not expressly required. Article 4(7) and 4(8) also create universal jurisdiction over the crimes listed in the Convention for the Suppression of Unlawful Seizure of Aircraft, the Convention for the Suppression of Unlawful Acts against the Safety of Civil Aviation,[24] and the Convention for the Suppression of Unlawful Acts against the Safety of Maritime Navigation[25] and its Protocol,[26] if the alleged offender is present in

[16] During the parliamentary discussion of the bill relating to the introduction into the penal code of a separate offence of aircraft hijacking the Minister of Justice said that 'under the principle of universality, it is also possible that a State, wishing to protect a hijacker, could bring the man to trial as soon as he entered the country, then impose a not too severe punishment on him or, possibly, even acquit him and then say: no one can be prosecuted twice for the same offence. And this must then be recognized…' (quoted in (1972) 3 *Netherlands Ybk Int'l L* 210).

[17] See, extensively, JJE Schutte, 'Enforcement Measures in International Criminal Law' (1981) 52 *Revue internationale de droit pénal* 441; see also AHJ Swart, *De berechting van internationale misdrijven* (1996) 23–6 and MR Mok, 'Het Europese verdrag tot bestrijding van terrorisme' (1977) 27 *Nederlands Juristenblad* 665.

[18] Orie *et al.* (n 2 above) 416.

[19] Ibid 412.

[20] See eg the Netherlands' reservation to the Convention on the Prevention and Punishment of Crimes against Internationally Protected Persons, including Diplomatic Agents.

[21] Orie *et al.* (n 2 above) 412.

[22] Gerritsen (n 2 above) 65.

[23] Mok and Duk (n 7 above) 146–7.

[24] Montreal, 23 September 1971; 974 UNTS 177.

[25] Rome, 10 March 1988; 1678 UNTS 29004.

[26] Protocol for the Suppression of Unlawful Acts Against the Safety of Fixed Platforms Located on the Continental Shelf (Rome, 10 March 1988; 1678 UNTS 29004).

the Netherlands[27] and a request for extradition has been received and refused. The latter condition follows from Dutch reservations to these conventions. Universal jurisdiction has also been established by a number of statutes not part of the penal code, two of which are discussed below.

Wet Oorlogsstrafrecht

The Crimes in Wartime Act (*Wet Oorlogsstrafrecht*)[28] was adopted primarily to implement the Geneva Conventions. By virtue of article 3(1) in combination with article 8(1) Dutch criminal law applies to anyone who commits outside the Netherlands a 'violation of the laws and customs of war'. By criminalizing all violations of the laws and customs of war, the legislature went further than the requirements of the 1949 Geneva Conventions.[29] This is surprising in the light of what has been said above. On the other hand, it should be noted that in 1949 the Special Criminal Court of the Netherlands opined that universal jurisdiction over war crimes exists as a matter of customary international law.[30] Until recently, however, there was controversy[31] over whether the Act also applied to war crimes committed in wars in which the Netherlands was not engaged. The issue was settled by the Dutch Supreme Court in the *Knesevic* case, which is discussed below.

Uitvoeringswet Folteringsverdrag

As the title indicates, the Act Implementing the Torture Convention (*Uitvoeringswet Folteringsverdrag*)[32] implements the UN Torture Convention. The adoption of a special statute deviates from the normal Dutch practice of implementing *aut dedere aut judicare* conventions through the addition of

[27] A reported case of universal jurisdiction over aircraft hijacking on the basis of article 4(7) is *Public Prosecutor* v *SHT*, summarized in (1987) 74 *Int'l L Reports* 162.

[28] Staatsblad 1952, No 408. For comments, see BVBA Röling, 'Enkele volkenrechtelijke aantekeningen bij de Wet Oorlogstrafrecht' [1959] *Nederlands Tijdschrift voor Internationaal Recht* 263; MW Mouton, 'La protection pénale des conventions internationales humanitaires' [1953] *Revue internationale de droit pénal* 851, 851–8; MW Mouton, 'De Wet Oorlogsstrafrecht en het internationale recht' [1960] *Nederlands Tijdschrift voor Internationaal Recht* 59; GL Coolen, 'De Wet Oorlogsstrafrecht: Een wet met gebreken' (1996) 26 *Delikt en Delinkwent* 43.

[29] Cf the discussion of the 1949 Geneva Conventions in ch 3 s A above.

[30] *In re Rohrig, Brunner, and Heinze*, Special Criminal Court, Amsterdam, 24 December 1949, English translation reprinted in (1950) 17 *Int'l L Reports* 393, 397: 'There was a rule of customary international law by which those who violate the rules of war can be punished by those into whose hands they have fallen (the so-called theory of detention). This rule has the same universality as that applied internationally in the rule which treats pirates as enemies of mankind.' The decision refers to the practice of American tribunals as evidence.

[31] Röling (n 28 above) 271–2; Mouton 1960 (n 28 above) 65–71; Coolen (n 28 above) 47–53; AH Klip, 'Strafrechtelijke reactie op ernstige schendingen van mensenrechten in het buitenland' in CH Brants, C Kelk, and M Moerings (eds) *Er is meer: Opstellen over mensenrechten in internationaal perspectief* (1996) 93, 95–7.

[32] Staatsblad 1988, no 478.

a new subsection in article 4 of the penal code. The obligation imposed by the Convention to establish universal jurisdiction over torture met with severe criticism in the Netherlands.[33] Nonetheless, the Netherlands did not make the usual reservation and article 5 of the Act provides for universal jurisdiction regardless of whether a decision regarding extradition has been taken.[34]

33 The following observations can be found in the parliamentary records: 'Special attention should be paid to the obligation arising from the Convention to establish universal criminal jurisdiction and to the way in which it is suggested this obligation should be fulfilled. It should first of all be stated that the reasons for imposing an obligation to establish such a far-reaching form of extraterritorial jurisdiction for torture are not obvious ones.

The criminal offence of torture is not intrinsically one which tends to involve more than one country. On the contrary, cases having an international aspect, either because the offender and victim possess different nationalities or because the offender has fled abroad or even because the criminal offence has had tangible effects on the territory of another State, are highly exceptional. Experience shows that it is much more typical for offender and victim to be of the same nationality, for the criminal offence to take place on the territory of the State whose nationality they possess, and for the offender to have little reason to flee the country as long as he feels he is supported by his social or political environment.

Furthermore, many instances of torture occur in secrecy, that is to say, in the absence of incidental witnesses, and it may therefore be extremely difficult for a third State which has detained a suspected torturer and has acquired the competence to try him, to obtain the necessary evidence to ensure a successful prosecution, particularly in cases where no co-operation may be expected from the State where the criminal offence took place in providing such evidence under the terms of a mutual legal assistance agreement.

Viewed in this light, the basic conditions which would justify the establishment of universal jurisdiction (ie over offences committed by foreign nationals outside the Netherlands) are lacking. Only rarely, in fact, will multinational features be inherent in the offence and will the required international solidarity and common interest exist between the States most involved. The mere fact that torture is an extremely serious offence which arouses great indignation and concern is not in itself sufficient justification for subjecting it to universal jurisdiction. This, at any event, is the traditional Dutch standpoint on this issue.

In this context, the basic principle to which we should continue to adhere is that the suppression of such practices is the responsibility of the States whose demonstrable connection with the offence in question constitutes grounds for the exercise of jurisdiction. Where such States are deemed by other States to be failing to exercise their jurisdiction sufficiently, this can easily create the temptation to intervene in the affairs of that State and can even lead to a political conflict, and the criminal law is hardly the most appropriate instrument for tackling political differences' (quoted in the initial report of the Netherlands to the Committee against Torture, UN Doc CAT/C/9/Add.1. 20 March 1990, para 40).

34 The parliamentary records elucidate why the Netherlands deviated from a standing policy: 'The reasons for deciding to honour the obligation [to establish universal criminal jurisdiction] despite the above considerations are twofold. In the first place, the social and political situation in a country where torture has been practised can always change dramatically, which would immediately lead to two of the necessary conditions (readiness to co-operate and shared code of values) being fulfilled. [...] [T]he second ground on the basis of which the establishment of universal jurisdiction could be accepted [...] rests on the intolerable nature of the idea that as long as torturers are protected by the regime in their own country, they may travel freely and may, with impunity, come face to face with their victims who have fled to other countries.

In this hypothesis, the exercise of extraterritorial jurisdiction is not to be construed as a means of acting on behalf of another, more closely concerned State. On the contrary, the prosecution of a public official representing the State for acts which he performed there with the approval or acquiescence of his superiors will be seen in essence as amounting to the prosecution and condemnation of the regime as a whole. In this way the administration of criminal justice goes far

The Act does not say that the foreign suspect must be present in the Netherlands, but it is clear that *seeking* extradition of an alien to stand trial in the Netherlands for a totally foreign offence would be irreconcilable with the Dutch understanding of *aut dedere aut judicare*.

Before reviewing cases a few remarks are needed about Dutch criminal procedure.[35] The Public Prosecution Service is the only body empowered to bring a prosecution for a criminal offence and is never obliged to do so (opportunity or expediency principle). Interested parties can, however, complain against decisions by the prosecution service not to prosecute before a court. If the court thinks that the accused should be prosecuted, it will order the public prosecutor to bring a prosecution. Dutch law does not forbid trials *in absentia*[36] and such proceedings occur relatively frequently.[37]

B. CASE-LAW

Chili Komitee Nederland v *Pinochet*

Chili Komitee Nederland v *Pinochet*[38] appears to have been one of the first attempts by a non-governmental organization to set in motion the criminal justice system of a third country to hold former Chilean president Augusto Pinochet accountable for the torture and disappearance of thousands in Chile during his rule. When the former head of state was on a private visit in Amsterdam in 1994 the Chile Committee (Chili Komitee) Netherlands filed a criminal complaint on the basis of the UN Torture Convention, which Chile and the Netherlands ratified respectively in September 1988 and January 1989. The complaint related to complicity in two cases of torture committed in Chile in November 1989, when Pinochet was still President. The allegations were

beyond the boundaries of a specific case to become an instrument in an international political conflict. There are thus very powerful objections to such a use of the Dutch criminal justice system. However, understandable scepticism concerning the effectiveness and credibility of criminal judgments in connection with a conflict in the international political arena stands in opposition to the sense of justice of Dutch society ruled by law, which should find its purest expression in the judgments of the courts. A veritable shock wave would go through the Dutch legal order if, faced with the presence in this country of a foreign national recognized as a torturer by witnesses and victims, the courts were to declare themselves incompetent to hear the case' (quoted in initial report of the Netherlands to the Committee against Torture (ibid) para 40).

[35] For an account in English of criminal procedure in the Netherlands, see AHJ Swart, 'The Netherlands' in C Van den Wyngaert (ed) *Criminal Procedure Systems in the European Community* (1993) 279–316.

[36] Article 280 of the code of penal procedure (*Wetboek van Strafvordering*).

[37] Swart (n 35 above) 313–14. The remedy is opposition (*verzet*), which leads to a complete retrial by the court that rendered the original decision.

[38] Public Prosecutor of Amsterdam, 6 June 1994; Court of Appeal of Amsterdam, 4 January 1995. Excerpts of both decisions are published in English in (1997) 28 *Netherlands Ybk Int'l L* 363–5.

taken from a publication of a Chilean human rights organization.[39] The Public Prosecutor declined to investigate, for the following reasons.

Universality principle The Convention against torture and cruel, inhuman or degrading treatment or punishment (UN Convention of 10 December 1984) grants jurisdiction in four cases to try offences which must be capable of being tried in a State Party under the Convention (Article 5 of the Convention). In the present case the Netherlands would obtain jurisdiction under Article 5, paragraph 2, from the presence of the alleged offender in Dutch territory. Article 5, paragraph 2, requires in this situation that the State Party does not extradite the alleged offender (to the State where the offence was committed or to the State of which the alleged offender or the victim is a national). There is nothing to show that the Netherlands has not taken the decision to extradite Pinochet. It is for this reason that in my view the Netherlands does not have jurisdiction.

In addition, it has not been established that Pinochet was in the Netherlands (or is still in the Netherlands) at the time that the request was made to the Public Prosecutor in Amsterdam. The complainant is twisting things around by demanding that the Public Prosecutor should have an investigation into precisely this matter. This is all the more relevant since it would follow from the complainant's submission that anyone who travels in an aircraft through Dutch airspace and who has possibly committed offences would have to be prosecuted by the Dutch criminal justice authorities (leaving aside for the moment the practical matter of how such people could be arrested).

In short, I believe that the Netherlands does not have jurisdiction in this case, or in any event that this has not been adequately established.

Other aspects In the first place, Pinochet was President of Chile in the period from 20 January 1989 to 11 March 1990. A head of State is entitled to invoke immunity. Furthermore, according to the complainant, Pinochet is still head of the Chilean armed forces, which would make it impossible to prosecute him in Chile. A prosecution would in my view be illusory, since it follows from the nature of the alleged torture that all or virtually all proof would have to be gathered in Chile. The Netherlands does not have a treaty with Chile that allows for the gathering of evidence in criminal proceedings. Moreover, a prosecution would entail many (different) practical problems. In my view, the Dutch criminal justice authorities cannot be expected to tackle these problems seriously and arrive at a solution.

There is also another reason why the Dutch criminal justice authorities cannot be required to institute criminal proceedings. German, Japanese and Yugoslavian war criminals have always been and are still being prosecuted and tried before international tribunals. The Netherlands has only prosecuted and tried Dutch war criminals and is still doing so. Viewed in this light, the prosecution of Pinochet by the Dutch criminal justice authorities would be disproportionate and presumptuous.

Finally, a prosecution, trial and execution of sentence would very probably founder because of the problems of implementation. All formal acts in the course of a prosecution must be served in the correct manner. Furthermore, even assuming that this goes well and that the evidence collected is complete, the sentence imposed could not

[39] This factual summary is based on the introduction to the case in *Netherlands Ybk Int'l L* (ibid).

be executed. Chile could not after all be compelled to extradite one of its own nationals. If the convicted person is not in the Netherlands, the Dutch criminal justice authorities have no means whatever of effectuating the sentence...[40]

On appeal, the Court of Amsterdam held:

The complaint is manifestly ill founded, even if it is assumed that the complainant CKN [Chile Committee Netherlands], according to its objects and as evidenced by its actual work, represents an interest that is directly affected by the decision not to prosecute Pinochet. It is, after all, evident that prosecution of Pinochet by the Dutch Public Prosecutions Department would encounter so many legal and practical problems that the Public Prosecutor was perfectly within his right to decide not to prosecute...[41]

Chili Komitee Nederland v *Pinochet* illustrates the practical problems created by the transitory presence in a third country of a person suspected of a crime to which an *aut dedere aut judicare* convention applies. Because the UN Torture Convention merely requires that the foreign suspect is 'present' (the drafters could have chosen the less ambiguous term 'reside') Pinochet's stay in an Amsterdam hotel arguably triggered the application of articles 5(2) and 7(1) of the Convention. However, the complaint was apparently based solely on a publication of a non-governmental source, without supporting affidavits. Article 7(2) of the Convention provides that '[i]n the cases referred to in article 5, paragraph 2, the standards of evidence required for prosecution and conviction shall in no way be less stringent than those which apply in the cases referred to in article 5, paragraph 1'. Arguably, this applies also to pre-trial arrest. Unless we are prepared to hold Pinochet responsible as a commander[42] for any act of torture that occurred in Chile during his rule it is difficult to see how the Dutch authorities could have detained him without lowering the ordinary standards of evidence for pre-trial arrest.

Public Prosecutor v *Knesevic*

The case of *Public Prosecutor* v *Knesevic*[43] arose out of the war and ethnic violence in the former Yugoslavia in the first half of the 1990s. The Netherlands

[40] Decision of the Public Prosecutor of Amsterdam (n 38 above); translation from *Netherlands Ybk Int'l L* (ibid).

[41] Court of Appeal of Amsterdam (n 38 above); translation from *Netherlands Ybk Int'l L* (ibid). Critical of the decision to dismiss are MT Kamminga and M Tijssen, 'Pinochet, Nederland en het VN-Verdrag tegen foltering' [1995] *Nederlands Juristen Comité voor de Mensenrechten-Bulletin* 986 and C Ingelse and H van der Wilt, 'De Zaak Pinochet: Over Universele Rechtsmacht en Hollandse Benepenheid' [1996] *Nederlands Juristenblad* 280. For a concurring opinion, see Klip (n 31 above) 102–5. For the noticeable lack of reaction by the UN Committee against Torture following the Dutch decision not to prosecute, see C Ingelse, *The UN Committee Against Torture: An Assessment* (2001) 347–8.

[42] Neither the UN Torture Convention nor the Dutch implementing statute provide for command responsibility.

[43] Examining magistrate, 1 December 1995; Hoge Raad der Nederlanden, 11 November 1997, published in (1998) XCI *Militair Rechterlijk Tijdschrift* 198–221 with note by H van der Wilt;

has at least three links with the conflict: it participated in the UN peacekeeping operation, it is the host country of the International Criminal Tribunal for the former Yugoslavia, and it admitted a considerable number of war refugees.[44] Among them was Knesevic, whom other refugees denounced as a war criminal. The office of the prosecutor requested an examining magistrate (*Rechter-Commissaris*) to open a preliminary judicial inquiry into possible 'violations of laws and customs of war' by the accused on the basis of the Crimes in Wartime Act.[45] The request characterized the events in the former Yugoslavia as 'an armed conflict not of an international character'.[46] In line with the traditional Dutch attitude towards extraterritorial jurisdiction, the investigative magistrate declared the application inadmissible on the ground that the Crimes in Wartime Act only applies to armed conflicts in which the Netherlands is involved.[47]

After several appeals and a remand the case ended up before the Supreme Court (Hoge Raad). The Court held that the Crimes in Wartime Act applied and that the Netherlands had jurisdiction. The Court found that it was clear from the parliamentary records that the legislature intended to comply in full with the 1949 Geneva Conventions, which require that all States parties search for suspects and bring them to justice before its own courts, regardless of their nationality.[48]

Although the Dutch Supreme Court in *Public Prosecutor* v *Knesevic* merely clarified an ambiguity in a municipal statute without interpreting international law, the decision has international legal significance. A country traditionally averse to extraterritorial jurisdiction claims universal jurisdiction over war crimes beyond the grave breaches provisions of the Geneva Conventions and Additional Protocol I. After the *Knesevic* decision the Dutch government transformed the special investigation unit for war criminals from the former Yugoslavia into a war crimes investigation unit without territorial restriction. A year later the unit had identified eighty-five foreign residents against whom there were indications that they were involved in war crimes or crimes against humanity in their country of origin,[49] but no prosecutions have been brought so far.[50]

English translation in (1998) 1 *Ybk Int'l Humanitarian L* 601 with note by N Keijzer at 483; see also R van Elst, 'De zaak Darco Knezevic: Rechtsmacht over Joegoslavische en andere buitenlandse oorlogsmisdadigers' [1998] *Nederlands Juristenblad* 1587.

[44] R van Elst, 'Afscheid van Joegoslavië: Over oorlogsmisdrijven en misdrijven tegen de menselijkheid begaan in voormalig Joegoslavië en de Nederlandse rechter' [1994] *Nederlands Juristenblad* 1401–10 examines the possibilities under Dutch law to prosecute refugees suspected of war crimes in the former Yugoslavia.

[45] Taken from the decision of the Hoge Raad der Nederlanden (n 43 above).

[46] Ibid.

[47] Order of the examining magistrate (n 43 above).

[48] Hoge Raad der Nederlanden (n 43 above) at 5.2.

[49] Tweede Kamer, vergaderjaar 1998–1999, 26 262, no 1 and no 2.

[50] The whereabouts of Knesevic are said to be unknown (R van Elst, 'Implementing Universal Jurisdiction Over Grave Breaches of the Geneva Conventions' (2000) 13 *Leiden J Int'l L* 815, 847).

Wijngaarde et al. v *Bouterse*

The defendant in *Wijngaarde* et al. v *Bouterse*[51] is the long-time leader of Surinam, Desiré Delano Bouterse. Since the country became independent from the Netherlands in 1975, Bouterse seized power twice by military coups. These days he is an elected member of parliament and the leader of Surinam's main political party.

In 1999, after long-drawn-out proceedings, a Dutch court tried and convicted Bouterse in his absence for conspiring to import cocaine into the Netherlands. While these proceedings were going on, a complaint in the Netherlands laid the basis for *Wijngaarde* et al. v *Bouterse*, which is of importance for this study.

The case arose out of the 'December killings', the arrest and summary execution in Surinam during the night of 8/9 December 1982 of fifteen prominent opponents of the Bouterse regime. At least one of the victims was a Dutch national. The December killings have been investigated and documented by numerous non-governmental and intergovernmental organizations,[52] yet have not led to criminal proceedings in Surinam.

In January 1996 a relative of the Dutch victim filed a criminal complaint against Bouterse for having ordered the December killings.[53] The complaint was not based on the nationality of the victim—that basis is firmly rejected in the Netherlands—but on the nationality of the alleged perpetrator. The plaintiff asserted that at the time of the offence Bouterse was still a Dutch national and that accordingly article 5 of the penal code should apply.

The Public Prosecutor in Amsterdam, however, believed that Bouterse had lost his Dutch citizenship by joining the Surinam armed forces in 1975, and therefore declined to open an investigation. A prolonged debate ensued on Bouterse's nationality.[54] The plaintiff then tried a different approach. On appeal, he advanced the position that the Netherlands could exercise *universal* jurisdiction over the crimes against all fifteen victims.

In an interlocutory order the Court of Amsterdam took judicial notice of the reports about the December killings of several non-judicial (international) bodies[55] and concluded that the 'suspicions and allegations are so serious that

[51] District Court of Amsterdam (sitting on appeal against a decision of the office of the Public Prosecutor), interlocutory order of 3 March 2000 and order of 20 November 2000 (District Court order) (copies on file with author), case note by E van Sliedregt and N Keijzer in (2000) 3 *Ybk Int'l Humanitarian L* 548, English translation of the order of 20 November published in ibid 677; Hoge Raad der Nederlanden, 18 September 2001 (Supreme Court decision) (copy on file with author).

[52] See n 55 below.

[53] Copy of complaint on file with author. A second Dutch plaintiff by the name of Hoost later joined in the proceedings.

[54] The question *when* Bouterse lost his Dutch nationality could not be resolved without the collaboration of the Surinam authorities, which they refused. It was ultimately ruled that Bouterse had 'almost certainly' lost his Dutch citizenship on 25 November 1975.

[55] *Inter alia* the report of Mr S Amos Wako, UN Special Rapporteur on summary or arbitrary executions (UN Doc E/CN.4/1985/17).

Bouterse should be held accountable before a criminal tribunal'.[56] The Court then considered the question whether the Netherlands was an appropriate forum.

To begin with, the Court states that the investigation of criminal offences committed in Surinam and that constitute violations of human rights is in principle incumbent on the Republic of Surinam by virtue of the International Covenant of Civil and Political Rights, to which it became a party in 1977. We accept, however, the position of plaintiffs that it cannot be expected that Bouterse will be brought to justice any time soon, in Surinam or elsewhere, for the conduct complained of. The Netherlands has close historical links with Surinam. A large Surinam community lives within the Netherlands.[57] The events of December 1982 shocked this community, but also the larger public in the Netherlands. There are indications that at least one victim was a Dutch national. Moreover, plaintiffs, who are relatives of two of the victims, live in the Netherlands. Because it cannot be expected that Bouterse will be prosecuted elsewhere any time soon, the plaintiffs have turned to the most appropriate authority. For these reasons, prosecution in the Netherlands would be opportune.[58]

Having concluded that prosecution by the Netherlands would be opportune the Court decided to ask expert advice on the international legal aspects of the case. The following questions were put to Professor John Dugard. (1) Under customary international law as it was in 1982, can the alleged acts be considered torture, crimes against humanity, or war crimes for which the perpetrator can be held criminally liable? (2) Can it be said that under customary international law as it was in 1982, or at any time later, the alleged crimes were imprescriptible? (3) Does customary international law as it was in 1982, or at any time since then, provide a State with extraterritorial jurisdiction over torture and crimes against humanity, if the suspect is not a national? (4) Does it make any difference, for the previous question, whether the suspect is present on the territory of that State? (5) Does it make any difference, for question (3), whether the victims are nationals of that State? (6) Does customary international law as it was in 1982, or at any time since then, oblige a State to exercise jurisdiction under the circumstances set out in questions (3), (4), and (5)? The court's final order, which follows the expert opinion,[59] deserves quotation at length.[60]

Opportunity of prosecution in the Netherlands

3.1 [...]

3.2 According to recent press reports judicial authorities in Surinam have launched their own investigation against Bouterse. This raises the question whether prosecution in the Netherlands is still opportune, as this Court held in its interlocutory order.

[56] Interlocutory order (n 51 above) para 3.8.

[57] Nearly half of the Surinamese population lives in the Netherlands.

[58] Interlocutory order (n 51 above) para 4.2.

[59] Copy of Professor Dugard's opinion on file with author.

[60] District Court order (n 51 above). The numbers refer to the paragraph numbers in the original.

3.3 This Court did not receive any official communication about such an investigation in Surinam and it is impossible to predict the possible outcome of such an investigation [...] Therefore, there are insufficient grounds for the Court to change its decision of 3 March 2000 regarding the opportunity of prosecution in this country.

3.4 This prosecution can, with the approval of this Court, always be suspended if legal developments in Surinam give cause to that. [...]

No immunity for Bouterse as head of State

4.1 Counsel for Bouterse argues that his client cannot be prosecuted for the alleged facts because he was head of State at the time.

4.2 The Court can leave aside the insufficiently supported submission that Bouterse was indeed the head of State. The commission of very serious crimes, like the ones in this case, cannot be attributed to the official functions of a head of State.

Criminality of the acts under international law and applicability of the universality principle

5.1 The Court accepts the remarks and conclusions of the expert to the effect that the acts can be considered crimes against humanity/torture under customary international law, in that they were committed in a systematic manner as part of an organized plan by the military authorities, of which Bouterse was commander, against a group of civilians, with the intent to obtain confessions or to intimidate or coerce members of the civilian population.

5.2 The Court also sides with the expert on the following points:
—that torture was already a crime under international customary law back in 1982 for which the perpetrator can be held individually and criminally accountable;
—that back in 1982, crimes against humanity (probably) could be committed not only during war or armed conflict, but also in time of peace;[61]
—that crimes against humanity are imprescriptible;
—that customary international law, as it was in 1982, provides a State with extra-territorial (universal) jurisdiction over a foreigner suspected of a crime against humanity.

5.3 The Court further understands from the report of the expert that it is not a requirement for the exercise of jurisdiction that the victim(s) is (are) a national of the prosecuting State, but that—as in the present case where plaintiffs are related to the victims—this would strengthen the legal basis for the exercise of jurisdiction.

5.4 The Court has found insufficient grounds in the report of the expert for the view that prosecution of Bouterse in this country would be impermissible under international (customary) law as long as he is not present in the Netherlands.[62]

[61] Professor Dugard had reservations in this respect. His opinion at 4.2.3 states that 'whether this was the position in 1982 is not entirely free from doubt, particularly in respect of armed conflict'.

[62] Professor Dugard had stated at 5.6.5 in his opinion:
'It is not clear whether this requirement prevents a State in whose territory the offender is not present from requesting extradition of the offender from a State in whose territory the offender is present, but which elects not to try him itself, when the sole basis for the exercise of jurisdiction

Torture

6.1 [...]

6.2 In the interlocutory order the Court raised the question whether the Act Implementing the UN Torture Convention can be applied to acts committed in December 1982, thus before the coming into force of the Act on 20 January 1989. The Court was concerned that this could violate the legality principle. [...]

6.3 The expert has voiced the opinion [...] that the UN Torture Convention has a declaratory character. In other words: the Convention only confirmed existing customary international law in respect of the prohibition on torture, its criminalization, and its recognition as a crime against humanity. In follows, in the opinion of the expert, that the Act Implementing the UN Torture Convention can be applied retrospectively to conduct which was already criminal under Dutch law, though not under the name torture, like assault and murder. In this respect, the expert has made a distinction between *retroactive* and *retrospective* legislation. A retroactive law renders an act criminal which was not punishable when committed. A retrospective law, on the other hand, does not create new offences.

6.4 The Court concurs with the expert's considerations and conclusions. This means that, the possible exercise of universal jurisdiction over Bouterse by a Dutch judge on the basis of the retrospective application of the Act Implementing the UN Torture Convention—which in the opinion of the Court is not only feasible but also appropriate—does not violate Article 15 of the International Covenant on Civil and Political Rights.

6.5 For these reasons, it cannot be concluded that the prosecution and possible punishment of Bouterse would violate the legality principle and/or that Bouterse could not have known that one day he could be prosecuted outside Surinam, in particular in the Netherlands. [...]

The notion of torture in the Act Implementing the UN Torture Convention

7.1 In the interlocutory order the Court raised questions regarding the applicability of the Act Implementing the UN Torture Convention to the killing of the victims. [...]

7.2 Upon closer consideration the Court finds insufficient indications to exclude the 'independent' killing, ie apart from the preceding torture, from the application of the Act.

7.3 In this respect, it is important that Article 1, paragraph 2, of the Act equates ill-treatment with the intentional infliction of a condition of severe angst or other form of mental desperation, which would be the case when one confronts the victims with an imminent execution. As already said, it would be inconceivable that this infliction would be considered torture but not the execution—the ultimate ill-treatment. [...]

is the principle of universality. Some have argued that it is objectionable to allow extradition requests of this kind as this would permit a particular state to acts as "policeman" of the world by requesting extradition of torturers from any country. This objection was not raised in the Pinochet proceedings and a number of English courts were prepared to entertain a request from Spain to exercise jurisdiction on grounds of universality. A State that requests extradition of a torturer would probably be wise to stress the presence of some connecting factor between it and the crime to ensure that this objection would not be raised against it.'

7.4 This leads to the conclusion that all alleged acts—torture, whether it results in death or not, as well as murder as an independent delict—can be prosecuted in the Netherlands on the basis of the Act Implementing the UN Torture Convention.
7.5 [. . .]
7.6 The Court recognizes, however, that there may be differences of opinion on this point and that it cannot be excluded that the criminal judge construes the Act more narrowly.
7.7 [. . .]

Other basis for prosecution

8.1 The events of 8/9 December cannot be qualified as war crimes. [. . .]
8.2 [. . .] The Court concurs with the view of the expert that crimes against humanity, outside the scope of the Act Implementing the UN Torture Convention, are only punishable in the Netherlands under the Wartime Criminal Law Act. The latter, however, does not consider them separate offences but aggravating circumstances in connection with war crimes. The alleged facts, however, cannot be qualified as war crimes.
8.3 These considerations lead the Court to conclude that there is no reason to open an investigation against Bouterse on a different or broader basis than the Act Implementing the UN Torture Convention.
8.4 The Court is, however, of the opinion that the judge who will decide this case on the merits should remain free to qualify the facts in accordance with his own views. The prosecution order will therefore not specify the precise legal grounds on which the prosecution should be brought.

9. [. . .]
10. [. . .]

Decision

The Court of Appeal:

—orders the public prosecutor in the district of Amsterdam to prosecute Desiré Delano Bouterse [. . .] for the offences to which the complaint relates and which were committed in Paramaribo, Surinam, on or about 8/9 December 1982;
—directs the public prosecutor to file an application with the examining magistrate responsible for dealing with criminal cases in the district of Amsterdam for the institution of a preliminary examination into the offence concerned;

—[. . .]

The order was sharply criticized by a prominent Dutch commentator because it broke with the traditional dualistic approach of the Netherlands regarding international criminal law.[63] The exercise of universal jurisdiction *in absentia* constitutes a further deviation from well-established Dutch practice.[64] On

[63] For a comprehensive critical analysis, see GAM Strijards, 'Neerlands dualisme en zijn strafmacht', [2000] *Nederlands Juristenblad* 2113–22.
[64] See above section A of this country study.

appeal by the Procurator-General[65] the Supreme Court quashed the order on no less than five grounds;[66] first, the application of the Act Implementing the Torture Convention to facts that had occurred before its adoption in 1988 violated article 16 of the Constitution (legality principle);[67] second, the killing of a person without first torturing him does not constitute torture in the sense of article 1 of the Act Implementing the Torture Convention;[68] third, the jurisdiction clause of the Act Implementing the Torture Convention (article 5) cannot be applied retroactively;[69] fourth, prosecution is barred by the domestic statute of limitation;[70] and finally, based upon a careful examination of the drafting history of the Act Implementing the Torture Convention, the Court opined that 'prosecution and punishment in the Netherlands of a person suspected of an offence under articles 1 and 2 of the Act Implementing the Torture Convention is only possible if one of the links mentioned in the Convention exists, for example when the offender or victim is a Dutch citizen, *or when the suspect is present in the Netherlands at the time of his arrest*'[71] (emphasis added).

The Supreme Court in *Wijngaarde* et al. v *Bouterse* did not decide any points of international law (dualism versus monism is a matter of domestic law). The court held though that the exercise of universal jurisdiction under the Act Implementing the Torture Convention is only possible if the suspect can be arrested on Dutch territory. With this requirement the Dutch Supreme Court is on the same wavelength as the chief prosecutor of Denmark in *Pinochet*, the French Court of Cassation in *Javor*, and the Brussels court of appeals in *Sharon* and *Ndombasi*.[72] No attention was apparently paid to the fact that the territorial State is not a party to the UN Torture Convention.

C. SUMMARY

The review of Dutch law and practice shows a relatively narrow ambit of municipal criminal law. The reluctance to exercise extraterritorial jurisdiction is motivated by human rights concerns and international comity. Ratification of international criminal law conventions does not usually lead to any extension of jurisdiction, unless the convention contains an unequivocal obligation to do so. Even then a reservation is usually made to the effect that the Netherlands will only prosecute a foreign suspect if a request for extradition has been received and refused.

[65] The Procurator-General is the Supreme Court's advisor on legal matters; he appealed against the order of the District Court by way of 'cassation in the interest of law'.

[66] Hoge Raad der Nederlanden (n 51 above). [67] Ibid para 4. [68] Ibid para 5.

[69] Ibid para 6. [70] Ibid para 7. [71] Ibid para 8.5.

[72] See the respective country studies above.

Chili Komitee Nederland v *Pinochet* illustrates the dilemmas created by the transitory presence in a third country of a person suspected of a crime to which an *aut dedere aut judicare* convention applies. In *Public Prosecutor* v *Knesevic* it was held that a foreign asylum seeker can be prosecuted in the Netherlands on the basis of universal jurisdiction for violations of the laws and customs of war committed during an armed conflict in which the Netherlands were not engaged. In *Wijngaarde* et al. v *Bouterse* the Supreme Court held that a foreigner suspected of torture abroad cannot be prosecuted in the Netherlands unless he is voluntarily present on Dutch territory. *In absentia* proceedings on the basis of universal jurisdiction are thus out of the question, as is the retroactive application of a domestic statute penalizing international crimes.

13

Senegal

A. AMBIT OF THE CRIMINAL LAW

The extraterritorial application of Senegalese criminal law is limited to active personality and protective jurisdiction. The relevant provisions can be found in Title XII ('*Des crimes et délits commis à l'étranger*') of the code of penal procedure (*Code de procédure penal*, or CPP). CPP article 664 provides for jurisdiction over *crimes* and, in the case of double criminality, also over *délits* committed by Senegalese nationals abroad. Protective jurisdiction is provided for in CPP article 669. In both cases, *ne bis in idem* applies (CPP article 667). The code contains neither a passive personality clause nor a general enabling clause for treaty crimes. Special statutes implementing international criminal law treaties do not appear to exist either. In short, any basis for universal jurisdiction seems to be lacking, but attention should be drawn to article 79 of the Constitution, which provides for the supremacy of duly ratified treaties over domestic law. A recent case put this constitutional provision to the proof.

B. CASE-LAW

Guengueng et al. v *Habré*

The case of *Guengueng* et al. v *Habré*[1] involves the former leader of Chad, Hissène Habré, who led the country from 1982 until his overthrowal in 1990. His regime was characterized by widespread and systematic repression. An official Chadian commission of inquiry into the crimes of his regime called for immediate prosecution. The successor government never indicted him nor pursued his extradition from Senegal, where he has lived since his ouster from power.

In January 2000 seven individual Chadians as well as a Chadian organization representing victims of the *Habré* regime filed a *constitution de partie civile* with an examining magistrate in Dakar (Senegal).[2] The complaint

[1] Court of Appeals of Dakar (Chambre d'Accusation), 4 July 2000 (Appeals judgment); Court of Cassation, First Chamber, 20 March 2001 (Cassation judgment); copies of decisions on file with author. My discussion of the *Habré* case draws heavily on R Brody and H Duffy, 'Prosecuting Torture Universally: Hissène Habré, Africa's Pinochet?' in H Fischer, C Kreß, and SR Lüder (eds) *International and National Prosecutions of Crimes under International Law: Current Developments* (2001) 817.

[2] Copy of complaint on file with author. On the initiation of criminal proceedings through the mechanism of *constitution de partie civile* see the Belgium and France country studies above.

alleged that the accused was personally responsible for crimes against humanity, torture and 'barbarous acts', and forced disappearances. The plaintiffs argued that general international law obliges Senegal to repress crimes against humanity wherever committed; furthermore, articles 5(2) and 7 of the UN Torture Convention require Senegal to repress torture independently of the *locus delicti*. It should be noted that Senegal and Chad ratified the UN Torture Convention in 1987 and 1995 respectively and that torture did not become a specific offence under Senegalese law until 1996. After favourable advice by the public prosecutor the examining magistrate indicted Habré on torture charges.

The accused moved to dismiss the case before the *Chambre d'Accusation* of the Dakar Court of Appeals, on three grounds: lack of extraterritorial jurisdiction under domestic law, violation of the legality principle (*nullum crimen sine lege*), and prescription under Senegalese law.[3] It is noteworthy that he did not claim immunity as a former head of State, nor did he raise the fact that Chad was not a party to the UN Torture Convention at the time of the alleged crimes.

The Court granted the appeal on the first ground and therefore did not address the legality and prescription arguments. The Court took the view that the UN Torture Convention, and article 5 in particular, could not be directly applied and that the absence of enabling legislation was thus fatal.[4] Article 5 prescribes that States parties must take the necessary measures to establish (extraterritorial) jurisdiction over torture.

On appeal in cassation the *avocat général* argued[5] that the requirement of prior implementing legislation disregards article 79 of the Senegalese Constitution[6] and, in so doing, also article 5(2) of the UN Torture Convention. The *Cour de Cassation* held the Convention not to be self-executing and accordingly rejected the appeal.[7]

The decision to dismiss in *Guengueng* et al. v *Habré* was based solely on domestic law, or better, on a lack thereof. Article 27 of the Vienna Convention on the Law of Treaties provides in this respect that internal law may not be invoked as justification for failing to perform a treaty. It is interesting to note that a 1995 Senegalese report to the UN Committee Against Torture states that Senegalese law complies with article 5 of the UN Torture Convention.[8] The *Habré* ruling holds the opposite, and the failure to adopt the necessary enabling legislation constitutes a violation of article 5(2) of the Convention.

The inaction by the Senegalese criminal justice authorities arguably also violates article 7(1) of the UN Torture Convention, which obliges a State party in whose territory a person alleged to have committed torture is found

[3] This summary of the defendant's arguments is adapted from the Appeals judgment (n 1 above).
[4] Very critical of the decision are Brody and Duffy (n 1 above) 826–42.
[5] Copy of brief on file with author.
[6] See section A above in this chapter.
[7] Cassation judgment (n 1 above).
[8] CAT/C/17/Add.14 of 11 July 1995, para 39.

to submit the case to its competent authorities for the purpose of prosecution, if it does not extradite him. As shown earlier it was the drafters' intent that jurisdiction must be established also in cases like the instant one where no extradition request is made by any other State. Senegal ratified the UN Torture Convention in 1987, thus towards the end of the *Habré* regime.[9] The Vienna Convention on the Law of Treaties provides in article 28 for the non-retroactivity of treaties. Since the allegations contained in the complaint took place after 1987 Senegal was indeed obliged to submit the case to its competent authorities for the purpose of prosecution.

Chad, for its part, did not become a party to the UN Torture Convention until after the *Habré* regime but the issue of non-ratification by the territorial State, and thus of the effect of treaties on third States, was not touched upon. It can be argued though that the individual's right to invoke an argument based thereon is derivative of the territorial State's right to protest. If the latter fails to register an official protest the former loses the right to raise the issue in proceedings against him. No protest was reported in the instant case. After the indictment was quashed the plaintiffs chose Belgium as a forum for further legal action against the former leader of Chad.[10]

C. SUMMARY

The ambit of Senegalese criminal law is nearly strictly territorial. Apart from protective jurisdiction there is no basis in Senegalese law for prosecuting a foreigner for a crime committed abroad, not even for crimes which Senegal has undertaken by treaty to repress. A case in point is *Guengueng* et al. v *Habré* where it was held that the UN Torture Convention is not self-executing and that in the absence of enabling legislation the suspect could not be prosecuted in Senegal.

[9] See ch 3 s A above.

[10] See the Belgium country study above n 82.

14

Spain

A. AMBIT OF THE CRIMINAL LAW

The scope of Spanish criminal law follows from the jurisdiction of the courts as spelled out in Book I, Title I (‘*De la extension y limites de la jurisdicción*’) of the 1985 Organic Law of the Judicial Power (*Ley Orgánica del Poder Judicial*, or LOPJ).[1] LOPJ article 23.1,[2] in conjunction with article 8.1 of the civil code,[3] establishes the territoriality of criminal law. LOPJ article 23.2 creates general active personality jurisdiction over *delitos* if the offence is also punishable in the territorial State, and a complaint by the victim or the foreign authorities has been received, and the offender has not yet been tried. Protective jurisdiction over nine specific offences is provided for in LOPJ article 23.3. General passive personality jurisdiction is conspicuously lacking. Thus Spanish courts ordinarily do not have jurisdiction over extraterritorial offences against Spanish nationals. The universality principle can be found in LOPJ article 23.4.

Ley Orgánica del Poder Judicial, article 23.4

LOPJ article 23.4 provides:

> Furthermore, Spanish courts have jurisdiction over acts committed abroad by Spaniards and foreigners, if these acts constitute any of the following offences under Spanish law: (a) genocide; (b) terrorism; (c) sea or air piracy; (d) counterfeiting; (e) offences in connection with prostitution and corruption of minors and incompetents; (f) drug trafficking; (g) any other offence which Spain is obliged to prosecute under an international treaty or convention.

The structure and content of this provision are similar to §6 of the German penal code.[4] All the listed offences are the subject of an international convention but in the case of genocide, terrorism, and offences in connection with prostitution, the Spanish legislature, like the German legislature, has gone further than is required by the terms of the relevant convention. LOPJ article 23.4 does not expressly require the presence of the foreign offender for

[1] In force since 1 July 1985.

[2] LOPJ article 23.1 reads: ‘Spanish courts are competent to try cases involving serious and lesser offences committed on Spanish territory or on board Spanish ships or aircraft, without prejudice to the provisions of the international treaties to which Spain is a party’.

[3] Article 8.1 of the civil code states ‘the penal, police, and public security laws are binding on every person within Spain’.

[4] See the Germany country study above.

the initiation of proceedings. However, trials *in absentia* are not allowed except in certain exceptional circumstances.[5]

The investigation of extraterritorial offences is the responsibility of a central examining magistrate (*juez central de instrucción*) who can be seized by the public prosecutor, by the victim, or by *any* private citizen or organization exercising the *acción popular*.[6] This right is unabridged in cases of extraterritorial offences.[7] Appeals against the magistrate's decisions are heard by the *Audiencia Nacional* (*Audiencia*), which is also the trial court for extraterritorial offences (LOPJ article 65).

B. CASE-LAW

Unión Progresista de Fiscales de España et al. v *Pinochet*

The landmark case of *Unión Progresista de Fiscales de España* et al. v *Pinochet*[8] has received ample attention in academic, diplomatic, and human rights circles. Compilations of the primary sources as well as a thorough analysis of the Spanish proceedings and their context are available in English.[9] The present analysis is limited to the controversy about jurisdiction during the proceedings in Spain and thus does not go into the questions of State immunity and retrospective application of the Organic Law of the Judicial Power.

In July 1996 the *Unión Progresista de Fiscales de España* (Progressive Union of Prosecutors of Spain) lodged a criminal complaint in Spain against General Augusto Pinochet and other junta leaders, who had ruled Chile by dictatorship between 1973 and 1989.[10] During their rule the loss of life exceeded 3,000 according to the official count. Parallel complaints were filed against the Argentine military junta for the murder or disappearance of up to

[5] Articles 791(4), 789(4), and 793 of the code of penal procedure (*Ley de Enjuiciamiento Criminal*).

[6] The legal basis of the *acción popular* is article 125 of the Constitution and articles 101 and 270 of the code of penal procedure.

[7] For an overview in English of Spanish criminal procedure, see R Vogler, 'Spain' in CM Bradley (ed) *Criminal Procedure: A Worldwide Study* (1999) 361; ER Vadillo, 'Spain' in C Van den Wyngaert (ed) *Criminal Procedure Systems in the European Community* (1993) 383.

[8] Audiencia Nacional (central investigating tribunal no 5), decisions of 16 and 18 October and 3 November 1998 (copies on file with author); Audiencia Nacional (criminal division) (plenary session), 5 November 1998 (copy on file with author), case note by M Carrasco and J Fernández in (1999) 93 *Am J Int'l L* 690, English translation published in R Brody and M Ratner (eds) *The Pinochet Papers: The Case of Augusto Pinochet in Spain and Britain* (2000) 95.

[9] Brody and Ratner (ibid) is an extremely useful chronological compilation of the primary sources translated into English. RJ Wilson, 'Prosecuting Pinochet: International Crimes in Spanish Domestic Law' 21 (1999) *Human Rights Q* 927 offers a thorough analysis of the Spanish proceedings and their context.

[10] This section draws on Wilson (ibid) 931–7 and on N Roht-Arriaza, 'The Pinochet Precedent and Universal Jurisdiction' (2001) 35 *New England L Rev* 311.

30,000 persons during the Argentine 'Dirty War' (1976–83). In both countries the military decreed amnesties before relinquishing power.

Among the victims were a number of foreign nationals.[11] It does not appear that any of them were victimized because of their nationality but it nonetheless adds an international legal element to the cases. As originally filed, the complaints for both Argentine and Chile named only Spanish citizens as victims. As noted above, the LOPJ does not provide for passive personality jurisdiction. The complaints subsequently added non-Spanish citizens, thus forcing the issue into the terrain of universal jurisdiction.

The examining magistrate in the Chile case declared himself competent to investigate charges of genocide, terrorism, and torture *regardless of the nationality* of the victims and issued a warrant for the arrest of Pinochet. When in London on a private visit British authorities detained Pinochet pursuant to the Spanish request.[12] The famous and highly complex British—Spanish *Pinochet* case was born. Chile, the territorial State, vehemently contested Spain's right to try its former head of State and Senator for Life.

The chief public prosecutor appealed to the Audiencia Nacional. The panel of eleven judges of the Audiencia upheld Spain's universal jurisdiction. Genocide was the first of the offences for which jurisdiction was approved. The Audiencia concluded that article VI of the Genocide Convention, ratified by Spain in 1968, does not prevent the exercise of extraterritorial jurisdiction.

> Article VI of the Convention does not rule out the existence of judicial organs with jurisdiction other than the domestic courts of the country in whose territory the crime was committed, or an international tribunal. Article VI of the Convention announces an international penal tribunal and imposes on the States parties the obligation of ensuring that genocide will necessarily be tried by the judicial organs of the State in whose territory the crimes were committed. Yet it would be contrary to the spirit of the Convention—which seeks a commitment on the part of the Contracting Parties to use their respective criminal justice systems to prosecute genocide as a crime under international law, and to prevent impunity in the case of such a crime—to interpret Article VI as limiting the exercise of jurisdiction by excluding any jurisdiction not treated therein. That the Contracting Parties have not criminalized this offence universally in each of their domestic jurisdictions does not stand in the way of a State party establishing such a category of jurisdiction for an offence that has a major impact worldwide, and that affects the international community directly, all of humanity, as is made clear in the Convention itself.[13][. . .]
>
> It should be recognized, considering the prevalence of international treaties over municipal law (article 96 of the Spanish Constitution and article 27 of the Vienna Convention on the Law of Treaties of 1969), that article VI of the Convention on the

[11] France, Germany, and Switzerland instituted proceedings against Pinochet on the basis of passive personality jurisdiction (see the respective country studies).

[12] An English translation of the Spanish request of 16 October 1998 to arrest Pinochet is published in Brody and Ratner (n 8 above) 57.

[13] Audiencia (n 8 above) s 2; translation taken from Brody and Ratner (ibid) 98.

Prevention and Punishment of the Crime of Genocide makes the action of jurisdictions others than those provided for at article VI subsidiary, such that a State must refrain from exercising jurisdiction over acts that constitute genocide where they are already being tried by the courts of the country in which they occurred or by an international penal tribunal.[14]

As to the question of jurisdiction over terrorism, the Audiencia's ruling relies largely on its legal reasoning with regard to genocide, in that both offences are found on the list of crimes for which universal jurisdiction exists under LOPJ article 23.4.[15] Regarding torture, the Audiencia held that the offence is clearly within the court's jurisdiction by virtue of LOPJ article 23.4(g) in conjunction with article 5(2) of the UN Torture Convention. Moreover, reasoned the Audiencia, any such acts are subsumed in the greater offences of genocide and terrorism, for which there is clear jurisdiction.[16] Finally, the Audiencia dealt very briefly with an argument by the prosecutor that article 2(1) of the UN Charter, which provides that the United Nations is 'based on the principle of sovereign equality of all its Members' bars interference by Spain in Chilean affairs.

When the Spanish judicial organs apply that provision [LOPJ article 23.4], they neither invade nor interfere in the sovereignty of the State in which the offence was committed; rather, they exercise Spain's own sovereignty in relation to international crimes.

Spain has jurisdiction to hear the facts, derived from the principle of universal prosecution of certain offences—categorized in international law—which has been incorporated into our domestic law. Moreover, Spain has a legitimate interest in the exercise of its jurisdiction, as more than fifty Spaniards were killed or disappeared in Chile, victims of the repression denounced in the record.[17]

The Audiencia's ruling on jurisdiction permitted the case to proceed in the Spanish court, whatever might be the outcome of the extradition litigation in the United Kingdom. British authorities decided that Pinochet could be extradited to Spain on charges of torture, irrespective of the nationality of the victims. The accused was, however, released on medical grounds and returned to Chile where litigation commenced under Chilean law.[18]

Unión Progresista de Fiscales de España et al. v *Pinochet* was the catalyst for legal actions in several other European countries, and ultimately also in Chile.[19] Belgium requested Pinochet's extradition too, but on the ground that he was responsible for crimes against humanity. The chief prosecutor of Denmark, on the other hand, decided against universal jurisdiction because

[14] Audiencia (n 8 above) s 2; translation taken from Brody and Ratner (ibid) 98.

[15] Ibid s 6. [16] Ibid s 7.

[17] Ibid s 9; translation taken from Brody and Ratner (n 8 above) 107.

[18] See correspondent's report by H Salinas Burgos and C Dettleff Beros in (2000) 3 *Ybk Int'l Humanitarian L* 447.

[19] Salinas Burgos and Dettleff Beros (n 18 above); Roht-Arriaza (n 10 above) 315–16 describes the catalyzing process that took place within Chile.

the accused was not present in Denmark. French and Swiss judicial authorities launched investigations into common offences (murder) against nationals on the basis of a general passive personality clause in their domestic law; along the same lines the German Federal Supreme Court ruled that Germany has jurisdiction over common offences in Chile during the Pinochet dictatorship against German nationals.[20] In Spain the judicial authorities and plaintiffs could not rely on a passive personality provision in the LOPJ to investigate crimes against Spaniards. This jurisdictional constraint offers the best explanation for the Spanish decision to characterize the offences as genocide and to investigate atrocities irrespective of the nationality of the victim.[21]

The decision of the Audiencia raises several questions. The characterization of the alleged offences as genocide is, to say the least, questionable[22] and 'leads to an absurdity that trivializes the very nature of genocide'.[23] The comprehensive Report of the Chilean National Commission on Truth and Reconciliation does not mention genocide.[24] Even if the acts were correctly qualified as genocide, would Spain be competent under international law? The Audiencia interpreted the Genocide Convention, which is binding on both Chile and Spain, as a treaty not excluding the exercise of universal jurisdiction under general international law. There is indeed a trend in other countries to construe the Convention that way.[25] But what does universal jurisdiction under general international law mean? Chapter 2 above demonstrated that the universality principle in doctrine stands for three different notions. One of them is the primary and unconditional right of *any* State to try breaches of international law. However, a so broad right was never envisaged during the drafting of the Genocide Convention, not even by the proponents of universal jurisdiction.[26] State practice so far examined, with the possible exception of Germany, requires an objective and material link consisting of the voluntary presence of the suspect in the forum State.

The characterization of the acts as torture seems appropriate, yet questions arise. First, the Audiencia failed to address the issue that the UN Torture Convention did not become binding between the two countries until 1988, long after the most repressive episode of the Pinochet regime. Second, articles 5(2) and 7 of the Convention create an obligation for the custodial State to prosecute

[20] See the respective country studies in this book.

[21] Carrasco and Fernández (n 8 above) 695 write that 'the Court's far-fetched interpretation of genocide may be viewed as a means of overcoming the jurisdictional lacunae of Spanish municipal law, rather than the jurisdictional strictures of international law'.

[22] Compare with the definition of genocide by the International Criminal Tribunal for Rwanda just months before in *Prosecutor* v *Akayesu* (ICTR-96-4-T) 2 September 1998, paras 492–524.

[23] WA Schabas, *Genocide in International Law* (2000) 150.

[24] Report of the Chilean National Commission on Truth and Reconciliation, 2 vols, translated by PE Berryman (1993).

[25] See the Australia, Austria, Canada, Belgium, France, Germany, Israel, and Swiss country studies in this book.

[26] Cf the discussion of the Genocide Convention in ch 3 s A above.

a suspect if it does not extradite him to either the territorial State, the State of nationality of the suspect, or the State of nationality of the victim. The Convention does not provide a third country's right to punish.

One could argue though that torture, like genocide, is subject to universal jurisdiction under general international law. Then the question arises again what universal jurisdiction under general international law means. As shown above, State practice requires an objective and material link between the forum State and the suspect. Noteworthy in this respect is a judgment of the International Criminal Tribunal for the former Yugoslavia handed down shortly after the decision of the Audiencia. In *Prosecutor* v *Furundzija* it was held that the prohibition against torture has acquired the status of *jus cogens* and that one of the consequences is that 'every State is entitled to investigate, prosecute and punish or extradite individuals accused of torture, *who are present* in a territory under its jurisdiction' (emphasis added).[27]

This is not to say that Spain could not, like France or Switzerland, exercise jurisdiction over offences committed against its nationals. The Chilean authorities were clearly unwilling to investigate these cases and article 5(1)(c) of the UN Torture Convention seems to be a basis for passive personality jurisdiction. Still the omission of the Spanish legislature to take the necessary measures to establish passive personality jurisdiction in domestic law does not justify the overreaching by the judicial authorities.

Menchú Tum et al. v *Montt* et al.

The case of *Menchú Tum* et al. v *Montt* et al.[28] arose out of the thirty-four year long civil war (1962–96) in Guatemala between insurgency groups and an authoritarian government dominated by the military. The numerous atrocities committed during this conflict are well documented by UN special rapporteurs and independent experts, the Human Rights Office of the Archbishop of Guatemala, and the Guatemalan Commission for Historical Clarification. In its report *Guatemala: Memory of Silence*[29] the Commission found that between 1981 and 1983 agents of the State of Guatemala committed acts of genocide against groups of Mayan people.[30] The country was ruled during most of that period by General Ríos Montt.

[27] *Prosecutor* v *Furundzija* (IT-95-17/1-T) 10 December 1998, para 153, reprinted in (1999) 38 *Int'l L Materials* 317.

[28] Audiencia Nacional, 13 December 2000 (copy on file with author), English translation published in (2000) 3 *Ybk Int'l Humanitarian L* 691. For a thorough comment, see M Cottier, 'What Relationship Between the Exercise of Universal Jurisdiction and Territorial Jurisdiction? The Decision of 13 December 2000 of the Spanish National Court Shelving the Proceedings Against Guatemalan Nationals Accused of Genocide' in H Fischer, C Kreß, and SR Lüder (eds) *International and National Prosecutions of Crimes under International Law: Current Developments* (2001) 843.

[29] The report was made public on 25 February 1999.

[30] See J Perlin, 'The Guatemalan Historical Clarification Commission finds Genocide' (2000) 6 *ILSA J Int'l & Comparative L* 389.

Ten months after the publication of *Guatemala: Memory of Silence*, a number of organizations and individuals, including Guatemalan Nobel Peace Prize winner Rigoberta Menchú Tum, filed a complaint in Spain against Montt and other former military leaders for their role in the atrocities. The complaint was based largely on the findings of the Commission.[31]

By order of 27 March 2000 the examining magistrate declared himself competent to investigate charges of genocide, and by connexity also of terrorism and torture. As in the *Pinochet* case, the public prosecutor appealed. The Audiencia granted the appeal on the ground that Spanish jurisdiction over genocide abroad is *subsidiary* to the jurisdiction of the territorial State.[32] This follows from Article VI of the Genocide Convention which 'imposes the subsidiarity (*subsidiaridad*) of the exercise of jurisdictions different from those mentioned by the provision, so that the judicial authorities of a State should abstain from exercising jurisdiction over acts constituting genocide which are being tried by the courts of the country in which they occurred by an international tribunal'.[33] Before Spain can exercise subsidiary universal jurisdiction it must be shown that the competent authorities of the territorial State are 'inactive', a term which the Court explains as follows:

> The inactivity (*inactividad*) of the judicial authorities of the State on whose territory the alleged genocide took place can result *either* from the adoption of a law [...] which prevents them from initiating a prosecution, as would be laws of amnesty or oblivion, *or*, although the legal possibility to prosecute exists, from pressures on the judiciary by governmental or *de facto* forces as a result of which it can be reasonably concluded that there exists a climate of intimidation or fear which does not allow justice to be administered in serenity and independence.[34]

The Court then proceeded to examine whether in the present case there are any such *legal* obstacles.

> In this respect it is important to note that although the Oslo Agreement[35] provides that the works, recommendations, and findings of the Commission for Historical Clarification have no legal effects, the Commission categorically affirms that nothing prevents State organs, in particular the entities of the criminal justice system, to base themselves on the elements contained in the Commission's report. The same reasoning applies to citizens whose rights to exercise legal action regarding the cases described in the report are fully preserved in their quality as victims. One of the recommendations of the Commission is that 'the State complies with and ensures compliance with the National Reconciliation Act so as to prosecute and try crimes such as genocide, torture, and forced disappearance, for whose commission penal responsibility does not extinguish under the Act.'

[31] Cottier (n 28 above) 843. [32] Audiencia (n 28 above) s 2 *in fine*. [33] Ibid.

[34] Ibid s 3.

[35] The basis of the Commission's work was the 'Agreement on the establishment of the Commission to clarify past human rights violations and acts of violence that have caused the Guatemalan population to suffer' ('Oslo Agreement') of 23 June 1994.

In fact, article 8 of the National Reconciliation Act [. . .] excludes the extinction of penal responsibility for genocide, torture, and forced disappearance, as well as for those crimes that are imprescriptible or do not allow the extinction of penal responsibility, in accordance with internal law or international treaties ratified by Guatemala.[36]

Having concluded that there are no legal obstacles to a prosecution in Guatemala the Court goes on to examine whether pressure from governmental or *de facto* forces might cause the Guatemalan judiciary not to act.

In this respect the Court wishes to point out that the [examining magistrate's] description of the situation of the Guatemalan justice system with respect to the acts committed refers to a time when the Guatemalan justice system was unable to accomplish its tasks and was hiding out of fear of one of the parties. What is not established, however, is that Guatemala's judges of *today* would refuse to act if a denunciation and annexed complaints like the ones presented before the [Spanish] Central Examining Court No 1 were filed with the Guatemalan judicial authorities competent for the prosecution of the crime of genocide and the related other crimes.

On this point it is noteworthy that the report of the Commission for Historical Clarification was presented to the parties and to the UN Secretary General on 25 February 1999 and that the initial complaint in the case was presented to the Central Examining Court No 1 on 2 December 1999.

There is no evidence of a rejection in the territorial State—which, we repeat, should exercise jurisdiction according to preferred criterion of article VI of the Genocide Convention—of the denunciation and annexed complaints that have been presented before Central Examining Court No 1. Furthermore, we cannot infer judicial inactivity from the passage of time, as was possible in the cases of Chile and Argentina where years had gone by since the end of the military dictatorships. The information on which the present case is based was made public on 25 February 1999 whereas the denunciation dates from 2 December 1999 and is not accompanied by a decision of the Guatemalan judicial authorities that they will not act.[37]

For these reasons, the Court does not deem that the current necessity is proven that Spain have recourse to the subsidiary criterion of universal repression of genocide to the detriment of the prevailing territorial principle embedded in article VI of the Genocide Convention on the Prevention and the Punishment of Genocide.[38]

Having found neither legal nor factual obstacles to a prosecution in Guatemala, the Court ordered the examining magistrate to stay the preliminary proceedings for lack of jurisdiction *at the moment*, thus possibly indicating its willingness to reconsider its position depending on the developments in Guatemala.

Menchú Tum et al. v *Montt* et al. essentially revisits *Pinochet* but nonetheless calls for two specific remarks. First, no one can fail to notice the historical irony of the prospect of a Spanish court trying a case of genocide committed

[36] Audiencia (n 8 above) s 3. [37] Ibid s 4. [38] Ibid s 5.

against a Native American group. Second, it seems at first sight paradoxical that in the present case, with evidence that genocide was committed, the Court declined jurisdiction, whereas in *Pinochet* it resorted to a frivolous qualification of the allegations as genocide in order to establish jurisdiction.

The Court in *Montt* advanced the 'subsidiary' nature of universal jurisdiction over genocide as a reason for divesting itself of jurisdiction. The Court asserted (without elaborating how it reached that view) that the principle of subsidiarity is no less than 'part of the international *jus cogens* that crystallized in Article VI of the Genocide Convention'.[39] Subsidiarity though, in the context of universal jurisdiction, traditionally means something totally different. In the *subsidiary* version of the universality principle the competence of the *judex loci deprehensionis* depends on double criminality and on some initiative of the territorial State in the form of an extradition request that was rejected or of a request to take over the criminal proceedings.[40] Conversely, in the *absolute* version these conditions need not be fulfilled. Subsidiary versus absolute universal jurisdiction in this sense was discussed during the drafting of the very Article VI of the Genocide Convention.[41]

Subsidiarity in *Montt* received a new meaning which draws on and combines the principles of exhaustion of local remedies in international human rights law[42] and of complementarity of the jurisdiction of the International Criminal Court.[43] This newly defined subsidiarity criterion substitutes the traditional meaningful link (presence) criterion. The Audiencia's jurisprudence resembles in this respect the German Code of Crimes Against International Law[44] and the principles and guidelines regarding the questions of impunity of perpetrators of gross human rights violations prepared by expert Joinet.[45]

C. SUMMARY

A general enabling clause in the Organic Law of the Judicial Power provides a basis for universal jurisdiction over any offence which Spain is obliged to prosecute under a treaty. In addition, several specific offences (including genocide) are made subject to the universal jurisdiction of Spanish courts. Spain is but one of several States parties to the Genocide Convention that have established a domestic legal basis for universal jurisdiction over

39 Ibid s 2.

40 C Van den Wyngaert, 'De toepassing van de strafwet in de ruimte: Enkele beschouwingen' in *Liber Amicorum Frédéric Dumon* (1983) 501, 516–18.

41 Cf the discussion of the Genocide Convention in ch 3 s A above.

42 See, for example, article 46 of the American Convention on Human Rights.

43 Article 17 ICC Statute.

44 See the Germany country study above.

45 See ch 3 s C above.

genocide, despite Article VI of the Convention. Spanish practice in this respect seems part of a recent and irreversible international trend.

Unión Progresista de Fiscales de España et al. v *Pinochet* was a rare example of the unilateral limited universality principle put into practice. The willingness of the judicial authorities in this case to stretch the international definition of genocide in order to arrest a suspect who has no link with Spain is clearly wrong. Later in *Menchú Tum* et al. v *Montt* et al. the highest court qualified the exercise of universal jurisdiction over genocide on the ground that Spanish jurisdiction is subsidiary to the jurisdiction of the territorial State.

Pinochet and *Montt* also took international venue shopping (as could be seen in some cases in Belgium) a step further. It is not only open to *victims* of international offences but to *any* person or private organization. Through the *acción popular* NGOs acted as pseudo-international prosecutors.[46] Another peculiarity of the cases was the fact that a former colonial power claims jurisdiction over human rights violations in its erstwhile colonies, while the crimes of a former repressive regime in the forum State remain covered with the cloak of tolerance.[47]

[46] According to Roht-Arriaza (n 10 above) 318 an international network of NGOs in Europe, Latin America, and the United States provided the evidentiary backbone of cases against the members of the former Chilean and Argentine junta.

[47] I refer here to the Franco regime (1939–75).

15

Switzerland

A. AMBIT OF THE CRIMINAL LAW

The ambit of the Swiss penal code (*code pénal suisse*, or CPS) is spelled out in its articles 3–7. The basic rule is embodied in article 3(1), which states that '[t]he present code applies to any person who commits a felony (*crime*) or misdemeanour (*délit*) in Switzerland'. Article 4 criminalizes extraterritorial offences against the State (protective principle). Swiss penal law also applies to extraterritorial felonies and misdemeanours against Swiss nationals (passive personality principle) (article 5) or by Swiss nationals (active personality principle) (article 6).[1] In both cases, jurisdiction is limited by the conditions of double criminality, the presence of the accused in Switzerland (either voluntarily or through extradition), *ne bis in idem*, and *lex mitior*. A recent case of passive personality jurisdiction involved former Chilean president Augusto Pinochet.[2]

Universal jurisdiction is limited to international offences. The official Swiss policy is that perpetrators of such crimes are to be extradited to the territorial State whenever possible.[3] The Federal Law on International Assistance in Criminal Matters[4] provides a basis for the extradition of foreigners in the absence of an extradition treaty with the requesting State. However, extradition must be refused when it is foreseeable that the individual will be subject to unfair procedures (article 2) or when the requesting State does not guarantee that the individual will not be executed or will not be submitted to any treatment affecting his or her physical integrity (article 37).

The provisions endowing Swiss courts with universal jurisdiction are scattered over the CPS and the military penal code (*code pénal militaire*, or CPM).

I warmly thank Cap Claude Nicati for his comments and suggestions.

[1] Active personality jurisdiction can be explained by the fact that extradition or surrender of a Swiss citizen without his written consent is forbidden under article 7 of the Federal Law on International Assistance in Criminal Matters of 20 March 1981 (*Loi fédérale sur l'entraide internationale en matière pénale, Recueil systématique du droit fédéral* 351.1).

[2] Switzerland was one of the countries which in 1998 requested Pinochet's extradition from the United Kingdom for crimes committed against its nationals in Chile; see the letter from the British Home Office to the Swiss Ambassador, 2 March 2000, reprinted in R Brody and M Ratner, *The Pinochet Papers: The Case of Augusto Pinochet in Spain and Britain* (2000) 478.

[3] JD Schouwey, 'Suisse' (1989) 60 *Revue internationale de droit pénal* 465, 482.

[4] Note 1 above.

Code pénal suisse, article 6bis

CPS article 6bis, introduced in 1982 when Switzerland ratified the European Convention on the Suppression of Terrorism, is a domestic enabling clause for treaty offences.[5] It provides:

> Other felonies and misdemeanours committed abroad
>
> 1. The present code is also applicable to whomever commits abroad a felony and misdemeanour which the Confederation is obliged to repress by virtue of an international convention, if the act is also punishable in the territorial State and if the perpetrator is present in Switzerland and is not extradited (*si l'auteur se trouve en Suisse et n'est pas extradé à l'étranger*). However, the foreign law is applicable if it is more lenient for the accused.
>
> 2. The perpetrator can no longer be punished in Switzerland if:
>
> he has been acquitted in the territorial State, for the same act by a final judgment;
> he has served the sentence imposed abroad, if the sentence has been remitted, or if the sentence has lapsed;
> he has served abroad only part of the sentence pronounced against him, that part will be deducted from the sentence which may be imposed here.

In contrast to most other domestic enabling clauses, article 6bis requires double criminality and provides for the application of the *lex mitior*. Prosecution in Switzerland will only take place if the suspect is present and cannot be extradited for legal or factual reasons. Therefore, seeking the extradition of a foreign suspect on the basis of article 6bis is out of the question.

Code pénal suisse, title 12bis

Title 12bis was added in 2000[6] to implement the Genocide Convention and to be a first step in the adaptation of Swiss law to the ICC Statute.[7] Hence the heading: Offences Against the Interests of the International Community (*Délits contre les intérêts de la communauté internationale*). In a second phase, the legislature will introduce the notion of crimes against humanity and will possibly also revise the existing war crimes legislation.[8] For now, title 12bis only deals with genocide (article 264).

[5] See, extensively, JD Schouwey (n 3 above) 479–82 and by the same author 'Crimes de guerre: Un état des lieux du droit suisse' (1995) XLVIII *Revue internationale de criminologie et de police technique* 46.

[6] *Loi fédérale concernant la modification du code pénal, du code pénal militaire et de la procédure pénale fédérale* of 24 March 2000, Recueil officiel des lois fédérales 2000 2725. For comments, see extensively M Cottier, 'The Case of Switzerland' in C Kreß and F Lattanzi (eds) *The Rome Statute and Domestic Legal Orders: General Aspects and Constitutional Issues* (2000) 219, 227–32.

[7] Cf the motifs set out in *Message du 31 mars 1999 relatif à la Convention pour la prévention et la répression du crime de génocide, et révision correspondante du droit pénal*, Feuille fédérale 1999 4911.

[8] Feuille fédérale 1999 4911, 4919.

Article 264, paragraph 1 makes genocide an offence punishable by between ten years and life imprisonment. By virtue of paragraph 2, Swiss law extends to genocide abroad 'if the suspect is present in Switzerland and cannot be extradited' (*s'il se trouve en Suisse et qu'il ne peut être extradé*).[9] The claim of universal jurisdiction is remarkable given that the law purports to implement the Genocide Convention, which is, as was shown in chapter 3 above, negative on universal jurisdiction. The Swiss Federal Council justifies this by reference to 'the imperative character (*jus cogens*) of the prohibition of genocide and its effect *erga omnes*'.[10]

Code pénal militaire, articles 9(1) and 109(1)

Universal jurisdiction under the military penal code results from a combination of CPM article 9(1), which states that the code applies to acts committed 'in Switzerland or abroad', and CPM article 109(1), which provides: 'Whoever acts contrary to the provisions of any international agreement governing the laws of war or the protection of persons and property, or whoever acts in violation of any other recognized law or custom of war shall be punished with imprisonment, except in cases where other provisions involving more severe sanctions are applicable. For offences of high gravity the penalty is penal servitude'.[11]

Because no reference is made to the nationality of the offender or the victim, articles 9(1) and 109(1) establish prima facie universal jurisdiction over violations of the laws and customs of war.[12] Some scholars, however, argue that foreign military personnel do not fall under the CPM unless Switzerland is at war,[13] while another commentator takes the view that Swiss military law is inapplicable to foreign civilians.[14] The issue was settled by the military tribunal of cassation in *Niyonteze*.[15] The court held that foreigners (whether civilians or military) fall under the jurisdiction of Swiss military courts[16] for violations of the laws and customs of war, but not for common crimes.

[9] Article 264, paragraph 2 also provides that CPS article 6bis applies (see above).

[10] Feuille fédérale 1999 4911, 4925–6.

[11] Translation taken from (1998) 1 *Ybk Int'l Humanitarian L* 512, n 190.

[12] Schouwey 1995 (n 5 above) at 2.2. See also, generally, AR Ziegler, 'La mise en œuvre du droit international humanitaire par la Suisse' (1997) XXXVI *Revue internationale du droit militaire et droit de la guerre* 245.

[13] R Roth and M Henzelin, 'The repression of violations of international humanitarian law' (1997), unpublished paper presented at a Meeting of Experts on 'National Repression of Violations of International Humanitarian law', Geneva 23–5 September 1997, organized by the International Committee of the Red Cross.

[14] K Hauri, *Militärstrafgesetz: Kommentar* (1983) commentary on CPM article 9.

[15] See the discussion of the *Niyonteze* case below.

[16] The Swiss military judiciary, apart from its head, comprises civilian lawyers who perform their annual mandatory military service. See, extensively, B Sträuli, 'The repression of violations of international humanitarian law in Switzerland: Aspects of criminal procedure' (1997), unpublished paper presented at a Meeting of Experts on 23–5 September 1997 (n 13 above).

Alternatively, Swiss civilian courts could exercise universal jurisdiction over foreign war criminals on the basis of CPS article 6bis and the 1949 Geneva Conventions and Additional Protocols. The difference between universal jurisdiction under the CPM and universal jurisdiction under CPS is that the former does not expressly require that the suspect be present in Switzerland and cannot be extradited.[17]

B. CASE-LAW

Two Swiss prosecutions for war crimes in foreign conflicts have been reported. It should be noted that Switzerland, as the depository of the Geneva Conventions and the host country of the International Committee of the Red Cross, is in a sense the cradle of international humanitarian law.

Military Prosecutor v *Gabrez*

The case of *Military Prosecutor* v *Gabrez*[18] arose out of the war and ethnic violence in the former Yugoslavia in the first half of the 1990s. Gabrez, a citizen from Bosnia-Herzegovina, was accused of having beaten and injured civilian prisoners in the concentration camps of Omarska and Keraterm. At the time of his arrest he was living in Switzerland where he had asked for political asylum. The prosecutor considered the allegations to fall within the scope of the Third and Fourth Geneva Conventions of 1949 and Additional Protocols I and II, and accordingly charged the accused with violations of the laws and customs of war (CPM article 109). The accused did not challenge Switzerland's jurisdiction. The trial court held that the provisions regarding international armed conflict of the relevant international conventions were applicable to the alleged conduct, but acquitted the accused on the ground that the evidence was insufficient to establish that he was in the camps at the time of the crimes.

Military Prosecutor v *Niyonteze*

The case of *Military Prosecutor* v *Niyonteze*[19] followed shortly after the *Gabrez* case. The conviction of Niyonteze for war crimes committed in an

[17] A letter of the office of the Judge Advocate General of the Swiss army (*auditeur en chef*) to the author states that the presence of the accused is a condition for launching an investigation. See also Schouwey 1995 (n 5 above) at 2.2.

[18] Tribunal militaire, Division 1, Lausanne, 18 April 1997 (copy on file with author), case note by AR Ziegler in (1998) 92 *Am J Int'l L* 78. The summary of the factual allegations and the charges is taken from the judgment.

[19] Tribunal militaire, Division 2, Lausanne, 30 April 1999 (trial judgment); Tribunal militaire d'appel 1A, Geneva, 26 May 2000 (appeals judgment); Tribunal militaire de cassation, 27 April 2001 (cassation judgment) (copy of decisions on file with author). A longer version of this case note appeared in (2002) 96 *Am J Int'l L* 231–6; permission to republish is acknowledged.

internal armed conflict was the first by a municipal court exercising universal jurisdiction under the 1949 Geneva Conventions and Additional Protocol II. It was also the first conviction by such a court with respect to the genocide against the Tutsi and the massacres of moderate Hutu in Rwanda during the armed conflict between government forces (Forces Armées Rwandaises, or FAR) and the rebel army of the Rwandan Patriotic Front (RPF) from April to July 1994.[20]

After the defeat of the FAR, Fulgence Niyonteze and his family fled to Switzerland. Fellow countrymen reported him to the Swiss authorities, who launched an investigation. The International Criminal Tribunal for Rwanda did not take over the proceedings. Rwanda reportedly requested the extradition of the defendant, but Switzerland declined the request.[21] Nevertheless, the Rwandan government lent its full support to the Swiss proceedings, which included what appears to be the first site visit by a municipal court exercising universal jurisdiction.

There were three sets of factual allegations underlying the charges against Niyonteze, the mayor of Mushubati (prefecture of Gitarama) during the conflict in Rwanda.

1. Upon his return from a trip to France,[22] Niyonteze convened a town meeting on Mushubati hill, reported that his commune had received 'a bad mark' because many Tutsi and moderate Hutu had escaped the massacres, and urged the population to eliminate them.
2. Thereafter, escorted by members of the FAR, the communal police, and the Interahamwe militia (a Hutu group), he made several visits to the Kabgayi refugee camp in order to induce the refugees to leave the camp and return home. While at the camp, he ordered specific persons to be killed. The refugees who left the camp were massacred.
3. He failed to attempt in any way to prevent or stop the killings in his commune, although he had the authority and responsibility to do so.[23]

The prosecutor argued[24] that the defendant was criminally responsible for the following violations of the CPM: murder (article 116), incitement to murder

[20] In 1994 Switzerland had expelled an alleged Rwandan *génocidaire*. See Ziegler (n 18 above) 258–9. In 1995 Switzerland had to defer to the International Criminal Tribunal for Rwanda with respect criminal proceedings against another Rwandan refugee: *Prosecutor* v *Musema* (ICTR-96-5-D) Application by the Prosecutor for a Formal Request for Deferral by Switzerland, (4 March 1996).

[21] Rwanda and Switzerland have an extradition agreement, but the Swiss Federal Law on International Assistance in Criminal Matters bars extradition on several human rights grounds (see section A of this chapter above). The Rwandan special genocide law, *Loi organique No 8196 du 30/8/96 sur l'organisation des poursuites des infractions constitutives du crime de génocide ou de crimes contre l'humanité, commises à partir du 1 er octobre 1990*, Journal Officiel de la République Rwandaise no 17 of 1 September 1996, however, provides for the death penalty for certain categories of *génocidaires*.

[22] The defendant was in France from mid-March to mid-May 1994.

[23] This summary of the factual allegations is adapted from the Cassation judgment (n 19 above) at 2.

[24] Ibid at 3.

(articles 22 and 116), and violations of the laws and customs of war (article 109). Counts of war crimes were brought under common article 3 of the 1949 Geneva Conventions and article 4(2)(a) of Additional Protocol II.

Shortly before the opening of the trial before the military tribunal in Lausanne,[25] the prosecutor amended the indictment by adding six counts based on the same factual allegations: genocide, incitement to commit genocide, complicity in genocide, crimes against humanity, incitement to commit crimes against humanity, and complicity in crimes against humanity. For these new counts the prosecutor relied on customary international law. The tribunal granted the defence motion to quash the amendment, however, on grounds of lack of jurisdiction *ratione materiae et loci* over genocide and crimes against humanity under domestic law. The notions of genocide and crimes against humanity under customary international law were not, the tribunal held, directly applicable in the Swiss legal order.[26]

The defence also challenged the tribunal's extraterritorial jurisdiction over murder and incitement to murder.[27] The tribunal ruled on the basis of a historical and teleological interpretation that the wording of CPM article 109(1) provides for jurisdiction *inter alia* over murder committed in conjunction with war crimes. This defence motion was therefore dismissed.

Shortly before the trial, as part of a procedure called *administration anticipée d'une preuve*, the entire tribunal went to Rwanda in order to hear witnesses and visit the crime scene. Some two dozen witnesses, including eight expert witnesses, subsequently testified during the three-week trial. From the judgment it is clear that in assessing the evidence the tribunal gave great weight to its own impressions of the site, particularly with respect to the first charge.

The tribunal found virtually all of the factual allegations to be proven.[28] Basing its competence over violations of common article 3 and Additional Protocol II on CPM article 108(2),[29] the tribunal held that international humanitarian law applied in all of Rwanda during the conflict, whether or not actual combat took place in Mushubati, and that it bound both civilians and members of the armed forces. The defendant was sentenced to life

[25] Trial judgment, n 19 above.

[26] Switzerland has since ratified and implemented the Genocide Convention. See s A of this chapter above.

[27] The maximum sentence for murder and incitement to murder is life imprisonment (CPM article 116(1)), whereas war crimes are punishable by a maximum of twenty years' imprisonment (CPM articles 28 and 109(1)).

[28] The exceptions were the killing of a particular individual under the second set of allegations and the distribution of weapons to facilitate the massacres under the third set of allegations.

[29] CPM Article 108 provides in part:

(1) The provisions of this chapter are applicable to declared wars and other armed conflicts between two or more states [...];

(2) The violation of international conventions is also punishable if they have a wider field of application.

imprisonment, the maximum sentence under the CPM, and expulsion from Switzerland for fifteen years following the completion of the main sentence.

The *Tribunal militaire d'appel* (appeals tribunal), after a full new trial,[30] concurred with all of the lower tribunal's factual findings (except the killing of one named individual) but reversed all convictions for common crimes (murder and incitement to murder) because of lack of jurisdiction *ratione personae* over civilians under the CPM.[31] However, the appeal tribunal did uphold the war crimes conviction of a civilian because the evidence showed that the defendant had (1) regularly exercised effective control not only over his *administrés*, but also over some FAR and militia members in his commune, and (2) convened the meeting at Mushubati hill and had, *in his capacity as state agent*, ordered FAR members to kill two named refugees in Kabgayi.

Because his conviction for common crimes was overturned, the defendant faced a substantially lower maximum penalty.[32] The appeal tribunal took into account both aggravating and mitigating factors,[33] and sentenced him to fourteen years' imprisonment followed by expulsion from Switzerland for fifteen years.

On appeal to the *Tribunal militaire de cassation* (cassation tribunal),[34] the defendant argued that the allegations, even if proven, could not be considered war crimes in the absence of a close link with the armed conflict. The tribunal articulated two constitutive elements of a war crime committed in an internal armed conflict. First, the class of perpetrators extends to 'all individuals lawfully invested with authority and who are expected to further or participate in the war effort because of their capacity as officials or agents of the state, or as persons holding a position of responsibility or as *de facto* representatives of the government'.[35] Second, the link between the offence and the armed conflict must be close, 'which means that it may not be vague or undetermined'.[36] The court concluded that both conditions were satisfied in the instant case.[37]

[30] Appeals judgment (n 19 above).

[31] The tribunal explained, ibid 33, that article 109(1) 'is not intended to subject a civilian to the general application of military penal law. In fact, the provision addresses itself to persons ordinarily subject to the military penal law and aims to prevent such a person from claiming that he can be punished only under the Geneva Conventions and thereby get around the possible application of the more severe military penal law'.

[32] See n 27 above.

[33] Appeals judgment (n 19 above) at 44: '[His] professional situation and his status as mayor obliged him to protect his *administrés*, [...] or at least to abstain from harming them. The Appeals Tribunal considers this an aggravating factor. However, the Tribunal cannot ignore the fact that [...] the defendant confronted a chaotic situation that left him relatively limited freedom of decision and action.'

[34] Cassation judgment (n 19 above).

[35] Ibid 43.

[36] Ibid 42.

[37] It found, however, that in the initial trial, the tribunal had erred in ordering the defendant's expulsion after the execution of the prison sentence without considering a suspension (*sursis*) of the measure. This partial cassation of the judgment does not affect the guilty verdict or the sentence of imprisonment.

The trial of Niyonteze was in many respects the 'twin' of the first trial and conviction before the ICTR in the *Akayesu* case.[38] The indictment reads almost as a copy of that for Akayesu. Both defendants were mayors in the prefecture of Gitarama and belonged to the MDR (Mouvement Démocratique Républicain) political party. The factual allegations were similar. Like Niyonteze, Akayesu convened the population of his commune and addressed them in the now well known doublespeak. Also like Niyonteze, Akayesu went to the refugee camp in Kabgayi in pursuit of specific individuals.[39] The defences showed strong similarities, too: 'syndicates of informers',[40] widespread lawlessness, and claims of having saved some lives. Several of the expert witnesses in the Swiss case had previously testified before the ICTR. For particular points—for example, the historical context of the 1994 events and the powers of a mayor in Rwanda—the Swiss tribunals relied heavily on *Akayesu*.[41]

Whereas the Akayesu trial dragged on for fifteen months, the Swiss judiciary, although faced with similar logistical challenges, disposed of the case in the first instance in less than a month. The sentences were markedly different: fourteen years for Niyonteze, life imprisonment for Akayesu.

This trial provides a basis for responding to some frequently heard objections to the exercise of universal jurisdiction. With regard to evidentiary problems, the Swiss authorities, who had learned from the *Gabrez* case, managed to present clear evidence of guilt, in spite of cultural differences and geographic distance, using such techniques as expert testimony and site inspection. With regard to the arbitrary determination of forum, it may seem cruel to try a suspect and subject him to a long prison sentence in the country of his coincidental arrest. But in this case the defendant came to Switzerland voluntarily, and his immediate family still lived there. It is by no means clear that it would be more humane to send him back to Rwanda either for trial or to serve his sentence.

C. SUMMARY

The Swiss common penal code provides for universal jurisdiction over genocide and any offence which Switzerland is obliged to prosecute under a treaty. The military penal code, for its part, establishes universal jurisdiction over

[38] *Prosecutor* v *Akayesu* (ICTR-96-4-T) 2 September 1998, partially reprinted in (1998) 37 *Int'l L Materials* 1411, case note by DM Amann in (1999) 93 *Am J Int'l L* 195.

[39] *Prosecutor* v *Akayesu*, paras 258, 267.

[40] It is noteworthy that the allegation that the prosecution witnesses belonged to 'syndicates of informers' was brought forward by the same witness in both cases.

[41] For the context of the 1994 events, the tribunal also took judicial notice of the works of Gérard Prunier, Alain Ribaux, and in particular Human Rights Watch and International Federation of Human Rights Leagues, *Leave None to Tell the Story: Genocide in Rwanda* (1999).

violations of the laws or customs of war, whether committed in an international or a non-international armed conflict. Switzerland is thus yet another country to endow its courts with universal jurisdiction over the core ICC crimes, but only if the suspect is present in Switzerland and cannot be extradited. Furthermore, the rules of *lex mitior* and *ne bis in idem* apply.

In *Military Prosecutor* v *Gabrez* and *Military Prosecutor* v *Niyonteze* victims and perpetrators of atrocities committed in foreign wars came face to face in the forum State. The competent international tribunal did not take over the proceedings and extradition to the territorial State was legally or factually impossible. Prosecution by Switzerland took place in a spirit of international solidarity and collaboration, with due respect for the interests of other States and of the defendants. Both cases demonstrate that with the necessary expertise and resources perpetrators of crimes under international law can be tried fairly and speedily in a third State.

16

The United Kingdom

A. AMBIT OF THE CRIMINAL LAW

'The territorial extent of English criminal jurisdiction is a subject that has evoked more attention from international lawyers than from domestic lawyers.'[1] Territoriality of criminal jurisdiction is so self-evident for British jurists (and by extension for most other common law jurists) that the subject hardly draws scholarly attention[2] and codification is not deemed necessary. Archbold restates the position of English courts very succinctly:

> [S]ubject to statutory exceptions to the contrary, a person, whether English or not, who commits crime abroad is not indictable here. In construing Acts of Parliament there is a well-established presumption that, in the absence of clear and specific words to the contrary, an 'offence-creating section' of an Act is not intended to make conduct taking place outside the territorial jurisdiction of the Crown an offence triable in England. *The presumption against a Parliamentary intention to make acts done by foreigners abroad offences triable in English criminal courts is even stronger*[3] (emphasis added).

The rule that criminal law is primarily territorial is linked historically with the function of the criminal courts,[4] with the requirement that the jury should be summoned from the locality where the incident occurred,[5] and last but not least, with evidentiary rules.[6] This preference for territorial prosecutions explains why the United Kingdom is willing to extradite anyone, including its own nationals, to stand trial abroad for an extraterritorial offence, even when no extradition treaty exists.[7]

I warmly thank John RWD Jones for providing a copy of his unpublished report on jurisdiction in England and Wales over international crimes and for his suggestions and critical comments.

The United Kingdom of Great Britain and Northern Ireland constitutes a single State but contains several legal systems. The system under consideration here is that of England and Wales.

[1] G Williams, 'Venue and the Ambit of Criminal Law' (1965) 81 *LQ Rev* 276.

[2] Exceptions are G Williams (ibid), who offers a full reasonable statement of the ambit of English criminal law in 1965, and G Gilbert, 'Crimes sans Frontières: Jurisdictional Problems in English Law' (1992) 63 *British Ybk Int'l L* 413. See also two governmental reports: The Law Commission, *Report on the Territorial and Extraterritorial Extent of the Criminal Law* (1978), and Home Office, Steering Committee Report, *Review of Extra-Territorial Jurisdiction* (July 1996).

[3] Archbold, *Criminal Pleading, Evidence and Practice* (2000) para 2–33 (citations omitted).

[4] '[I]t being the function of the English courts to maintain the Queen's Peace within her realm': ibid.

[5] The original conception was that the jurors were supposed to speak from their own knowledge. See Williams (n 1 above) 276.

[6] In particular the hearsay rule and the reliance on oral testimony. Because of this, the prosecution in England of an extraterritorial offence would necessitate the appearance in person of all (foreign) witnesses, which evidently poses logistical and financial challenges.

[7] Section 15 of the Extradition Act 1989 allows *ad hoc* extradition arrangements.

English legal circles increasingly recognize though that jurisdictional isolationism is gradually being superseded. This is evidenced by Lord Griffiths's *dictum* in *Somchai Liangsiriprasert* that 'crime has ceased to be largely local in origin and effect. Crime is now established on an international scale and the common law must face this new reality'.[8] A 1996 report of the Home Office states in the same vein that:

> In the age of the Internet and other technological advances, it may be inevitable that the law will be left to catch up with new developments in crime; the question is whether there needs to be a consistent basis for making exceptions to the principle of territoriality, and whether it is defensible in the long term to maintain a territorial policy to which it is known that many exceptions will have to be made, particularly where there is no established principle against which the case for these exceptions can be judged.[9]

Parliament, however, is not limited in its powers by any doctrine of territory. Various statutes extend English criminal jurisdiction in respect of specific crimes.[10] Most of them are designed to punish acts aimed against fundamental national interests (protective jurisdiction).[11] The Offences against the Person Act 1861 establishes jurisdiction over murder and manslaughter (section 9) and bigamy (section 57) committed anywhere in the world by British subjects (active personality jurisdiction).[12] The prosecution of a national for murder or manslaughter abroad only takes place when the defendant returns voluntarily to the United Kingdom after the commission of the offence[13] and prosecution by the territorial State is not possible.[14] The United Kingdom traditionally opposes passive personality[15] and universal jurisdiction.

As for the latter, it will be remembered that during the drafting of the Genocide, Apartheid, and Torture Conventions, the United Kingdom consistently argued against such jurisdiction.[16] In line with this attitude, Parliament

[8] *Somchai Liangsiriprasert* v *United States Government* et al. [1990] 2 All ER 866, 871–2.

[9] Home Office (n 2 above) 11, para 2.17. The report concludes, however, that 'the essential territorial basis of jurisdiction within the UK appeared to be right for its particular circumstances' and recommends that it should be retained (36, para 5.2). The assumption of wholesale extraterritorial jurisdiction, according to the report, would require changes to the existing rules of evidence. 'Without such changes, the Committee considered that the commitment of resources required to prosecute individual cases would prove too great, with the result that the majority of cases would not be prosecuted' (ibid). In effect, legislation would be unenforceable, which would 'undermine the authority of the criminal law' (36, para 5.1).

[10] For a list, see Archbold (n 3 above) para 2–33.

[11] See, extensively, Williams (n 1 above) 396–9 and I Cameron, *The Protective Principle of International Criminal Jurisdiction* (1994) 299–301.

[12] For rationales and historical background see, in detail, Williams (n 1 above) 399–408.

[13] Ibid 296.

[14] T Vander Beken, *Forumkeuze in het internationaal strafrecht: Verdeling van misdrijven met aanknopingspunten in meerdere staten* (1999) para 284.

[15] H Donnedieu de Vabres, *Les principes modernes du droit pénal international* (1928) 369–70 reports that in 1852 the United Kingdom officially protested against a French bill introducing general passive personality jurisdiction.

[16] See ch 3 s A above.

only enacts statutes with universal application if required by an international convention. Among the statutes so enacted are the Geneva Conventions Act 1957, the Geneva Conventions (Amendment) Act 1995, the Aviation Security Act 1982,[17] the Taking of Hostages Act 1982,[18] and section 134 (Torture) of the Criminal Justice Act 1988.[19]

These Acts provide that grave breaches, aircraft hijacking, hostage taking, and torture *by whomever committed, in the United Kingdom or outside*, may be prosecuted in English courts,[20] as long as the foreign suspect is voluntarily—albeit temporarily—in the United Kingdom. The latter condition is not expressly required, but seeking extradition of an alien to stand trial in the United Kingdom for a totally foreign offence would be antithetic to long-standing British policy, which precisely consists in *returning* suspects to the territorial State if at all possible.

That a transitory presence suffices follows *a contrario* from the jurisdiction clauses in a number of other statutes that provide for extraterritorial jurisdiction over certain offences by foreigners who, after the crime, *have become British residents* or citizens. This limited form of universal jurisdiction can be found in the Sex Offenders Act 1997, the War Crimes Act 1991, and the International Criminal Court Act 2001. The following paragraphs briefly elaborate on the latter two.

War Crimes Act 1991

Concerns about the presence of Nazi war criminals[21] also prompted the establishment of a commission of inquiry in the United Kingdom in 1988.[22] The commission recommended that legislation should be introduced to give British civilian courts jurisdiction over acts of murder and manslaughter committed as war crimes (violations of the laws and customs of wars) in Germany or in German-occupied territory during the period of World War II by persons who are now British citizens or resident in the United Kingdom.[23] Acting upon that recommendation Parliament enacted amidst great controversy the War Crimes Act 1991.[24] Section 1 of the Act provides as follows.

[17] The Aviation Security Act 1982 enacts the 1971 Convention for the Suppression of Unlawful Acts against the Safety of Civil Aviation.

[18] The Taking of Hostages Act 1982 enacts the 1979 International Convention against the Taking of Hostages.

[19] Section 134 of the Criminal Justice Act 1988 enacts the 1984 UN Torture Convention.

[20] Prosecution under these Acts may only be instituted with the consent of or on behalf of the Director of Public Prosecutions or the Attorney General.

[21] Similar concerns led to the appointment of commissions of inquiry and the adoption of special legislation in Australia and Canada; cf the Australia and Canada country studies above.

[22] *Report of the War Crimes Inquiry* (1989) ('the Hetherington Report').

[23] Had they been British citizens at the time of the alleged offences, British courts would have jurisdiction under the Offences Against the Person Act 1861 (see above).

[24] The Bill encountered great opposition in the House of Lords and was finally passed without its consent. For commentaries, see C Greenwood, 'The War Crimes Act 1991' in H Fox and

(1) Subject to the provisions of this section, proceedings for murder, manslaughter or culpable homicide may be brought against a person in the United Kingdom irrespective of his nationality at the time of the alleged offence if that offence
   (a) was committed during the period beginning with 1st September 1939 and ending with 5th June 1945 in a place which at the time was part of Germany or under German occupation; and
   (b) constituted a violation of the laws and customs of war.
(2) No proceedings shall by virtue of this section be brought against any person unless he was on 8 March 1990, or has subsequently become, a British citizen or resident in the United Kingdom, the Isle of Man or any of the Channel Islands.
(3) [...]

The scope of the Act is in nearly every aspect narrower than the scope of its Australian and Canadian counterparts. The War Crimes Act 1991 is limited *ratione loci* to places which at that time were part of Germany or under German occupation,[25] *ratione materiae* to 'murder, manslaughter or culpable homicide which constituted a violation of the laws and customs of war',[26] *ratione personae* to current citizens and residents,[27] and *ratione temporis* to World War II.[28]

The remark made above that the Australian Act is a limited exercise of universal jurisdiction also holds true for the British Act. First, the United Kingdom's participation in World War II creates a constructive link with any war crime committed during that conflict; second, a strong link with the foreign offender (residence) is required at the time of prosecution. Only two prosecutions have reportedly been brought under the Act.[29] The War Crimes Unit created by the Act has meanwhile been dissolved.

International Criminal Court Act 2001

The International Criminal Court Act 2001[30] incorporates the core ICC offences into domestic law. Sections 51 and 68 define the scope *ratione loci* and *personae*.

MA Meyer (eds) *Armed Conflict and the New Law. Vol II: Effecting Compliance* (1993) 215; AT Richardson, 'War Crimes Act 1991' (1992) 55 *Modern L Rev* 73.

[25] The Australian Act extents to all of Europe; the Canadian Act has no geographical limits (see the respective country studies above).

[26] The Australian Act is applicable to 'war crimes', of which the definition resembles the provisions of the Nuremberg Charter; the Canadian Act applies to 'war crimes' and 'crimes against humanity', as defined by international law (ibid).

[27] In this respect, the British and Australian Acts are identical; the Canadian Act applies also to non-residents who are 'present' (ibid).

[28] The British and Australian Acts are identical in this respect too; the Canadian Act applies retroactively, but not limited to World War II, and prospectively.

[29] JL Garwood-Cutler, 'National Prosecutions for International Crimes: The British Experience' in MC Bassiouni (ed) *International Criminal Law* (2nd edn, 1998) III, 325–30.

[30] The Act was adopted on 11 May 2001 and entered into force on 1 September 2001; the United Kingdom ratified the ICC Rome Statute on 4 October 2001.

Section 51 Genocide, crimes against humanity and war crimes

(1) It is an offence against the law of England and Wales for a person to commit genocide, a crime against humanity or a war crime.
(2) This section applies to acts committed—
  (a) in England or Wales, or
  (b) outside the United Kingdom by a United Kingdom national, a United Kingdom resident or a person subject to UK service jurisdiction.

Section 68 Proceedings against persons becoming resident within the jurisdiction

(1) This section applies in relation to a person who commits acts outside the United Kingdom at a time when he is not a United Kingdom national, a United Kingdom resident or a person subject to UK service jurisdiction and who subsequently becomes resident in the United Kingdom.
(2) Proceedings may be brought against such a person in England and Wales or Northern Ireland for a substantive offence under this Part if—
  (a) he is resident in the United Kingdom at the time the proceedings are brought, and
  (b) the acts in respect of which the proceedings are brought would have constituted that offence if they had been committed in that part of the United Kingdom.

Like the War Crimes Act 1991, universal jurisdiction is limited to foreigners who are either resident at the time of the offence or who become resident after the crime and still reside in the United Kingdom when the proceedings are brought. Non-residents could still be extradited to another State, or be surrendered to the ICC.

B. CASE-LAW

No cases of universal jurisdiction have been reported, but British authorities arrested former Chilean President Pinochet at the request of Spain.[31] In chapter 1 above it was submitted that if a State issues an *ultra vires* arrest warrant, other countries may treat the warrant as invalid and accordingly not execute it. To what degree does the arrest legitimize the Spanish proceedings?

Extradition of Pinochet

Former Chilean President Augusto Pinochet was placed under arrest in the United Kingdom with a view to extraditing him to stand trial in Spain in respect of crimes committed in Chile during his tenure of office.[32] The arrest was made on the execution of two provisional arrest warrants issued by a

[31] See the Spain country study above.

[32] For an overview of the protracted British proceedings, see C Warbrick, EM Salgado, and N Goodwin, 'The Pinochet Cases in the United Kingdom' (1999) 2 *Ybk Int'l Humanitarian L* 91.

British magistrate at the instance of a central examining magistrate of the Spanish Audiencia Nacional.[33] The warrants were issued on the basis that there was evidence that the accused was responsible for torture, hostage taking, and murder.[34]

The General claimed immunity from arrest and extradition proceedings as a former head of State in respect of acts committed when he was head of State. Second, he argued that the warrants disclosed no 'extradition crimes' as required by the Extradition Act 1989 and the relevant international agreement, the European Convention on Extradition.[35]

In a historical decision, Britain's highest court, the House of Lords, ruled against the General.[36] The issue of individual criminal responsibility of a head of State for crimes under international law is not relevant to this study and is therefore not discussed here. Still, does *Pinochet* contain arguments for the proposition that such crimes are subject to universal jurisdiction? It is submitted that it does not.

Let us list the relevant points. Spain and the United Kingdom are both parties to the European Convention on Extradition. Article 2(1), entitled *Extraditable Offences*, provides that '[e]xtradition shall be granted in respect of offences punishable under the laws of the requesting Party and of the requested Party by deprivation of liberty or under a detention order for a maximum period

[33] See the Spain country study above.

[34] Copies of the warrants are reproduced in R Brody and M Ratner, *The Pinochet Papers* (2000) 61, 67. The first warrant was issued on the basis that there was evidence that the accused 'between the 11th of September 1973 and the 31st of December 1983 within the jurisdiction of the Fifth Central Magistrate of the National Court of Madrid did murder Spanish citizens in Chile within the jurisdiction of the Government of Spain'. The second warrant was issued on the basis that there was evidence that the accused 'between 1st of January 1988 and December 1992 being a public official intentionally inflicted severe pain and suffering on another in the performance or purported performance of his official duties within the jurisdiction of the Government of Spain'. A schedule attached to the warrant sets out particulars of other offences:

Between the 1st day of January 1988 and 31st December 1992 being a public official, conspired with persons unknown intentionally to inflict severe pain or suffering on another in the performance or purported performance of his official duties.

Between the 1st day of January 1982 and 31st January 1992, detained other persons (the hostages) and in order to compel such persons to do or to abstain from doing any act, threatened to kill, injure or continue to detain the hostages.

Between the 1st day of January 1982 and 31st January 1992, conspired with persons unknown to detain other persons (the hostages) and in order to compel such persons to do or to abstain from doing any act, threatened to kill, injure or continue to detain the hostages.

Between January 1976 and December 1992 conspired together with persons unknown to commit murder in a convention country.

All within the jurisdiction of the Government of Spain.

[35] Paris, 13 December 1957; ETS No 24.

[36] United Kingdom House of Lords: *Regina* v *Bartle and the Commissioner of Police for the Metropolis and Others* ex parte *Pinochet* 24 March 1999, reprinted in (1999) 38 *Int'l L Materials* 581, case notes by CM Chinkin in 93 *Am J Int'l L* (1999) 703 and by M Ratner in Brody and Ratner (n 34 above) 33.

of at least one year or by a more severe penalty....' This is the well known double criminality rule of extradition law. Article 7(2), entitled *Place of Commission*, provides that '[w]hen the offence for which extradition is requested has been committed outside the territory of the requesting Party, extradition may only be refused if the law of the requested Party does not allow prosecution for the same category of offence when committed outside the latter Party's territory or does not allow extradition for the offence concerned'.

The proceedings in the United Kingdom were governed by the Extradition Act 1989, which among other things implements the European Convention on Extradition.[37] The Act contains a provision to the effect that an extraterritorial offence against the law of a foreign State (in this case Spain) is an extradition crime if equivalent conduct would constitute an extraterritorial offence against the law of the United Kingdom.[38]

Hostage taking[39] and torture[40] constitute extraterritorial offences against the law of the United Kingdom, whatever the offender's nationality. The

[37] For a discussion of the extradition aspects of *Pinochet*, see C Warbrick, 'Extradition Law Aspects of Pinochet 3' (1999) 48 *Int'l & Comparative L Q* 958.

[38] Section 2 of the Extradition Act 1989 provides:

(1) In this Act, except in Schedule 1, 'extradition crime' means—
  (a) conduct in the territory of a foreign state, a designated Commonwealth country or a colony which, if it occurred in the United Kingdom, would constitute an offence punishable with imprisonment for a term of 12 months, or any greater punishment, and which, however described in the law of the foreign state, Commonwealth country or colony, is so punishable under that law;
  (b) an extra-territorial offence against the law of a foreign state, designated Commonwealth country or colony which is punishable under that law with imprisonment for a term of 12 months, or any greater punishment, and which satisfies—
    (i) the condition specified in subsection (2) below; or
    (ii) all the conditions specified in subsection (3) below.

(2) The condition mentioned in subsection (1)(b)(i) above is that in corresponding circumstances equivalent conduct would constitute an extra-territorial offence against the law of the United Kingdom punishable with imprisonment for a term of 12 months, or any greater punishment.

(3) The conditions mentioned in subsection (1)(b)(ii) above are—
  (a) that the foreign state, Commonwealth country or colony bases its jurisdiction on the nationality of the offender;
  (b) that the conduct constituting the offence occurred outside the United Kingdom; and
  (c) that, if it occurred in the United Kingdom, it would constitute an offence under the law of the United Kingdom punishable with imprisonment for a term of 12 months, or any greater punishment.

(4) [...]

[39] Section 1(1) of the Taking of Hostages Act 1982 provides:
A Person, whatever his nationality, who, in the United Kingdom or elsewhere—

(a) detains any other persons ('the hostage'), and
(b) in order to compel a State, international governmental organisation or person to do or abstain from doing any act, threatens to kill, injure or continue to detain the hostage, commits an offence.

[40] Section 134(1) of the Criminal Justice Act 1988 provides: 'A public official or person acting in an official capacity, whatever his nationality, commits the offence of torture if in the

hostage-taking charge against Pinochet was quashed because the warrants did not disclose any offence under the Taking of Hostages Act 1982. The court found, however, that torture committed in Chile or elsewhere after the entry into force of section 134 of the Criminal Justice Act 1988 is an extraditable offence as defined in the Extradition Act 1989. This finding, that the conduct alleged is an extraditable offence *under English law*, is correct and constitutes the *ratio decidendi*.

Reference by the majority to 'a worldwide universal jurisdiction' under the UN Torture Convention (Lord Browne-Wilkinson) is a mere *obiter dictum*, which seemed primarily intended to bolster the court's principal ruling, that there is no head of State immunity for international crimes.

Apart from being an *obiter dictum*, the majority's construction of the jurisdiction provisions in the UN Torture Convention[41] is questionable. The Convention provides for the jurisdiction of the territorial State, the State of nationality of the offender, the State of nationality of the victim (article 5(1)), and as a last resort the custodial State (article 5(2)). Jurisdiction is universal in the sense that *any* custodial State can put the suspect on trial. There can, however, be only *one* custodial State. Because Pinochet was in London only the United Kingdom could base jurisdiction on article 5(2). Spain's claim was therefore *ultra vires* under the Torture Convention. This does not mean that by extraditing Pinochet the United Kingdom would have breached a norm of international law. Barring some human rights considerations, a country is free to accede to any extradition request. It implies, however, that Spain could not legally enforce Pinochet's extradition under the Convention.

The dubious interpretation of the Torture Convention in an *obiter dictum* does not affect the *ratio decidendi* that the conduct alleged is an extraditable offence under English law. It does, however, undermine *Pinochet* as an authoritative decision on the issue of universal jurisdiction.[42]

C. SUMMARY

The United Kingdom continues to adhere strongly to the common law rule that all crime is local. For the problem of extraterritorial crime it

United Kingdom or elsewhere he intentionally inflicts severe pain or suffering on another in the performance or purported performance of his official duties'.

[41] For the text of these provisions, see ch 3 s A above.

[42] A similar view is held by H Fox, 'The Pinochet Case No. 3' (1999) 48 *Int'l & Comparative L Q* 687, 688; JY de Cara, 'L'affaire Pinochet devant la chambre des lords' (1999) XLV *Annuaire Français de Droit International* 72, 96–100; MC Bassiouni, 'Universal Jurisdiction for International Crimes: Historical Perspectives and Contemporary Practice' (2001) 42 *Virginia J Int'l L* 81, 125.

relies primarily on extradition. However, this has not kept the legislature from establishing piecemeal extraterritorial jurisdiction over specific offences. Statutes that provide for universal jurisdiction require a link with the United Kingdom. Some require that the foreign offender is a resident; for other crimes it suffices that the foreign suspect is simply present. The executive retains absolute discretion over prosecutions under any of these statutes. No prosecutions on the basis of universal jurisdiction have been reported.

17

The United States of America

A. AMBIT OF THE CRIMINAL LAW

The federal criminal code (18 USC (United States Code) Part I) does not specifically spell out its scope of application,[1] leaving room for interpretation. In the nineteenth and early twentieth centuries the Supreme Court repeatedly affirmed the common law rule of territoriality of criminal law: 'The laws of no nation can justly extend beyond its own territories, except so far as regards its own citizens. They can have no force to control the sovereignty or rights of any other nation, within its own jurisdiction. And, however general and comprehensive the phrases used in our municipal laws may be, they must always be restricted in construction, to places and persons, upon whom the Legislature have authority and jurisdiction'.[2]

It was considered that international comity required the strict territorial application of municipal law:

> [T]he general and almost universal rule is that the character of an act as lawful or unlawful must be determined wholly by the law of the country where the act is done [...] For another jurisdiction, if it should happen to lay hold of the actor, to treat him according to its own notions rather than those of the place where he did the acts, not only would be unjust, but would be an interference with the authority of another sovereign, contrary to the comity of nations, which the other state concerned justly might resent.[3]

The views of the judiciary nowadays are markedly different: federal and state regulatory and criminal provisions have potential worldwide application[4] if a perceived United States interest is at stake, even without clear and specific statutory language. The executive for its part has not recoiled from forcibly apprehending foreign suspects abroad for trial in the United States.[5]

I warmly thank Professor Christopher Blakesley for his suggestions and critical comments.

The law under consideration here is United States federal law only.

[1] The proposal for a new criminal code by the National Commission of Reform of Federal Criminal Laws (1971) contained a section on extraterritorial jurisdiction. The reform effort was abandoned in the early 1980s.

[2] *The Apollon*, 1824, 9 Wheat. (US) 361, 370; see also *The Schooner Exchange* v *M'Faddon*, 1812, 7 Cranch (US) 116, 135–6.

[3] *American Banana Co* v *United Fruit Co* 213 US 347 (1909) 365; see also *The Antelope* 1825, 10 Wheat. (US) 66, 122–3.

[4] EW Morgan, 'Retributory Theater' (1988) 3 *Am. University J Int'l L and Policy* 1, 29–30.

[5] See eg *United States* v *Noriega*, 746 F. Supp. 1506 (S.D. Fla. 1990); *United States* v *Alvarez-Machain*, 112 S. Ct. 2188 (1992); see also s B of this chapter below.

Under these circumstances, describing within the limited scope of the present study the United States system of jurisdiction—if there is a 'system' at all—is simply not possible. Other authors have made significant contributions in this respect. The process of expansion of United States jurisdiction during the last thirty years, mainly by judicial stretching of the territorial and protective principles, has been thoroughly studied by Blakesley[6] in particular and by Cameron.[7] Watson has written superbly on the increased acceptance in the United States of passive personality jurisdiction.[8] The same author has argued for the introduction of active personality jurisdiction since the United States abandoned in the first half of the twentieth century something akin to it: consular jurisdiction.[9]

In a nutshell, United States criminal law is at face value less far-reaching than the criminal law of many continental European countries; broadly applied active or passive personality jurisdiction, for example, are foreign to it. On the other hand, courts have been willing to assert extraterritorial jurisdiction in the absence of explicit statutory language to that effect.

As matters of domestic law, a person cannot be extradited unless there is an extradition treaty with the requesting State,[10] nor can a person be tried in a federal court for a (international) crime unless a federal statute defines and punishes the offence. By virtue of article I, section 8, 10° of the Constitution, Congress has the power 'to define and punish Piracies and Felonies committed on the High Seas, and Offenses against the Law of Nations'.[11]

Ne bis in idem is recognized by the Fifth Amendment of the Constitution, which states that no person 'shall be subject for the same offense to be put twice in jeopardy of life or limb'. The double jeopardy clause, however, protects only against multiple prosecutions by the *same* sovereign State. Because conduct can violate the laws of more than one sovereign State the perpetrator can be punished by each of them ('dual sovereignty doctrine').[12] As a result,

[6] See CL Blakesley's consecutive publications: 'United States Jurisdiction Over Extraterritorial Crime' (1982) 73 *J Crim L & Criminology* 1109; 'A Conceptual Framework for Extradition and Jurisdiction Over Extraterritorial Crimes' [1984] *Utah L Rev* 685; (together with O Lagodny) 'Finding Harmony Amidst Disagreement over Extradition, Jurisdiction, The Role of Human Rights, and Issues of Extraterritoriality Under International Criminal Law' (1991) 24 *Vanderbilt J Transnational L* 1; 'Extraterritorial Jurisdiction' in MC Bassiouni (ed) *International Criminal Law* (2nd edn, 1998) II, 33.

[7] I Cameron, *The Protective Principle of International Criminal Jurisdiction* (1994) 210–92.

[8] GR Watson, 'The Passive Personality Principle' (1993) 28 *Texas Int'l L J* 1.

[9] GR Watson, 'Offenders Abroad: The Case for Nationality-Based Criminal Jurisdiction' (1992) 17 *Yale J Int'l L* 41.

[10] 18 USC §3181; see also *Valentine* v *United States* ex rel *Neidecker*, 299 US 5, 8–9 (1936). An exception to this rule is the 'surrender' of persons other than citizens or permanent residents who have committed violent crimes in foreign countries against US nationals (18 USC §3181 (b)).

[11] On the question of constitutionality of extraterritorial jurisdiction, see AF Lowenfeld, 'US Law Enforcement Abroad: The Constitution and International Law' (1989) 83 *Am J Int'l L* 880.

[12] T Vander Beken, *Forumkeuze in het internationaal strafrecht: Verdeling van misdrijven met aanknopingspunten in meerdere staten* (1999) 271–4; see also *United States* v *Rezaq* in s B of this chapter below.

a person can be prosecuted at the federal level after a prosecution at the state level (and *vice versa*) and *a fortiori* after a prosecution abroad.

With these remarks in mind we turn to universal jurisdiction and start with the American Law Institute's views on the matter. Its Restatements of the Law purport to be unofficial codifications of United States law, but in reality contain a healthy dose of attempts to influence the development of the law. The previous Restatement of the Foreign Relations Law of the United States (1965) cited only piracy as an offence subject to universal jurisdiction. The current Restatement (1986) considerably expands what the commentary calls 'the class of universal offenses'. Section 404, titled *Universal Jurisdiction to Define and Punish Certain Offenses*, reads: 'A State has jurisdiction to define and prescribe punishment for certain offenses recognized by the community of nations as of universal concern, such as piracy, slave trade, attacks on or hijacking of aircraft, genocide, war crimes, and perhaps certain acts of terrorism, even when none of the basis of jurisdiction indicated in §402[13] is present.'

The commentary states that '[u]niversal jurisdiction over the specified offenses is a result of universal condemnation of those activities and general interest in cooperating to suppress them, as reflected in widely accepted international agreements and resolutions of international organizations'. Thus the reasoning is that *universal condemnation* (the words and actions of States) makes certain activities *universal offenses* which are then *ipso facto* subject to *universal jurisdiction*. The commentary adds that '[t]hese offenses are subject to universal jurisdiction as a matter of customary international law'. This is a different argument for which little evidence is put forward. Section 404 makes no reference to the whereabouts of the accused, and therefore does not exclude *a priori* the possibility of exercising universal jurisdiction over a foreign suspect who is not in the United States. In chapter 2 above this was labelled the unilateral limited universality principle.

As for the United States government, the executive now supports universal jurisdiction over certain international offences. It will be remembered that during the drafting of the Genocide Convention, the United States delegate called the principle of universal punishment 'one of the most dangerous and unacceptable

[13] Section 402, titled 'Bases of Jurisdiction to Prescribe', reads:
Subject to §403, a State has jurisdiction to prescribe law with respect to

(1) (a) conduct that, wholly or in substantial part, takes place within its territory;
(b) the status of persons, or interest in things, present within its territory;
(c) conduct outside its territory that has or is intended to have substantial effect within its territory;
(2) the activities, interests, status, or relations of its nationals outside as well as within its territory; and
(3) certain conduct outside its territory by persons not its nationals that is directed against the security of the State or against a limited class of other State interests.

of principles'.[14] Thirty years later the United States 'strongly supported'[15] the universal jurisdiction provision in the UN Torture Convention. At a 2000 symposium[16] David Scheffer, United States Ambassador at Large for War Crimes Issues, stated that 'as a government, the United States recognizes universal jurisdiction for certain crimes under certain circumstances', cited efforts by his government to find one or more (European) countries willing to prosecute the leadership of the Cambodian Khmer Rouge, Iraqi President Saddam Hussein, Kurdish rebel leader Ocalan, and former Ethiopian leader Mengistu, and added that the United States had not raised objections to the final ruling of the British House of Lords in the *Pinochet* case.[17] Finally, it should be mentioned that during the drafting of the War Crimes Act 1996 and Expanded War Crimes Act 1997, which implement *inter alia* the 1949 Geneva Conventions and Additional Protocols, the State Department and the Defense Department recommended to endow United States courts with extraterritorial jurisdiction where neither the victim nor the perpetrator are American, as long as the perpetrator is present in the United States.[18]

The position of Congress is more ambiguous. Unlike the legislatures in Australia, Canada, and the United Kingdom,[19] Congress did not enact special legislation to allow the criminal prosecution of alleged Nazi war criminals who had immigrated after World War II. Instead, the United States opted for denaturalization, extradition, and deportation.[20] Second, the War Crimes Act 1996 and Expanded War Crimes Act 1997[21] are the only 1949 Geneva Conventions implementation laws studied in this survey that do not provide for universal jurisdiction.[22] Third, Congress has enacted anti-ICC legislation even though

[14] See above ch 3.

[15] Message of the President of the United States transmitting the UN Torture Convention to the United States Senate for ratification (23 May 1988), comment on article 5 of the Convention.

[16] Symposium 'Universal Jurisdiction: Myths, Realities, and Prospects', Fall 2000, New England School of Law.

[17] David Scheffer, 'Opening Address' (2001) 35 *New England L Rev* 233, 234–6. The official US position as expressed by Scheffer clashes with the views of former Secretary of State HA Kissinger, 'The Pitfalls of Universal Jurisdiction: Risking Judicial Tyranny' (2001) 80 *Foreign Affairs* 86.

[18] United States House of Representatives, Report 104-698 to accompany HR 3680, 7–8.

[19] See above the respective country studies.

[20] See JM Wagner, 'US Prosecution of Past and Future War Criminals and Criminals Against Humanity: Proposals for Reform Based on the Canadian and Australian Experience' (1989) 29 *Virginia J Int'l Law* 887.

[21] The War Crimes Act 1996 and Expanded War Crimes Act are enacted as 18 USC, Part I, Chapter 118, §2441.

[22] A number of recent scholarly articles argue for an expansion of United States jurisdiction over the core international crimes; see, for example, D Cassel, 'Empowering United States Courts to Hear Crimes Within the Jurisdiction of the International Criminal Court' (2001) 35 *New England L Rev* 421; MS Zaid, 'Will or Should the United States Ever Prosecute War Criminals? A Need For Greater Expansion in the Areas of Both Criminal and Civil Liability' (2001) 35 *New England L Rev* 447.

the President has signed the ICC Treaty.[23] The American Servicemembers' Protection Act 2002[24] authorizes the President to use 'all means necessary and appropriate' to bring about the release from captivity of United States personnel detained or imprisoned against their will by or on behalf of the Court.[25] It is paradoxical that the executive recognizes the exercise by a single State of universal jurisdiction over the core international crimes, but that Congress refuses any surrender of jurisdiction over United States nationals to the ICC.

Nevertheless, Congress has ratified and implemented a number of *aut dedere aut judicare* conventions.[26] Accordingly, Titles 18 and 49 USC provide for jurisdiction over *inter alia* hostage taking,[27] torture,[28] unlawful seizure of aircraft,[29]attacks against aircraft,[30] and attacks against internationally protected persons.[31] United States jurisdiction exists independently of the *locus delicti* and the nationality of victim or offender, as long as the latter is 'afterwards found in the United States'.[32]

As a final point, the United States are in the vanguard of universal civil jurisdiction over gross human rights committed anywhere in the world. Many a (former) foreign official has been convicted in the United States on the basis of the Alien Tort Statute 1789 (28 USC §1350) and the Torture Victim Protection Act 1991.[33]

[23] The United States signed the ICC treaty on 31 December 2001 but in a communication received on 6 May 2002 the United States informed the UN Secretary-General 'that the United States does not intend to become a party to the treaty. Accordingly, the United States has no legal obligations arising from its signature on December 31, 2000. The United States requests that its intention not to become a party, as expressed in this letter, be reflected in the depositary's status lists relating to this treaty.' Letter reprinted in (2002) 41 *Int'l L Materials* 1014.

[24] HR (House of Representatives) 4775; entry into force 2 August 2002.

[25] Section 2008(a).

[26] See above ch 3.

[27] 18 USC, Part I, Chapter 55, §1203 implements the 1979 International Convention Against the Taking of Hostages.

[28] 18 USC, Part I, Chapter 113C implements the 1984 UN Torture Convention.

[29] 49 USC, Subtitle VII, Part A, subpart iv, Chapter 465, §46502 implements the 1970 Convention for the Suppression of Unlawful Seizure of Aircraft.

[30] 18 USC, Part I, Chapter 2, §32 implements the 1971 Convention for the Suppression of Unlawful Acts against the Safety of Civil Aviation.

[31] 18 USC, Part I, Chapter 51, §1116 implements the 1973 Convention on the Prevention and Punishment of Crimes Against Internationally Protected Persons, including Diplomatic Agents.

[32] This is the wording used in every one of the aforementioned sections of Titles 18 and 49 USC, except for the provision on torture (18 USC §2340A) which states that the alleged offender must be 'present'.

[33] For a thorough analysis see eg B Stephens and M Ratner, *International Human Rights Litigation in US Courts* (1996) and RG Steinhardt and A D'Amato (eds) *The Alien Tort Claims Act: An analytical anthology* (1999); see also JL Garwood-Cutler, 'Enforcing International Criminal Law Violations with Civil Remedies: The US Alien Tort Claims Act' in MC Bassiouni (ed) *International Criminal Law* (2nd edn, 1998) III, 343–91.

B. CASE-LAW

Matter of Extradition of John Demjanjuk

Matter of Extradition of John Demjanjuk[34] is the United States component of *Attorney General of Israel* v *Demjanjuk*.[35] In 1983 Israel requested the United States to extradite the accused, a naturalized United States citizen from the Ukraine, to stand trial for acts falling under the Nazi and Nazi Collaborators (Punishment) Law. Under United States law a person can only be extradited if he is charged with an offence 'within the jurisdiction' of the requesting State.[36] This is part of a broader United States policy not to co-operate if it does not recognize the competence of the requesting State. Thus, if Israel lacked jurisdiction, the accused could not be extradited.

Citing §404 of the Restatement as authority, the US District Court and the Sixth Circuit Court of Appeals, federal tribunals, held that Israel's assertion of jurisdiction is proper under international law. The District Court found that 'Israel's assertion of jurisdiction over the respondent based on the Nazi statute conforms with the international law principle of "universal jurisdiction". [. . .] The power to try and punish an offense against the common law of nations, such as the law and customs of war, stems from the sovereign character of each independent State, not from the State's relationship with the perpetrator, victim or act.'[37]

The Court of Appeals found that the accused could be handed over to Israel because in case of war crimes and crimes against humanity 'neither the nationality of the accused or the victim(s), nor the location of the crime is significant. The underlying assumption is that the crimes are offenses against the law of nations or against humanity and that the prosecuting nation is acting for all nations. This being so, Israel or any other nation, regardless of its status in 1942 or 1943, may undertake to vindicate the interest of all nations by seeking to punish the perpetrators of such crimes.'[38]

Whether or not Israel's prosecution of Nazis is an exercise of universal jurisdiction,[39] the decisions and the subsequent extradition constitute important affirmations by the United States judiciary and executive of §404 of the Restatement in respect of genocide, crimes against humanity, and war crimes,

[34] *Matter of Extradition of John Demjanjuk*, 612 F.Supp. 544 (D.C. Ohio 1985) (District Court judgment); *Demjanjuk v Petrovsky*, 776 F.2d 571 (1985) (appeal judgment), case notes by M Leigh in (1986) 80 *Am J Int'l L* 645 and by S Lutnick in (1986) 10 *Suffolk Int'l L J* 607. For an analysis of both *Demjanjuk* decisions see RH Reiss, 'The Extradition of John Demjanjuk: War Crimes, Universality Jurisdiction, and The Political Offense Doctrine' (1987) 20 *Cornell Int'l L J* 281.

[35] See the Israel country study above.

[36] 18 USC §3184.

[37] District Court judgment (n 34 above) under section 'Israeli Jurisdiction'.

[38] Appeal judgment (n 34 above) 582–3.

[39] Cf the discussion of the *Eichmann* and *Demjanjuk* cases in the Israel country study above.

and therefore of the third doctrinal conception of universal jurisdiction: the unilateral limited universality principle.[40]

United States v *Yunis, United States* v *Yousef,* and *United States* v *Rezaq*

United States v Yunis,[41] *United States v Yousef,*[42] and *United States v Rezaq*[43] are three unrelated cases of unlawful seizure of or attack on foreign civilian aircraft in the Middle East and the Far East. The criminal actions were not directed against the United States. The defendants, one of whom had already been convicted on the same facts by a foreign court, were forcibly brought to the United States.[44] Once on United States territory they were indicted under the municipal statutes implementing the Hague Hijacking Convention[45] and/or the Montreal Convention for the Suppression of Unlawful Acts against the Safety of Civil Aviation.[46] These statutes provide for United States jurisdiction when the foreign offender is 'afterwards found in the United States';[47] they also provide under certain circumstances for the death penalty. In two of the cases the State of nationality of defendant was not a party to the relevant international instrument.[48]

The defendants argued that jurisdiction was manufactured and that they were not 'found' in the United States within the meaning of the statute.[49] In each case federal courts held that jurisdiction was proper under domestic and international law. Because *Yousef* and *Rezaq* essentially revisit *Yunis* only the last is discussed.

The District Court in *Yunis* held that the United States could exercise jurisdiction under the universality principle which 'recognizes that certain offenses are so heinous and so widely condemned that any State if it captures the offender may prosecute and punish that person on behalf of the world community regardless of the nationality of the offender or victim or where the

[40] See ch 2 s C above.

[41] 681 F.Supp. 896 (D.D.C.) (trial judgment); 924 F.2d 1086 (1991), reprinted in (1991) 30 *Int'l L Materials* 403 (appeals judgment).

[42] 927 F.Supp. 673 (S.D.N.Y. 1996).

[43] 134 F.3d 1121 (D.C. Cir. 1998).

[44] Yunis was lured through the efforts and strategem of FBI agents into international waters off the coast of Cyprus, where they arrested him. Yousef was detained in Pakistan by local authorities who quickly surrendered him to United States agents. Rezaq was sentenced to 25 years' imprisonment for his role in a hijacking by a court in Malta. After seven years he was released, and when he landed on board an aeroplane in Nigeria, local authorities placed him in the custody of FBI agents, who transported him on a waiting aircraft to the United States. These facts are taken from the judgments.

[45] See the discussion of this convention in ch 3 s A above.

[46] Montreal, 23 September 1971; 974 UNTS 177.

[47] For an overview of United States anti-terrorism statutes and their ambit, see R Boed, 'United States Legislative Approach to Extraterritorial Jurisdiction in Connection with Terrorism' in MC Bassiouni (ed) *International Criminal Law* (2nd edn, 1998) II, 145–76.

[48] MP Scharf, 'Application of Treaty-Based Universal Jurisdiction to Nationals of Non-Party States' (2001) 35 *New England L Rev* 363, 379–80.

[49] Arguments adapted from the judgments.

crime was committed'; the Court cited with approval §404 of the Restatement which specifically identifies aircraft hijacking as a universal offence; it rejected the defendant's argument that forcible return to the forum State does not create jurisdiction.

Once a defendant is brought within the jurisdiction of the Court he is subject to prosecution for all federal offenses. Yunis was seized for alleged violation of the hostage taking statute. Physical presence in United States territory is not a necessary element for exercising subject matter jurisdiction over that offence. Only after he stepped onto American soil was the defendant charged with aircraft piracy. Indeed, once he was within the boundaries of the United States, the government was obliged by statute and the Montreal Convention to prosecute him for destroying the aircraft. As discussed earlier, both the Hague Convention and the Montreal Convention require all contracting States to exercise jurisdiction over individuals charged with seizing control of an aircraft. Any State that secures custody of the alleged hijackers is obliged to prosecute or extradite them.[50]

In addition, the Court found that jurisdiction was justified under the passive personality principle since two passengers on board the hijacked aircraft were Americans. It was stated that although the latter principle was the most controversial of the jurisdictional principles in international law, 'the international community recognizes its legitimacy'.[51] It was pointed out that although the United States had historically opposed passive personality jurisdiction, it had been accepted by the United States and the international community in recent years in the sphere of terrorist and other internationally condemned crimes.[52]

The Court of Appeals affirmed, noting that:

The Antihijacking Act of 1974 was enacted to fulfil this nation's responsibilities under the Convention for the Suppression of Unlawful Seizure of Aircraft (the 'Hague Convention'), which requires signatory nations to extradite or punish hijackers 'present in' their territory. [...] This suggests that Congress intended the statutory term 'found in the United States' to parallel the Hague Convention's 'present in [a contracting State's] territory,' a phrase which does not indicate the voluntariness limitation urged by Yunis.[53]

The decisions stretch the *aut dedere aut judicare* formulas of the relevant conventions to the extreme; formal extradition (*dedere*) was bypassed and one defendant had already been tried and convicted (*judicare*) abroad. Earlier in this book it was submitted that the relevant conventions provide for the jurisdiction of the territorial State, the State of nationality of the offender, the State of nationality of the victim, and as a last resort the custodial State; they do not provide a third country's right to punish. As we have seen, judicial authorities

[50] Trial judgment (n 41 above) 906. [51] Ibid 901. [52] Ibid 902.
[53] Appeals judgment (n 41 above) 408.

in Belgium, Denmark, France, Germany, and the Netherlands have ruled against the exercise of universal jurisdiction through extradition, let alone through forcible apprehension.

C. SUMMARY

Once an adherent of the common law rule that crime is territorial, the United States now increasingly claims extraterritorial jurisdiction. The expansion is as much the work of prosecutors and courts as it is of the legislature. United States practice has sanctioned what in chapter 2 above was called the unilateral limited universality principle. In the *Extradition of John Demjanjuk* authorities assisted and recognized the requesting State's assertion of universal jurisdiction over genocide, crimes against humanity, and war crimes.

In *United States* v *Yunis*, *United States* v *Yousef*, and *United States* v *Rezaq*, the United States itself exercised universal jurisdiction over aircraft hijackers/attackers after apprehending them abroad and, in the case of Rezaq, even after a foreign conviction. The United States has also actively lobbied other governments to exercise universal jurisdiction over the likes of Pol Pot and Saddam Hussein. It remains to be seen whether United States practice can stand the test of an important principle of international law: reciprocity. This question actually applies to all the countries studied in this book. There is, however, a specific reason for asking it now. If Congress is horrified by the thought of an international tribunal trying a United States agent for, let's say, war crimes, one must wonder how it would react were another country to do so.

Conclusions

This study was prompted by several countries' efforts to investigate and prosecute non-nationals for crimes committed abroad against non-nationals. It centered around two questions: (1) what international legal limitations are there upon a State's ability to do so, and (2) what is the municipal legal basis for the exercise of universal jurisdiction? Part I of this study dealt primarily with the first question, and Part II with the second. It remains now to summarize the results of Part II and to connect them with those of Part I.

As we saw in Part II, territoriality of criminal jurisdiction is the basic rule in all the countries here examined. Various European countries, however, have historically claimed extensive extraterritorial jurisdiction over offences of a certain gravity. More generally, the trend in most States, including common law countries, has been steadily to expand the ambit of the criminal law, thereby eroding the basic rule. The expansion is the result either of new legislation or of judicial stretching of the territoriality and protective principles in existing laws.

Municipal laws providing for universal jurisdiction can be classified into three groups. The first comprises the *aut dedere aut judicare* clauses applicable to all extraditable offences if the foreign suspect cannot be extradited. These clauses, which represent the co-operative general universality principle, are often as old as the codes in which they are found. Moreover, they can be (and have been) used as a concurrent basis for universal jurisdiction over international offences. *Aut dedere aut judicare* implies that the foreign suspect must be voluntarily present in the forum State before it can exercise jurisdiction.

The second group comprises the general enabling clauses in civil law countries which establish domestic jurisdiction over all offences that are the subject of an international convention ratified by the country in question. Enabling clauses of this type—falling under the co-operative limited universality principle—were introduced from the 1970s onward in response to the multiplication of international criminal law treaties. As was apparent from the review of those treaties, their jurisdictional provisions vary and are sometimes ambiguous. By opting for a general enabling clause, national legislatures leave to national judges the ultimate interpretation of a treaty's jurisdictional provisions. None of the domestic enabling clauses examined makes an exception for offences committed on the territory of a non-party State.

The third group comprises statutes covering specific crimes, whether or not in implementation of a treaty. Among the crimes that a significant number of national legislatures have made subject to universal jurisdiction—under either

I warmly thank Dr Stephen Sher for his comments and suggestions.

the co-operative or the unilateral limited universality principle, *without* looking for permission in conventional international law—are the core international crimes: war crimes, crimes against humanity, and genocide. An important catalyst for municipal legislative action was the adoption of the International Criminal Court Statute in 1998. Since then, nearly half of the countries surveyed have established universal jurisdiction over genocide, notwithstanding a provision to the contrary in the Genocide Convention. The great majority of statutes covering specific offences do not make the exercise of jurisdiction dependent upon the suspect's not having been extradited. Under municipal statutes it is usually a necessary and sufficient condition that the foreign suspect be 'present'. What is understood by the expression 'present' remains uncertain, however, because no legislature has defined it. As in the case of general enabling clauses, the ultimate interpretation is left to municipal courts, with arguably unpredictable results; in one case it was held that a suspect who had been forcibly apprehended abroad by the forum State was 'present' for the purpose of establishing jurisdiction. In what may prove to be an important shift, however, Germany's recently enacted Code of Crimes Against International Law deliberately eliminates the judge-made presence doctrine. Significantly, this German statute comes at a moment when many States parties to the ICC Statute are considering drafting and adopting implementing legislation. Some of them will look for examples abroad, and especially to the more powerful States such as Germany.

Until recently, the number of cases in which States exercised universal jurisdiction to prosecute foreign nationals for crimes committed abroad was negligible. In the past ten years, however, some twenty cases of universal jurisdiction have been reported. The catalyst was the creation of the *ad hoc* international tribunals for the former Yugoslavia and for Rwanda. Faced with the presence of refugees who had allegedly committed acts within the jurisdiction of these tribunals, both national authorities and human rights organizations were successful in establishing a plausible foundation under domestic and international law for launching criminal proceedings. Once aware of these avenues, victims of gross human rights violations tried to locate forums willing to exercise universal jurisdiction over those at whose hands they had suffered.

The exercise of universal jurisdiction over gross human rights violations is primarily victim driven, through either simple denunciation or, where available, the mechanism of *constitution de partie civile*. An important difference was noted between common and civil law countries. In the former, universal jurisdiction can be exercised only by or on behalf of the Attorney General, who is part of the executive branch of the national government. In the latter, however, the ordinary rules of criminal procedure usually apply. Either a local prosecutor or a victim (through the mechanism of *constitution de partie civile*) can initiate an investigation into extraterritorial offences, with the executive having no authority to intervene in order to prevent or end the investigation. In one country surveyed, the power to initiate an investigation is vested in *any* person or organization, thus creating the possibility of a true *actio criminalis popularis*.

In the cases that have gone to trial, the determination of the forum was generally neither arbitrary nor unreasonable. Indeed, nearly all defendants had strong links with the forum States, and extradition to the territorial States was impossible because of either legal or factual obstacles. Under such circumstances the only alternatives to prosecution were to leave an alleged (international) offender in peace, or to expel him. In a few rare cases, however, the defendants had no strong link to the forum State, and that State obtained personal jurisdiction only through rendition or forcible apprehension abroad. In one such case the defendant was tried again after a foreign conviction.

There have also been a few 'cases' that created a lot of commotion but went nowhere: the victim-driven attempts to exercise universal jurisdiction *in absentia* over (former) foreign officials. In addition to raising substantive legal questions concerning State immunity, these cases raise policy and ideological issues concerning forum shopping by the victim (resulting in a totally arbitrary determination of the forum) and Western judicial imperialism. The reader can scarcely have failed to notice the one-way traffic between Western and developing countries. In view of their lack of resources, of institutional capacity, and, it must be said, of military and political power, the latter are unlikely to take an active role in these legal developments. The 'universal' in 'universal jurisdiction' may remain wishful thinking for a long time.

A series of three questions will enable us to connect up the results of Parts I and II: (1) to what extent are the different doctrinal views on universal jurisdiction discernible in municipal State practice? and (2) what international legal conclusions can be drawn from municipal State practice? and (3) what is the impact of recent State practice on the establishment of the ICC, and vice versa?

As for the first question, municipal State practice predictably reflects all three doctrinal notions of the universality principle. Three of the countries examined follow the co-operative general universality principle. This approach makes sense if one looks at their overall system of jurisdiction, which includes active personality jurisdiction. The claim of secondary universal jurisdiction over all offences of a certain gravity guarantees equal treatment of nationals and foreigners. It would meet with incomprehension in those countries that a national could be prosecuted after committing a crime abroad, while a foreign fugitive would be left in peace because for some reason he could not be extradited. An international legal limit on the custodial State's right to punish in those circumstances would undermine the trust of citizens in the legal order, both domestic and international. Provided that the principles of double criminality, *ne bis in idem*, and *lex mitior* are respected, prosecution by the custodial State interferes with no legitimate expectations of the offender. He chose to leave the territorial State and prefers not to return. If prosecution is undertaken, the double criminality and *ne bis in idem* rules preclude the criminal proceedings from constituting an unwarranted interference with the domestic affairs of the territorial State.

The practice of most States discussed in this study—their statutes and cases—falls under the co-operative limited universality principle. Since this principle applies to international offences, the comments made above concerning the co-operative general universality principle are also applicable here. The third doctrinal version of the universality principle, that of unilateral limited universality, is unknown to conventional international law, is rarely supported by *opinio juris*, and is equally rarely evident in municipal State practice. Only in a few countries is there a discernible trend in favour, with Germany at the forefront.

It is difficult to draw any significant international legal conclusions from the above discussion of State practice—which is itself, moreover, only one of the two elements of customary law.[1] Although the primary criterion for including a State in this study was merely that of its having some record of legislative or judicial practice in relation to universal jurisdiction, the resulting number of States is only a small fraction of the world's total. It therefore follows that in the great majority of States relevant practice is negligible or non-existent. In addition, customary law is established not just through a pattern of States making a particular type of claim, but also through the acquiescence of other States and, most especially, through the absence of protest by States particularly interested in the matter at hand. As noted by one commentator, the problem is that it is difficult to determine whether a government has repeatedly objected to, or acquiesced in, another government's practice.[2] The relevant material may consist of confidential diplomatic notes or classified internal memoranda.[3] Consequently, the only questions that can be answered are whether and how States have reacted *publicly* to the exercise of universal jurisdiction by other States.

As suggested above, one must distinguish between the position of the territorial State, which was invariably also the State of nationality of the offender, and that of the States that are, to varying degrees, merely observers. Territorial States have reacted in two different ways: with acquiescence, or even full support, when proceedings were launched against nationals present voluntarily in the forum State; and with strong protests (and in one case, even legal action) whenever universal jurisdiction was exercised *in absentia*. Here, as elsewhere, politics and international law are interconnected. In the first type of situation, based on other States' claims of territorial jurisdiction, defendants and the acquiescing governments were typically on opposite sides

[1] Cf the Introduction, s D above.

[2] GR Watson, 'The Passive Personality Principle' (1993) 28 *Texas Int'l LJ* 1, 39.

[3] Ibid.

of the very conflict in which the crimes were committed. The *Eichmann* case is arguably an exception, but he symbolized a totally discredited former regime. In the second type of situation, jurisdiction exercised *in absentia* by another State, diplomatic incidents resulted because supporters of the defendant either remained in power or still exercised considerable political influence in the territorial State. In the *Pinochet* case there was also a noteworthy difference in the reaction of States that were not directly involved in one way or another. European countries endorsed the proceedings in Spain while South American heads of State denounced them. Perhaps more important, or at least more influential, than these expressions of regional solidarity was the United States' decision not to protest.

Although the reported cases of universal jurisdiction *in absentia* have generated much controversy, the fact remains that there have been very few of these cases. A customary right to exercise such jurisdiction has arguably not (yet) materialized. A nascent, supportive trend, albeit with a powerful country like Germany at the forefront, does not constitute custom, and both the legality and the appropriateness of exercising jurisdiction *in absentia* remain controversial. Of much less concern is the uncertain, not fully determinate legal status of other versions of the universality principle, and the question of whether they have achieved the status of customary law. Because they satisfy the requirements of justice and effectively protect the interests of the States and individuals concerned, they may reasonably be considered useful 'signposts' for national legislatures and courts.[4]

By contrast, the unilateral limited universality principle has an intrinsically arbitrary character. The totally random determination of the forum (and hence of the applicable procedural and substantive law) runs counter to the fundamental principle of the predictability of criminal law. Unilateral limited universality also does not adequately protect the interests of States which are more directly concerned. To be sure, the *in absentia* proceedings in these cases do not interfere with the domestic affairs of other States since the alleged crimes are indeed crimes under international law. Nevertheless, the fact is that jurisdiction exercised by a State without its having an objective or legal link with either the offence or the offender erodes the very concept of jurisdiction. Unlimited (hence arbitrary) jurisdiction is a *contradictio in terminis* and runs counter to one of the fundamental goals of international law: a rational distribution of competences among equal sovereigns. Thus, while not violating the non-interference principle, universal jurisdiction *in absentia* contravenes the more fundamental principle of sovereign equality of States, of which non-interference is only one aspect. Critics may ask how a right recognized in *every* State can possibly violate the principle of sovereign equality. The answer was given by the International Court of Justice in the

[4] Cf the discussion in ch 1 s F above.

Corfu Channel case, which concerned the forcible extraterritorial collection of evidence. The Court held that such actions would 'from the nature of things... be reserved for the most powerful States, and might easily lead to perverting the administration of international justice itself'.[5] This pronouncement seems no less relevant for the problem of universal jurisdiction *in absentia*, and existing State practice certainly does not undercut the argument.

The third and final question concerns the impact of recent State practice on the establishment of the ICC on 1 July 2002, and vice versa. The catalyst for the adoption in 1998 of the ICC Statute[6] was undoubtedly the creation in 1993 and 1994 of the first *ad hoc* international criminal tribunals since World War II: the ICTY and the ICTR. The recent tribunals were, in turn, catalysts for the exercise of universal jurisdiction by States, first within the scope of the events in the former Yugoslavia and Rwanda, later also over atrocities committed in other conflicts and independently of the suspects' whereabouts and their actual or former status. Some cases (*Pinochet, Ndombasi, Sharon*) generated controversy, but it seems that the very depth of the dissension may have persuaded a significant number of States of the urgent need to establish the ICC. The actions of the Belgian and Spanish judicial authorities, though arguably illegal, may therefore have accelerated the ratification process of the ICC Statute.

What will be the probable impact of the establishment of the ICC on State practice in respect of universal jurisdiction? The ICC Statute provides in its preamble and in article 1 that the jurisdiction of the Court will be 'complementary to national criminal jurisdictions'. Clearly, this provision does not preclude the exercise of jurisdiction over the core ICC crimes by the *judex loci deprehensionis*. This consequence can be drawn from a joint reading of the Statute and the Draft Code of Crimes against the Peace and Security of Mankind,[7] both of which originated from the International Law Commission. Some argue, however, that the ICC Statute does not exclude the exercise of universal jurisdiction *in absentia*. This view must be rejected. The creation of the ICC brings much-needed legal security and equality into an area of law where might was right. To advocate that a single State has similar, if not broader, powers than the treaty-based Court is tantamount to maintaining the status quo.

Future State practice, like that of the past, is likely to be greatly influenced by the transnational campaign to achieve accountability for gross human rights violations.[8] Exercises of universal jurisdiction under circumstances similar to the Rwanda and Bosnia refugee cases can and should be expected,

[5] ICJ Reports 1949, 4, 35.

[6] Rome, 17 July 1998; reprinted in (1998) 37 *Int'l L Materials* 999.

[7] See ch 3 s C above.

[8] On this campaign see N Roht-Arriaza, *Transnational Justice* (Pennsylvania Press; forthcoming 2004).

as should exercises of universal jurisdiction over common offences when extradition is impossible. Whether the *Pinochet* and *Ndombasi* scenarios will be repeated is more doubtful. In the end it may well be that they were an aberrant intermezzo between Nuremberg and the ICC. But perhaps not: who knows if the next case is already being planned; the world is surely not short of the dictators, tyrants, and others whose actions sometime call out for unilateral criminal prosecution. Here, as always, the development of the law will reflect not just theory, but also history.

Postscript

Everybody interested in the subject-matter of this book no doubt looked forward keenly to the judgment of the International Court of Justice in the case concerning the *Arrest Warrant of 11 April 2000* (*Democratic Republic of the Congo* v *Belgium*).[1] Alas, the Court left us out in the cold. By thirteen votes to three the Court ruled in favour of Congo on the basis of the sovereign immunity argument. It abstained from considering Congo's initial—but later abandoned—claim that the *in absentia* proceedings were an excessive exercise of universal jurisdiction. All that can be done in these circumstances is to look for indications in the judgment and opinions of how the Court would have decided had it considered Congo's other argument.

The facts underlying the case are described in *Public Prosecutor* v *Ndombasi* et al. in the Belgian country study above. In a nutshell, an examining magistrate in Brussels, seized by the public prosecutor and private parties, issued on 11 April 2000 an arrest warrant against the then acting Congolese minister of foreign affairs on the basis of the Belgian Act Concerning the Punishment of Grave Breaches of International Humanitarian Law. There were no links between Belgium and the alleged crime or suspect. Thus the Belgian proceedings, like the Spanish proceedings in *Pinochet*, were an exercise of universal jurisdiction *in absentia*, in accordance with the third doctrinal version of the universality principle.[2] That a Belgian appeals' court, after the ICJ judgment, invalidated the proceedings under municipal law gives the case an odd twist.

Congo relied in its ICJ application on two separate legal grounds. First, it claimed that '[t]he *universal jurisdiction* that the Belgian State attributes itself under Article 7 of the law in question' constituted a '[v]iolation of the principle that a State may not exercise its authority on the territory of another State and of the principle of sovereign equality among all Members of the United Nations, as laid down in Article 2, paragraph 1, of the Charter of the United Nations'. Second, it claimed that '[t]he non-recognition, on the basis of Article 5 [...] of the Belgian Law, of the immunity of a Minister of Foreign Affairs in office' constituted a '[v]iolation of the diplomatic immunity of the Minister of Foreign Affairs of a sovereign State, as recognized by the jurisprudence of the Court and following from Article 41, paragraph 2, of the Vienna Convention of 18 April 1961 on Diplomatic Relations'.

[1] Judgment of 14 February 2002, reprinted in (2003) 41 *Int'l L Materials* 536; case note by A Orakhelashvili in (2002) 96 *Am J Int'l L* 677; see also C Kreß, 'Völkerstrafrecht und Weltrechtspflegeprinzip im Blickfeld des Internationalen Gerichtshofs' (2002) 114 *Zeitschrift für die gesamte Strafrechtswissenschaft* 818.

[2] See ch 2 above.

Belgium, for its defence with regard to the first legal ground, relied essentially on international customary law. A subsidiary argument was that in the absence of any treaty or custom prohibiting universal jurisdiction *in absentia*, it enjoyed total freedom of action. To this end it invoked the '*Lotus* principle' that States have a right to do whatever is not prohibited by international convention or custom.[3]

In its Memorial and final oral submissions, however, Congo abandoned the excessive universal jurisdiction argument and referred only to the second legal ground, sovereign immunity. Belgium then contended that the *non ultra petita* rule limits the jurisdiction of the Court to the latter issue. The Court accepted the argument yet reserved itself the right to 'deal with certain aspects of that [universal jurisdiction] question in the reasoning of its Judgment, should it deem this necessary or desirable'.[4] It did not, but seven judges addressed the issue in separate opinions or declarations.[5]

President Guillaume, who has a longstanding interest in the matter,[6] noted that universal jurisdiction *in absentia* is unknown to international conventional law.[7] Looking at State practice, he found that the national legislation and jurisprudence cited by Belgium[8] (most of which are discussed in this book) do not support the argument that international customary law allows universal jurisdiction *in absentia*. Belgium's subsidiary argument (the '*Lotus* principle'), he observed, was hardly persuasive because the situation today 'is totally different'.[9] 'The adoption of the United Nations Charter proclaiming the sovereign equality of States, and the appearance on the international scene of new States, born of decolonization, have strengthened the territorial principle.'[10] His opinion ends in no uncertain terms:

> [A]t no time has it been envisaged that jurisdiction should be conferred upon courts of every State in the world to prosecute such crimes, whoever their authors and victims and irrespective of the place where the offender is to be found. To do this would moreover risk judicial chaos. It would also be to encourage the arbitrary for the benefit of the powerful, purportedly acting as agents for an ill-defined 'international community'. Contrary to what is advocated by certain publicists, such a development would represent not an advance in the law but a step backward.[11]

[3] Cf the discussion in ch 1 s A above. [4] Judgment (n 1 above) para 43.

[5] The opinions of the *ad hoc* judges chosen by the litigants are not considered here.

[6] See his publications 'Terrorisme et droit international' (1989) 215 *Receuil des cours de l'académie de droit international* 287 and 'La compétence universelle, formes anciennes et nouvelles' in *Mélanges offerts à Georges Levasseur: Droit pénal, droit européen* (1992) 23. As the French delegate to the diplomatic conferences on the suppression of the unlawful seizure of aircraft (The Hague, 1970) and on the suppression of unlawful acts against the safety of civil aircraft (Montreal, 1971) Judge Guillaume was directly involved with the drafting of the first post-World War II *aut dedere aut judicare* conventions. [7] Separate opinion of Judge Guillaume para 9.

[8] See Counter-Memorial of Belgium, 28 September 2001, chapter 3.

[9] Separate opinion of Judge Guillaume para 15. [10] Ibid. [11] Ibid.

Judge Rezek observed along the same lines that '[i]f the application of the universality principle would not presuppose the presence of the accused person on the territory of the forum State, all co-ordination becomes impossible and the very international system of co-operation in the repression of crime would collapse'.[12] His opinion does not fail to notice the possible North–South tension on the issue: 'It is not without reason that the Parties before the Court have discussed the question how certain European countries would react if a judge from Congo had indicted their officials for crimes supposedly committed on their orders in Africa'.[13]

Belgium's arguments also did not convince Judge Ranjeva.[14] Accordingly, he concluded that 'it would have been difficult, in the present state of positive law, not to validate Congo's first legal ground'.[15]

Judges Higgins, Kooijmans, and Buergenthal, in a joint separate opinion, conceded that neither international conventional law nor international customary law provides a basis for universal jurisdiction *in absentia* and that the writings of publicists 'cannot of themselves and without reference to the other sources of international law, evidence the existence of a jurisdictional norm'.[16] But, the opinion continues, 'there is equally nothing in this case law which evidences an *opinio juris* on the illegality of such jurisdiction. In short, national legislation and case law,—that is, State practice—is neutral as to the exercise of universal jurisdiction.'[17] Having found neither a permissive nor a prohibitive (customary) rule the opinion turns to the *Lotus* dictum, relied upon by Belgium, that '[f]ar from laying down a general prohibition to the effect that States may not extend the application of their laws and the jurisdiction of their courts to persons, property and acts outside their territory, it leaves them in this respect a wide measure of discretion which is only limited in certain cases by prohibitive rules'. The application of this dictum 'represents a continuing potential in the context of jurisdiction over international crimes'.[18] The opinion subscribes to the concept that States who claim the right to act unilaterally to assert a universal jurisdiction over international crimes act as 'agents for the international community' and goes on to say that '[t]his vertical notion of authority of action is significantly different from the horizontal system of international law envisaged in the *Lotus* case'.[19]

Regarding the question whether the presence of the accused is a precondition of the assertion of universal jurisdiction, the joint opinion states that the treaty *obligation* to extradite or try a suspect who is present 'cannot be interpreted *a contrario so as to exclude* a voluntary exercise of universal jurisdiction [over a suspect who is not present]'.[20] The judges concluded that '[i]f the underlying purpose of designating certain acts as international crimes is to authorize

[12] Separate opinion of Judge Rezek para 10. [13] Ibid para 9.
[14] Declaration of Judge Ranjeva paras 8 and 9. [15] Ibid para 12.
[16] Joint separate opinion of Judges Higgins, Kooijmans, and Buergenthal para 44.
[17] Ibid para 45. [18] Ibid para 50. [19] Ibid para 51. [20] Ibid para 57.

a wide jurisdiction to be asserted over persons committing them, there is no rule of international law (and certainly not the *aut dedere* principle) which makes illegal co-operative overt acts designed to secure their presence within a State wishing to exercise jurisdiction'.[21]

Judge Koroma stated (without elaborating how he had reached that view) that 'Belgium is entitled to invoke its criminal jurisdiction against anyone, save for a Foreign Minister in office. It is unfortunate that the wrong case would appear to have been chosen in attempting to carry out what Belgium considers its international obligation.'[22]

The opinions of Judges Guillaume, Rezek, and Ranjeva being in line with this book's findings, the present comments are limited to the joint opinion of Judges Higgins, Kooijmans, and Buergenthal. That opinion and this study concur on several points. Neither international conventional law nor international customary law provide a basis for universal jurisdiction *in absentia*. Writings of publicists, however unanimous and numerous they may be, cannot of themselves and without reference to the other sources of international law evidence the existence of a norm of international law.

The present author respectfully disagrees, however, on the following points. State practice as to the exercise of universal jurisdiction *in absentia* is not all that neutral. In the few precedents (*Sharon, Ndombasi*, and *Pinochet*) the States of nationality of the suspects protested vigorously, and not merely on immunity grounds.

Another point of disagreement is the contention that the *aut dedere aut judicare* clauses in treaties cannot be interpreted *a contrario* so as to exclude a voluntary exercise of universal jurisdiction in cases where a suspect is not present. As shown in chapter 3 above, a textual analysis of *aut dedere aut judicare* clauses in conventions and a review of commentaries by eminent jurists involved with the drafting suggest otherwise. The Judges' suggestion that the parties to the numerous *aut dedere aut judicare* treaties and to the ICC Statute silently reserved themselves a supposed *right* to exercise universal jurisdiction *in absentia* is unpersuasive, especially with regard to the ICC. The author cannot agree more with President Guillaume that this would encourage the arbitrary for the benefit of the powerful.

The conclusion of Judges Higgins, Kooijmans, and Buergenthal is perhaps not as far-reaching as it may appear. What they do not rule out is a *co-operative* exercise of universal jurisdiction *in absentia*. The author submits that this implies the consent of the State(s) involved, on a case-by-case basis. Without such consent any exercise of universal jurisdiction *in absentia* is doomed to be unilateral and risks weakening the very international order that it pretends to guard.

[21] Joint separate opinion of Judges Higgins, Kooijmans, and Buergenthal para 58.
[22] Separate opinion of Judge Koroma para 8.

The sharp division among the judges[23] and the first scholarly comments on the judgment[24] are a vivid illustration of the reality of Beckett's words quoted at the beginning of this book: 'The exercise of criminal jurisdiction over foreigners is a sphere in which juridical literature and speculation abound and are conflicting even in the matter of first principles, but international precedent is rare and indecisive.'[25] It is nonetheless the author's hope that this study can offer a useful frame of reference, advance the discussion, and contribute to progress in this matter.

[23] Cf the split court in the *Lotus* case. [24] N 1 above.
[25] WE Beckett, 'Criminal Jurisdiction over Foreigners' (1927) 8 *British Ybk Int'l L* 108, 109.

Bibliography

BOOKS

Ahlbrecht H and Ambos K (eds) *Der Fall Pinochet(s): Auslieferung wegen Staatsverstärkter Kriminalität?* (Baden-Baden, 1999)

American Law Institute, *Restatement of the Law (Third), The Foreign Relations Law of the United States* (St Paul, MN, 1987) 2 vols

Archbold, *Criminal Pleading, Evidence and Practice* (London, 2000)

Badi J (ed) *Fundamental Laws of the State of Israel* (New York, 1961)

Bassiouni MC, *A Draft International Criminal Code and Draft Statute for an International Criminal Court* (Dordrecht, 1987)

——*International Criminal Law Conventions and their Penal Provisions* (Irvington-on-Hudson, NY, 1997)

——and Wise EM, *Aut Dedere Aut Judicare: The Duty to Extradite or Prosecute in International Law* (Dordrecht; Boston, 1995)

Bevan D, *A Case to Answer: The story of Australia's first European war crimes prosecution* (Kent Town, South Australia, 1994)

Bindung K, *Handbuch des Strafrechts, 1. Band* (Leipzich, 1885)

Bin-Nun A, *The Law of the State of Israel: An Introduction* (Jerusalem, 1992)

Bosly HD and Vandermeersch D, *Droit de procédure pénale* (Brussels, 1999)

Boulesbaa A, *The UN Convention on Torture and the Prospects for Enforcement* (The Hague; Boston; London, 1999)

Brody R and Ratner M (eds) *The Pinochet Papers: The Case of Augusto Pinochet in Spain and Britain* (The Hague; London; Boston, 2000)

Brownlie I, *Principles of Public International Law* (Oxford, 4th edn, 1990)

Burgers JH and Danelius H, *The United Nations Convention against Torture: A Handbook on the Convention against Torture and Other Cruel, Inhuman or Degrading Treatment or Punishment* (Dordrecht; Boston, 1988)

Cameron I, *The Protective Principle of International Criminal Jurisdiction* (Aldershot, England; Brookfield, VT, 1994)

Dahm G, *Zur Problematik des Völkerstrafrechts* (Göttingen, 1956)

D'Amato A, *The Concept of Custom in International Law* (Ithaca; London, 1971)

De Hoogh A, *Obligations* erga omnes *and International Crimes: A Theoretical Inquiry into the Implementation and Enforcement of the International Responsibility of States* (The Hague, 1996)

de La Pradelle P, *La Conférence Diplomatique et les Nouvelles Conventions de Genève du 12 Août 1949* (Paris, 1951)

Desportes F and Le Gunehec F, *Le nouveau droit pénal* (Paris, 1995)

de Vattel E, *Le droit des gens ou les principes de la loi naturelle appliqués à la conduite et aux affaires des Nations et des Souverains* (1758) (translated by J Chitty, *The Law of Nations or Principles of Natural Law Applied to the Conduct and Affairs of Nations and Sovereigns* (Philadelphia, 1839))

de Visscher C, *Theory and Reality in Public International Law* (translated from the French by PE Corbett) (Princeton, 1968)

Donnedieu de Vabres H, *Les principes modernes du droit pénal international* (Paris, 1928)

Drost PN, *Genocide: United Nations Legislation on International Criminal Law* (Leiden, 1959)

Foregger E and Kodek G, *Strafgesetzbuch: Kurzkommentar* (Vienna, 6th edn, 1997)

Friedmann W, *The Changing Structure of International Law* (New York, 1964)

Glaser S, *Infraction internationale: Ses éléments constitutifs et ses aspects juridiques* (Paris, 1957)

Grotius H, *De Jure Belli ac Pacis Libri Tres* (1625) (translated by FW Kelsey, *The Law of War and Peace* (Oxford, 1925))

Hauri K, *Militärstrafgesetz: Kommentar* (Bern, 1983)

Henrich A, *Das passive Personalitätsprinzip im deutschen Strafrecht* (Freiburg i. Br., 1994)

Henzelin M, *Le principe de l'universalité en droit pénal international* (Basel; Geneva; Munich; Brussels, 2000)

Higgins R, *Problems and Process: International Law and How We Use It* (Oxford, 1994)

Høyer G, Spencer M, and Greve V, *The Danish Criminal Code* (Copenhagen, 1997)

Huet A and Koering-Joulin R, *Droit pénal international* (Paris, 1994)

Human Rights Watch and International Federation of Human Rights Leagues, *Leave None to Tell the Story: Genocide in Rwanda* (New York; Washington; London; Brussels; Paris, 1999)

Ingelse C, *The UN Committee Against Torture: An Assessment* (The Hague; Boston; London, 2001)

Janis MW, *An Introduction to International Law* (Gaithersburg, NY, 3rd edn, 1999)

Jescheck HH and Weigend T, *Lehrbuch des Strafrechts, Allgemeiner Teil* (Berlin, 5th edn, 1996)

Keck ME and Sikkink K, *Activists Beyond Borders: Advocacy Networks in International Politics* (Ithaca; London, 1998)

Kelsen H, *Principles of International Law* (New York; Chicago; San Francisco, Toronto; London, 2nd edn, 1966)

Kohler J, *Internationales Strafrecht* (Stuttgart, 1917)

Koskenniemi M, *From Apology to Utopia: The Structure of the International Legal Argument* (Helsinki, 1989)

Lauterpacht E, *International Law: Being the collected papers of Hersch Lauterpacht, Systematically arranged and edited by E Lauterpacht* (Cambridge, 1970)

Li H, *Die Prinzipien des internationalen Strafrechts: Eine vergleichende Untersuchung zwischen dem internationalen Strafrecht der Volksrepublik China und dem der Bundesrepublik Deutschland* (Pfaffenweiler, 1991)

Lambert JJ, *Terrorism and Hostages in International Law: A Commentary on the Hostages Convention 1979* (Cambridge, 1990)

Lemkin R, *Axis Rule in Occupied Europe: Laws of Occupation, Analysis of Government, Proposals for Redress* (Washington, DC, 1944)

Les Novelles, Corpus Juris Belgici, Procédure Pénale, vol. I (Brussels, 1946)

Lombois C, *Droit pénal international* (Paris, 1971)

Mann FA, *Further Studies in International Law* (Oxford; New York, 1990)

Meili F, *Lehrbuch des internationalen Strafrechts und Strafprozeßrechts* (Zurich, 1910)
Nguyen Quoc Dinh, Daillier P, and Pellet A, *Droit Public International* (Paris, 4th edn, 1992)
Oehler D, *Internationales Strafrecht. Geltungsbereich des Strafrechts. Internationales Rechtshilferecht. Recht der Gemeinschaften, Völkerstrafrecht* (Cologne; Berlin; Bonn; Munich, 2nd edn, 1983)
Oppenheim L, *International Law: A Treatise, vol. I, Peace* (London; New York, 3rd edn, 1920)
Orie AMM, van der Meijs JG, and Smit AMG, *Internationaal Strafrecht* (Zwolle, 2nd edn, 1991)
Panken H and Wouters J (eds) *De Genocidewet in internationaal perspectief* (Brussels, 2002)
Pappas C, *Stellvertretende Strafrechtspflege* (Freiburg i. Br., 1996)
Pictet J, *The Geneva Conventions of 12 August 1949: Commentary published under the general editorship of Jean S. Pictet, I, Geneva Convention for the Amelioration of the Condition of the Wounded and Sick in Armed Forced in the Field* (Geneva, 1952)
Ragazzi M, *The Concept of International Obligations* Erga Omnes (Oxford; New York, 1997)
Robinson N, *The Genocide Convention: A Commentary* (New York, 1960)
Rosswog E, *Das Problem der Vereinbarkeit des aktiven und passiven Personalgrundsatzes mit dem Völkerrecht* (Bonn, 1965)
Rubin AP, *The Law of Piracy* (Irvington-on-Hudson, NY, 2nd edn, 1997)
——*Ethics and Authority in International Law* (Cambridge, 1998)
Schabas WA, *Genocide in International Law* (Cambridge, 2000)
Schwaighofer K, *StGB-Kommentar: System und Praxis* (Vienna, 1997)
Shelton D, *Remedies in International Human Rights Law* (Oxford, 1999)
Shubber S, *Jurisdiction Over Crimes On Board Aircraft* (Dordrecht, 1973)
Simma B (ed) *Kommentar zur Charta der Vereinten Nationen* (Munich, 1991)
Solna G, *Das Weltrechtsprinzip im internationalen Strafrecht* (np, 1925)
Steinhardt RG and D'Amato A (eds) *The Alien Tort Claims Act: An analytical anthology* (Ardsley, NY, 1999)
Stephens B and Ratner M, *International Human Rights Litigation in US Courts* (Irvington-on-Hudson, NY, 1996)
Strijards GAM, *Internationaal Strafrecht: Strafmachtsrecht* (Arnhem, 1984)
Swart AHJ, *De berechting van internationale misdrijven* (Deventer, 1996)
Swart B and Klip A (eds) *International Criminal Law in the Netherlands* (Freiburg i. Br., 1997)
Traub M, *Das Universelle Schutzprinzip und das Prinzip der identische Norm, als ein regulierender Faktor der staatlichen Strafkompetenz* (Breslau, 1913)
Travers M, *Le droit pénal international et sa mise en oeuvre en temps de paix et en temps de guerre, tome I, Principes, Règles générales de compétence des lois répressives* (Paris, 1920)
Vander Beken T, *Forumkeuze in het internationaal strafrecht: Verdeling van misdrijven met aanknopingspunten in meerdere staten* (Antwerp; Apeldoorn, 1999)

Vermeulen G, Vander Beken T, Zanders P, and De Ruyver B, *Internationale samenwerking in strafzaken en rechtsbescherming: Pleidooi voor een geïntegreerde nationale en internationale benadering* (Brussels, 1995)

Wendt W, *Das passive Personalitätsprinzip* (Kiel, 1965)

Williams SA and Castel JG, *Canadian Criminal Law: International and Transnational Aspects* (Toronto, 1981)

Wolswijk HD, *Locus delicti en rechtsmacht* (Deventer; Utrecht, 1998)

ARTICLES

Ambos K and Wirth S, 'Genocide and War Crimes in the Former Yugoslavia Before German Criminal Courts' in Fischer H, Kreß C, and Lüder SR (eds) *International and National Prosecutions of Crimes under International Law: Current Developments* (Berlin, 2001) 769–97

Akehurst M, 'Jurisdiction in International Law' (1972–73) 46 *British Ybk Int'l L* 145–257

Andries A, Van den Wyngaert C, David E, and Verhaegen J, 'Commentaire de la loi du 16 juin 1993 relative à la répression des infractions graves au droit international humanitaire' (1994) 74 *Revue de Droit Pénal et de Criminologie* 1114–84

Baauw P, 'Ne bis in idem' in Swart B and Klip A (eds) *International Criminal Law in the Netherlands* (Freiburg i. Br., 1997) 75–84

Bassiouni MC, 'Universal Jurisdiction for International Crimes: Historical Perspectives and Contemporary Practice' (2001) 42 *Virginia J Int'l L* 81–156

Baxter RR, 'Jurisdiction over War Crimes and Crimes Against Humanity: Individual and State Accountability' in Bassiouni MC and Nanda VP (eds) *A Treatise on International Criminal Law* (Springfield, IL, 1973) 65–96

Beckett WE, 'The Exercise of Criminal Jurisdiction over Foreigners' (1925) 6 *British Ybk Int'l L* 44–60

—— 'Criminal Jurisdiction over Foreigners' (1927) 8 *British Ybk Int'l L* 108–28

Bein D, 'Criminal Law' in Zamir I and Colombo S (eds) *The Law of Israel: General Surveys* (Jerusalem, 1995) 128–96

Benavides L, 'The Universal Jurisdiction Principle: Nature and Scope' (2001) 1 *Anuario Mexicano de Derecho Internacional* 19–96

Berman PS, 'The Globalization of Jurisdiction', (2002) 151 *University of Pennsylvania LR* 311–530

Bertram G, 'Sextourismus und Strafverfolgung' (1996) 49 *Neue Juristische Wochenschrift* 436–8

Bigay J, 'Extrader ou punir' [1980] *Revue de Droit Pénal et de Criminologie, numéro spécial* 'Extradition et terrorisme' 113–46

Blakesley CL, 'United States Jurisdiction Over Extraterritorial Crime' (1982) 73 *J Crim L and Criminology* 1109–63

—— 'A Conceptual Framework for Extradition and Jurisdiction Over Extraterritorial Crimes' [1984] *Utah L Rev* 685–761

—— 'Extraterritorial Jurisdiction' in Bassiouni MC (ed) *International Criminal Law* (Ardsley, NY, 2nd edn, 1998) II, 33–106

Blakesley CL, 'Autumn of the Patriarch: The Pinochet Extradition Debacle and Beyond—Human Rights Clauses Compared to Traditional Derivative Protections such as Double Criminality' (2000) 91 *J Crim Law and Criminology* 1–98

—— and Lagodny O, 'Finding Harmony Amidst Disagreement over Extradition, Jurisdiction, The Role of Human Rights, and Issues of Extraterritoriality Under International Criminal Law' (1991) 24 *Vanderbilt J Transnational L* 1–73

Blewitt GT, 'National Prosecutions for International Crimes: The Australian Experience' in Bassiouni MC (ed) *International Criminal Law* (Ardsley, NY, 2nd edn, 1998) III, 301–24

Boed R, 'United States Legislative Approach to Extraterritorial Jurisdiction in Connection with Terrorism' in Bassiouni MC (ed) *International Criminal Law* (Ardsley, NY, 2nd edn, 1998) II, 145–76

Bosniak L, 'Multiple Nationality and Postnational Transformation of Citizenship' (2002) 42 *Virginia J Int'l L* 979–1004

Bowett DW, 'Jurisdiction: Changing Patterns of Authority over Activities and Resources' (1982) 53 *British Ybk Int'l L* 1–26

Brody R and Duffy H, 'Prosecuting Torture Universally: Hissène Habré, Africa's Pinochet?' in Fischer H, Kreß C, and Lüder SR (eds) *International and National Prosecutions of Crimes under International Law: Current Developments* (Berlin, 2001) 817–42

Cameron I, 'The Protective Principle of Criminal Jurisdiction in Nordic Criminal Law' in Lahti R and Nuotio K (eds) *Criminal Law Theory in Transition: Finnish and Comparative Perspectives* (Helsinki, 1992) 544–70

Carnegie AR, 'Jurisdiction over Violations of the Laws and Customs of War' (1963) 39 *British Ybk Int'l L* 402–24.

Cassel D, 'Empowering United States Courts to Hear Crimes Within the Jurisdiction of the International Criminal Court' (2001) 35 *New England L Rev* 421–46

Clark RS, 'Offenses of International Concern: Multilateral State Practice in the Forty Years Since Nuremberg' (1988) 57 *Nordic J Int'l L* 49–118

—— 'Apartheid', in Bassiouni MC (ed) *International Criminal Law* (Ardsley, NY, 2nd edn, 1998) I, 643–62

Coolen GL, 'De Wet Oorlogsstrafrecht: Een wet met gebreken' (1996) 26 *Delikt en Delinkwent* 43–55

Cornils K, 'The use of foreign law in domestic adjudication', in Jareborg N (ed) *Double Criminality: Studies in International Criminal Law* (Uppsala, 1989) 70–83

—— 'Zur Regelung des raümlichen Geltungsbereichs im finnishen Strafgesetzentwurf' in Lahti R and Nuotio K (eds) *Criminal Law Theory in Transition: Finnish and Comparative Perspectives* (Helsinki, 1992) 571–86

Costello D, 'International Terrorism and the Development of the Principle *Aut Dedere Aut Judicare*' (1975) 10 *J Int'l L and Economics* 483–501

Cotterell HD, 'Harm Dost en uitlevering' (1976) 51 *Nederlands Juristenblad* 830–1

Cottier M, 'The Case of Switzerland' in Kreß C and Lattanzi F (eds) *The Rome Statute and Domestic Legal Orders: General Aspects and Constitutional Issues* (Baden-Baden, 2000) 219–46

—— 'What Relationship Between the Exercise of Universal Jurisdiction and Territorial Jurisdiction? The Decision of 13 December 2000 of the Spanish National Court Shelving the Proceedings Against Guatemalan Nationals Accused of Genocide' in Fischer H, Kreß C, and Lüder SR (eds) *International and National Prosecutions of Crimes under International Law: Current Developments* (Berlin, 2001) 843–57

Cowles WB, 'Universality of Jurisdiction Over War Crimes' (1945) 33 *California L Rev* 177–218

d'Argent P, 'La loi du 10 février 1999 relative à la répression des violations graves du droit international humanitaire' (1999) 118 *Journal des Tribunaux* 549–55

de Cara JY, 'L'affaire Pinochet devant la chambre des lords' (1999) XLV *Annuaire Français de Droit International* 72–100

Dinstein Y, 'International Criminal Law' (1985) 20 *Israel L Rev* 206–42

Donnedieu de Vabres H, 'Les leçons de l'histoire et le progrès du droit pénal international' [July–September 1951] *Revue de Science Criminelle et de Droit Pénal Comparé* 1–20

Dugard J and Van den Wyngaert C, 'Reconciling Extradition with Human Rights' (1998) 92 *Am J Int'l L* 187–212

Epp H, 'Austria' (1989) 60 *Revue internationale de droit pénal* 115–26

Eser A, 'Grundlagen und Grenzen "stellvertretender Strafrechtspflege" (§7 Abs. 2 Nr. 2 StGB). Zur Problematik der "indentischen Tatortnorm" bei Auslandstaten, insbesondere bei Amnestierung am Tatort' [1993] *Juristenzeitung* 875–84

Fawcett JES, 'The Eichmann Case' (1962) 27 *British Ybk Int'l L* 181–215

Feller SZ, 'Jurisdiction over Offenses with a Foreign Element' in Bassiouni MC and Nanda VP (eds) *A Treatise on International Criminal Law* (Springfield, IL, 1973) II, 5–64

—— 'Concurrent Criminal Jurisdiction in the International Sphere' (1981) 16 *Israel L Rev* 40–74

Fitzmaurice G, 'The Law and Procedure of the International Court of Justice, 1951–54: General Principles and Sources of Law' (1953) 30 *British Ybk Int'l L* 7–70

Fox H, 'Jurisdiction and Immunities' in Lowe V and Fitzmaurice M (eds) *Fifty Years of the International Court of Justice* (Cambridge; New York, 1996) 210–34

—— 'The Pinochet Case No. 3' (1999) 48 *Int'l and Comparative LQ* 687–702

Gardocki L, 'The Principle of Universality' in Jareborg N (ed) *Double Criminality: Studies in International Criminal Law* (Uppsala, 1989) 57–69

Garwood-Cutler JL, 'Enforcing International Criminal Law Violations with Civil Remedies: The US Alien Tort Claims Act' in Bassiouni MC (ed) *International Criminal Law* (Ardsley, NY, 2nd edn, 1998) III, 343–91

—— 'National Prosecutions for International Crimes: The British Experience' in Bassiouni MC (ed) *International Criminal Law* (Ardsley, NY, 2nd edn, 1998) III, 325–30

George BJ, 'Jurisdiction Over Embassies, Consulates, International Organizations and Their Personnel, and Armed Forces Stationed Abroad' in Bassiouni MC (ed) *International Criminal Law* (Ardsley, NY, 2nd edn, 1998) I, 107–44

Gerritsen MT, 'Jurisdiction' in Swart B and Klip A (eds) *International Criminal Law in the Netherlands* (Freiburg i. Br., 1997) 49–73

Gilbert G, 'Crimes sans Frontières: Jurisdictional Problems in English Law' (1992) 63 *British Ybk Int'l L* 413–42

Graefrath B, 'Universal Criminal Jurisdiction and an International Criminal Court' (1990) 1 *Eur J Int'l L* 67–88

Graven J, 'Les crimes contre l'humanité' (1950) 76 *Receuil des cours de l'académie de droit international* 427–538

Greenwood C, 'The War Crimes Act 1991' in Fox H and Meyer MA (eds) *Armed Conflict and the New Law, vol II, Effecting Compliance* (1993) 215–31

Greve V, 'Denmark' in Van den Wyngaert C (ed) *Criminal Procedure Systems in the European Community* (London; Brussels; Dublin; Edinburgh, 1993) 51–72

Grynfogel C, 'Le concept de crime contre l'humanité: Hier, aujourd'hui et demain' (1994) 74 *Revue de droit pénal et de criminologie* 13–51

Guillaume G, 'Terrorisme et droit international' (1989) 215 *Receuil des cours de l'académie de droit international* 287–371

—— 'La compétence universelle, formes anciennes et nouvelles' in *Mélanges offerts à Georges Levasseur: Droit pénal, droit européen* (Paris, 1992) 23–36

Harnon E and Stein A, 'Israel' in Bradley CM (ed) *Criminal Procedure: A Worldwide Study* (Durham, NC, 1999) 217–44

Higgins R, 'The Role of Resolutions of International Organizations in the Process of Creating Norms in the International System' in Butler W (ed) *International Law and the International System* (Dordrecht; Boston, 1987) 21–30

Holdgaard Bukh M, 'Prosecution Before Danish Courts of Foreigners Suspected of Serious Violations of Human Rights or Humanitarian Law' (1994) 6 *Eur Rev Public L* 339–52

Huber B, 'Criminal Procedure in Germany' in Hatchard J, Huber B, and Vogler R (eds) *Comparative Criminal Procedure* (London, 1996) 96–175

Ingelse C and van der Wilt H, 'De Zaak Pinochet: Over Universele Rechtsmacht en Hollandse Benepenheid' (1996) *Nederlands Juristenblad* 280–5

Jennings RY, 'Nullity and Effectiveness in International Law' in *Cambridge Essays in International Law: Essays in honour of Lord McNair* (London; Dobbs Ferry, NY, 1965)

—— 'General Course on Principles of International Law' (1967) 121 *Receuil des cours de l'académie de droit international* 323–605

Jung H, 'Zur Internationalisierung des Grundsatzes ne bis in idem' in Albrecht PA, Ehlers APF, Lamott F, Pfeiffer C, Schwind H-D, and Walter M (eds) *Festschrift für Horst Schüler-Springorum* (Cologne; Berlin; Bonn; Munich, 1993) 493–502

Kamminga MT and Tijssen M, 'Pinochet, Nederland en het VN-Verdrag tegen foltering' (1995) *Nederlands Juristen Comité voor de Mensenrechten-Bulletin* 986–95

—— 'Lessons Learned from the Exercise of Universal Jurisdiction in Respect of Gross Human Rights Offenses' (2001) 23 *Human Rights Q* 940–74

King HT, 'Universal Jurisdiction: Myths, Realities, Prospects, War Crimes and Crimes Against Humanity: The Nuremberg Precedent' (2001) 35 *New England L Rev* 281–6

Kissinger HA, 'The Pitfalls of Universal Jurisdiction: Risking Judicial Tyranny' (2001) 80 *Foreign Affairs* 86–96

Klip AH, 'Strafrechtelijke reactie op ernstige schendingen van mensenrechten in het buitenland' in Brants CH, Kelk C, and Moerings M (eds) *Er is meer: Opstellen over mensenrechten in internationaal perspectief* (Arnhem, 1996) 93–106

Kobrick ES, 'The Ex Post Facto Prohibition and the Exercise of Universal Jurisdiction Over International Crimes' (1987) 87 *Columbia L Rev* 1515–38

Koering-Joulin R and Huet A, 'Compétence des tribunaux répressifs français et de la loi pénale française: Infractions commises à l'étranger' in *Editions Techniques: Juris-Classeurs* (Paris, 1991) Fascicule 20, procédure pénale, articles 689–696

Kos-Rabcewicz-Zubkowski L, 'Canada' (1989) 60 *Revue internationale de droit pénal* 195–213

Koskenniemi M, 'The Pull of the Mainstream' (1990) 88 *Michigan L Rev* 1946–62

Kremnitzer M, 'Criminal Law' in Shapira A and DeWitt-Arar KC (eds) *Introduction to the Law of Israel* (The Hague; London; Boston, 1995) 253–66

Kreß C, 'Völkerstrafrecht in Deutschland' (2000) 20 *Neue Zeitschrift für Strafrecht* 617–24

—— 'Völkerstrafrecht und Weltrechtspflegeprinzip im Blickfeld des Internationalen Gerichtshofs' (2002) 114 *Zeitschrift für die gesamte Strafrechtswissenschaft* 818–49

Krikke A, 'De zaak-Dost: De rechtsmacht van de Bondsrepubliek bij de bestrijding van verdovende middelen' (1976) *Recht en Kritiek* 249–67

Kühne HH, 'Germany' in Van den Wyngaert C (ed) *Criminal Procedure Systems in the European Community* (London; Brussels, Dublin; Edinburgh, 1993) 137–62

Liebscher V, 'Die neue Struktur des Internationalen Strafrechtes (§§62 bis 67 StGB)' (1974) 94 *Juristische Blätter* 393–402

Linke R, 'Grenzen der Strafgerichtsbarkeit: Zugleich Besprechung der zweiten Auflage von Oehler, Internationales Strafrecht' (1984) 39 *Österreichische Juristenzeitung* 487–90

Lippman M, 'The Drafting of the 1948 Convention for the Prevention and Punishment of Genocide' (1985) 3 *Boston University Int'l LJ* 1–65

Lombois C, 'De la compassion territoriale' (1995) *Revue de Science Criminelle et de Droit Pénal Comparé* 399–403

Lowenfeld AF, 'US Law Enforcement Abroad: The Constitution and International Law' (1989) 83 *Am J Int'l L* 880–93

Lüder SR, 'Eröffnung der deutschen Gerichtsbarkeit für den Völkermord im Kosovo?' (2000) 53 *Neue Juristische Wochenschrift* 269–70

Mahmoudi S, 'The International Court of Justice and Nuclear Weapons' (1997) 66 *Nordic J Int'l L* 77–100

Maier HG, 'Jurisdictional Rules in Customary Law' in Meessen KM (ed) *Extraterritorial Jurisdiction in Theory and Practice* (London; Boston, 1996) 64–99

Maison R, 'Les premiers cas d'applications des dispositions pénales des Conventions de Genève par les jurisdictions internes' (1995) 6 *Eur J Int'l L* 260–73

Mann FA, 'The Doctrine of Jurisdiction in International Law' (1964) 111 *Receuil des cours de l'académie de droit international* 9–158

—— 'The Doctrine of International Jurisdiction Revised after Twenty Years' (1984) 186 *Receuil des cours de l'académie de droit international* 11–115

—— 'Reflections on the Prosecution of Persons Abducted in Breach of International Law' in Dinstein Y (ed) *International Law at a Time of Perplexity: Essays in Honour of Shabtai Rosenne* (Dordrecht; Boston, 1989) 407–21

Marschik A, 'The Politics of Prosecution: European National Approaches to War Crimes' in McCormack TLH and Simpson GJ (eds) *The Law of War Crimes: National and International Approaches* (The Hague; London; Boston, 1997) 65–102

Massé M, 'Ex-Yugoslavie, Rwanda: une compétence "virtuelle" des juridictions françaises?' (1997) *Revue de Science Criminelle et de Droit Pénal Comparé* 893–8

Mayerhofer C, 'Können Kriegverbrechen auf dem Gebiet des ehemaligen Jugoslowien von österreichischen Gerichten verfolgt werden?' (1994) 116 *Juristische Blätter* 567–659

Méndez JE and Meintjes G, 'Reconciling Amnesties with Universal Jurisdiction' (2000) 2 *Int'l L Forum* 76–97

Mercier A, 'Le conflit des lois pénales en matière de compétence' (1931) I *Annuaire de l'Institut de Droit International* 87–147

Merlung E, 'National Implementation: The Universal Jurisdiction. The Saric Case' in *The Punishment of War Crimes. International Legal Perspectives* (1996) 12–17

Meron T, 'The International Criminalization of Internal Atrocities' (1994) 89 *Am J Int'l L* 554–77

Meyer J, 'The Vicarious Administration of Justice: An Overlooked Basis of Jurisdiction' (1990) 31 *Harvard Int'l LJ* 108–16

Mikliszanski K, 'Le système de l'universalité du droit de punir et le droit pénal subsidiaire' (1936) *Revue de Science Criminelle et de Droit Pénal Comparé* 331–41

Mok MR, 'Het Europese verdrag tot bestrijding van terrorisme' (1977) 27 *Nederlands Juristenblad* 665–71

——and Duk RAA, 'Toepassing van Nederlands strafrecht op buiten Nederland begane delicten' in *Handelingen der Nederlandse Juristen-Vereniging deel 1, tweede stuk* (Zwolle, 1980) 2–149

Morgan EW, 'Retributory Theater' (1988) 3 *Am University J Int'l L and Policy* 1–63

Mouton WM, 'La protection pénale des conventions internationales humanitaires' (1953) *Revue internationale de droit pénal* 851–73

——'De wet oorlogsstrafrecht en het internationale recht' (1960) *Nederlands Tijdschrift voor Internationaal Recht* 59–71

Nelson A, 'Swedish and Foreign Crimes in the Swedish Criminal Justice System' in Jareborg N (ed) *Double Criminality: Studies in International Criminal Law* (Uppsala, 1989) 11–42

Oehler D, 'Immunität, Exterritorialität und Asylrecht im Internationalen Strafrecht' (1979) 91 *Zeitschrift für die gesamte Strafrechtswissenschaft* 395–429

——'Perspectives on the Contents of the Special Part of the Draft International Criminal Code' (1981) 52 *Revue internationale de droit pénal* 407–38

——'Auslieferungsersuchen, Einlieferung und der Geltungsbereich des Strafrechts' in *Festschrift der Rechtswissenschaftlichen Fakultät zur 600-Jahr-Feier der Universität zu Köln* (Cologne; Berlin; Bonn; Munich, 1988) 489–504

Orie AMM, 'Internationaal strafrechtelijke aspecten van de Dost-affaire' (1976) 30 *Nederlands Juristenblad* 1045–59

——Rüter CF, Schutte JJE, and Swart AHJ, 'Netherlands' (1989) 60 *Revue internationale de droit pénal* 395–417

Pella V, 'La répression de la piratérie' (1926) 15 *Receuil des cours de l'académie de droit international* 149–275

Perlin J, 'The Guatemalan Historical Clarification Commission finds Genocide' (2000) 6 *ILSA J Int'l and Comparative L* 389–414

Peters P, 'Volkenrechtelijke aspecten van extraterritoriale wetgeving' in Peters P and Kotting R (eds) *Extraterritoriale wetgeving* (Deventer, 1984) 1–109

Pradel J, 'France' in Van den Wyngaert C (ed) *Criminal Procedure Systems in the European Community* (London; Brussels; Dublin; Edinburgh, 1993) 105–36

Puttler A, 'Extraterritorial Application of Criminal Law: Jurisdiction to Prosecute Drug Traffic Conducted by Aliens Abroad' in Meessen KM (ed) *Extraterritorial Jurisdiction in Theory and Practice* (London; Boston, 1996) 103–21

Randall KC, 'Universal Jurisdiction under International Law' (1988) 66 *Texas L Rev* 785–841

Rayfuse R, 'The Draft Code of Offences Against the Peace and Security of Mankind; Eating Disorders at the International Law Commission' (1997) 8 *Crim L Forum* 43–86

Reiss RH, 'The Extradition of John Demjanjuk: War Crimes, Universality Jurisdiction, and The Political Offense Doctrine' (1987) 20 *Cornell Int'l L J* 281–315

Reydams L, 'Universal Jurisdiction over Atrocities in Rwanda: Theory and Practice' (1996) 4 *Eur J Crime, Crim L and Crim Justice* 18–47

——'Universal Criminal Jurisdiction: The Belgian State of Affairs' (2000) 11 *Crim L Forum* 183–216

——'Prosecuting Crimes Under International Law on the Basis of Universal Jurisdiction: The Experience of Belgium' in Fischer H, Kreß C, and Lüder SR (eds) *International and National Prosecutions of Crimes under International Law: Current Developments* (Berlin, 2001) 799–816

Richardson AT, 'War Crimes Act 1991' (1992) 55 *Modern L Rev* 73–86

Roach K, 'Canada' in Bradley CM (ed) *Criminal Procedure: A Worldwide Study* (Durham, NC, 1999) 53–80

Roberts AE, 'Traditional and Modern Approaches to Customary International Law: A Reconciliation' (2001) 95 *Am J Int'l L* 757–91

Rodley NS, 'Torture, Extra-Legal Execution and "Disappearance" as Crimes under International Law' in David PR, *Crime and Criminal Policy: Papers in Honour of Manuel López-Rey Y Arrojo* (1985) 587–604

Röling BVA, 'Enkele volkenrechtelijke aantekeningen bij de wet oorlogsstrafrecht' (1959) *Nederlands Tijdschrift voor Internationaal Recht* (special issue) 263–91

Roht-Arriaza N, 'The Pinochet Precedent and Universal Jurisdiction' (2001) 35 *New England L Rev* 311–20

Rubin AP, 'Actio Popularis, Jus Cogens and Offenses Erga Omnes' (2000) 35 *New England L Rev* 265–80

Sadat Wexler L, 'The Interpretation of the Nuremberg Principles by the French Court of Cassation: From Touvier to Barbie and Back Again' (1994) 32 *Columbia J Transn'l L* 288–380

Saldaña Q, 'La justice pénale internationale' (1925) 10 *Receuil des cours de l'académie de droit international* 221–429

Sandoz Y, 'Penal Aspects of International Humanitarian Law' in Bassiouni MC (ed) *International Criminal Law* (2nd edn, Ardsley, NY, 1998) I, 393–414

Schabas WA, 'Canadian Implementing Legislation for the Rome Statute' (2000) 3 *Ybk Int'l Humanitarian L* 337–46

Scharf MP, 'Application of Treaty-Based Universal Jurisdiction to Nationals of Non-Party States' (2001) 35 *New England L Rev* 363–82

Schmitz R, '§7 II Nr. 2 StGB und das Prinzip der stellvertretenden Strafrechtspflege' in Samson E (ed) *Festschrift für Gerald Grünwald* (Baden-Baden, 1999) 619–40

Schouwey JD, 'Suisse' (1989) 60 *Revue internationale de droit pénal* 465–89

Schouwey JD, 'Crimes de guerre: Un état des lieux du droit suisse' (1995) XLVIII *Revue internationale de criminologie et de police technique* 46–56

Schultz H, 'Compétences des jurisdictions pénales pour les infractions commises à l'étranger' (1967) 22 *Revue de science criminelle et de droit pénal comparé* 305–38

Schutte JJE, 'Enforcement measures in international criminal law' (1981) 52 *Revue internationale de droit pénal* 441–53

Schwarzenberger G, 'The Problem of an International Criminal Law' in Mueller GOW and Wise EM (eds) *International Criminal Law* (South Hackensack, NJ, 1965) 3–36

Shachor-Landau C, 'Extra-Territorial Penal Jurisdiction and Extradition' (1980) 29 *Int'l and Comparative LQ* 274–95

Simma B, 'International Human Rights and General International Law' in *Collected Courses of the Academy of European Law* (Florence, 1993) IV, Book 2, 153–236

—— and Paulus AL, 'The Responsibility of Individuals for Human Rights Abuses in Internal Conflicts: A Positivist View' (1999) 93 *Am J Int'l L* 302–16

Sponsler TH, 'The Universality Principle of Jurisdiction and the Threatened Trials of American Airmen' (1968–1969) 15 *Loyola L Rev* 43–67

Stern B, 'La compétence universelle en France: Le cas des crimes commis en ex-Yougoslavie et au Rwanda' (1997) *German Yearbook of International Law* 280–99

Stessens G and Van den Wyngaert C, 'The International Non Bis In Idem Principle: Resolving Some of the Unanswered Questions' (1999) 48 *Int'l and Comparative LQ* 779–804

Strijards GAM, 'Neerlands dualisme en zijn strafmacht' (2000) *Nederlands Juristenblad* 2113–22

Swart AHJ, 'De Nederlandse strafrechtspleging en het internationale recht' in *Internationalisering van het strafrecht. Ars Aequi Libri. Serie Strafrecht en criminologie, VI* (Utrecht, 1986) 37–66

—— 'Jurisdiction in Criminal Law: Some Reflections on the Finnish Code from a Comparative Perspective' in Lahti R and Nuotio K (eds) *Criminal Law Theory in Transition: Finnish and Comparative Perspectives* (Helsinki, 1992) 527–43

—— 'The Netherlands' in Van den Wyngaert C (ed) *Criminal Procedure Systems in the European Community* (London; Brussels; Dublin; Edinburgh, 1993) 279–316

Terry J, 'The Canadian Criminal Code, Universal Jurisdiction, and the Prosecution of Foreign Human Rights Offenders in Canadian Courts' (1989) (unpublished LLM thesis, Harvard Law School)

Thomas F, 'De burgerlijke vordering wegens misdrijven met een buitenlands element' (1982) 19 *Tijdschrift voor Privaatrecht* 13–40

—— 'De internationale gelding van de strafwet in de ruimte', in De Nauw A, D'Haenens J, and Storme M (eds) *Actuele problemen van strafrecht* (Antwerp; Arnhem, 1988) 195–214

Thun K, 'Zur Strafverfolgung Pinochets in der Bundesrepublik Deutschland' in Ahlbrecht H and Ambos K (eds) *Der Fall Pinochet(s): Auslieferung wegen staatsverstärkter Kriminalität?* (Baden-Baden, 1999) 19–23

Träskman PO, 'Should We Take the Condition of Double Criminality Seriously?' in Jareborg N (ed) *Double Criminality: Studies in International Criminal Law* (Uppsala, 1989) 135–55

—— 'Provisions on jurisdiction in criminal law: The reform of the law caught in the tension between tradition and dynamism' in Lahti R and Nuotio K (eds) *Criminal law theory in transition: Finnish and comparative perspectives* (Helsinki, 1992) 511–26

Triffterer O, 'Efforts to Recognize and Codify International Crimes' (1989) 60 *Revue internationale de droit pénal* 29–88

Triggs G, 'Australia's War Crimes Trials: All Pity Choked' in McCormack TLH and Simpson GJ (eds) *The Law of War Crimes: National and International Approaches* (The Hague; London; Boston, 1997) 121–50

Vadillo ER, 'Spain' in Van den Wyngaert C (ed) *Criminal Procedure Systems in the European Community* (London; Brussels; Dublin; Edinburgh, 1993) 383–400

Vandemeulebroeke O and Gazan F, 'Traite des êtres humains—exploitation et abus sexuels: Les nouvelles lois des 27 mars et 13 avril 1995' (1995) 75 *Revue de Droit Pénal et de Criminologie* 973–1077

Van den Wyngaert C, 'De toepassing van de strafwet in de ruimte: Enkele beschouwingen' in *Liber Amicorum Frédéric Dumon* (Antwerp, 1983) 501–25

—— 'Belgium' (1989) 60 *Revue internationale de droit pénal* 153–68

—— 'Double Criminality as a Requirement to Jurisdiction' in Jareborg N (ed) *Double Criminality: Studies in International Criminal Law* (Uppsala, 1989) 43–56

—— 'Belgium' in Van den Wyngaert C (ed) *Criminal Procedure Systems in the European Community* (London; Brussels; Dublin; Edinburgh, 1993) 1–50

Vandermeersch D, 'La répression en droit belge des crimes de droit international' (1997) 68 *Revue internationale de droit pénal* 1093–135

——'Les poursuites et le jugement des infractions de droit humanitaire en droit belge' in *Actualité du droit international humanitaire* (Brussels, 2001) 123–80

van Elst R, 'Afscheid van Joegoslavië: Over oorlogsmisdrijven en misdrijven tegen de menselijkheid begaan in voormalig Joegoslavië en de Nederlandse rechter' (1994) *Nederlands Juristenblad* 1401–10

—— 'De zaak Darco Knezevic: Rechtsmacht over Joegoslavische en andere buitenlandse oorlogsmisdadigers' (1998) *Nederlands Juristenblad* 1587–93

—— 'Implementing Universal Jurisdiction Over Grave Breaches of the Geneva Conventions' 2000 13 *Leiden J Int'l L* 815–54

van Heeck S, 'Der aktuelle Fall: Die Anwendung deutschen Strafrechts auf Balkankriegsverbrechen' [2000] *Humanitäres Völkerrecht-Informationsschriften* 27–33

Verhoeven J, 'M. Pinochet, la coutume internationale et la compétence universelle' (1999) 118 *Journal des Tribunaux* 308–15

Vogler R, 'Criminal Procedure in France' in Hatchard J, Huber B, and Vogler R (eds) *Comparative Criminal Procedure* (London, 1996) 14–95

—— 'Spain' in Bradley CM (ed) *Criminal Procedure: A Worldwide Study* (Durham, NC, 1999) 361–94

von Cleric GF, 'Das Weltrechtsergreifungsprinzip' (1920) 22 *Schweizerische Juristen-Zeitung* 345–52

Wagner JM, 'US Prosecution of Past and Future War Criminals and Criminals Against Humanity: Proposals for Reform Based on the Canadian and Australian Experience' (1989) 29 *Virginia J Int'l Law* 887–936

Warbrick C, 'Extradition Law Aspects of Pinochet 3' (1999) 48 *Int'l and Comparative LQ* 958–65

——, Salgado EM, and Goodwin N, 'The Pinochet Cases in the United Kingdom' (1999) 2 *Ybk Int'l Humanitarian L* 91–118

Watson GR, 'Offenders Abroad: The Case for Nationality-Based Criminal Jurisdiction' (1992) 17 *Yale J Int'l L* 41–84

—— 'The Passive Personality Principle' (1993) 28 *Texas Int'l L J* 1–46

Weigend T, 'Germany' in Bradley CM (ed) *Criminal Procedure: A World Wide Study* (Durham, NC, 1999) 187–216

Wenig JM, 'Enforcing the Lessons of History: Israel Judges the Holocaust' in McCormack TLH and Simpson GJ (eds) *The Law of War Crimes: National and International Approaches* (The Hague; London; Boston, 1997) 103–22

Williams G, 'Venue and the Ambit of Criminal Law' (1965) 81 *L Q Rev* 276–88, 395–421, 518–38

Williams SA, 'Laudable Principles Lacking Application: The Prosecution of War Criminals in Canada' in McCormack TLH and Simpson GJ (eds) *The Law of War Crimes: National and International Approaches* (The Hague; London; Boston, 1997) 151–70

Wilkitzki P, 'Federal Republic of Germany' (1989) 60 *Revue internationale de droit pénal* 263–90

Wise EM, 'Note on International Standards of Criminal Law and Administration', in Mueller GOW and Wise EM (eds) *International Criminal Law* (South Hackensack, NJ, 1965) 135–63

Zaid MS, 'Will or Should the United States Ever Prosecute War Criminals? A Need For Greater Expansion in the Areas of Both Criminal and Civil Liability' (2001) 35 *New England L Rev* 447–70

Ziegler AR, 'La mise en œuvre du droit international humanitaire par la Suisse' (1997) XXXVI *Revue internationale du droit militaire et droit de la guerre* 245–66

Zoller E, 'Territorial Effect of the Norm on Responsibility', in Ginsburgs G and Kudriavtsev VN (eds) *The Nuremberg Trial and International Law* (Dordrecht; Boston; London, 1990) 106–11

REPORTS

Bos A, 'The Extraterritorial Jurisdiction of States: Preliminary Report' (1993) 65 *Ybk Institute Int'l L*, I, 14–44

Brierly JL, 'Report on Jurisdiction over Extraterritorial Crime' (1926) 20 *Am J Int'l L* 253–8

Chilean National Commission on Truth and Reconciliation, 2 vols, translated by PE Berryman (Notre Dame, IN, 1993)

Commission of Inquiry on War Criminals (Canada), *Report, Part I: Public* (1986)

Consultative Assembly of the Council of Europe, 'Report on the Settlement of Conflicts in Criminal Matters' (1965) Doc 1873

Council of Europe, European Committee on Crime Problems, *Extraterritorial criminal jurisdiction* (1990)

Grützner H, *Le champ d'application du droit pénal: Aperçu comparatif élaboré en vue de la préparation d'une Convention européenne portant unification des dispositions relatives au champ d'application du droit pénal* (1964)

Harvard Research in International Law, 'Piracy' (1932) 26 *Am J Int'l L* 739–1013

Harvard Research in International Law, 'Jurisdiction with Respect to Crime' (1935) 29 *Am J Int'l L* 435–651

Home Office (UK), Steering Committee Report, *Review of Extra-Territorial Jurisdiction* (1996)

International Law Association, 'The Exercise of Universal Jurisdiction in Respect of Gross Human Rights Violations: Final Report on the Exercise of Universal Jurisdiction in Respect of Gross Human Rights Offences' in *Report of the 69th Conference of the International Law Association* (2000) 403–31

Law Commission (UK), *Report on the Territorial and Extraterritorial Extent of the Criminal Law* (1978)

Law Reform Commission of Canada, *Extraterritorial Jurisdiction, Working Paper 37*, (1984)

Menzies A, *Review of Material Relating to the Entry of Suspected War Criminals into Australia* (1987)

Report of the War Crimes Inquiry (UK) (1989)

Trousse PE, 'La compétence extraterritoriale des jurisdictions répressives belges' in *Rapports belges au VIIe Congrès international de droit comparé* (1966) 511–38

Index